Introduction to Environmental Economics

Introduction to
Environmental
Economics

Professor Nick Hanley

Professor of Environmental Economics, University of Glasgow

Professor Jason F. Shogren

Stroock Distinguished Professor of Natural Resource Conservation and Management,
and Professor of Economics, University of Wyoming

Dr Ben White

Senior Lecturer in Agricultural Economics, University of Newcastle and Adjunct Senior Lecturer in
Agricultural Economics, University of Western Australia

OXFORD
UNIVERSITY PRESS

OXFORD

UNIVERSITY PRESS

Great Clarendon Street, Oxford OX2 6DP

Oxford University Press is a department of the University of Oxford.
It furthers the University's objective of excellence in research, scholarship,
and education by publishing worldwide in

Oxford New York

Athens Auckland Bangkok Bogotá Buenos Aires Calcutta
Cape Town Chennai Dar es Salaam Delhi Florence Hong Kong Istanbul
Karachi Kuala Lumpur Madrid Melbourne Mexico City Mumbai
Nairobi Paris São Paulo Shanghai Singapore Taipei Tokyo Toronto Warsaw

with associated companies in Berlin Ibadan

Oxford is a registered trade mark of Oxford University Press
in the UK and in certain other countries

Published in the United States
by Oxford University Press Inc., New York

A catalogue record for this book is available from the British Library

Library of Congress Cataloging in Publication Data
(Data available)
ISBN 0-19-877595-4

10 9 8 7 6 5 4 3 2 1

Typeset in Swift
by RefineCatch Limited, Bungay, Suffolk
Printed in Great Britain
on acid-free paper by
Bath Press Ltd., Bath, Avon

N. Hanley
For Charlie, Fiona, and Rose

J. Shogren
For Deb, Maija, and Riley

B. White
For Jane, Catherine, Steven, and Dominic

Acknowledgements

This book would not have been completed without the help of many people. Nick Hanley would like to thank Linda Goodall for art work, editing and general organization; Felix Fitzroy for comments on Chapter 9; Ceara Nevin for research assistance; and Fiona for reading all his chapters with the expert eyes of a non-economist. Jason Shogren would like to thank Tom Crocker (for advice) and Bob Dylan (for different advice). Ben White thanks Elizabeth Moore for work on the rainforest chapter and Katherine Falconer for comments. We all thank staff at OUP for all their hard work and encouragement.

Contents

Part One **Economic Tools**

Part Two **Applying the Tools**

List of Boxes

List of Figures

List of Tables

Part I

Economic Tools

Chapter 1

Economics for the Environment

WELCOME! The title of this chapter is *Economics for the Environment*. Why? Because economics has an important contribution to make to helping us understand and solve the many environmental problems facing people throughout the world today. Economists are often portrayed as the bad guys in the environmental debate. One of us was once sitting on a plane when someone asked them what they did. On hearing the answer 'I'm an environmental economist,' the response came back: 'Isn't that a contradiction in terms?' People often equate 'economics' with 'financial and commercial', yet economics is as much about Main Street as it is about Wall Street. We believe that economic arguments can often be used to help the environment, rather than harm it. In Part I of this book, we set out the principle insights that economics has to offer. Then, in Part II, we take important environmental problems, and show how these insights can improve how people respond to these problems. We believe strongly that an environmental policy which does not address economics is likely to get things wrong; but also that economic actors should be encouraged to take into account their impacts on the environment, by getting prices right. Economic and environmental systems are closely interlinked: by ignoring economic insights, we are unlikely to produce sensible outcomes for either system.

People are paying more attention to the environmental consequences of economic activity, and to the economic value of the environment. Partly, this is due to greater public awareness of environmental issues such as climate change or the loss of treasured local landscapes. Partly, it is a consequence of the increasing interest of policymakers to understand the benefits and costs of environmental regulation. People have started to care and know more about environmental degradation, yet the costs of protecting the environment keep getting pointed out to us (witness industrial opposition to the introduction of a carbon tax in the European Union). Sustainable development has become a buzzword for governments at all levels, yet few understand exactly what it means; whilst predictions of impending doom due to world population increases continue to circulate. Given our belief that economics has an important, indeed vital, contribution to make in understanding these issues and the trade-offs that lie behind them, a book which tries to get the basic ideas across to a wide audience seemed a good idea.

In the rest of this chapter, we:

■ Discuss the connections between the economy and the environment.

■ Review ten key insights from environmental and resource economics that environmental scientists, managers, and politicians ought to be aware of.

■ Explain how this book is best used.

■ Provide an overview of what happens in the rest of the book.

1.1 The Economy and the Environment

THIS book explores why economics matters more to environmental and natural resource policy than many people think. To begin with, it's important to say that economics is not just about financial comings and goings: the 'unpriced' services which the natural environment provides us with are equally its concern. The value of protecting wetlands for their biodiversity, flood defence, and pollution treatment functions is just as much an economic value as this week's production of oil from the North Sea.

Next, we need to better appreciate how the economy and the environment are interlinked. The economy operates from inside the environmental system, with conditions in the two systems being simultaneously determined. By 'the economy', we mean all the firms that make up industry; households (people) in their twin roles as consumers and suppliers of labour; governments; the institutions that govern interactions between these groups, such as markets; the state of technology; and our stocks of produced capital (such as roads and space stations). By 'the environment', we mean all natural resources, including land, land cover, and ecosystems (flora and fauna); resource deposits under the land surface; the world's oceans and atmosphere; and natural climate and nutrient cycles. As Figure 1.1 shows, there are many links between these two systems.

First, the environment provides the economic system with *inputs* of raw material and energy resources, including minerals, metals, food, hydrocarbons, and fibres such as wood and cotton. These resources may be either non-renewable (such as coal or iron ore), or renewable such as fisheries or forests. Inputs are often transformed by the economic system into outputs which consumers demand: wood into paper and oil into petrol, for example.

Second, the economy uses the environment as a *waste sink*. Wastes may originate from either production processes, such as CO_2 from electricity generation, or from consumption activities, for instance when households put out the garbage for collection and disposal. Wastes may be of a number of basic types: solid, air-, or waterborne; whilst the environment has a limited assimilative capacity to absorb and transform some wastes into harmless substances. Pollution is typically said to occur when emissions exceed assimilative capacity, and produce some undesirable impact.

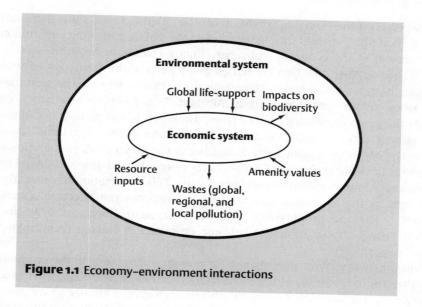

Figure 1.1 Economy–environment interactions

Third, the environment provides households with a direct source of *amenity*. People derive utility (happiness, satisfaction) from the contemplation of scenic beauty and wildlife, and from hiking and fishing. As Chapter 3 makes clear, these direct utility impacts are both important and highly relevant from an economics viewpoint.

Finally, the environment provides the economic system with basic *life-support services*. These include climate regulation, the operation of the water cycle, the regulation of atmospheric composition, and nutrient cycling.

One obvious point is that if the economy increases its demand on the environment with regard to any one of these four service flows, then this can impact on the environment's ability to provide other services. For example:

- An increase in the use of the environment as a waste sink due to increased emissions of pollutants may reduce the environment's ability to supply basic life-support by interfering with climate regulation; or may reduce the amenity value of the environment by degrading wildlife populations.

- An increase in demand on the environment for resource inputs may mean a reduction in amenity flows, if for example quarries are developed in national parks or as logging reduces the area of rainforest.

- We also show a link in Figure 1.1 between the economy and *biodiversity*. This shows that economic activity can affect natural diversity, most notably by taking over habitats (for example, when a rainforest is turned into a gold mine). Diversity is thought to be an important property of natural systems, especially with regard to their ability to withstand shocks such as drought and fire (this property is sometimes known as *resilience*).

An important feature of the interdependent economic-environmental system is *co-evolution*. This means that the way in which the economic subsystem evolves over time depends on the changing conditions of the environmental subsystem, and vice versa. A good illustration of this, in terms of impacts of the changing environment on the evolution of the economy, concerns climate change in neolithic Scotland. In around 4000 BC, neolithic farmers settled many parts of the west coast of Scotland, including islands such as Arran. The prosperity of this society may be seen from the large stone monuments they erected. Substantial land cover alterations occurred, notably the onset of clearing land of trees.[1] However, as the climate became cooler crop growth rates declined and the land became harder to subsist in. Areas of peat bog began to expand. Settlements became abandoned as people moved east and south: thus the evolution of economic activity was profoundly changed by exogenous alterations in environmental conditions. This explanation has recently been challenged as too simplistic, however, since it ignores the effects of cumulative cultivation on land productivity, and the short-term climate and acidity fluctuations brought about by major volcanic eruptions in Iceland (Whittington and Edwards, 1997).

Environmental systems may change for reasons endogenous to the economic system as well as in response to exogenous factors such as climate change in the preceding example. For instance, in nineteenth-century Egypt, a change to irrigated agriculture in the Nile valley to produce cotton for exporting, away from the system of natural flooding which had been in use since 5000 BC, resulted in the increasing salinity of farm land, and its eventual abandonment. Overexploitation of farmlands in areas as diverse as Mesopotamia, Easter Island, the Indus valley, and the Mayan civilization of Central America, caused food production crashes which changed the course of the development of entire societies (Ponting, 1991).

Economic changes impact on ecosystem evolution too. Examples include:

■ species introductions. For instance, the introduction of possums from Australia to New Zealand, and earlier introductions of cats, has changed the types and abundance of flora and fauna there.

■ changes in aquatic ecosystems as the industrial revolution unfolded in nineteenth-century Britain. The resultant increased sulphur deposition via acid rain reduced pH values in lakes and lochs, changing the composition of vertebrate and invertebrate fauna over time.

---

[1] There were in fact many phases of change in the woodland area up to 2,000 years ago, whilst the exact causes of change are still much debated. See Whittington and Edwards (1997).

1.2 Ten Key Insights from Economics which Environmental Scientists, Environmental Managers, and even Politicians should be aware of

THE previous section set out the interactions between the economy and the environment. What do economists have to say about these interactions? In the rest of this book, we will be explaining the contribution that economics can make to understanding and solving environmental problems. But suppose someone was too busy to read the rest of this book. What, at a minimum, would we wish to leave them with? The following list is one possibility:

1. Economic and environmental systems are determined simultaneously. This means that to fully understand these systems, economics must incorporate the mechanical underpinnings of the natural sciences, and the natural sciences must incorporate the behavioural underpinnings of economics.

2. The behavioural underpinnings of economics can be summed up as follows. First, people respond to incentives, as do firms. The most important incentives tend to be prices. Second, people make decisions 'at the margin': in other words, they try to balance out the costs and benefits of going one step further. Finally, expect firms and households to usually act in their own best interests. For firms, this typically means maximizing profits and for households it means maximizing their well-being (their *utility*). This implies that we should not be surprised when either behaves strategically: for example, when someone free-rides when asked to make a donation for an environmental good cause (see Chapter 2); or when a farmer threatens to destroy a wetland in return for a compensation payment not to do so. Institutions need to be designed which take these kinds of responses into account.

3. Environmental resources are scarce, and using them in one way has an opportunity cost. By 'scarce', we mean that there are not enough environmental resources around to simultaneously meet every possible demand on them. By 'opportunity cost', we mean the net benefits forgone from the next-best use. For example, suppose a piece of land has three possible uses, namely agriculture, forestry, and recreation, which have returns of £2,000/ha., £3,000/ha., and £4,000/ha. respectively. These activities we will assume to be mutually exclusive, in that the land cannot be used for more than one purpose at the same time. Deciding to use the land for recreation purposes forgoes a return from either agriculture or forestry, and the opportunity cost is the next-best return forgone, namely £3,000/ha. This cost should be taken account of when evaluating the net benefits of using the land for recreation.

4. Left to itself, the free market system can generate the 'wrong' level of environmental quality. Too many environmental bads (e.g. too much pollution) and too
few environmental goods (such as beautiful landscapes) will result from the point
of view of social optimality. Why should this be? Because the system of property
rights in existence means that no market price exists either to discourage economic agents from polluting, or to encourage them to produce environmental
benefits. This problem is known in economics as market failure: Chapter 2
investigates this issue in detail, and suggests alternative ways of solving such
problems. Another way of thinking about this is to say that the environment is
valuable in many ways, but not all of these show up in market values or prices.
For example, it is hard for a private landowner to charge for the landscape benefits his farm 'produces', and no market price exists for many aspects of landscape
beauty.

5. However, markets have proved to be the best way of allocating a vast range of
resources: Adam Smith's invisible hand still has much to recommend it. Markets
are extremely good at coordinating actions and at transmitting information. For
many resources, the market system is also very good at responding to changes in
relative scarcity. For example, the significant hikes in oil prices in the 1970s produced automatic adjustments in supply and demand. Finally, markets allow
people the opportunity to trade, which turns out to be a very good way of increasing social welfare on the whole. Markets can also be made to work for the
environment: see, for example, the discussion of the idea of tradable pollution
permits in Chapter 11 on water pollution.

6. Government intervention does not always make things better, and can make
things worse. The Common Agricultural Policy of the European Union has been
frequently criticized as giving farmers an incentive to damage the environment:
this might be called 'government failure'. When governments interfere with the
free operation of markets, they need to be aware that they are likely to bring
about coordination and information problems. Government intervention may
well hinder the responsiveness of markets to changes in relative scarcity, for
example if they keep prices at levels other than the market-clearing rate
(Chapter 2).

7. Environmental protection costs money. Scarcity means that opportunity costs
exist for all choices, even those driven by moral imperatives. Protecting
endangered species costs money, both directly (e.g. in monitoring) and indirectly
(in that land can no longer be used for development). Spending more public
money on public transport systems to reduce air pollution may mean less money
available to spend on schools. What is more, the costs of protecting the environment typically increase at the margin. As emissions from industrial sources are
progressively cleaned up, each extra reduction gets more and more expensive to
achieve.

8. When managing renewable resources such as fish and forests, choosing the maximum sustainable yield as the best level at which to harvest is rarely optimal. This
is because this rule ignores the economic costs and benefits of renewable
resource management. For instance, the maximum sustainable yield in a fishery

may be to catch 20,000 tonnes of fish per season. However, if costs rise faster than revenue at this point, then the government should reduce catches to below this level: catching at the maximum sustainable yield usually means too many boats chasing too few fish.

9. Whilst economic growth may not solve all environmental problems, and may be the cause of some, very few people would swap their position today with the equivalent 200 years ago. Think about that the next time you watch a wildlife programme on satellite TV.

10. Many of the world's most serious environmental problems are global in nature; however, economics predicts that getting countries to agree to do something about these together is going to be tough (Chapter 7). This is because game theory shows us that countries have an incentive to 'free-ride' on the actions of others, and so to avoid signing up for international agreements to cut global pollutant emissions, for example. However, economists can help in designing institutional arrangements to reduce these problems.

Box 1.1 Key Insights from Ecology that Economists ought to be aware of?

Above, we set out ten lessons that economists would like to teach natural scientists concerned with the environment. Naturally, such folk probably think their disciplines have much to teach economists! Environmental economists work with natural scientists from a wide range of disciplines, including population biology, freshwater chemistry, hydrometrics, and ecology. Joan Roughgarden (1995) has produced an account of key insights from ecology that economists would benefit from an awareness of, in the context of protecting biodiversity. These include:

- Ecologists are not good at predicting what will happen to ecosystems and the services they provide if species are gradually removed, since that is not a question they have been trying to answer. However, they do know something about the role that species currently play within systems.

- Ecosystems generate services which are important to society, and which may be lost if the system is damaged.

- Within any system, some species are redundant at points of time in terms of providing these services, yet may become essential if circumstances change.

- Economists should know more about the fundamental causes of biodiversity loss, if they are to say anything useful about reducing it.

- Habitat size is an important determinant of how many species one expects to find in an area, but is not the only determinant

- Many species are important for their potential as a source of new drugs. This potential is a function of diversity, with greater diversity being associated with greater levels of bio-active chemicals;

- In terms of the stability of ecosystems to shocks, not all species are equally important. Loss of 'keystone species' will produce bigger changes than loss of non-keystone species.

1.3 The Rest of This Book: An Overview

Wᴇ divide the book into two parts. Part I explores some important concepts in economics, and illustrates why they matter for environmental issues. Chapter 2 explores the role of markets in determining the level of environmental quality. The practice of placing monetary values on the environment has become controversial, but is an important component of the economist's toolbox: Chapter 3 deals with this issue. In Chapter 4 we set out the basic procedures of a very widespread technique of analysing policy and project choice, namely cost-benefit analysis. Problems encountered in using this methodology are also reviewed. Many environmental decision-making problems are characterized by high levels of risk and uncertainty, so Chapter 5 introduces economic approaches to these issues. Sustainable development is a fashionable buzzword in environmental and development debates at present: Chapter 6 investigates what economics has to contribute, in the context of older arguments over the environmental implications of economic growth. In Chapter 7, game theory techniques are introduced (at a very simple level!) as a good way of understanding situations where we have strategic interactions between players, be they countries arguing over climate change conventions, or fishermen competing over harvests. Finally, Chapter 8 lays out some basic economics of the debate over free trade: does free trade always increase people's well-being? Can trade restrictions be justified on environmental grounds?

In Part II, we show how economics can help us understand the causes of a series of important environmental problems, and more importantly, to cast light on the best way of managing them. The problems studied are:

- Transport and the environment
- Protecting the rainforests
- Controlling water pollution
- Climate change
- Biodiversity
- Energy policy and resources

These chapters are brief considerations of these important and complex issues, so we only have time and space to highlight how economics can be useful in thinking about our impacts on the natural world. Yet the material in Part II does show (we hope!) the richness of analysis that economics can bring to these problems.

Finally, in the last chapter we ask the questions: what happens when environmental considerations get left out of economics? And what happens when economics gets left out of environmental policy-making and resource management decisions?

1.4 Using This Book for Teaching and Learning

THIS book is aimed at a wide audience. Very little background by way of economics is assumed, and the use of mathematical explanations is downplayed as much as possible. The book is therefore suitable for introductory courses in environmental and natural resource economics, both for economics students and non-economists. It should also be suitable for undergraduate- and M.Sc.-level interdisciplinary courses where many students lack a background in economics.

Instructors will see that we do not follow a traditional path in explaining the subject: for example, there is no chapter on the economics of renewable resources *per se*, nor on the economics of the mine. However, the basic ideas may all be found either in Part I (e.g. in Chapter 7 on game theory, for renewables) or in the case studies in Part II (e.g. in the energy chapter for non-renewables and the rainforest chapter for forestry economics). Clearly there are costs to presenting things this way, but we feel these are outweighed by the benefits: an initial introduction to important economic concepts; and then a look at important environmental issues which draws on these concepts and develops others.

References

Roughgarden, J. (1995). 'Can economics protect biodiversity?' in T. Swanson (ed.), *The Economics and Ecology of Biodiversity Decline* (Cambridge: Cambridge University Press).

Whittington, G. and Edwards, K. (1997). 'Climate change' in K. Edwards and I. Ralston, (eds.), *Scotland: Environment and Archaeology, 8000 BC–AD 1000* (Chichester: John Wiley & Sons).

Suggestions for Further Reading

- Boulding, K. (1966). 'The economics of the coming spaceship earth', in H. Jarrett (ed.), *Environmental Quality in a Growing Economy* (Baltimore: Johns Hopkins University Press).

- Crocker, T. (1999). 'A brief history of environmental and resource economics', in J. van den Bergh (ed.), *Handbook of Environmental and Natural Resource Economics* (Cheltenham: Edward Elgar).

- Ponting, C. (1991). *A Green History of the World* (London: Penguin Books).

Chapter 2
Markets for the Environment

2.1 Introduction

WE all use markets in our everyday life, and some of us without knowing it. Many people even champion their use as the most useful way to organize economic activity. Most of us appreciate the choices and opportunities that markets provide to our families. We embrace markets daily—voluntary exchange regulated by competition is a big part of how we all live our lives. Almost everyone likes choice.

What is a market anyway? To most, a market is a neighbourhood mall or global website where one can buy and sell apples or armchairs. A market is a concrete place to spend money. To economists, the idea of a market is more exotic—they see the market as a spontaneous tool of exchange. Markets arise spontaneously in all cultures because people find value in trade. Market trading creates wealth through voluntary exchange of scarce resources, in which prices guide the terms of trade. Wealth is created when resources move from low-value to high-value uses. Markets *create* wealth, rather than *redistribute* wealth.

We should all appreciate markets for another reason. Markets are an effective channel of communication. Many scientists dedicated to protecting the environment believe that markets are the most effective tool humans have 'discovered' to organize and coordinate the diffuse set of information spread throughout society (see Hayek, 1945). Markets use prices to communicate both the laws of nature and the laws of man. Prices send signals to coordinate efficiently decentralized economic decisions. Markets succeed when prices accurately define the trade-offs we face such that resources are allocated to their highest-valued use in society.

But markets can fail too. Society confronts unacceptable environmental risks when a market price fails to communicate social desires and physical constraints accurately. Prices might misstate the economic value of a reduction in health risk from an environmental threat, or prices might not even exist to signal the value. Left alone, a market might produce too few or too many goods or services. A wedge is driven between what people want individually and what society wants as a collective.

Endangered species protection on private land is a classic example of market failure. About half of the listed endangered species in the USA have 80 per cent of their habitat on private land. But the benefits of protecting endangered species accrue to an entire nation, while a sizeable share of costs fall on private landowners. And since the market price of private land does not capture the social benefits of such species, landowners have more incentive to protect their own investment than to protect endangered species. The market fails when private decisions generate a less protected habitat than society as a whole desires.

But even when markets are a problem, they can be the cornerstone of the solution. Rather than turning to more government regulation or stakeholder-participation processes, society can adjust existing or create new markets to manage our environment and natural resources. A market is a tool whose precision depends on how society defines the rules to regulate its behaviour, i.e. property rights, liability, and information. People who are unhappy with the prices that a market produces need to see the connection between the signals sent and the underlying rules that we defined. We can work together to change these rules. We should view markets as our slave not our master.

This chapter explores the nature of markets, market failure, and market redemption. We discuss the power of markets, and why economists like them so much. We then dissect how markets can fail the environment due to externalities, public goods, common property, thresholds, and hidden information. We end by exploring how we can use elements of markets to correct market failure, or policy failure due to government subsidies.

2.2 The Power of Markets

A **MARKET** serves society by efficiently organizing economic activity. Markets use prices to communicate the wants and limits of a diffuse and diverse society so as to bring about coordinated economic decisions in the most efficient manner. The power of a perfectly functioning market rests in its decentralized process of decision-making and exchange; no omnipotent central planner is needed to allocate resources. Rather, market prices ration resources to those who value them the most, and in doing so, people are swept along by Adam Smith's invisible hand to achieve what is best for society as a whole. Self-interest is the driving power, competition the regulator of that power—together they work to improve the life of common people.

A key idea behind the power of markets and free exchange is *comparative advantage*. A person has a comparative advantage over another person in one good relative to another good if his relative *efficiency* in the production of the first good is greater than the other person's. Alternatively, a person has a comparative advantage if his opportunity cost is less than the other person's. Recall *opportunity cost* is the economic cost as measured by what one has to give up to do something else.

Should Bob Dylan shovel his own snow for example? No—even though his Bobness could probably shovel as well as the next guy, his opportunity costs are too great. Say he could blow the snow in two hours; in the same time he could have written a new song and earned $500,000. A neighbour's child might take four hours and would cost his Bobness $60. The child could have earned $24 in those four hours working for his parents. Both are better off if the child next door shovels the snow.

Absolute advantage does not necessarily translate into *comparative advantage*. Everyone has a comparative advantage at something because opportunity costs differ among people. Markets and free trade can benefit everyone in society because they allow people to specialize in activities in which they have a comparative advantage. See Chapter 8 for an extension of this idea to the benefit of trade between nations.

A market is successful when it produces an efficient allocation of resources. Efficiency in economics is most commonly defined as *Pareto optimality*—the inability to reallocate resources without making at least one person worse off. If consumers and producers act to maximize their private net benefits, a complete set of markets in which people freely exchange goods and services will generate a socially optimal allocation of resources. See Box 2.1 for a discussion of market equilibrium and the gains from trade.

Property rights are crucial to a successful market system. A well-defined property rights system represents a set of entitlements that define the owner's privileges and obligations for use of a resource or asset and have the following four characteristics:

Comprehensive—all resources are either privately or collectively owned, and all entitlements are defined, well known, and enforced.

Exclusive—all benefits and costs from use of a resource should accrue to the owner, and only to the owner, either directly or by sale to others. This applies to both private and common property resources.

Transferable—property rights should be transferable from one owner to another through a voluntary exchange. The owner thus has incentive to conserve the resource beyond the time he or she expects to make use of it.

Secure—property rights to resources should be secure from involuntary seizure or encroachment by other people, firms, and the government. Security provides the owner with an incentive to improve and preserve a resource while it is in his or her control rather than exploit the assets.

These four conditions represent an ideal scenario in which all gains from trade are found and captured by people looking for opportunities to trade. Economists do not blindly presume this is the real world, rather they work with the idea of complete markets to set a theoretical benchmark against which they can judge the effectiveness of different plans to organize economic activity. This confining orthodoxy of maximization and equilibrium to capture the interactions of intelligent self-interested people is a necessary fiction rather than literal truth, and should be recognized as such.

Markets also force people to make a distinction between rhetoric and action in the context of environmental assets. We all have opinions. Markets help separate those opinions we are willing to back up with real resources from those we are not. The

Box 2.1 Market Equilibrium and the Gains from Trade

Consider the following simple market. Suppose a market for a classic Ansel Adams photo of the Grand Tetons exists with eight buyers and eight sellers. Each buyer has his or her maximum willingness to pay (WTP) for one photo; each seller has his or her minimum willingness to accept compensation (WTA) for one photo:

Buyer ID	WTP	Seller ID	WTA
B1	$300	S1	$250
B2	$200	S2	$350
B3	$50	S3	$150
B4	$500	S4	$450
B5	$300	S5	$250
B6	$250	S6	$100
B7	$400	S7	$200
B8	$100	S8	$100

Using the WTP and WTA data, we can graph the market demand and supply curves, and then calculate the equilibrium price and quantity, and the total gains from trade. First, rank-order the buyers from highest to lowest WTP, and draw them as a set of downward steps. This is the market demand curve. Now rank-order the sellers from lowest to highest WTA, and graph them as a set of upward steps. This is the market supply curve. Where the market demand and supply cross is the market equilibrium.

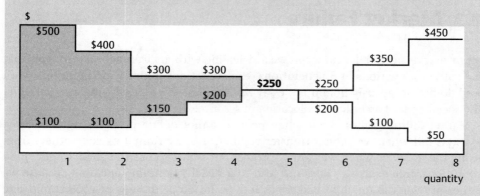

We say that when supply equals demand the market is in equilibrium. In this example then, the equilibrium market price equals $250, and the equilibrium quantity is 4 or 5.

The total gains from trade is defined as the sum of *consumer surplus* and *producer surplus*. Consumer surplus (CS) represents the gains to each buyer, and is represented as the difference between each buyer's WTP and the market price:

$$CS = (\$500 - 250) + (\$400 - 250) + (\$300 - 250) + (\$300 - 250) + (\$250 - 250) = \$500.$$

For example, buyer 7 was willing to pay $400; but since the market was in place he only had to pay $250; his benefits from the market, i.e. his consumer surplus, was therefore $150 (= $400 − 250). The sum of each buyer's consumer surplus is the benefits to all the consumers.

Producer surplus (PS) is the difference between the market price and each seller's WTA:

$$PS = (\$250 - 100) + (\$250 - 100) + (\$250 - 150) + (\$250 - 200) + (\$250 - 250) = \$450$$

For example, seller 7 was willing to accept $100; but since the market was in place she received $250; her benefits from the market, i.e. her producer surplus, was therefore $150 (= $250 − 100). The sum of each seller's producer surplus is the benefits to all the producers.

Total surplus equals the sum of consumer and producer surplus, which equals $950 = ($500 + 450), which is represented by the shaded area between the demand and supply curve.

discipline provided by the market forces people to relate their choices to the choices of others and to the consequences the sum of these choices produce.

People often overstate their real willingness to cooperate or to contribute to saving threatened tree frogs or critical wetlands when asked a hypothetical question. And in many contexts, understanding the gap between actions and intentions can make all the difference between whether an environmental project actually makes sense. Markets do not sustain cheap talk backed by either deep or shallow pockets.

2.3 Market Failure

BUT markets can fail. And when we are dealing with environmental resources that cut across nations and generations, the conditions under which markets work well do not necessarily hold up. We say markets fail when private means contradict the social ends of an efficient allocation of resources.

Market failure comes about when people cannot define property rights clearly. Markets fail when we cannot transfer rights freely, we cannot exclude others from using the good, or when we cannot protect our rights to use the good. Under these conditions, free exchange does not lead to a socially desirable outcome because we either provide too much of bad goods like pollution or too few of good things like open space. Since everyone 'owns' the right to clean air and good climates and bio-diversity, nobody owns the right and therefore it is impossible for a market to exist so people can trade freely. The market system is thus incomplete, and we have the problem of 'missing markets'.

Most societies do not currently have well-defined rights to produce or consume hog odour (i.e. the smell of manure) from a corporate hog factory. Those up- or down-wind currently cannot buy or sell tickets for fragrant air. The hog factory upwind cannot sell fresh air, those downwind cannot buy fresh air. As such, since the factory does not bear the downwind costs, it can effectively ignore these costs. With incomplete markets, the hog factory lacks a motivating economic incentive to control emissions or to switch to less polluting practices.

Similarly, there may be no legal or institutional basis that allows people who use polluted river water to receive compensation from upstream farmers whose sediments, pesticides, or fertilizers impose downstream costs in the form of contaminated drinking water, poor fishing, or reduced recreational opportunities. Farmers can thus impose 'external costs' on these other users of the river.

Economists have developed a taxonomy to identify and categorize the different types of market failure for environmental and natural resource issues. Understanding how and why a market fails is the first step to correct the problem. Consider now four types of market failure for environmental resources—externalities, public goods, common property, and hidden information. Note that you will see some blur between the types of market failure. We do not consider market power or monopoly in our discussion.

Externalities. Externalities are the classic case of market failure. An externality exists when a person does not bear all the costs or receive all the benefits of his or her action. An externality exists when the market price or cost of production excludes its social impact, cost, or benefit. Externalities are everywhere. Look around and think of all the times your actions affect others, for better or worse, and you did not pay or receive compensation for the costs or benefits. The market fails because no exchange institution exists—read market—in which the person pays for the external benefits or pays a price for imposing the external costs.

Driving your car around town creates numerous externalities. The exhaust contributes to air pollution, driving at rush hour adds to congestion, road rage increases the risk to others and yourself, the beautiful racing flames painted on the side adds to civic pride. No explicit markets exist to exchange the good for the bad. You live with it. But from an efficiency viewpoint in which society is trying to get the most out of its limited resources, the lack of a market leads to too much exhaust, too much congestion, too much road rage, too few racing flames.

Consider an example of a negative externality, or external cost, in a local environment. The untamed village of Centennial sits at the base of the Wild Mountains. The village currently has limited development and those houses that do exist usually sit below the ridgeline so that most people cannot see them. People enjoy the wide-open space that the current form of development promotes. But now a newcomer has moved into the valley and wants to build a new house on his private property. This property sits on a prominent ridge, a 'hogback', and the proposed house will be a two-storey starter mansion that will be visible to everyone in the valley.

Ole lives below the ridge and currently has an undisturbed view of the hogback and the valley beyond. If Riley builds his house, the sense of open space will disappear and Ole's view will be ruined for sure. Riley's action will reduce Ole's well-being but no compensation will be paid for his or anyone else's lost views. Riley's private decision to build his mansion does not account for the losses suffered by the rest of the community who treasured their open space—a wedge is driven between the private and socially optimal allocation of resources.

Figure 2.1 illustrates this example. Riley accounts for his own incremental benefits

Box 2.2 An Example of an Externality: Air Pollution in Ecuador

As we have seen, failing to put the correct 'price' on using the environment can lead to too much environmental degradation. Factory owners who decide to increase output face no cost for any resultant increase in pollution. This suggests that they have no economic incentive to cut down on emissions, and then society has too much pollution. Another example is the air pollution arising from driving to work. When people drive to work, they pay no immediate price for the pollution coming from their cars.

Jurado and Southgate (1999) explore these factory and auto externalities in a recent study of air quality in Quito, the capital of Equador. Quito lies high up in an Andean mountain valley, which exacerbates its air quality problem. The table below shows that major sources of pollutants are vehicles and factories. Neither factory nor vehicle owners face any immediate economic price for the pollution they are responsible for.

Table B2.1

	Total suspended particulates (TSP)	Sulphur dioxide (SO_2)	Nitrous oxides (NO_x)
Vehicles	1,069	659	5,298
Factories	7,170	18,707	5,023

These levels of air pollution exceed the World Health Organization (WHO) maximum recommended levels. The concentrations of TSP in 1991 averaged 149.9 : g/m^3, compared with the WHO standard of 60 : g/m^3.

The authors estimated the economic costs of air pollution as measured by the impact on human health. Pneumonia and other respiratory ailments are the leading cause of death in all age groups in the city, and are exacerbated by high TSP levels. The study used statistical relationships between TSP levels and three standard measures of ill-health: restricted activity days, work days lost, and excess mortality.

The predicted increases in ill-health from pollution were valued in economic terms using several approaches, including the value of working time, and the cost of illness (e.g. hospital resources used up in treating patients; see rows 2 and 3 of Table B2.2). Extra deaths were valued as the discounted value of lifetime earnings, a somewhat dated approach. This yields a value of $16,887 per avoided death. This gives the values in row 4 of Table B2.2.

We have used the more modern 'value of statistical life' estimates based on how much people are willing to pay for risk reductions (see Chapter 5 for details). The value of reduced risk is increased by an order of magnitude in row 5. These new estimates are based on the figure of $130,000 per avoided death from Fankhauser et al., (1998) for developing countries. Whatever the values used, the message is clear: externalities due to private air pollution decisions impose social costs on the citizens of Quito.

Table B2.2

	Annual costs to citizens of Quito, US$s
Restricted activity day costs (given 3,433,000 restricted days)	$14,418,600
Working days lost costs (given 1,765,000 working days lost)	$12,708,000
Excess mortality costs, as per study (given 94 extra deaths per year)	$1,587,378
Excess mortality costs, revised	$12,220,000

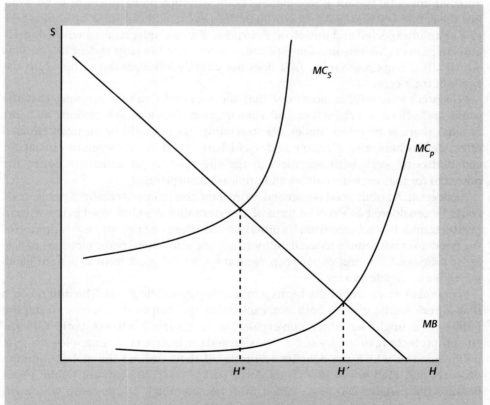

Figure 2.1 Marginal benefits and marginal costs: private and social

and costs, and chooses to develop his house at level H'. If he had accounted for the social costs of lost open space suffered by Ole and the rest of the community, Riley would have developed at level H^*—a smaller house built below the ridge. Since $H' > H^*$, the market is said to have failed to allocate resources efficiently—too much housing on the ridge in Centennial valley.

Obviously this example did not involve life and death, only a loss of aesthetics. But many externalities in the environment do increase the risks to life and limb. Toxic waste dumps that leach into drinking water are a vivid example; urban air pollution due to transportation that curtails the activities of young children is another. All actions that alter the risk to others in which no compensation is paid or received create externalities that are left unattended by the market.

Most standard examples of pollution reflect a direct externality—you breathe or drink polluted air or water and you have a direct impact on your health. But over the last century tracking the effects of an externality has become more complicated as humanity develops new technologies to separate itself from the whims of nature. Determining the cause and potential effects is less obvious in many cases. The effects are often less direct and more roundabout.

The idea of *ecosystem externalities* captures these indirect impacts. An action affects an environmental system at one obvious point in which no harm seems to be done. But the action is working its way through the system, and can show up somewhere else as an unexpected and unwelcome surprise. For example, citizens who kill predators to protect children and domestic animals can generate large rodent infestations which affect crops and sanity. DDT does not directly kill birds but rather thins the shells of their eggs.

Ecosystem externalities point out that the economist cannot presume that the cause and effect of production and consumption decisions are obvious and just because there is no effect 'under the streetlamp' there might be an unanticipated effect somewhere else (Crocker and Tschirhart, 1993). It is therefore crucial for economists to work with scientists in the life sciences to anticipate better the potential for indirect externalities and unpleasant surprises.

Public goods. A public good is a second form of market failure. Actually, a public good could be considered as a special form of an externality. A public good exists when a person cannot be excluded from its provision and when one person's consumption of the good does not reduce its availability to anyone else. These two conditions of *non-excludability* and *non-rival consumption* separate a public good from a private good, which is excludable and rival.

Economists make use of the terms *pure* and *impure* public goods. The difference is that a pure public good is both non-excludable and non-rival; whereas an impure public good might be either non-excludable or non-rival but not both. Climate-change protection, ozone layer, biodiversity, and the high seas are examples of a pure public good in which the benefits accrue to all those around the globe. Common property and club goods like rivers, local parks, lakes, are impure public goods because the benefits can be excluded from non-members of the group who owns the resource. We focus here first on pure public goods, and then turn to common property in the next section.

Non-exclusion depends on the physical characteristics of the good and the property rights regime. Climate-change protection is the most obvious form of public good in the environment. No nation can be excluded from the emission reduction efforts of another nation. Biodiversity preservation is another example of a public good. No person can be excluded from the public benefits created from a stable ecosystem created by preserving species. For wildlife viewing, unless the species exist only on private reserves, then it is difficult to exclude potential beneficiaries from enjoying the prospect of seeing them. And if people derive value simply from the existence of a species, exclusion is impossible. This holds for many environmental resources—if air quality in a city improves, nobody who lives in or visits the city can be excluded from the benefits. Note that other environmental resources are excludable in consumption. For example, market prices control recreational access to downhill skiing at a resort.

Non-rivalness also depends on the characteristics of the good. The benefits gained from the resource is independent of the number of other people who wish to use it. For example, better air quality increases one person's well-being, no matter how many other citizens there are. If an endangered species is protected, the number of people affected does not reduce the benefits to each person. Some environmental resources do not completely possess this property. If designating a wilderness area as a recreational resource protects it from future development, more people implies more congestion and fewer benefits for many visitors. Many people visiting Yellowstone National Park for example feel that congestion is a disamenity. Too many people, too little solitude, at least for those restricted to their mobile.

What is the relevance of these properties for the socially optimal provision of public goods and market failure? Let's revisit the Centennial open space issue as a public goods problem. Open spaces are a public good if defined as an aesthetic available to all people in the same amount—my visual consumption of open space does not reduce your access nor reduce the amount of open space. The potential problem with using the market to provide this public good voluntarily is *free-riding*—since he or she cannot be excluded from the same amount of the good, each person has an incentive to let someone else provide the public good. Everyone has an incentive to free-ride off the efforts of others.

Free-riding can lead to what is commonly called the classic and well-known case of the *prisoner's dilemma*, also called the *social trap* or the *tragedy of the commons* (the next chapter expands on this theme). The dilemma exists when people find that their individual incentives lead them to the worst outcome possible—for themselves and society. The idea is compelling enough—a person looking out for his own self-interest and who is fully aware that other people are doing the same, still cannot avoid shooting himself in the foot. In public good terms, this means that a person knows he should not free-ride because he can do better by being a good citizen; but he still feels compelled to because if he doesn't free ride and everyone else does, he is left holding the bag.

Of course, in reality people do contribute to the provision of some public good voluntarily everyday. Whether people contribute to the public good is not the question. The question is whether they voluntarily contribute an amount of effort or money that equals the amount they actually benefit from the good. If so, market works in allocating a public good. If not, by definition the market fails. The market fails because people have undersupplied the socially optimal level of the public good. Free-riding can be partial or complete, so the market might fail by a little or a lot. But technically, the market still fails. Market failure occurs with voluntarily public good provision when people contribute any amount less than their true benefits for the good.

Consider the incentives to free-ride on open space provision. Suppose Ole and the citizens of Centennial are considering pooling their resources and using the market to buy out Riley to stop him from building his new mansion on the hogback. Since no one can be excluded from the potential benefits of open space, the incremental benefit to society from one more unit of visibility equals the summed incremental benefits from each person who gains enjoyment from the view.

Social incremental benefits reflects how much society values each extra unit of the good. Economists then ask about the 'optimal level' of the public good: what is the level of this good that will maximize net benefits to society? The optimal level is when the social incremental benefits equal the incremental cost to provide one more unit of the good. This optimal level is called the *Lindahl equilibrium*, named after the Swedish economist who first identified it.

If the market fails to generate the optimal level of the public good, how could it then be supplied? One possibility is to build a club: everyone who benefits from the good gets together to provide the good, and the benefits of this provision are then restricted to those people belonging to the club. This seems attractive since only the beneficiaries of the good pay for it, and government is not forced to intervene. Organizations like the RSPB in Britain, and the Sierra Club in the USA, are partial examples of this. The RSPB buys and safeguards nature reserves using funds generated by club members (see Foster, Bateman, and Harley, 1997).

But while club members get reduced fees for entry to sites, non-members also benefit from environmental preservation. The non-excludability of benefits means less nature reserves would be provided than optimal if their provision was left solely to the RSPB. What is more, club financing is likely to be less than optimal, in that people do not have to join and pay, even though they know they will benefit anyway. The strategic incentive to free-ride still exists.

The Commons. The commons are an impure public good if the resource is defined by rivalrous consumption and non-excludability or *open access*. If one person's use reduces the total available to all, everyone has an incentive to capture the benefits as quickly as possible before someone else gets them. This free-for-all leads to the economically inefficient use of the resource. The moratorium on fishing for cod and witch flounder off the Grand Banks in the North Atlantic is a prime example.

By inefficiency we mean that the fishers harvest to the point at which the incremental costs exceed the incremental revenue (i.e. market price) of harvesting. Overuse implies that the market price has failed to signal the true scarcity of the asset. Since a fish caught by one fisher is one fewer fish for all others, fishers have no private incentive to account for the scarcity value of the resource. They expend too

Box 2.3 The Tragedy of the Commons

Biologist Garrett Hardin coined the phrase 'the tragedy of the commons' in the journal *Science* in 1968. The word 'tragedy' meant a 'remorseless working of things'.

Hardin was concerned with unchecked global population growth, which he saw as unsustainable especially for common property. His example of a pasture open to all graziers to let their cattle roam over leads to overgrazing. Each grazier gets the full benefit of adding one more animal to the common (the profit per beast). But as cattle numbers rise, overgrazing occurs, which then causes everyone to lose. Each person thus rushes headlong down a path that eventually leads to social ruin, destroying the idea of Adam Smith's beneficial but invisible hand. This tragedy only gets serious, Hardin argues, as population rises, since rising population equates to more people wanting to graze their animals.

Hardin's analysis has been praised, criticized, and extended. We now know that overgrazing of common areas is not new—it happened in ancient Mayan civilization and ancient Egypt. We also know that the price of the good produced on the commons matters more to the rate of exploitation than Hardin thought. We also know that many commons throughout the world are regulated by rules set by those who have access to the area (see Chapter 3). The common grazing moorland in England is an example of commons without environmental destruction.

Yet Hardin's message is powerful. We can find many examples of open-access resources damaged by overuse. A recent example is a study of common grazing areas in the Northern Isles off the Scottish coast. On Shetland, common grazings seem to suffer higher levels of environmental damage than comparable privately owned areas (Hanley *et al.*, 1998).

much effort and end up overharvesting the fish stock relative to what is economically efficient and potentially biologically inefficient.

What happens in open access commons? Each fisher has an incentive to catch as many fish before someone else catches the same fish. He has no incentive to value the scarcity of the fish because if he does not catch them someone else will. His decision to leave the fish be is not respected by others because they have as much right to the fish as he does. So he starts expending effort and in doing so his effort is such that his incremental costs end up exceeding his incremental revenue. This violates the standard efficiency condition that says that net benefits are maximized when incremental revenue equals incremental costs.

Why? Efficiency is breached because each fisher imposes an external cost on all the other fishermen. This external cost arises because each time a fish is caught it makes it more costly for everyone else to catch the next one. This is like a variant of the infamous 90–10 rule of diminishing returns to effort—you get 90 per cent of the fish with 10 per cent of the effort, but catching the remaining 10 per cent takes 90 per cent of the effort because they are harder to find. And when everyone else is out fishing as well, this rule comes into play even more quickly because you are all out there trying to catch the fish.

When do the fishers stop their effort in open access? A fisher stops when his incremental costs equal the average revenue, or when his economic profits are zero. In this case, even though net profits to fishers are zero, the net social value is negative because the scarcity value of the fish has been ignored in the free-for-all. In this case, each fisher does not earn the economic rent that would reflect the scarcity value of the fish to society.

Open access is the case in which we might witness a 'tragedy of the commons'. Since everyone has access, all have the rights to the resource and scarcity value is ignored. But the reality is that most commons have a property-right scheme, either formal or informal, that works to allocate resources in a more economically efficient manner. There are numerous documented examples of self-governing commons in which people work as a collective unit and respect the scarcity value of the resource. These groups succeed when they establish common property rights that include sharing rules, exclusion principles, and enforcement and punishment schemes (see Ostrom 1990).

Market failure need not always occur with the commons. People have and continue to define rules to capture the scarcity value of a resource shared by many people. Be aware that often market failure is associated with the commons when people use the term 'the commons' or the 'global commons' when they actually mean a global or regional public good that is both non-rival and non-excludable. Pure public goods are much more of a challenge to handle because of the need for a larger coalition of affected parties. We also expand on this in the climate-change Chapter 14.

Hidden information. Market failure can occur when people cannot observe what other people are doing. *Moral hazard* confounds market operations because one person cannot observe the hidden actions of others. *Adverse selection* frustrates markets because a person cannot observe the hidden type of a person or the hidden quality of some good or service. Both types of hidden action retard the creation of markets that could be used to allocate resources to more efficient use, such as the reduction of environmental risk.

Moral hazard implies that a regulator cannot perfectly monitor pollution abatement, and therefore a firm could shirk on pollution control. The firm has an incentive to shirk if it bears all the control costs in return for a fraction of the benefits. The result again is too much pollution relative to the economically efficient level. Also moral hazard can lead to an inefficient 'pooling' of environmental risk.

Environmental risks are part of life, and it would be better to find markets to allow those who are less willing to bear risk to sell the risk to those who are willing to buy it. But moral hazard reduces the ability to reallocate risk among different economic agents. When the private market cannot monitor actions, an insurer will withdraw from the pollution liability market because the provision of insurance will also affect the individual's incentives to take precautions.

Given that accidental spills or storage of pollution can create potential financial liabilities (e.g. clean-up costs, medical expenses), a firm would like to pay to pass these risks on to a less risk-averse agent such as an insurer. But since there is a trade-off between risk-bearing and incentives, the market for pollution liability insurance will be incomplete as insurers attempt to reduce the information rents of the better-informed individual. The market will produce an inefficient allocation of risk.

Adverse selection affects the environment too. One key recommendation of environmental policy is sustainable production of products. These products should be produced using methods that will support some 'high' quantity and quality resource supply. The challenge facing these sustainable products is that these products are more expensive and thus demand a higher market price. But if buyers cannot be guaranteed that they really are getting their 'sustainability' bang for their buck, they will not buy them. Just saying that a product is sustainable is not enough for many consumers.

If a consumer cannot distinguish the sustainable product from a similar product produced using standard practices, he has no incentive to pay the price premium. Why should he or she pay more than average when he or she cannot distinguish high-quality from low-quality products?

The problem then is if the buyers disappear, the sellers have to withdraw from the market. The sellers with an above-average quality product who cannot get a price premium have no incentive to stay in the market because they could do better investing elsewhere with greater returns. And if enough high-price paying buyers disappear, the sellers disappear too, and the market will collapse. Preventing this collapse often requires a voluntary or government-sponsored certification scheme.

2.4 Markets for the Environment

MARKET failure can create environmental problems. But even if markets fail, we can still use the ideas behind markets to address the problems that might exist. We do not necessarily need to turn to command-and-control government intervention or collaborative stakeholder processes. Rather we can rewrite the rules to create new markets to address the failings of existing markets. Except in those cases in which government intervention is demonstrably superior, market-based policy serves as a ready substitute for technocratic or stakeholder processes, which have their own set of successes and failures.

Think about other kinds of real issues, like financial assets for instance, in which we are much less willing to delegate decision-making authority to the government or stakeholders. The fact that people have been creating and using markets to manage many assets constructively for the last three centuries should send a signal of their power, especially given that the odds and consequences of uncertainty in financial assets exceed most health and environmental risks. The relative stakes per percentage risk are much larger in financial assets than risks from environmental dilemmas. But we do not ask the government to regulate stock prices. We ask the government to help establish, monitor, and enforce the trading rules of the market, but not the market price itself.

Box 2.4 Government Intervention Failure: The Common Agricultural Policy

This chapter discusses how market failure can lead to undesirable consequences for the environment. Governments have a case for some level of intervention to do something about it. Sometimes, however, government intervention can make things worse for the environment. A good example of this is the Common Agricultural Policy of the European Union, affectionately known as the CAP.

Through a highly complex system of import levies, export subsidies, and intervention buying, the CAP offered farmers throughout the EU higher prices for their outputs than the free market would generate. The official reasons given were to support farm incomes, stabilize crop prices, and increase self-sufficiency rates for major food products. Casting aside the dubious economic arguments which could be made in support of these goals, let us focus instead on what the implications were for the environment. Farmers naturally responded to higher prices by increasing output, both by cultivating more land and increasing the intensity of production on all farmland. Coupled with technological progress, this had profound impacts on the countryside, especially in a country such as the UK, where farmland accounts for about 80 per cent of the total land area.

Bowers and Cheshire (1983) produced a powerful account of the impacts of the CAP, and previous domestic farm support measures which had been in place since 1949. Most important among the impacts on farming were:

- The removal of hedgerows, the ploughing of field margins, and the loss of farm woodlands
- Replacement of permanent pasture with temporary pastures and arable
- Land drainage
- Significant increases in the use of pesticides, herbicides, and fertilizers

The effects of these changes in farm practices on wildlife and landscape were extensive.

Figures from the Nature Conservancy Council published in 1983 showed, for example:

- A 50–60 per cent loss in lowland heaths since 1949
- A 95 per cent loss in herb-rich flower meadows
- An 80 per cent loss in chalk grasslands of high ecological value

Since 1983, environmental damage has continued to be felt, for instance in the loss of farmland bird species. Most of these changes could be attributed to changes in farming practices. As the English poet John Betjeman eloquently put it:

> We spray the fields and scatter
> The poison on the ground
> So that no wicked wild flowers
> Upon our farm be found.
> We like whatever helps us
> To line our purse with pence;
> The twenty-four-hour broiler-house
> And neat electric fence.

> *We fire the fields for harvest,*
> *The hedges swell the flame,*
> *The oak trees and the cottages,*
> *From which our fathers came.*
> *We give no compensation,*
> *The earth is ours today,*
> *And if we lose on arable*
> *Then bungalows will pay.*
>   *(to be sung to the tune, 'Harvest Home')*

Thus the CAP actually exacerbated an environmental problem, rather than solving it. By encouraging farmers to increase production and change how they produced, the CAP increased the external costs that farmers imposed on the countryside. Only recently have moves been taken to reduce these impacts, through agri-environmental schemes which actually pay farmers to produce environmental goods (see Dabbert *et al.*, 1998).

We now consider three basic ways we can create new markets to address market failure associated with environment. A basic market has a supply side and a demand side, which together produce quantity exchange at a market price that reflects the value of the asset. Working from this basic construction, we consider three options. First, we can assign property rights for environmental assets and let people negotiate over the price and quantity of the good. Second, we can work through regulators to set a market price per unit of the environmental asset and let people decide how much of the asset they want to buy. Third, we can use regulators to set the quantity of the asset that can be bought and let the people decide what price they are willing to pay for the fixed quantity. Consider each in turn.

Assign property rights and bargain over price and quantity. In 1960, economist Ronald Coase argued that we can create new markets for non-market goods like the environment as long as we are willing to remove institutional constraints to assigning well-defined property rights. Coase noted that two parties have an incentive to negotiate an economically efficient and mutually advantageous solution to a dispute provided that one party is given unilateral property rights to the asset in question. The key point is that it does not matter which party gets the property rights, only that they are assigned to someone. The outcome will be the same—an efficient allocation of resources. This is the Coase theorem, which holds provided that transaction costs are low and legal entitlements can be freely exchanged and enforced. Transaction costs are the price paid to organize economic activity, including information, negotiation, writing and enforcing contracts, specifying property rights, and changing institutional designs.

Consider our open space example. Riley and Ole obviously disagree about the amount of open space in Centennial valley. Riley owns the right to build his house on the hogback, Ole owns his own land below. All the citizens own the right to the view of the valley and ridge around Wild Mountain. But here is the rub. If everyone owns the right to the view, it is the same as saying that no one owns the right.

One solution to the conflict is for the government to intervene and restrict Riley's development, or to tell Ole to grow up and live with it. This command and control approach would allow a third party to select the winner and loser(s). The government could instead work with the community to create a dispute resolution process in which everyone could sit down at the bargaining table, and try to come to some agreement. This would require all stakeholders to agree to some solution. It would promote collaboration and by avoiding polarization produce creative solutions with political momentum. This could support local leadership and collaborative efforts to help Riley and the others enhance the environment and achieve economic productivity; or it could collapse into a bitter confrontation with no resolution.

Alternatively, we promote a Coasean solution that would create a market for open space by assigning property rights to either Riley or Ole. First suppose a third party assigns the property rights to Ole. Ole now has the right to keep the open spaces as he sees fit. This means he could choose to keep the open spaces to his liking, and have the legal power to ask Riley to build a house that would not disturb the open spaces. This makes Ole the supplier of development. And he would have to decide how much open space to surrender to development under a specific price schedule. Ole's supply schedule of development space would reflect his incremental costs from development, which are usually increasing in development. The more development, the greater loss of well-being as measured by more incremental costs.

Riley would now have to come to Ole to buy the use of open space for development. Riley would have to decide how much open space he would demand for a specific price. His demand schedule for development space would reflect his incremental benefits from development, which are assumed to be decreasing in development. More development, fewer incremental benefits.

The market for development space would clear at the market price in which all the space demanded would equal all supplied. Both Ole and Riley benefit from the trade: Ole earns benefits pay receiving a price for open space that exceeds his opportunity cost; Riley benefits from paying for space that is less than his benefits for developing. The market leads to an efficient outcome—the incremental benefits from development equal the incremental costs.

Now suppose instead that the third party assigned the property rights to Riley. The roles are reversed—Riley has the right to use up open space as he sees fit; Ole has the right to try and buy open space. The power of the Coase theorem is that the outcome would be exactly the same as before—same market price, same market quantity, same efficiency result. Economic efficiency is the same. Note, however, that the distribution of wealth differs. Now Riley receives the payment from Ole. Whether this is preferable to Ole receiving the wealth is a question of ethics.

What happens is that we simply redefine Ole and Riley's schedules to reflect the new property-right structure. Ole's supply curve for development now becomes his demand curve for open space. Ole now demands open space—different levels for specific prices. Riley's demand curve for development now becomes his supply curve for open space. He chooses to sell different amounts of open space at specific prices.

The market for open space would again clear at the identical market price in which all the space demanded would equal all supplied. Both Ole and Riley capture the same benefit from the trade: Ole earns benefits by paying a price for open space that is less than his opportunity cost of development; Riley benefits from selling open space at a price that exceeds his costs for forgoing developing. Again the market is efficient—the incremental benefits from open space preservation equal the incremental costs.

The Coase theorem is more likely to work the fewer people involved in the dispute. More people increase the transaction costs necessary to come to an agreement, and make the market less efficient. It is also hard to identify responsible parties in some cases; and people have more incentive to free-ride in larger groups. In the case of larger numbers, one can still use the market. Now one either can set the price of trade, or the quantity traded and allow the market to work.

Set the price of social damage—green taxes. For nearly a century economists have promoted the idea that we can adjust market prices to fix environmental dilemmas. We create new economic incentives in the market by altering the relative price of pollution or an otherwise unpriced environmental asset. The economist Alfred Pigou first suggested that an effective solution to pollution problems is to add a tax on to the market price. This Pigovian tax, or now more commonly called a *green tax*, would be set to equal the external cost, or incremental damage, suffered by those affected by the pollution.

In principle, society can alter a person's choices by imposing a green tax. The person will continue to produce and pay the tax as long as the incremental benefits he receives from the output exceed the tax. Once the green tax exceeds the incremental benefits, he cuts off his production. Ideally, if the green tax is set such that it reflects the equilibrium level of incremental damage, the person will voluntarily select the level of output that is the social optimum.

For Riley and Ole, a regulator could set the green tax at the equilibrium level of Ole's incremental damage suffered from the loss of open space. Now Riley would develop the space up to the point at which the tax exceeded his incremental benefits, and then he would stop. This would result in the same level of development as the Coasean solution.

Some economists have argued that there is a 'double dividend' with green taxes. A double dividend exists when a green tax (i) reduces the amount of pollution emitted; and (ii) when the revenues raised by the taxes are used to offset other distortionary taxes like the income or capital gains taxes. A distortionary tax is a charge on an activity society wants to promote rather than discourage, like work and investing. If we can use green taxes to reduce pollution and then use the extra revenue to reduce income taxes, society has two hits with one shot.

Unfortunately, the double dividend story has a twist. We know environmental protection benefits society. But this protection also raises prices and the overall cost of living, which cuts into a person's wages. Environmental protection is like a second labour tax added on to the already distortionary income tax. Now our worker has even more reason to decrease his labour supply, which is an additional cost to society—less labour, less wealth created. The open question remains whether the environmental benefits of the green tax will be large enough to offset the losses from the decreased labour supply. The double dividend moral is this: correcting one mistake can make a second even worse.

In addition, green taxes have been historically set to raise small amounts of revenue not induce big changes in behaviour. Taxes have been set too low to induce people to increase significantly either pollution abatement or environmental protection (Hanley, Shogren, and White, 1996). This reality is in part affected by the lack of information required to successfully implement an incentive to approach some social goal. Setting an efficient green tax requires information on the incremental costs and benefits schedules. One also needs information on the environmental fate and transport systems and the monetary value of risks to life and limb. The information required to find this incremental damage function is not free, as had been presumed in the original green tax models.

In fact, costly information for green taxes prompted Coase to propose his ideas of property rights, markets, and negotiations. Coase pointed out that if one could assign an efficient green tax, information costs must have been very low. If that is so, people could most likely use that information to find their own agreement, provided property rights were assigned to one of the disputing parties.

Set the quantity of social damages—tradable permit systems. An alternative to setting a Pigovian tax is to set a fixed quantity of the environmental good in question, and to allow people to trade the good on the open market. Thomas Crocker and J. Dales introduced the idea of tradable permits for environmental protection independently in the mid-1960s. Emission markets work by assigning the property rights to pollute to firms, governments, and people. These rights create value to something that was otherwise a free good, e.g. clean air or water.

Tradable permits focus on the quantity side of the market equation. A regulator selects a fixed quantity of pollution or development, and then sets the number of permits available for trade accordingly. These permits are then allocated to firms and people in the affected area. People then buy and sell these permits on the open market. People who keep pollution or development below their allotted permit level can sell or lease their surplus permits. People who exceed their allocation must buy permits from those who either produce less or find less polluting technologies.

What makes a tradable permit system effective? Economists have identified the conditions under which such a system is more likely to work. Permits must be well defined and scarce so their value can be estimated accurately. Free trade should dominate the permit market. Government intervention, bottlenecks, and transaction costs that limit the scope of trading should be minimal. Less friction increases the odds that people who value the permits the most will be able to buy or keep them. Permits should be 'bankable', such that people have the flexibility to save and spend permits as the market conditions fluctuate. People should be allowed to keep any profits they earn from the trade of permits. Penalties for violating a permit must exceed the permit price to help make sure people play by the rules.

Again for Riley and Ole, the regulator would select the amount of development allowable: ideally the efficient level, in which incremental benefits equal incremental cost. The regulator would then allocate permits to the Centennial community based on some predetermined rule—perhaps the number of acres or years spent in the valley. The permits are then free to be traded. If Riley wants to develop open space by more than his allotment, he would be free to buy more development permits on the

Box 2.5 Trading Pollution Permits

The USA is the nation with the most extensive experience of using Tradable Pollution Permit markets (TPPs) to control pollution. The initial moves towards use of TPPs came in the 1970s, due to conflicts between achieving national targets for clean air, and allowing economic growth in heavily industrialized states which were in violation of these national targets. Policy initiatives such as offsets, netting, and banking were brought together under the Emissions Trading Program in 1986. This allowed for limited permit trading in 'emission credits' for seven pollutants in 247 control regions across the USA.

In 1992, amendments to the Clean Air Act paved the way for a nationwide TPP system for sulphur dioxide emissions from power stations. The aim was to reduce total emissions to 50 per cent of existing levels. The market began in 1995. Some 110 of the largest power stations were allocated permits based on historical emissions, and then allowed to trade. Even though SO_2 is a non-uniformly mixed pollutant, permits traded at a one-for-one rate. In 2000, 800 additional power stations were to be brought into the scheme.

Evidence suggests that the scheme has performed well. First, total emission fell by more than the target level in phase 1, as firms banked permits for future use. The market in permits grew steadily, and permits prices fell from an initial high of around $1,000/tonne to around $100/tonne. The increasing volume of trading, reducing transactions costs, and falling abatement costs probably caused this price fall. This last was due to suppliers of abatement equipment cutting their prices since firms now had an alternative (buying permits), and by reductions in the price of low-sulphur coal due to deregulation.

Overall, the cost savings of the sulphur trading programme have been estimated at up to 50 per cent of what the costs would had been if regulation had been employed instead. This implies a saving to the US economy of between $225 million and $375 million (Ellerman *et al.*, 1998). Finally, the total costs of the scheme seem to be substantially less than the benefits, which include the economic value of avoided damage to human health, ecosystems, and recreational activities (Burtraw, 1998). Tradable permits have provided very good value for the money.

open market. In theory, the equilibrium permit price would equate the incremental costs to the incremental benefits of development. Again the efficient outcome is achieved.

Whether tradable permit markets will flourish as a tool to manage environmental and health dilemmas will be determined in time. Conceived in the 1960s, tested in the 1970s and 1980s, implemented in the 90s, discussions of tradable pollution permits are now commonplace in discussions on how to manage the environment. The most visible example is the acid rain trading programme that reduced sulphur dioxide emissions by 50 per cent at one-half to one-third the cost of a command-and-control approach. Such success stories raise the costs to policy-makers who neglect how effective markets can be at managing risk to society (see Sorrell and Skea, 1998).

Even climate change policy has rallied around the 'carbo' market, that is the market for carbon emissions, as an integral part of the cost-effective risk reduction strategy. The USA has proposed creating an international market to trade carbon emissions. This carbo market would allow buyers the flexibility to find low-cost carbon emissions from around the world. Estimates suggest that a perfectly functioning market would cut the costs of reaching the Kyoto targets by between 50 to 80 per cent (see Chapter 14). The interesting twist here is the biggest advocates for carbon markets are non-economists. In contrast, economists question whether the property rights regimes could be constructed such that the market would function as predicted.

2.5 Conclusion

FOR 5,000 years the best humans could do was to increase our life expectancy by five years. About 200 years ago, however, something changed, and since then Western culture has witnessed a thirty-year increase in how long we might live. Is it a coincidence that around the same time Adam Smith published his classic work *The Wealth of Nations* which explained the power of the market? Maybe not. Maybe understanding the undeniable role of markets as collector, codifier, and disseminator of diffuse information has helped to create the social order to improve the quality of life.

Herein we have examined how markets can work against and for the environment. Markets are a process of discovery. Markets allow us to create wealth, which in turn allows us to create more health. And even when one market fails, a new market can be constructed to manage the environment. Markets do not substitute for good environmental policy; rather they can be a good tool to promote more protection for less wealth. Markets can make good environmental policy better by allowing for the flexibility to protect valuable resources cost-effectively. We must remember that markets work for us and not the other way around. Identifying when and where markets can be created or corrected to address environmental problems is a major task for us all.

References and Further Reading

Anderson, T., and Leal, D. (1991). *Free Market Environmentalism* (Boulder, Colo.: Westview Press).

Arrow, K. (1969). 'The organization of economic activity: issues pertinent to the choice of market versus nonmarket allocation', *The Analysis and Evaluation of Public Expenditures: The PPB System* (Washington, DC: Joint Economic Committee, 91st Congress). 47–64.

Baumol, W., and Oates, W. (1988). *The Theory of Environmental Policy*, 2nd edn. (Cambridge: Cambridge University Press).

Bowers, J. K., and Cheshire, P. (1983). *Agriculture, the Countryside and Land Use: An Economic Critique* (London: Methuen).

Burtraw, D. (1998). 'Cost savings, market-performance and economic benefits of the US Acid Rain Program', in Sorell and Skea (1998).

Coase, R. (1960). 'The problem of social cost', *Journal of Law and Economics* 3: 1–44.

Cornes, R., and Sandler, T. (1986). *The Theory of Externalities, Public Goods, and Club Goods* (Cambridge: Cambridge University Press).

Crocker, T. (1966). 'The structure of atmospheric pollution control systems', in H. Wolozing (ed.), *The Economics of Air Pollution* (New York: W.W. Norton): 61–86.

—— and Tschirhart, J. (1993). 'Ecosystems, externalities, and economies', *Environmental and Resource Economics* 2: 551–68.

Dabbert, S., Dubgaard, A., Slangen, L., and Whitby, M. (1998) *The Economics of Landscape and Wildlife Conservation* (Oxford: CAB International).

Dales, J. (1968). *Pollution, Property, and Prices* (Toronto: University of Toronto Press).

Ellerman, D., Schmalensee, R., Joskow, P., Montero, J., and Bailey, M. (1998). 'Summary evaluation of the US SO_2 emissions trading programme as implemented in 1995', in Sorrell and Skea (1998).

Foster, V., Bateman, I., and Harley, D. (1997) 'Real and hypothetical willingness to pay for environmental preservation', *Journal of Agricultural Economics* 8(2): 123–38.

Frankhauser, S., Pearce, D., and Toll, R. (1998). 'Extensions and alternatives to climate-change impact valuation: on the critique of IPCC impact estimates', *Environment and Development Economics* 3(1): 59–82.

Gordon, S. (1954). 'The economic theory of a common property resource: the fishery', *Journal of Political Economy* 62: 124–42.

Hanley, N., Kirkpatrick, H., Simpson, I., and Oglethorpe, D. (1998). 'Principles for the provision of public goods from agriculture: modelling moorland conservation in Scotland', *Land Economics* 74: 102–13.

—— Shogren, J., and White, B, (1996). *Environmental Economics in Theory and Practice* (London: Macmillan).

Hardin, G. (1968). 'The tragedy of the commons', *Science* 162: 1243–48.

Jurado, J., and Southgate, D. (1999). 'Dealing with air-pollution in Latin America: The case of Quito, Ecuador', *Environment and Development Economics* 4(3): 375–89.

Ledyard, J. (1987). 'Market failure', in J. Eatwell, M. Milgate, and P. Newman (eds.), *Allocation, Information, and Markets* (New York: W.W. Norton & Co.)

Ostrom, E. (1990). *Governing the Commons* (Cambridge: Cambridge University Press).

Samuelson, P. (1954). 'The pure theory of public expenditure', *Review of Economics and Statistics* 36: 387–9.

Sorrell, S., and Skea, J. (eds.) (1998). *Pollution for Sale: Emissions Trading and Joint Implementations* (Cheltenham: Edward Elgar).

Stavins, R. (2000). 'Market-based environmental policies', in P. Portney and R. Stavins (eds.), *Public Policies for Environmental Protection* (2nd edn.) (Washington, DC: RFF Press).

Weitzman, M. (1974). 'Prices vs. quantities', *Quarterly Journal of Economics* 41: 477–91.

Chapter 3
Valuing the Environment and Natural Resources

IN this chapter, we are going to consider:

- What does 'economic value' mean?
- In what ways the environment has economic value.
- How, in principle, these values might be measured.
- How, in practice, environmental values are measured.
- What we might do with estimates of environmental value.

3.1 What Does Economic Value Mean?

ECONOMICS is often described as the study of how to allocate limited resources in the face of unlimited wants. The fact that resources are scarce means that using up resources in one way prevents us from using them in another way. This cost is called an *opportunity cost*, that is a cost in terms of the best alternative use forgone. This is very relevant to the environment: using a river as a waste disposal facility implies an opportunity cost of lost recreation and wildlife benefits, since the river is now polluted. Designating a mountain area as a national park which may be used for informal recreation alone may mean we forgo mineral extraction opportunities. In other words, deciding to use the environment in one way entails a sacrifice, which is the benefits we could have got by using it in some other way. Using the environment in one way may also imply non-environmental sacrifices too: for example, the decision to impose an energy tax on grounds of air-pollution may mean poor households forgo significant consumption possibilities. However, if society decides to go ahead with the tax, then a judgement must have been reached, either explicitly or implicitly, that the air quality benefits are 'worth it': the benefits of better air quality being judged as being higher than the costs of the tax policy.

The idea that the value of something is dependent on what we are willing to give up to have it is a key economic principle. But in what terms should we express what is being given up in any instance? In the above example, poor households could be giving up a wide variety of consumption goods. In the case of preserving a mountain area from mineral extraction, the profits from such extraction could have funded a wide variety of consumption too. One approach therefore is to take the most general measure of what is being sacrificed, *income*. The simplest way to see this is by considering an example. Suppose poor households were asked whether they would support the energy tax, given that its objective was to improve air quality in their city. One way of putting this question would be to ask if their willingness to pay (to give up income) for the air quality improvement was higher than the cost to them of the tax. An important point to note here is what is being valued: a prospective *change* in environmental quality. Economic value really only has any meaning when it is defined over such a change: that is, when it is measured with regard to more or less of a good being provided. This means we need a full description of what the world looks like without such a change, which in turn implies that economic value is context-dependent. Willingness to pay (WTP) (or, more exactly, *maximum* willingness to pay) would, in this case, measure the benefits to them of the increase in air quality. An objection that could be made straightaway is that, if WTP is used as a measure of value to an individual, then this measure depends not just on their preferences (how much do they dislike air pollution) but also on their income. A rich household, with the same preferences, could clearly afford to pay more than a poor household. Economic values based on WTP would therefore always be biased in favour of the rich.

Economists usually answer 'Yes, that's right. But willingness to pay is a pretty useless concept unless backed up by ability to pay. At the level of the economy as a whole, we clearly cannot give up more than we actually have or expect to earn.' Avoiding the temptation of making the somewhat dubious assumption that the existing distribution of income is optimal, we are therefore left with the position that value, as measured by WTP, is a function of the existing income distribution, and may change as this distribution changes. However, it is still very useful to know the relative values of things (potential resource uses) at the existing income distribution. Efficiency concerns (the business of comparing benefits and costs) and equity concerns (whether and by what means to change the distribution of income) are typically kept firmly separate in economics.

To recap, given that resources are scarce, using them in one way implies an opportunity cost. The value of a particular resource use can be measured in terms of the sacrifice people are willing to make to have it. At the most general level, this sacrifice is in terms of income, so therefore WTP makes sense as a measure of economic value to the individual. However, we have to accept that this measure is sensitive to changes in the distribution of income. If preferences differ, then people with similar income amounts will be WTP different amounts for the same resource allocation. For example, if Joe is sensitive to urban air quality because his kids suffer from asthma, but Josephine has no kids, then if their incomes are equal, Joe's WTP for a given improvement in air quality may well be higher than Josephine's.

Another measure of the economic value of something, based on the same principles of scarcity, is to ask what compensation an individual would accept to give that thing up. This is a very familiar idea in everyday life. For example, the value you place on your favourite guitar is equal to the *minimum* you would accept to go without it (sell or rent it), your minimum Willingness To Accept Compensation (WTAC).[1] For workers, the value of their working time is measurable by the minimum hourly wage they would accept to work. This compensation-for-loss concept of value can also be extended to environmental resources, although this is often more difficult in both practice and in principle (see Chapter 5, Sec. 5). The value you place on your garden could be estimated by the minimum compensation you would accept to sell it to your neighbour. But asking people the minimum compensation they would accept to allow a species to become extinct pushes this concept of value to its limits.

Whether we use WTP or WTAC as value concepts may matter. According to a famous paper by Robert Willig (1976), the differences between WTP and WTAC for most goods should be small, and should depend on the relationship between income and demand, and on how much of one's income was spent on the good. However, experimental findings in both environmental and standard microeconomics have revealed quite large differences between WTP and WTAC, which seem to violate these findings.[2] Two competing explanations have emerged. The first, based on work by Michael Hanemann (1991), shows that the difference is explicable in terms of how good a substitute exists for a commodity. If there are no good substitutes, then we could expect quite large differences between WTP and WTAC, whereas if close substitutes exist, then WTP and WTAC should not be that different. The second explanation is rooted in psychology, in the concept of loss aversion. This suggests that people systematically value what they already have more highly than what they could acquire, so that losses are always valued more highly than equivalent gains. It seems likely therefore that choices will often have to be made between WTP and WTAC. Such choices should preferably be made in terms of the allocation of property rights. If people have a right to the current level of supply of a good, then we should not ask them their WTP to prevent a reduction, but instead ask how much compensation they would demand to agree to this reduction. If people do not have the right, however, to an increased level of supply, then it is proper to ask for their WTP for such an increase, rather than their WTAC to forgo such an increase.

Summarizing, if an increase in an environmental good is being valued, we can 'ask' either what people's maximum WTP is to have this increase, or their minimum WTAC to forgo this increase. If a reduction in the same good is being valued, we can ask either their maximum WTP to prevent such a reduction, or their minimum WTAC to tolerate it. This allows a money value to be placed on an environmental gain/loss, which is an estimate of the underlying utility gain/loss (see Chapter 4 for more discussion). For an individual, we could experiment by asking their maximum WTP for a succession of increases in an environmental good. For one such person, Gavin, we might get results such as are shown in Figure 3.1(a). As the quantity of the

[1] For the author of this chapter, this is the current list price of his Martin D0001R plus $10,000 for grief and suffering if he ever had to sell it.
[2] Although the differences do get smaller in some cases the more experience people have in trading in the good.

good rises (as an example, we might consider pairs of ospreys in Scotland), Gavin's total WTP increases: for example, he is WTP more to protect 100 pairs than for fifty pairs, since, as a birdwatcher, his utility is higher for 100 pairs than for fifty. Note that as the number of pairs 'offered' continues to rise, his total WTP (his total value) increases at a decreasing rate. Transforming 3.1(a) into a marginal WTP curve, by measuring the increase in total WTP as the number of pairs, Q, rises we get Figure 3.1(b), which shows marginal WTP decreasing but always positive[3] (no satiation is setting in). Marginal WTP declines as Q rises due to diminishing marginal utility. Figure 3.1(c) shows Gavin's marginal WTP curve, which we now term a marginal value curve, MV^G, since it indeed shows the value at the margin to him of increasing numbers of ospreys. His friend Kitty is also a birdwatcher who is even more fond of ospreys: her marginal value curve, MV^K, thus lies above Gavin's at every point (we assume, for simplicity, that Gavin and Kitty have equal incomes). Drawing MV curves as smooth and continuously decreasing is a theoretical assumption which makes the maths easier, but which may not be borne out in reality. However, the assumption of declining marginal utility does seem well supported by the evidence.

Figure 3.2 shows the derivation of WTP and WTAC for an individual who is offered an increase in environmental quality from Qo to Q1. This diagram shows utility as being a function of two things: environmental quality, Q, and income, Y. The curves

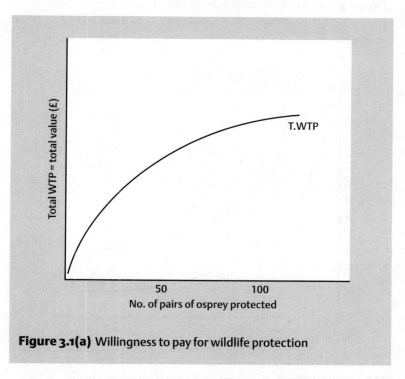

Figure 3.1(a) Willingness to pay for wildlife protection

---

[3] Marginal WTP for any value of Q, say Q^*, is equal to the slope of the total WTP curve at Q^*. It is the partial derivative of total WTP with respect to Q, evaluated at Q^*.

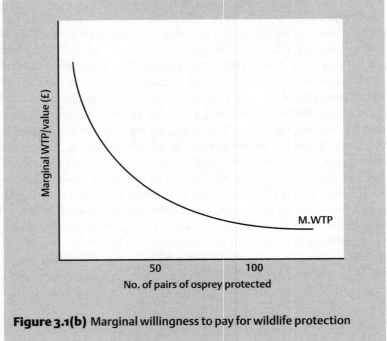

Figure 3.1(b) Marginal willingness to pay for wildlife protection

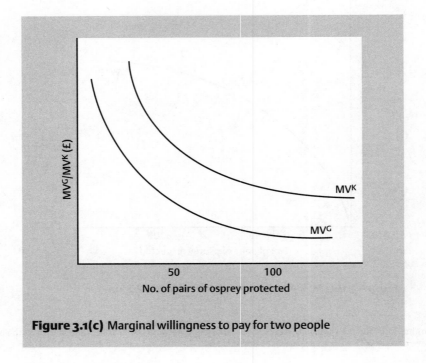

Figure 3.1(c) Marginal willingness to pay for two people

Uo and U1 are indifference curves. These have the property that along a given indifference curve, utility is constant (thus this individual is willing to swop income for environmental quality). Indifference curves are shaped the way they are drawn as we assume diminishing marginal utility, as in Figures 3.1. The further an indifference curve is away from the origin, the higher the level of utility, thus U1 is greater than Uo. We start at point a, with income of y and environmental quality of Qo. Now suppose environmental quality increases to Q1. With the same income, the individual moves to point b, on a higher indifference curve. They are thus better off. What is their maximum willingness to pay for this increase in environmental quality? This is the most income they could give up from point a and still have utility equal to UO. We can see that this amount is the vertical distance labelled WTP in the figure, that is the distance (bc). This diagram can also be used to work out the minimum compensation this individual would have to be offered to forgo the improvement in environmental quality. Starting at point b, if income rises by the amount shown as WTA, this keeps the individual at utility level U1, even when environmental quality stays at Qo. Thus the difference (da) is equal to WTA. Notice that, the way the diagram is drawn, WTP < WTA.

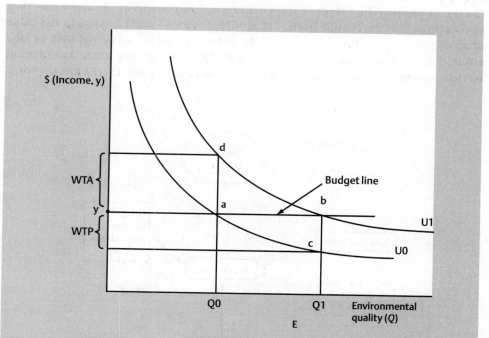

Note: Environmental quality increases from Q0 to Q1. This increases consumer utility from U0 to U1 along their fixed budget line, moving the consumer from point a to point b. This also implies consumers have a maximum willingness to pay of WTP. Alternatively they would be willing to accept compensation of WTA to forgo an improvement in environmental benefits. Note that WTA is greater than WTP.

Figure 3.2 Indifference curves and the value of an increase in environmental quality

3.2 In What Sense Does the Environment have Economic Value?

IN Chapter 1, we saw how environmental and economic systems are interlinked. Figure 1.1 shows that the environment provides four services to the economy: (i) as a source of energy and material resources (inputs) to production; (ii) as a waste sink; (iii) as a direct source of amenity; and (iv) as the provider of global life-support services. Services (i) and (ii) can be grouped together as they both provide inputs to the production process, of raw materials, energy, and waste disposal services. Figure 3.3 shows these inputs, combined with other inputs such as labour, produce useful goods and services. For example, inputs of bauxite, energy, and waste assimilation capabilities allow the production of aluminium. One monetary value of this output is its net benefit, measured as price minus production cost, multiplied by the quantity of the good produced. The value of a *change* in the level of environmental and resource inputs to the production of any good might thus be approximated by the value of the change in profits. The values of the environment in roles (i) or (ii) above can thus be determined as the change in the value of profits for a (small) change in the value of environmental inputs: in other words, if bauxite inputs were reduced by one tonne, what is the value of the associated profit decrease? For waste assimilation services, essentially the same question could again be asked: what is the loss in profits

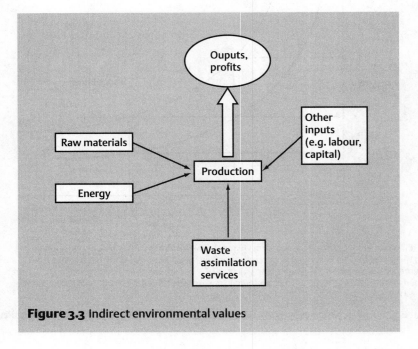

Figure 3.3 Indirect environmental values

associated with a unit reduction in emissions? This marginal productivity approach for determining environmental values of types (i) and (ii) is essentially no different from the approach used to determine the value of other inputs to production, such as labour and capital. Let us call these types of environmental values *indirect benefits*, since the environment is being valued indirectly through its role in the production process. Changes in these indirect benefits when resource quantities/qualities change could be expected to show up in the accounts of private firms: in this sense, then, natural resources generate what are known as *private benefits*.

For amenity values we need to consider more direct impacts of the environment on utility. As Figure 3.4 shows, individuals may derive utility (happiness, satisfaction) from a great number of different sources, including consumption goods and services (CDs, movies, haircuts) and environmental inputs. These environmental inputs may be related to the consumption of some activity, such as in fishing, sightseeing, or birdwatching, or less immediately through the knowledge that endangered species and habitats are being protected, or through watching wildlife films on TV.

We can speak of environmental 'goods' as those environmental inputs of which the individual prefers more to less (e.g. landscape quality, air quality). Environmental 'bads' would then be those environmental inputs which decrease utility as they increase: for example, noise or water pollution. Clearly, some environmental goods and bads are mirror images of each other, for example river water quality (a good) and river water pollution (a bad). The economic value of any environmental good can be thought of as the increase in utility if that environmental input is increased by a given amount; or the reduction in utility if the quantity/quality of that good is decreased. Similarly, for an environmental bad, we are interested in the amount by

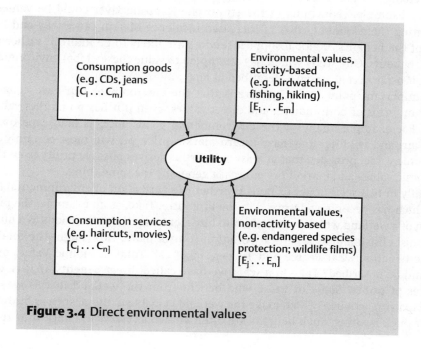

Figure 3.4 Direct environmental values

which utility increases if the environmental bad is reduced. Ideally, we would seek to measure the marginal utility of environmental goods (and bads), being the change in utility for a one unit increase in the good (although it is hard to specify units for some environmental goods such as landscape). These types of environmental values could be called *direct* benefits, since their impact is directly on utility, rather than indirectly through their role in the production of consumption goods and services.

There is no reason to suppose that a given environmental good is equally valuable to everyone. It is to be expected that the marginal utility of the good (that is, the change in utility when the level of the good itself changes by a small amount) will vary across individuals, whilst some individuals may derive no utility at all from some environmental resources. For example, if Joe is completely uninterested in bird-watching, then an increase in his local population of curlews may well have zero value to him. If his neighbour Jane is a keen ornithologist, then her marginal utility for this same increase may be very high. Such interperson differences in utility and value are returned to again below.

Finally, the economic process also benefits from the global life-support services provided by the environment, such as global climate regulation, the maintenance of a global atmospheric chemistry suitable to life, the stratospheric ozone layer, and nutrient and hydrologic cycles. In many way, it is harder to conceptualize the economic value of these types of services, since if they were absent, then life on the planet would cease to exist. In this sense, their value is infinite. However, it is possible to look at the value of preventing (small) changes in these services. For example, the value of preventing further changes in the global climate through enhanced warming could be measured by looking at the costs (and benefits) which would result from a given change in greenhouse gas emissions. Chapter 12 considers this in detail. As another example, reductions in the stratospheric ozone layer could be valued by estimating the economic costs of increased incidence of skin cancer. By and large, most of the benefits of global support services are likely to be indirect, rather than direct, benefits. One study which has attempted to value these global environmental values (Costanza *et al.*, 1997) is described in Box 3.1.

An important point to notice here is that the environment can have economic value, in terms of both indirect and direct values, even if it has no market value or price. For example, many of the environmental goods such as landscape quality, clean air, and wildlife, may have a zero market price yet will most certainly have economic value, provided that at least one person derives positive utility from them. Economic values and market prices are *not* generally the same thing.

Finally in this section, let us note a further categorization of environmental benefits which has become widespread in the literature. Take, as an example, the preservation of a wetland which is important to birds, but which also functions as a nursery for fish/shellfish and as a natural pollution control plant. How might the total economic benefits (what Pearce and Turner (1990) call Total Economic Value) of this wetland be described? Take first what we have called direct benefits, that is, direct sources of utility. Some of those who benefit from the wetland in this way may participate in activities which make the wetland valuable to them, such as birdwatching or duck hunting. Such benefits are often known as *use values*, since they require

Box 3.1 The Value of Everything or the Value of Nothing?

In 1997, Costanza and co-authors published a paper in *Nature* on 'The value of the world's ecosystem services and natural capital', which is the most ambitious application to date of ecosystem valuation methods. They try to estimate direct and indirect values for seventeen ecosystem services for sixteen biomes. Services included water supply, soil formation, food production, pollination, and climate regulation. Biomes covered all of the planet, with categories including open oceans, estuaries, temperate forests, and tundra. Non-renewable resources were excluded from the analysis. The authors argued that it makes no sense to value total services since their value is infinite (in that they are essential to life on earth). However, they claim that it does make sense to value *changes* in these services, for example, the impacts of given loss of coral reefs.

The authors came up with a figure of US$16–54 trillion per year (10^{12}) for the value of current ecosystem services (they did not, in the end, value marginal changes despite their claims) with a mean of $33 trillion. This is 1.8 times bigger than global GNP! Clearly, this has the unfortunate implication that it exceeds the most the world could be willing to pay to prevent the loss of all ecosystems.

Costanza *et al.* made it clear that they had their own reservations about these results:

- there are missing values in the literature for the value of many biomes, e.g. desert
- current prices are distorted, and so do not indicate the social value of ecosystem services
- the WTP estimates used are in any case based on incomplete knowledge and unsustainable consumption
- their aggregation procedure assumes no sharp discontinuities in ecosystem functions
- aggregating by area multiplication of average values is a problem, since it makes no account of diminishing marginal utility.

The biggest problem with these results is simple: they are meaningless. First, whilst the authors claim to value *changes* in ecosystems, they actually use a hotch-potch of average values gained in studies which typically looked at small, well-defined changes in local environmental quality, to measure the *total* worth of the global ecosystem. Yet, as we point out in this chapter, economic value is only defined over well-identified changes in environmental quality, and we don't know what the counter-factual is in the Costanza case (no nature anywhere?). What is more, the original study estimates were based on 'everything else being constant' assumptions: everything else clearly is not constant if we lose everything! Second, we have already said that the number $33 trillion makes no sense in a maximum WTP sense, since we don't have this much to spend. Does it make any sense in terms of WTAC? No. If all the world's natural systems disappeared overnight, then it might well take more than $33 trillion to compensate the world's citizens for this loss. In fact, one could say that in this sense, $33 trillion is a serious underestimate of infinity!

Since publication, these results have been subject to much comment. Amongst the views expressed are the following:

1. The results do not mean that the world is $33 trillion better off than we previously thought. Daly (1998) has pointed out that it is easy to confuse 'value in use' with 'value in exchange'. The former measures total utility, the latter marginal utility. Marginal utility depends on scarcity; as the amount of natural capital falls, its value in use declines although its value in exchange rises due to increased scarcity. The Costanza *et al.* number might, ideally, tell us how far we have got from the 'garden of Eden', when marginal value of natural capital was zero (a full stock). As the world's ecosystem value rises, this indicates we should do more to protect it since it is getting scarcer. A problem which arises here is that for non-market goods, there is no market price to rise as a scarcity indicator.

2. The approach taken ignores irreversibilities and future scarcity. It is not clear whether their number is an over- or under-estimate as a result.

3. Finally, if we are measuring the amount of anything, we need something meaningful to measure it in, a 'numeraire'. To compare two situations we need a numeraire which is not affected by the change from one to the other. The numeraire in the Costanza study is money, measured in today's prices and incomes. However, a loss in the world's ecosystems such as is implicit in their work would have such a huge effect on economic activity that prices and incomes would be way different from what they are now. So we cannot compare the situations that Costanza *et al.* implicitly need to compare using the measuring units which they employ!

Argument over this study and its implications seems likely to continue for some time.

actual participation to enjoy them. Use values may be consumptive (hunting) or non-consumptive (birdwatching). However, people other than those who actually visit the wetland may derive benefits, in terms of the utility they get from just knowing that the wetland is preserved. These types of benefit have become known as *non-use* or *existence values*. They may be motivated by selfish reasons, or by altruism, either for other members of the current generation, or for future generations. Existence values may be particularly high for unique, irreplaceable natural assets, such as the Grand Canyon in the USA, Stonehenge in England, or Kakadu National Park in Australia.

The sum of use and existence values gives the total direct benefits of preserving the wetland. The wetland's role as a nursery for fish and shellfish could be evaluated by estimating biological models of the contribution the wetland makes to fish/shell-fish populations, and then by looking at the economic (commercial) value of these species (for an example, see Ellis and Fisher, 1987). Changes in these economic values, in terms of gains/losses in consumers' surplus and producers' profits from some change in the wetland could be calculated. Finally, the wetland's pollution control function could be valued either by using the value of avoided pollution damages (say, from sedimentation of coral reef fisheries, or from nutrient enrichment), or the pollution control costs that would have to be incurred to replace the role currently being undertaken by the wetland. The sum of avoided pollution/pollution control costs, and commercial fisheries value, would give the indirect benefits of preserving the wetland. Adding the wetland's direct and indirect benefits gives its Total Economic Value

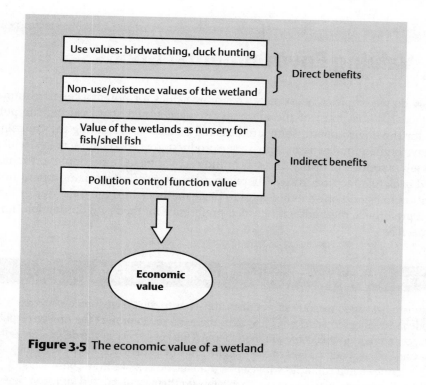

Figure 3.5 The economic value of a wetland

(see Figure 3.5). For an example of these sorts of calculations for actual wetlands, see Barbier, Burgess, and Folke (1994).

In some environmental economics texts,[4] a further, separate element of economic value is found, known as 'option value'. This is claimed to be akin to an insurance premium, which potential or actual users of an environmental resource are willing to pay to secure that resource's availability at some time in the future. However, economists now know that option value does not exist as a separate element of total economic value, and moreover that both its sign and size are uncertain (Ready, 1995). Instead, the term 'option price' is used to describe willingness to pay under conditions of supply uncertainty (where an individual does not know for sure how much of a public good such as a designated wilderness area will be supplied), or demand uncertainty, where the individual is not sure of their future demand (e.g. how many trips to the wilderness area they will make in the next two years). Chapter 5 returns to the treatment of risk and uncertainty in economics.

---

[4] e.g. Pearce and Turner, 1990.

3.3 Valuing Environmental Goods

How do we empirically estimate economic values for non-market environmental goods? Whilst most of the methods used are aimed at measuring the public's WTP for the environment, some are directed instead at evaluating the contribution the environment makes as an input to the production of goods and services, which are themselves sources of utility. Directly or indirectly then, all environmental values are traced back to effects on utility. There are many ways of categorizing environmental valuation methods: one useful way is to place methods into the following groups: (1) stated preference methods; (2) revealed preference methods; (3) production-function approaches.

Box 3.2 Valuing Environmental Benefits: Conservation in Africa

A debate has raged recently at meetings of parties to the Convention on International Trade in Endangered Species (CITES) as to the best way to protect the African elephant. Chapter 8 takes up this debate in more detail. One key aspect of the debate, though, is the value of elephants as part of the 'wildlife tourism' experience. Put more crudely, how much money could countries with elephant populations make from conserving elephants as tourism assets, rather than allowing them to be hunted for ivory? Several studies have been undertaken of the value of wildlife-based tourism. Brown and Henry (1993) used both the travel-cost method and contingent valuation to value elephant viewing by tourists in Kenya.

The travel-cost study was based on data from a large survey of overseas visitors to Kenya in 1989. Travel costs, including air travel, land travel, and time costs, were related to the number of visits per 1,000 population. This gave estimates of consumers' surplus per wildlife holiday to Kenya of around $194 for North American tourists and $822 for European tourists. Based on estimates of total visitor numbers, this implies a total value (consumers' surplus) of between $182m. and $218m. p.a. (in 1989 $s). Not all of this value can be attributed to the existence of elephants, since there are many other reasons to come on safari trips. To find out how much of this total value could be attributed to elephants, people were asked to apportion their reasons for coming on holiday into a number of categories, one of which was wildlife viewing. They were then asked to apportion this wildlife viewing amount across different types of wildlife, such as big cats and elephants. This allows a very rough estimate of the wildlife viewing value of elephants alone, which worked out at $20–24m. p.a. This amount represents the value of elephants *in situ* to the Kenyan government, in terms of potential additional tourist revenue that could be 'extracted'. Interestingly, the contingent valuation survey referred to above yielded estimates of total consumers' surplus which were very close to the travel-cost estimates, at $23–27m. p.a.

3.3.1 **Stated preference approaches**

This group includes the following methods:

- contingent valuation
- choice experiments
- contingent ranking

These methods have the common feature that they are all based on surveys in which the public is directly questioned about its WTP (or WTAC) for certain hypothetical changes in environmental quality, or about choices between different 'packages' of environmental quality and the price of each package. The contingent valuation method (CVM) is by far and away the most common of these approaches in practice, so most space is devoted to it here (for a fuller account, see Hanley and Spash (1993); or Bateman and Willis (1999)). CVM originated in the early 1960s, but did not become widely used until the mid-1970s. By 1995, Carson had identified over 2,000 CVM studies, and its use seems to be growing exponentially. CVM has now been sanctioned for use in government decision-making in the USA, for example by the Fish and Wildlife Service, and in environmental damage claims through the courts. In Europe, its use is also spreading, and many government agencies in, for example, the UK, Denmark, and Norway have commissioned its use. CVM studies are also growing rapidly in developing countries, especially as part of the assessment of externally funded environmental projects.

The method is, in principle, very simple. Given that the absence of market values for environmental goods is (obviously!) due to the absence of a market, CVM asks respondents how they would behave *if* such a market existed. For example, a CVM survey could ask:

Suppose the only way of improving water quality in this river was if all local residents agreed to pay a surcharge on their local council tax. What is the maximum that you would be willing to pay, per household per year, to have these water quality improvements go ahead?

Respondents are a random sample of the relevant population, which might in different settings comprise the general public, local residents, or visitors to a recreation area. The important point about CVM is that respondents are asked what they would be WTP (or WTAC) for a hypothetical increase or decrease in environmental quality.

There are several main design features of a CVM questionnaire:

- People must be given a reason why they might be asked to pay for something which they currently do not see themselves as paying for. For example, if the purpose of the CVM was to estimate the total economic value of a local wood, respondents could be told that raising money in the form of donations was essential to safeguard the wood from development threats.
- A bid vehicle must be used which is both credible and non-controversial. The bid vehicle is the means by which respondents pay in the hypothetical market (in the

Box 3.3 Valuing Environmental Costs: Quarrying

Quarrying rock, sand, and gravel to produce materials for building and road construction generates a number of environmental costs. These include disamenity to local residents, through dust and noise; and adverse effects on landscape quality, especially in national parks. In the UK, the government decided to introduce an environmental tax on quarrying to try to reduce these environmental impacts. The tax rate was to be decided using estimates of the environmental costs of quarrying to two groups: local residents living near quarries, and visitors to national parks such as the Yorkshire Dales with significant quarrying activity.

A large contingent valuation study was undertaken, giving 9,631 responses from residents and 1,019 responses from visitors to national parks. A payment card mechanism was used to elicit bids, with an increase in national taxes as the payment vehicle for landscape effects, and an increase in local taxes for the disamenity impacts on local people. Many *local residents* (around 80 per cent) said that they were not particularly bothered by the quarry. This led to a small percentage of respondents expressing a positive WTP to shut the quarry down early. WTP bids were collected as per household amounts, and once aggregated into population values were converted into a more policy-useful per-tonne amount by allowing for the production levels and lifespans at each type of quarry studied. The main results that emerged were:

	Mean WTP per household (£)	Implied mean WTP per tonne (£)
Local residents: hard rock quarries	10.23	0.34
Local residents: sand and gravel quarries	15.57	1.96
National survey: visitors to national parks	5.09	10.52

Sand and gravel quarries give rise to higher external costs per tonne, accoring to these results. Why is this? The study authors attribute it to (i) the much longer lifespan of hard-rock quarries; (ii) the fact that hard-rock quarries tend to be located in areas of lower population density; and (iii) the higher outputs of hard-rock quarries relative to sand and gravel operations.

The UK government announced the introduction of an environmental tax on quarrying, based on these values, in the 2000 Budget.

above example, it could be donations to a conservation trust). Bid vehicles must be credible in the sense that respondents feel that they could be applied in practice. For example, if the value of a large wilderness area with many access points was being studied, specifying an entrance fee as a bid vehicle would not be credible if people thought it would be impossible to enforce, or if it would be too politically unpopular to imagine it being introduced.

■ The CVM payment question should be asked in a way which minimizes incentives for respondents to behave strategically, for example by free-riding (underbidding) or by stating an amount in excess of their true WTP. One school of thought suggests that the best way to do this is to avoid voluntary donation bid vehicles, and use tax-based or entry-fee-based bid vehicles instead.

■ Respondents should be given adequate, unbiased information on the environmental good and its hypothetical market, in order to let them make an informed judgement.

■ A decision has to be made on how to ask the WTP/WTAC question. This can be done using an open-ended format ('what is the most you would be WTP?'), through payment cards, where respondents are shown a series of amounts and are asked to indicate their maximum WTP/minimum WTAC from amongst these amounts; and dichotomous choice formats, where respondents are asked to say whether they would be WTP/WTAC a specific amount, known as the bid price. This bid price is then varied across individuals, which yields yes/no responses to different amounts. Average WTP/WTAC for the sample can then be inferred statistically from this data.

■ 'Protest bids' should be identified. When respondents are asked how much they would be WTP (or WTAC), a proportion will give a zero response. For some people, this is because they do not value the good, in that it does not impact on their utility. If I am asked my WTP to protect a wildlife species which I don't care about, then I place zero value on it and accordingly will state a zero WTP. But I might bid zero, even if I care about the species, because I am protesting about being asked the question in this way, or because I do not find the hypothetical market to be credible. In a WTAC scenario, respondents who are asked their minimum WTAC to allow a local woodland to be felled may state a zero amount because they feel that no amount of monetary compensation would make up for the loss of the wood: this is another form of protest bid. Protest bidders are usually separated out from 'genuine zeros' and positive bidders before analysis progresses.

■ Many surveys now include debriefing questions, which seek to analyse how well respondents understood the survey questions, what exactly they thought they were paying for/being compensated for, how credible they found the survey, and whether it had changed their opinions on the issue at hand.

Given all these issues, CVM studies now begin by undertaking focus group sessions, where different scenarios, bid vehicles, information sets, and question formats can be tested out by the researcher in small groups before surveying begins. Surveys may be carried out by mail, telephone, or in face-to-face interviews. Once a sufficient sample has been collected, mean or median WTP/WTAC is calculated from the sample, using the individual responses (once protest bidders have been excluded). This sample average can then be aggregated into a population mean/median: this implies that the researcher has already defined the relevant population, which of course she must do before beginning the survey (see Chapter 4 for more discussion of what constitutes the 'relevant population'). A final stage is to undertake a 'bid curve' analysis, where WTP responses are statistically related, using regression analysis, to variables thought likely to influence them, such as education and income. The purpose of doing this would be to (i) see how much of the variation in WTP across the sample could be explained (and therefore how much is unexplained), and (ii) whether the signs on the variables of interest are in accord with such *a priori* expectations as we have: for example, income would be expected to be positively related with WTP, in that higher-income levels should, on average and other things being held equal, imply higher WTP amounts. For some CVM designs, notably dichotomous choice versions, bid curves must be estimated in order to calculate mean WTP.

The fact that CVM has become so widely used implies it has some advantages as a method. Principal amongst these are:

1. It is a very generalizable method in that it can be applied in an extremely wide range of situations, from the benefits of preserving global biodiversity, to the benefits of improving a city's air quality or protecting a local wetland.
2. It is capable of measuring both use and non-use values. Non-use (existence) values have been found to be very important in many cases (see, for example, Schulze *et al.*, 1983). CVM questionnaires can also be designed so that the researcher gains some insight into *why* people value a given environmental good, and how this valuation changes when, for example, uncertainty surrounding the supply of the good changes.

However, CVM has also attracted much criticism. This has in general focused on three issues. First, that CVM measures what people say they would do, which may be different to what they would actually do. Stated WTP could be greater or less than actual, true WTP for a number of reasons. First, if respondents think their answer may influence how much they would actually get charged, they may free-ride by understating their WTP. Second, if respondents believe that their answer is not linked to what they would actually be charged, but is linked to how likely the environmental change is to happen, then they may overstate their WTP for an environmental change which increases their utility. The issue of 'calibrating' CVM responses has thus attracted much attention. The NOAA panel (see Box 3.4) recommended that on average stated WTP values should be reduced by 50 per cent. More considered research has found that the extent to which hypothetical WTP over- or under-states actual WTP depends crucially on the type of environmental good being studied and the design of the CVM exercise itself. In a study comparing hypothetical WTP with actual WTP, Foster, Bateman, and Harley (1997) found that, for UK wild-life sites, actual and hypothetical WTP were very similar amongst those who made positive bids/donations.

Another criticism of CVM is that it produces estimates of WTP that are insensitive to the amount of the environmental good being bid for: the 'scoping' problem. One reason for people saying they would pay roughly the same to protect one lake in Ontario from acidification as they would pay to protect all lakes in Ontario is that their stated WTP is actually a symbolic number motivated by a feel-good factor. Attention has thus focused on the results of scope tests, which measure WTP for different quantities of the same good. For example, different subsamples of a population could be asked their WTP to protect 100, 500, or 1,000 hectares of forests from felling, and statistical tests performed to see whether WTP was indeed sensitive to the

Box 3.4 The Exxon Valdez Incident and the NOAA Guidelines

The wrecking of the oil tanker the *Exxon Valdez* off the coast of Alaska in 1989 was the somewhat unforeseen cause of a major spur to the development of the contingent valuation method (CVM) in terms of a legally acceptable method of valuing environmental damages in the USA. US law had gradually seen the introduction of damage claims for environmental losses, principally under the Comprehensive Environmental Response, Compensation and Liability Act regulations of 1980, and the Oil Pollution Act of 1990. Following a famous judgment by the DC Court of Appeals (State of Ohio vs. Department of the Interior), non-use values (or more strictly, what has been termed 'passive use' values, including the values derived from watching wildlife on TV, for example) were deemed relevant under this body of legislation, in that persons could sue responsible parties for lost passive use values. This clearly had an enormous implication for Exxon, since much of the environmental damage resulting from the Valdez spill (damage to wildlife and a pristine, fragile ecosystem) were likely to be passive use, as opposed to actual, active use values, since actual active use of the area was relatively modest.

As a counter to the possibly large size of damage claims being made against Exxon, the company funded a series of studies which basically tried to discredit CVM as a method for valuing losses in passive use values. The government body responsible for issuing regulations on the assessment of damage from oil spills, the National Oceanic and Atmospheric Administration (NOAA), convened a panel of distinguished economists thought to have no vested interest in the CVM method to conduct hearings on the validity of the CVM method in 1992. The panel's report on their findings was published in January 1993 (Federal Register, 15.1.93), and was basically a cautious acceptance of CVM for valuing environmental damage including lost passive use values. The principle recommendations were as follows:

1. A dichotomous choice format should be used.
2. A minimum response rate from the target sample of 70 per cent should be achieved.
3. In-person interviews should be employed (not mail shots), with some role for telephone interviews in the piloting stages.
4. WTP, not WTAC, measures should be sought.
5. After excluding protest bids, a test should be made of whether WTP is sensitive to the level of environmental damage.
6. CVM results should be calibrated against experimental findings, otherwise a 50 per cent discount should be applied to CVM results.
7. Respondents should be reminded of their budget constraints.

These measures are a mixture of theoretically based recommendation and rules of thumb. It would be unfortunate if all CVM practitioners felt constrained to stick to these guidelines in future research, since the guidelines pose some awkward questions. These include:

(i) are all 'protest' bids giving the same signals? How should these signals be interpreted and utilized in any case?; (ii) can the 50 per cent discount rule be justified empirically?; and (iii) is the preference for the DC design format justified?

area of forest protected. Carson (1997) found that the majority of CVM studies do indeed pass such tests of scope.

Thirdly, CVM results have been criticized as being dependent on the information they provide to respondents, and of asking respondents to undertake a task which they are not up to. In many cases, the population of interest may be quite uninformed about the environmental resource which is being studied: we would not expect people to be able to give a WTP figure for a function of an ecosystem they do not understand. For example, suppose a policy of protecting the population of an obscure species is being evaluated. We wish to know the value people place on this species, yet we expect that many folks will never even have heard of it before. To successfully implement the survey, researchers will need to inform respondents about the species, the threats to it, and what can be done to avert these threats. Yet this changes their knowledge in the process of undertaking the survey: thus by implementing a CVM survey, we are possibly changing the preferences that we wish to measure. Different types and amounts of information may significantly affect stated WTP (see, for example, Hanley and Spash, ch. 12). The question which CVM must answer then is 'how much information is enough, and what should it cover?'

Finally, some of the objections to CVM in this context are actually more general objections to the use of cost-benefit analysis to help decision-making over the environment. The views/preferences of the general public are said to be too ill-informed relative to those of 'experts', so that experts alone should be allowed to make the policy judgement. This is a debatable position which clearly flies in the face of democratic principles.

Two other stated preference methods will be briefly mentioned, namely choice experiments and contingent ranking. These share a particular view on how the demand for the environment goods is best pictured, a view known as the *characteristics theory of value*. This states that the value of, say, a forest, is best explained in terms of the characteristics or attributes of that forest. Different forests are actually different 'bundles' of attributes, and what people value is these bundles. The value of any particular forest then can be broken down into the value of its different attributes. In the choice experiment method, the researcher first of all identifies the main attributes that are relevant in describing the environmental good in question. This is done using focus groups. For forests, the attributes might include species composition, age, type of felling, and provision of recreational facilities. Different bundles of these attributes are then assembled, using statistical design principles. Bundles are then arranged in pairs or triads, and respondents asked to choose between them and some *status quo* alternative. For example, a recent study by Morrison *et al.* (1998) looked at the benefits of protecting wetlands in Australia. Each respondent was asked to choose most preferred alternatives amongst pairs of different wetland management options, such as shown in Table 3.1.

By including cost as one of the attributes, it is possible to calculate (i) the marginal WTP of people in the sample for each attribute which is a significant determinant of choice; and (ii) the value of any combination of attributes. For a review of choice experiments applied to the environment, see Hanley, Wright, and Adamowicz (1998).

Contingent ranking proceeds along similar lines. In this technique, different

Table 3.1 Choice experiment for valuing Australian wetlands

	Management option A	Management option B	Management option C (*status quo*)
Wetland area	1,000 ha.	800 ha.	700 ha.
Bird species (no.)	40	30	25
Jobs	15	16	20
Cost	$30/hsld.	$15/hsld.	$15/hsld.
Which would you prefer A, B, or C?			

bundles of environmental attributes (for example, different combinations of recreation intensity, wildlife quality, and timber production for a national forest park) are again presented to respondents, along with a price tag for each of these bundles (say, increases in local taxes to pay for park management). Each respondent might be given four of these bundles, and is then asked to rank them, from most preferred to least preferred. By statistically analysing these rankings, economists can again infer marginal WTP for changes in any significant attribute, and WTP for a particular bundle. An example of the use of the contingent-ranking technique to valuing the environmental impacts of pesticides used by farmers is Foster and Mourato (2000).

3.3.2 Revealed preference approaches

In revealed preference (RP) approaches, the analyst tries to infer the value people place on environmental goods from their behaviour in markets for related goods. A major difference between RP and stated preference approaches is thus that in the former we make use of people's *actual* behaviour, rather than their intentions. Two principle types of RP approach will be discussed here: the hedonic pricing method, and travel cost models.

The hedonic pricing method (HPM) has its basis in the same characteristics theory of value as choice experiments. In other words, people are pictured as valuing goods in terms of the bundles of attributes which these possess. For a house, these attributes might include the number of bedrooms, the age of the house, the size of garden, and whether it has a garage. These could all be called 'site characteristics', S_i. Also important to buyers and sellers will be the locational aspects of the house, such as how far it is from major employment areas, how good the local school is, and how good its transport links are. Call these 'neighbourhood characteristics', N_i. Finally, environmental characteristics (E_i) may also be an important determinant of house prices: for example, these could include noise levels, air quality, scenic views and proximity to landfill sites or quarries.

The basic assumption of the HPM is that people's valuation of environmental attributes can be inferred from the amount they are willing to pay for these attributes through the housing market. For example, other things being equal, a house in a quieter part of town may sell for more than a similar house in a noisier part of town. If I value peace and quiet, then I may be willing to pay this premium, whilst sellers will know this when advertising their house. For the buyer, the highest premium they would be WTP for any environmental attribute would be the maximum value they place on it: if these premia could be identified, this would thus tell us something about the value of those environmental attributes (like noise) which can be linked to house prices.

The HPM thus proceeds by collecting data on (most usually) house prices from sales records,[5] along with data on E_i, N_i, and S_i. A regression analysis can then be carried out to estimate the equation:

$$P_j = f(E_{ij} \ldots E_{mj}, N_{ij} \ldots N_{nj}, S_{ij} \ldots S_{qj}), \tag{3.1}$$

where there are m environmental attributes, n neighbourhood attributes, and q site attributes, and where P_j is the price of the jth house. For those attributes which turn out to have a statistically significant effect on house prices, the 'implicit price' (that is, the price premium) can be calculated. This might tell us, for example, that a 10 per cent improvement in air-quality levels increases house prices by 2 per cent on average: this could then be used to work out the implied WTP in money for this air-quality improvement. In this manner, money values can be placed on environmental attributes that are linked to house prices. In Figure 3.6, we show the kind of relationship one might find in the data: as the level of air pollution falls, and so air quality rises, house prices go up, other things being equal. In other words, to 'buy' an improvement in local air quality from E1 to E2, the house-buyer has to spend an additional amount equal to ΔP.

The HPM has been widely used to study the implicit prices of changes in air quality, noise, and proximity to waste sites. A fairly recent survey of much of this work can be found in Smith and Huang (1995), whilst Farber (1998) surveys work on proximity to waste sites specifically. However, a number of drawbacks can be identified with the technique. These are:

■ Many environmental goods are not linked to housing markets. For these goods, the HPM will not work. Even for those goods which are so linked, the method provides only an indication of partial value. For example, air-quality improvements may benefit visitors and commuters to a city, as well as those who own a house there, but only house-owners' values get picked up by the method.

■ The method assumes that the housing market is in equilibrium in a rather special sense: that, for every attribute, house-buyers are able to locate a house which allows them to equate their marginal value for each environmental attribute with the marginal cost (implicit price) of these attributes.

■ Good information: essentially, we must assume that all buyers and sellers are very well informed about how environmental attributes vary spatially across the area being studied.

---

[5] Rents can also be used.

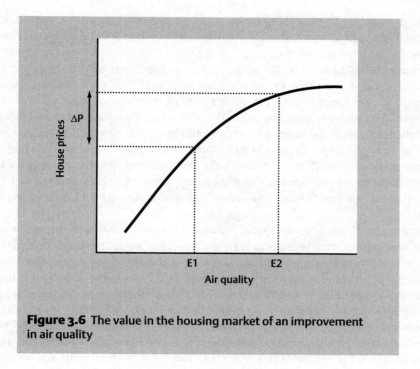

Figure 3.6 The value in the housing market of an improvement in air quality

- Current versus future changes: house purchases are investments, in the sense that people make them for a relatively long period of time, often in the anticipation of capital gains. Their maximum WTP for a house depends not just on current levels of environmental attributes, but also on expectations of changes in the levels of these attributes over the time during which they expect to own the house.

Travel cost models are amongst the oldest environmental valuation techniques. They originated in the USA, in the context of the planning and management of outdoor recreation in national parks. Informal outdoor recreation is clearly a source of utility for many people, and such recreation often takes place in areas managed or regulated by governments. Activities such as hillwalking, canoeing, angling, climbing, cross-country ski-ing, and rock-climbing have all increased in terms of participation in the last fifty years, and seem certain to be of increasing importance to land management in the future, along with more informal types of recreation such as picnicking and dog-walking. But how could the economic value of such activities be measured?

Stated preference approaches such as CVM have been intensively used to estimate WTP for outdoor recreation opportunities, and for changes in such opportunities (for example, for water-quality improvements in the context of recreational fishing). An alternative approach, though, is to use travel cost-type models. These are based on the observation that expenditure is typically necessary to partake in such recreational activities. These expenditures include time and money spent in travelling to recreational sites (it may seem odd to talk about time spent as an expenditure, but time is scarce for everyone, and using up scarce time has an opportunity cost). An individual can be pictured as being willing to spend up to the value in utility which they get from making such a trip. Typically, their actual spending will be less than the most they would be willing to spend.

For example, consider Orviedo National Park in the Spanish Pyrenees. Suppose we want to estimate the value of informal recreation in this area. Visitors would be irrational if they spent more in visiting the park than the utility they derive from their visit. For any individual, the total cost of visiting (time plus distance) will almost certainly be less than the maximum they would be willing to spend, which is equal to the value they place on a trip to the park. They thus enjoy a consumers' surplus[6] from visiting, equal to the difference between the most they would pay (per trip) and what they actually pay. By observing the relationship between visits and travel costs, it might thus be possible to infer the value (consumers' surplus) which recreationalists enjoy.

A simple travel cost analysis would proceed as follows. Visitors to the national park would be surveyed, and asked how far they had travelled to make this visit, and how often in the last twelve months they had visited the site. They might also be asked how many other similar sites they had visited in the area, and about their income, recreational experiences, and family size. In Figure 3.7(a), we show a possible relationship between the number of visits individuals make to the park (V_i) and the costs to them per visit (C_i). For example, visitor V_1 faces a cost per trip of 2,400 Pts. and makes only two trips per year, whilst visitor V_2 faces a cost of 1,200 Pts. per trip and makes six trips. These travel costs would be calculated by the researcher, by converting distances from miles to pesetas (by using an estimate of motoring costs per mile), and time from hours to pesetas (by using an estimate of the money value of an hour of leisure time: see below). If responses from, say, 1,000 visitors were collected, then this would probably allow us to estimate such a curve with reasonable precision. The curve in Figure 3.7(a) is really a demand curve for the site, since it shows, at any price, how many trips are taken. Since the area under a demand curve shows total value, we can measure the area under travel cost curves and use these to measure total value, or, more usually, consumers' surplus per visit.

We show visually how this could be done in Figure 3.7(b). Imagine that we select one individual (Begona) from the sample. Begona currently faces a travel cost of 2,000 Pts per visit, and makes three trips per year. However, the value she places on each visit is more than 2,000 Pts, so currently she enjoys a consumers' surplus. Using the average relationship between visits and travel costs in Figure 3.7(a), it is possible to see what would happen to the number of trips Begona would make if the cost to her was increased, for example if an admission fee to the park were introduced. At an admission fee of A1, her trips fall to V_1, whilst at a higher admission fee of A2 they fall further to V_2. By repeating this exercise, we could trace out the function shown originating at V^* and passing through the points (A1, V_1) and (A2, V_2). The area under this curve and above the horizontal line originating at Ao (the current cost she actually faces) is the consumers' surplus she enjoys from making V^*=3 trips per year. Notice

---

[6] Recall from Ch. 2 that this is the difference between the maximum you are WTP for something and what you actually pay for it.

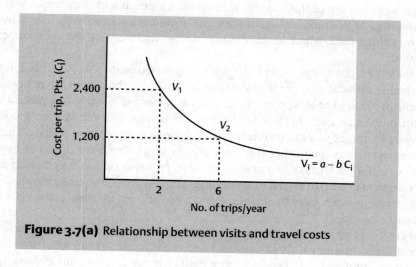

Figure 3.7(a) Relationship between visits and travel costs

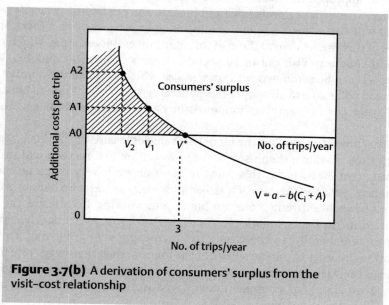

Figure 3.7(b) A derivation of consumers' surplus from the visit–cost relationship

that if Begona were only to make one trip per year, the marginal value to her of this trip would be higher than if she makes three trips per year, since the demand curve is downward-sloping.

In practice, it is not necessary to trace out the kind of curve shown in Figure 3.7(b) to calculate consumers' surplus, since it can be calculated mathematically from the equation relating actual trips to actual visits:

$$V_i = a - b\,C_i.$$

(3.2)

This simple version of the travel-cost model has a number of drawbacks, which we now investigate. We also look at some more recent advances in the use of models based on similar data, which also are concerned with estimating the value of outdoor recreation.

Substitute sites. The simple travel-cost model discussed so far was presented in terms of predicting visits at one single site. Suppose, however, that there are many similar sites within reach of at least part of our sample of visitors. Clearly, the more alternatives an individual has, the less likely they are to visit the site we are modelling. Moreover, we might want to estimate demand across a set of sites, which all differ in some respects from each other (for example, fishing rivers with different expected catches or different types of fish or accessibility). Two approaches may be noted. Most simply, if we are still interested in modelling demand for one site, we could allow for the influence of other sites by including the costs of trips to these other sites in the travel-cost equation.

However, this approach suffers from the fact that the alternative sites may all be different from the site we are interested in, in other respects than just travel costs. A more recent approach has been to more explicitly model site choice using *random utility models*. These adapt a probabilistic approach, and predict the probability that an individual will visit a given site out of a list of alternative sites, as a function of the attributes of this site relative to those of the alternatives: for example, which river(s) a person will choose to visit out of all salmon streams in British Columbia. Random utility models can be combined with *count models* which estimate the number of trips that a person will make to all sites of this general type (say all salmon-fishing streams in BC) in a year. For an example of random utility and count models in use, see Loomis (1995).

The value of travel time. What is the monetary value of leisure time? Above, we argued that since time is scarce, then using it up in travelling to a recreational site has an opportunity cost. But what is this equal to? This depends very much on individual circumstances. Imagine the case of a self-employed carpenter who likes to go fishing. Every hour he spends fishing is one less hour spent working. In this case, the value of his leisure time (in Deutschmarks per hour, say), is equal to his hourly earnings in work or more generally, to the wage rate. For people who are giving up working opportunities in order to pursue leisure at the margin, then their wage rate measures the value of their leisure time. However, for many people, this is not a good description of the situation. For example, unemployed workers, parents staying at home, and retired people do not give up work for leisure at the margin. This is also true for the majority of workers, who tend to be on fixed-hours contracts. For example, if Fanny is a schoolteacher, then she is unlikely to be giving up earnings (at the margin) during her holidays in order to go fishing. In such cases, where people are not making marginal wage/leisure choices, it is harder to know how to value leisure time.

Most research in this area has used either stated or revealed preference approaches to estimate leisure time values in contexts where people choose between faster, more expensive routes and slower, cheaper ones. These studies reveal that leisure time values are positively related, on the whole, to income, so that some fraction of the wage for an individual is a reasonable guess as to the monetary value of their leisure time. Commonly used fractions in the literature include 33 per cent and 43 per cent; however, the valuation of leisure time is still an inexact science. This is problematic for travel-cost-type models since consumer surplus estimates for recreation have been shown to depend on which value for leisure time is used.

Use values versus non-use values. Finally, it should be obvious that since the travel-cost approach infers values from expenditure, those who make no such expenditures have no inferred valuation for the good. If all values were use values, this would not be such a problem, except in terms of understanding participation decisions by those people who do not currently use the resource. However, if there are non-use values associated with an environmental resource such as a national park, then travel-cost approaches cannot pick up such values, since they can accrue to people who do not visit the site.

3.3.3 Production function approaches

In production function approaches, the environment is typically valued as an input to the production of some market-valued good or service. Changes in the quality or quantity of an environmental resource are valued by estimating the implications of this for outputs and prices of market goods/services, usually in terms of changes in consumers' surplus and producers' profits. This class of methods includes 'dose-response' models, which are used to study the impacts of pollution on market-valued outputs (for example, the effects of increases in low-level ozone on agricultural crops). More recent terminology discusses 'ecosystem function valuation' models, but the basic approach is similar. To take a simple example, consider the role that wetlands play in coastal fisheries. Wetlands provide important nursery areas for fish and shellfish, including crabs. Ellis and Fisher (1987) modelled the case of wetlands off the gulf coast of Florida. Human effort (in terms of numbers of traps set) and wetland acreage were found to jointly determine the output of blue crabs. Having identified this production function, the authors then found the profit-maximizing levels of effort for different levels of wetland acreage. It was then possible to see the effects on welfare, measured as changes in consumer and producer surplus, of reductions in wetland area. Their results are shown in Table 3.2.

Dose-response models have been very widely used in the literature, mainly to study the effects of air pollutants on agricultural crops and forests. Polluting emissions from a variety of sources are modelled in terms of their fate in the environment. For example, for SO_2, this might involve being blown from one country to another and then falling as acid rain. This constitutes the 'dose' of pollution, to which a physical response occurs. This physical response (e.g. crop damage, buildings damage, fisheries impacts) is estimated using models produced by natural scientists. An economic response to such damage can then occur, for example if farmers decide to grow less pollution-sensitive crops. Finally, the net effects on output, consumers' surplus, and producers' profits are evaluated, along with other elements of damage costs (for example, costs of restoring old buildings damaged by acid rain).

Box 3.5 Valuing Heritage Sites: Stonehenge

In many countries, the landscape we see now has been formed by a tremendous mixture of human and natural influences. For example, semi-natural habitats such as hay meadows and heather moorland are the product of a particular type of farming regime, combined with environmental conditions which make such habitats viable. The built environment is also part of landscapes, and historical remains are very important in this context. One of the most famous archaeological sites in Europe is Stonehenge, in the Salisbury Plain of England, a World Heritage Site. Stonehenge, as its name implies, is a henge monument (circle and surrounding ditch) made of stones, in this case massive Sarcen stones. It dates from 5000 to 3500 years ago.

Currently, the quality of the site for visitors is impaired by the proximity of an increasingly noisy and busy road, the A303. This state of affairs was described at a recent public enquiry as a 'national disgrace'. Accordingly, English Heritage, who manage the site jointly with the National Trust, proposed the construction of a covered tunnel for the A303 in the area around the site, which would essentially hide all of the passing traffic and greatly reduce noise levels. The cost of this project was estimated at £125 million: but was it worth it? To answer this question, a contingent valuation study was commissioned. Susana Mourato and David Maddison designed a survey whereby visitors and the general public were asked their WTP in higher taxes for the road tunnel project. The general public were included in order to capture non-use values. The most conservative estimate of benefits showed them to be worth £150 million, that is more than the cost of the tunnel. Accordingly, the UK government announced that it would fund construction.

Table 3.2 Results from a production function model of wetlands and a crab fishery

Wetland acreage	No. of traps	Change in combined consumer and producer surplus (US$/year)
100,000	29,575	192,658
200,000	30,986	295,290
300,000	31,842	358,290
400,000	32,464	404,139
500,000	33,000	437,688

Finally, ecosystem function valuation approaches have recently been put forward, particularly by ecological economists, as a preferred approach to environmental valuation. Proponents of this approach often express dissatisfaction with the other means of environmental valuation set out in this chapter, in particular over the information problem (uninformed citizens cannot be asked to value the environment, it should be left to 'experts') and over ethical unease at asking people to express environmental values in such an explicit way as WTP. The basic idea is to identify the different functions of an ecosystem, and then to try to put a money value on some of these. Where no monetary valuation is possible/appropriate, then effects are still retained in analysis, but expressed in qualitative terms. The approach is often used to look at management alternatives for ecosystems, and makes extensive use of systems analysis to represent the complex interlinkages within an ecosystem, and between this system and the economy. Money values typically come about through production function links to marketed outputs, and avoided damage cost or replacement cost approaches. The latter would involve valuing the pollution treatment capabilities of a wetland as the cost of providing a human-engineered replacement sewage treatment system.

There is some confusion over terminology amongst devotees of the approach. For instance, de Groot (1993) identified four types of environmental function:

- regulatory functions, for example the prevention of soil erosion;
- carrier functions (providing space for wildlife), such as nature protection;
- information functions, e.g. cultural, educational, scientific; and
- production functions, e.g. oxygen, genetic resources

However, many (most) of these functions are interdependent, and one may provide an input for the other. An alternative definition is that an environmental function is a set of ecological processes which produce an environmental good or service. Goods may be directly or indirectly supplied. Directly supplied goods include hunting and fishing opportunities in a wetland, whilst an example of indirect supply would be the wetland acting as a nursery for coastal fisheries. Services supplied by a wetland would include protection against storm events (coastal stabilization) and pollution reduction (e.g. of nutrients and sediments). A recent application was provided by Gilbert and Janssen (1998), who applied the method to the appraisal of management alternatives for mangrove wetlands in the Philippines. The value (both monetary and non-monetary) of different goods and services under different management alternatives is ranked; however, combining monetary and non-monetary measures in the same ranking turns out to be rather difficult. In addition, replacement costs are a poor measure of ecosystem value unless several conditions are fulfilled. These are (i) that the human-engineered substitutes provide identical services to the ecosystem; (ii) that they are the best way of substituting for its loss; and (iii) that people on aggregate would be willing to pay their cost (Bockstael et al., 1999).

3.4 Why Place Economic Values on the Environment?

Economic estimates of the value of changes in environmental and resource quality may be useful in a number of contexts. These include:

- policy appraisal;
- project appraisal;
- environmental management;
- environmental damage assessment;
- setting environmental taxes; and
- national accounting.

Let us look at each of these in more detail.

3.4.1 Policy appraisal

One way in which economists can be useful is through the provision of advice to policy-makers. Worldwide, much of the funding for environmental valuation studies has come from government departments and agencies with responsibilities for environmental policy design and implementation (for example, in the UK, with the Forestry Commission and the Environment Agency); or with responsibility for policies which impact on the environment (e.g. roads policy).

Within the UK, a formal commitment to engage in environmental cost-benefit analysis exists with respect to the national environment agencies (although varying degrees of importance are then attached to the results of these exercises). Government departments, since the publication of *Policy Appraisal and the Environment* in 1991, have all been encouraged to apply environmental CBA principles to policy design: this encouragement has been moved in the direction of a requirement by recent Cabinet Office guidelines. As has been shown by internal reports on this process, there are relatively few instances so far where a full-blown CBA has been applied to environmental policy decisions: however, cost-benefit thinking may be becoming more widespread.[7] It seems likely that environmental valuation will increasingly be called on by policy-makers; although it also appears that this is unlikely to be solely or mainly as part of a formal CBA. Within the European Union, Pearce (1998) has argued that until relatively recently, there was no or only little consideration given to

---

[7] e.g. The recent draft National Air Quality Standards were subject to a full economic appraisal (although the environmental valuation parts of this were poorly received by ministers).

comparing the environmental costs and benefits of draft directives, which has probably led to some expensive errors. Pearce observes that, since the Maastricht Treaty, attitudes towards CBA within the Commission have changed, with draft directives impacting on the environment being increasingly subject to some form of benefit–cost comparison. Examples include revisions to a directive on air pollution from municipal waste incinerators, and the planned EU Acidification Strategy.

3.4.2 Project appraisal

Much early work in environmental valuation was also carried out in a project appraisal context, which was to be expected given the increasing use of cost-benefit analysis in public project appraisal (see Chapter 4). A good example is the development of hydroelectric power in the USA (Krutilla and Fisher, 1985); and forestry planting decisions in the UK, where recreation and biodiversity impacts can be included in the list of costs and benefits.

3.4.3 Environmental management

Within the area of environmental management, a key feature may be the requirement to use environmental valuation to aid improvement in policy implementation. For example, in the Environmental Sensitive Areas scheme, farmers are paid subsidies to conserve or improve different environmental features within defined geographic areas of the country. Knowing the relative marginal values of, for example, wetlands compared to farm woodlands, may be very useful in this regard, implying a possible advantage for attribute-based valuation approaches, such as choice experiments, contingent-ranking, and random-utility travel-cost approaches. If a public forestry service is charged with managing forests in a manner which maximizes net social benefits, then decisions over species mix, age diversity, and the provision of recreation facilities would be helped if managers have estimates of the marginal values of these attributes.

3.4.4 Setting environmental taxes

Environmental valuation has been increasingly used in the UK for setting eco-taxes, for example with regard to the landfill tax and the putative tax on quarrying. Valuation has been used in both justifying a tax, and in determining its level. However, applying an estimate of average external cost at the current level of activity does not constitute the Pigovian tax which it is made out to be, since this would typically measure the marginal external cost at the optimal level of externality. Here, the crucial issue would appear to be knowing how marginal damages vary with the level of the externality-causing activity. This is essentially the question of scale in valuation. Whilst, as noted above, most contingent valuation studies are sensitive to scale, it is uncommon for more than a couple of quantities to be valued. Valuation functions can of course be estimated with scale as one independent variable, but choice experiments allow scale itself to be an attribute. Choice Experiments may thus be more useful for eco-tax setting, but again this is unproven at present.

3.4.5 Environmental damage claims

Under the CERLA and Oil Pollution Acts in the USA, firms that cause accidental environmental damages can be sued in the courts by states and the Federal government to recover the monetary value of such damage. The most famous such incident has been the Exxon Valdez oil spill in 1989 (see Box 3.4); however, another good example was the accident involving the oil tanker *American Trader*, which spilled up to 400,000 gallons of crude oil into the Pacific Ocean off the coast of California. The state of California sued the 'responsible parties', for damages. Interestingly, in this case, the two parties produced alternative sets of estimates of these damages, which resulted in the main from the temporary closure of a number of beaches. The state of California's experts estimated the value of a lost day's recreation on the beach to be around $15/visit; unsurprisingly, the defendants' economists came up with a lower value of $4–8 per visit. Arguments also raged about how many visits were lost. The jury ended up ruling more in favour of the state of California's estimates, and awarded costs against the delegates of $10.2 million.

3.4.6 National accounting

In Chapter 6, we discuss the issue of making 'green' adjustments to national accounting figures such as gross national product, as a way of producing a better measure of welfare, and (possibly) an indicator of sustainability. Governments can use environmental valuation in calculating such green adjustments to the national accounts, for example to take account of changes in the level of pollution between this year and the previous year, or to value the partial felling of a country's stock of forests.

3.5 Summary

CHANGES in the quantity or quality of environmental resources have economic value if they have an impact on utility. We can base our measures of these values upon either the most that people are willing to give up to acquire some (desirable) change, or the least they are willing to accept to forgo it (for an undesirable change, then we can use either the most people are willing to pay to prevent it, or the lowest compensation they would accept to put up with it). Actual methods for obtaining estimates of these values can be divided into stated and revealed preference approaches. In the former case, we can use hypothetical changes in environmental quality to measure willingness to pay/willingness to accept in the contingent valuation method, or by using choice experiments. In revealed preference methods, people's actual choices over recreation (the travel-cost model) or housing (the hedonic-price method) are studied. Ecosystem valuation methods are somewhat different, since on the whole they trace ecosystem impacts back to impacts on production (e.g. lost fisheries output), or the cost of replacements.

Governments can and have made extensive use of environmental valuation in a number of contexts, particularly policy and project appraisal. Other uses also exist, including the settling of environmental damage claims and calculating green tax rates.

References

Barbier, E., Burgess, J., and Folke, C. (1994). *Paradise Lost? The Ecological Economics of Biodiversity Decline* (London, Earthscan).

Bateman, I., and Willis, K. (eds.) (1999) *Valuing Environmental Preferences: Theory and Practice of the Contingent Valuation Method* (Oxford: Oxford University Press).

Bockstael, N., Freeman, A. M., Kopp, R., Portney, R., and Smith, V. K. (1999). 'On valuing nature'. Mimeo.

Brown, G., and Henry, W. (1993). 'The viewing of elephants', in E. Barbier (ed.), *Economics and Ecology: New Frontiers and Sustainable Development* (London: Chapman & Hall).

Carson, R. T. (1997). 'Contingent valuation and tests of scope insensitivity', in R. Kopp, W. Pommerhene, and N. Schwartz (eds.) *Determining the Value of Non-market Goods* (Boston: Kluwer).

Costanza, R. *et al.* (1997). 'The value of the world', ecosystem, and natural capital', *Nature* 387 (May): 253–60.

Daly, H. (1998). 'The return of Lauderdale's paradox', *Ecological Economics* 25(1): 21–4.

De Groot, R. (1993). *Function of Nature* (Groningen, Wolters-Noordhoff).

Desvouges, W., Smith, V. K., and Fisher, A. (1987). 'Option price estimates for water quality improvements', *Journal of Environmental Economics and Management* 14: 248–67.

Dunford, R. (1999). 'The American Oil trader spill', AERE Newsletter, May: 12–20.

Ellis, G., and Fisher, A. (1987). 'Valuing the environment as an input', *Journal of Environmental Management* 25: 149–56.

Farber, S. (1998). 'Undesirable facilities and property values: a summary of empirical studies', *Ecological Economics*, 24 (1): 1–14.

Foster, V., Bateman, I., and Harley, D. (1997). 'Real and hypothetical willingness to pay for environmental preservation', *Journal of Agricultural Economics* 48(2): 123–38.

—— and Mourato, S. (2000). 'Measuring the impacts of pesticide use in the UK: a contingent ranking approach', *Journal of Agricultural Economics* 51(1): 1–21.

Gilbert, A., and Jansson, R. (1998). 'Use of environmental functions to communicate the values of a mangrove ecosystem under different management regimes', *Ecological Economics* 25(3): 323–46.

Hanemann, M. (1991). 'Willingness to pay and willingness to accept: how much can they differ?', *American Economic Review* 81: 635–47.

Hanley, N., and Spash, C. (1993). *Cost-Benefit Analysis and the Environment* (Cheltenham: Edward Elgar).

—— Wright, R., and Adamowicz, W. (1998). 'Using choice experiments to value the environment: design issues, current experience and future prospects', *Environmental and Resource Economics* 11(3–4): 413–28.

Krutilla, J. V., and Fisher, A. C. (1985). *The Economics of Natural Environments* (Washington, DC: Resources for the Future).

London Economics (1999). *The Environmental Costs of the Supply of Aggregates*, Final report to DETR of phase-2 work (London: London Economics).

Loomis, J. (1995). 'Four models for determining environmental quality effects on recreational demand and regional economics', *Ecological Economics* 12: 55–65.

Morrison, M., Bennett, J., Blamey, R., and Louviere, J. (1998). *Choice Modelling and Tests of Benefit Transfer*. Choice Modelling Research Report 8, University College, University of New South Wales, Canberra.

Mourato, S., and Maddison, D. (2000). 'Valuing different road options for Stonehenge', in S. Navrud and R. Ready (eds.), *Valuing Cultural Heritage* (Cheltenham: Edward Elgar).

Pearce, D. (1998). 'Environmental appraisal and environmental policy in the European Union', *Environmental and Resource Economics* 11: 489–501.

—— and Turner, R. K. (1989). *Economics of Natural Resources and the Environment* (London: Harvester Wheatsheaf).

Ready, R. (1995). 'Environmental valuation under uncertainty', in D. Bromley (ed.), *The Handbook of Environmental Economics* (Oxford: Blackwell).

Schulze, W. D., Brookshire, D., Walther, E., MacFarland, K., Thayer, M., Whitworth, R., and Ben-David, S. (1983). 'The economic benefits of preserving visibility in the national parklands of the South West', *Natural Resources Journal* 23: 149–73.

Smith, V. K., and Huang, J. C. (1995). 'Can markets value air quality?', *Journal of Political Economy* 103: 209–27.

Willig, R. (1976) 'Consumers surplus without apology', *American Economic Review* 66: 589–97.

Chapter 4
Cost-Benefit Analysis and the Environment

I**N** this chapter, we introduce the most commonly used decision-making tool developed by economists, cost-benefit analysis. CBA has been extensively applied to environmental management problems by academics, and by policy makers too. This chapter:

- explains the theoretical background to CBA;
- sets out the stages of an actual CBA, with examples;
- considers the methodological problems of the technique, especially as it relates to the environment;
- provides a brief discussion on ethical objections to CBA; and finally
- looks at actual use of CBA in environmental policy-making.

4.1 Some Background

E**CONOMISTS** have long been intrigued by the problem of how to decide whether one outcome is better than another from society's point of view. Ideally, we would like to find decision-making rules which give consistent outcomes, that is outcomes which are the same when applied in the same circumstances. Rules are desirable if we are to avoid *ad hoc* decision-making. We would also like to find a method which is democratic, in some sense, and practical; and (as economists!) which can be shown to be consistent with economic theory.

The area of research known as 'welfare economics' developed out of the search for such a method. Cost-benefit analysis eventually emerged out of welfare economics as a practical application of a decision-making rule. Welfare economics is concerned with developing tools which allow outcomes to be compared according to a criterion taken from eighteenth century philosophy, known as utilitarianism. In case that sounds a bit esoteric, ask yourself whether this seems sensible: that we should com-pare outcomes on the basis of what gives the greatest benefit to the greatest number of people. Benefit here means utility: thus, welfare economics looks at ways of com-paring outcomes in terms of their contribution to the utility of the population as a whole. We are going to try and choose options, therefore, that give the biggest (net) pay-off to socienty in terms of utility.[1] Social welfare, or the well-being of society as a whole, is determined by adding up welfare (or utility) levels across people in differing circumstances. As will be seen, this poses some awkward problems, both conceptual and practical.

We have already come across the idea of representing the 'happiness levels' of individuals by reference to their utility level, and with the idea that one could repre-sent what determines an individual's utility through a utility function. Deciding how good some outcome is from the point of social welfare, and whether a reallocation of resources improves social welfare clearly requires us to be able to: (i) compare people's individual utility levels (Joe's with Joanne's) and (ii) add up utilities over all the individuals in a society.

Understanding the consequences of these two seemingly straightforward require-ments has kept economists busy for over a century, in particular the comparison of your well-being with my well-being. Let's pass over these difficulties here (see Box 4.1 for a discussion) and assume that it is acceptable to compare utility levels between people, and that we can add up utilities across individuals. Remember that in practice we actually use money equivalents of these underlying utility amounts (so that the increase in utility to you of having a new bike is measurable by the most you are willing to pay for it, for instance).

Given this, one early suggestion for how we could determine whether a project/policy improved social welfare was proposed by the Italian economist Pareto. A 'Pareto improvement' is where at least one person is made better off by a change and no one is made worse off. In such a situation, Pareto argued, most people would agree that society was better off. However, in practice it is hard to find a resource realloca-tion that does not impose costs on anyone. If the Pareto criterion is taken literally, then this implies that any project which makes just one person worse off should be turned down. Yet in almost all cases, there will be some 'losers'. How can this be handled? The most important solution was proposed independently, but at around about the same time, by Nicholas Kaldor and John Hicks in the late 1930s. Their principle is now known as the potential Pareto improvement (PPI) criterion. The important word here is 'potential', since applying the principle involves asking: 'Could the gainers (those who benefit from a resource reallocation) compensate the losers (those who are worse off as a result) and still be better off?'

No *actual* compensation of losers need take place—this is a distributional issue whereas the PPI criterion focuses solely on the efficiency of resource allocation. Should all losers actually get full compensation for their losses, then the potential Pareto improvement would be transformed into an actual Pareto improvement, but

---

[1] Notice straight away that by focusing solely on the implications of outcomes for people, we exclude all non-anthropocentric concepts of value.

Box 4.1 The Welfare Economics Background explored

As mentioned in the main text, the PPI test is the welfare economics foundation of CBA. This states that a resource allocation is efficient if gainers could compensate the losers and still be better off. Two points we could make straight away are that (i) the principle assumes all losses can be compensated for—this may not always be the case; and (ii) that costless transfers are possible. But transfers of what? At its most basic level, the principle is concerned with transfers of *utility*, since utility is assumed to be how we measure 'welfare'. Imagine an economy with a given technology and given resources composed of two people only. If we could convert all efficient production and consumption decisions into utility equivalents we might end up with a 'utility possibility frontier' as shown in Figure 4.B1.

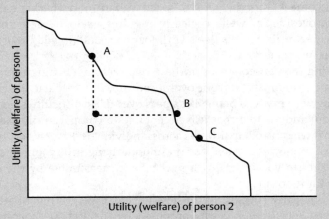

Figure 4.B1

Using the Pareto principle or the compensation test does not allow us to compare points A and B, since moving from A to B means one person getting better off with one getting worse off. Neither criterion can in fact rank points on the frontier. However, imagine that due to market failure or a market distortion we start off at D. Any movement to a point on the line segment AB improves both or at least one person's welfare, without making the other worse off. How about a move from D to C? This makes individual 1 worse off and individual 2 better off. But we could redistribute utility to individual 1 back to say point B, where he is no worse off than at D.

As readers will discover in Johansson (1991), problems do occur with the PPI criteria nevertheless. This led economists to search for other ways of comparing the social welfare implications of policies/projects. The Bergson Social Welfare Function (SWF) is one way of doing this. Such a function shows us conceptually how social welfare is composed. For example, a Utilization SWF would look like this:

$$W = U_1 + U_2.$$

Here, social welfare is just the sum of individual utilities (this is called 'welfarism'), and so that welfare increases as utility increases. This suggests that the best outcome in social welfare terms is where the marginal utility of one person is equal to that of everyone else. This does not necessarily imply that everyone should have the same level of income for an optimal outcome as might be first guessed. This is because income is not the same as utility, and utility functions (the relationship between income and utility) are not necessarily the same for everyone. Notice also that the utilitarian SWF implies that the only thing that matters for social welfare is individual utility—there is no 'common good'.

If we take the ethical view that making poor people (or otherwise disadvantaged people) happier is more socially valuable at the margin than an equal increase in happiness for rich people, then we might prefer a conceptual SWF like:

$$W = a.U_1 + b.U_2$$

where a and b are weights which are bigger for poor people, for example, than for rich people. Finally, a more extreme form of SWF follows from assuming that the *only* thing society cares about is the welfare of the least well-off members of society: this is known as a Rawlsian or maximin SWF.

Since in CBA we only measure money equivalents (approximations, to be more exact) of underlying utility changes, adding utility changes may not give the same result as adding monetary equivalents. Also, unless we know what SWF society implicitly 'uses', we cannot be sure that the $NPV > 0$ test is an improvement in social well-being, since we are unsure of the weights, for example, of the 'correct' SWF.

there is no requirement for this to take place on efficiency grounds. Another way of stating the PPI criterion is 'are the aggregate benefits bigger than the aggregate costs?', since losses and costs are taken to be synonymous, as are gains and benefits. It is this way of looking at the PPI criterion which provides the link between welfare economics as a theory and cost-benefit analysis as a practice.

The fundamental working assumptions behind the PPI criterion are that all losses are compensatable, and that gains and losses are comparable with each other (are symmetric). 'Losses' might be a worker giving up her leisure to work for a company, and clearly wages are offered in compensation which the worker can freely accept or reject. But losses could equally well be the destruction of a local nature reserve due to the building of a new road—losers here (those people who care about the nature reserve) might well refuse any amount of money in compensation if they feel the reserve is 'priceless'. We return to such ethical issues in CBA in Section 4.5.

By measuring gains as the money value of benefits, and costs as the money value of losses, the PPI criterion can be translated into a single number, namely the money value of the total net benefits of a project/policy. This, as we explain below, is the 'net present value' of the project/policy: if it is positive then the project/policy passes the CBA test, and by implication the PPI criterion. This means that the resultant resource reallocation is economically efficient: a government able to fund a series of economically efficient programmes would be improving the allocative efficiency of the economy, and by implication, social welfare. However, not everyone is necessarily made better off as a result, since as we have already noted, compensation is hypothetical rather than actual. The CBA test does not say anything about the fairness of the resource allocation, nor its political acceptability, nor (as we explain below) whether it improves the sustainability of the economy.

Students with some knowledge of management economics or finance may think at this point that CBA sounds much the same as the discounted cash flow (DCF) analysis routinely applied to firms' investment decisions. While many similarities exist, the key difference is the scope of whose welfare is being considered. In DCF analysis, the scope is narrower, since the only impacts of relevance are those on shareholder wealth, and the way these are valued in terms of the financial implications for the firm (its profits). In CBA, the scope is much broader, and the relevant impacts are those on anyone living in the society for which the CBA is being carried out (e.g. all UK residents). These impacts are valued in terms of their social cost or social benefit, which include costs and benefits not expressed through markets.

CBA has turned out to be one of the most useful economic tools. Why?

■ It addresses an important social concern (the efficiency of resource allocation), and is applicable in a wide range of circumstances.

■ A wide variety of impacts can be included, and compared in the same measurement units.

■ CBA can be used in both project and policy appraisal, and as a device for allocating scarce public money across competing uses.

■ CBA possesses an advantage over referendums, since it takes account of both the direction (approve/disapprove) and intensity of preferences (how much do you dislike this? How much do I like it?).

■ CBA allows us to emphasize both the economic value of environmental protection, as well as the opportunity cost of protecting the environment.

It has also attracted a high degree of criticism from both economists and non-economists. Certainly CBA has many weaknesses, and there are many problems in applying it to the environment (Section 4.3). One criticism is that resource allocation efficiency is just not of interest to people. However, many economists would counter that in a world of scarce resources and unlimited wants, it should be! CBA is also criticized as being technocentric and non-inclusive in terms of community decision-making. On the other hand, CBA does offer a formal and conceptually simple way of presenting the advantages and disadvantages of a policy or project option. Many of the criticisms of CBA indeed seem to set up a straw man—few economists would argue that CBA should ever be the *sole* guide to decision-making, but should just be viewed as one input to the decision-making process. For example, we might also want to use risk analysis, environmental impact analysis, and a referendum to make a decision over whether to abandon a nuclear energy programme. Let us now look at how a CBA is conducted.

4.2 Stages of a Cost-Benefit Analysis

Not all CBAs are carried out in exactly the same way. However, the 'routine' we set out below would be recognized by most practitioners.

4.2.1 Project/policy definition

This involves setting out exactly what is being analysed; whose welfare is being considered; and over what time period. For example, we could establish that the CBA is to be conducted on a proposed new sewage treatment plant for a seaside town; that we will consider impacts on all those who live in the town, since we will assume that they are paying for it through local taxes, and will benefit from cleaner bathing water, plus visitors to the beaches in the town since they will also enjoy higher-quality water. The analysis is to be carried out over the expected lifetime of the plant, say thirty years. Often, defining the 'relevant population' is an difficult issue. For instance, if the policy is to safeguard an internationally rare habitat located in Scotland, should benefits to non-Scottish conservationists also be counted in terms of their willingness to pay for this action? The relevant time-period may also be problematic. If nuclear waste storage proposals are being analysed, then it is necessary to make allowance for the very long half-life of some radioactive isotopes.

4.2.2 Identify physical impacts of the policy/project

Any project/policy has implications for resource allocation: labour used to build a road; additional electricity production due to the creation of a new power station; less waste being landfilled, and more recycled, because of a tax on landfill sites. The next stage of a CBA is to identify these outcomes in physical magnitudes: so many man-hours of labour, so many megawatts of electricity. For environmental impacts, environmental impact analysis will often be used to produce predictions. Frequently, these changes in resource allocation will not be known with certainty—for example, how many fewer tonnes will go to landfill because of a new tax? For environmental impacts, uncertainty in outcomes is to be expected to an even greater degree than with other impacts. The effects on invertebrate fauna from a reduction in acid deposition, or the effects of enhanced global warming on species migration are examples. CBA does not handle such uncertainty at all well, and we return to this in Section 4.5.

Once physical impacts have been identified and quantified, it is then necessary to ask which of them are relevant to the CBA. Essentially, anything which has an impact on the quantity or quality of resources, or on their price, may be said to be relevant if it can be traced back to a link with utility. The effects of price changes are measured by calculating changes in consumers' and producers' surplus (see Johansson, 1991, for more details). If significant price changes are not expected, then it is quality impacts that are of most interest. This is especially true in the context of government policy initiatives affecting the environment, or public/private investments which affect the environment: for instance, if policy leads to an improvement in the quality of river water, or to an increase in the area of wilderness designation. Excluded from a CBA are 'transfer payments', income transfers from the State to individuals, such as farm subsidies or unemployment benefits (see Sugden and Williams, 1974).

Since we specify relevant impacts in terms of utility impacts, it is not necessary to restrict attention to market-valued impacts, since non-market value changes (such as an improvement in air quality) are relevant if they affect people's utility. Environmental effects can also make their presence felt through production links with marketed goods: for instance, the effect of air pollution on farm crops.

4.2.3 Valuing impacts

One important feature of CBA is that all relevant effects are expressed in monetary values, so that they can then be aggregated. For environmental impacts, there has been a tradition of listing such changes in physical/qualitative terms: pressures still exist to continue with this practice, but as we saw in Chapter 3, it is now possible to place monetary values on many types of environmental change.

The general principle of monetary valuation in CBA is to value impacts in terms of their marginal social cost or marginal social benefit. 'Social' here means 'evaluated with regard to the economy as a whole'. Simple financial investment appraisal, in contrast, values costs and benefits in terms of their impact on firms and their shareholders only. But where are these marginal social benefits and costs derived from? Under certain conditions, market prices tell us about both, as was explained in Chapter 2. In Figure 4.1, we show equilibrium in the world market for coal. The demand curve Q^D shows the marginal WTP of buyers of coal at a range of quantities, which represents a schedule of marginal social benefits (MSB). The supply curve shows the marginal private cost (MPC) to mine-owners of producing coal. If there were no externalities in coal production, then this would also show the marginal social cost (MSC). Both MSB and MSC would then be equal to the equilibrium market price, p^e. However, if coal-mining does result in external costs, then the marginal social cost of coal, which should be used to value coal impacts in a CBA, is shown as p^* for quantity q^e.

The price p^*, representing the marginal social cost of coal as an input to a project, is often referred to as a *shadow price*. Shadow prices are estimates of marginal social costs/benefits when market prices are distorted in some way, either through externalities as in Figure 4.1, or due to government intervention in the market, as shown in Figure 4.2. Here, we show the market for a farm crop which is subject to price

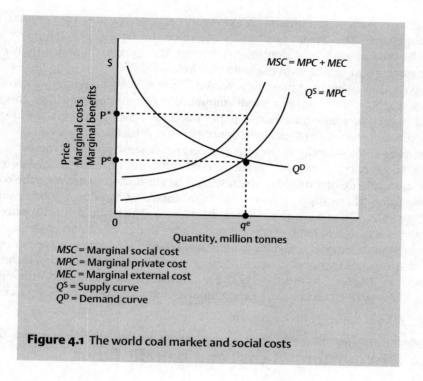

MSC = Marginal social cost
MPC = Marginal private cost
MEC = Marginal external cost
Q^S = Supply curve
Q^D = Demand curve

Figure 4.1 The world coal market and social costs

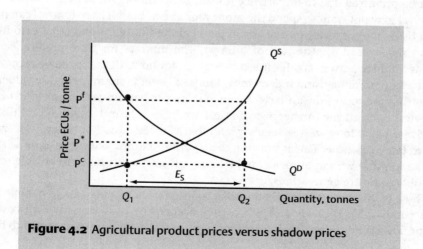

Figure 4.2 Agricultural product prices versus shadow prices

intervention. Such intervention is an extremely common feature in agricultural markets worldwide. The government holds the price the farmer gets (p^F) above what would be the free-market equilibrium p^e, through buying up the excess supply E^s and either storing it or selling it on the world market.

Suppose CBA is being applied to a project (such as land drainage) which would increase supply of this crop by a small amount. What economic value does this extra output have? The value to farmers is p^F per tonne, but part of this is a transfer payment (subsidy) from the government. Consumers are actually only WTP an amount p^c at the margin for quantity Q, so p^c is the correct shadow price for the extra farm output. In practice, economists often estimate the proportion of farm-gate prices which are made up of a subsidy, which should be eliminated to arrive at the correct shadow price. These support proportions are known as 'producer subsidy equivalents', or PSEs. These PSEs represent the extent to which the domestic price of a commodity is distorted from the world price, expressed as a percentage.

Environmental impacts, such as a landscape quality, air quality or species protection, can be valued in monetary terms through using the kind of valuation techniques outlined in Chapter 3 to estimate WTP for changes in the quantity of these public goods. These WTP estimates can be thought of as a special case of shadow pricing.

4.2.4 Discounting of cost and benefit flows

Once all relevant cost and benefit flows that can be expressed in monetary amounts have been so expressed, it is necessary to convert them all into *present value* (PV) terms. This necessity arises out of the time value of money, or time preference. To take a simple example, suppose an individual is asked to choose between receiving £100 today and receiving that same £100 in one year's time. The more immediate sum might be preferred due to impatience (I want to spend the money right now). Alternatively, I may not want to spend the money for a year, but if I have it now I can invest it in a bank at an interest rate of say 10 per cent, and have £100 x (1+i) = £110 in one year's time, where i is the rate of interest. The motives for time preference, and reasons for discounting, are discussed in Box 4.2: for now, all that need be recognized is that a sum of money, and indeed most kinds of benefit, are more highly valued the sooner they are received. Similarly, a sum of money to be paid out, or any kind of cost, seems less onerous the further away in time we have to bear it. A bill of £1 million to repackage hazardous wastes seems preferable if received in 100 years time rather than in ten years time. This is nothing to do with inflation,[2] but more to do with the expectation that we might expect to be better off in the future, or to be able to pass the bill onto future generations.

So how is this time effect taken into account, and how are cost-and-benefit flows made comparable regardless of when they occur? The answer is that all cost and benefit flows are *discounted*, using a discount rate which, for now, is assumed to be the

---

[2] For a discussion on how to handle inflation in CBA, see Hanley and Spash (1993. ch. 1).

Box 4.2 Discounting and the Discount Rate

Discounting, to non-economists, is one of the most controversial aspects of CBA. This is because of some of its impacts: a benefit far away in time (in say 100 years from now) becomes almost worthless in present-value terms, and so has a low weight in the decision even though it might be very important to the people who receive it in 100 years. For example, suppose investment in nuclear fusion is predicted to generate benefits of £100 million/year within seventy-five years. At a discount rate of 5 per cent this is only worth:

$$£100m * (1 + i)^{-75} = £2.57m/yr$$

now. Because discounting works in this negative exponential fashion, very large future benefits can have very small impacts on present decisions. What's true for benefits is true for costs as well: if, for example, repairing a nuclear waste site is likely to be required in 200 years at an expected cost of £300 billion, this is only worth £300 $(1.05)^{-200}$ or £0.017 billion now. Discounting has thus been criticized as being 'unfair to the future'.

The rights of future generations are a complicated matter. However, it is hard to escape the view that discounting operates to the disadvantage of such future people. Why do economists discount then? There are two main reasons: (i) because people do. Individuals generally view benefits as less valuable, as costs and less costly, the more they are postponed. The rate at which people trade off future against present cost/benefits is known as the marginal rate of time preference, and is a candidate for the discount rate the government should use in CBA; (ii) because, due to the productivity of capital, we expect society to get richer over time. If the marginal utility of consumption is declining, then an extra unit of benefit is worth less the further into the future it occurs. The rate at which capital productivity grows is another candidate for the social discount rate. For a detailed discussion of the discount rate, see Hanley and Spash (1993: ch. 8).

rate of interest, i. The present value of a cost or benefit (X) received in time t is calculated as follows:

$$PV(X_t) = X_t [(1 + i)^{-t}]. \tag{4.1}$$

The expression in square brackets in equation (4.1) is known as a discount factor. Discount factors have the property that they always lie between 0 and +1. The further away in time a cost or benefit occurs (the higher the value of t), the lower the discount factor. The higher the discount rate i for a given t, the lower the discount factor, since a higher discount rate means a greater preference for things now rather than later.

Discounting may be done in CBA in one of two ways: either by finding the net value of benefits minus costs for each time-period (usually each year), and discounting each of these annual net benefit flows throughout the lifetime of the project; or by calculating discounted values for each element of a project, then summing the discounted elements. For example, adding up total discounted labour costs, total discounted material costs, and total discounted energy saving benefits. Both approaches should give identical answers.

4.2.5 Applying the net present value test

The main purpose of CBA is to help select projects and policies which are efficient in terms of their use of resources. The criterion applied is the *net present value* (NPV) test. This simply asks whether the sum of discounted gains ($\Sigma B_t(1+i)^{-t}$ as it is written below) exceeds the sum of discounted losses (written as $\Sigma C_t(1+i)^{-t}$). If so, the project can be said to represent an efficient shift in resource allocation, given the data used in the CBA. The *NPV* of a project is thus:

$$NPV = \Sigma B_t(1+i)^{-t} - \Sigma C_t(1+i)^{-t} \qquad (4.2)$$

where the summations Σ run from $t=0$ (the first year of the project) to $t=T$ (the last year of the project). Note that no costs or benefits before year 0 are counted. The criterion for project acceptance is: accept if and only if $NPV > 0$. Based on the PPI criterion, any project passing the *NPV* test is deemed to be an improvement in social welfare.

There are a number of alternatives to the *NPV* criterion. The two most commonly employed are the internal rate of return (IRR) and the benefit–cost ratio. The *IRR* is a measure frequently employed in financial investment appraisal. It is the rate of interest which, if used as the discount rate for a project, would yield a *NPV* of zero, and is interpreted as the rate of return on the resources (investment funds) used in the project. This can be compared with the opportunity cost of these investment funds, which might be the market rate of interest. However, the *IRR* is flawed as a measure of resource allocation for two principal reasons. First, many projects can generate multiple IRRs from the same data set, so the analyst does not know which to select as the decision-making criterion. Second, the *IRR* is unreliable when comparing performance across many projects in a portfolio. This is because the *IRR* only compares the return on one project relative to the opportunity cost of funds. The benefit–cost ratio is simply the ratio of discounted benefits to discounted costs. The decision rule becomes: proceed if and only if the benefit–cost ratio exceeds unity.

An optional part of this stage involves changing the weights in the *NPV* function. As was noted in Chapter 3, economic measures of value based on WTP are dependent on the existing distribution of income. In this sense, it might be objected that the *NPV* measure only works as a welfare change measure if we assume that the existing distribution of income is, in some sense, optimal. Using the *NPV* as a measure of the contribution to social welfare made by a policy/project is also complicated by the fact that we do not know the correct marginal utilities of income with which to weight benefits and costs. For these reasons, an optional stage which follows the *NPV* calculation is to examine the effects of different weighting schemes on *NPV* values. Suppose that the impacts of a motorway project can be divided up according to which group in society they affect, groups being defined on income grounds alone. This might give the results shown in Table 4.1.

The conventional *NPV* calculation implicitly puts an equal weight (equal to one) on all these impacts, giving a *NPV* of +£1 million, so the project would be accepted.

Table 4.1 Road impacts by income group	
Group affected	Impact discounted (£) (– a loss, + a gain)
G1 Low income	–2.4 million
G2 Mid income	+1.1 million
G3 High income	+2.3 million

However, society might place more importance on each £1 of impact on poor groups than on rich groups. This could be reflected in a different weighting scheme. One possible set of weights would be $w = (Y^*/Y_i)$, where w is the weight to be attached to impacts on group i, Y^* is mean household income across all groups, and Y_i is mean income within group i. This gives a higher weight to poorer groups than to richer groups, and the *NPV* formula becomes:

$$NPV = w_1 B_1 + w_2 B_2 + \ldots wnBn \qquad (4.3)$$

where Bn are discounted net benefits to group n.

   This may seem like an attractive option, but there are severe problems here. First, what weights should be used in a practical context? Marginal utility of income weights are typically not known, and relative income is only one ground on which to differentiate between groups. How should these groups be defined, and how easy is it to work out how much each group will be affected? For these reasons, this unequal weighting procedure (sometimes known as 'revisionism') is rarely practised at the public agency level, with the exception of projects in developing country contexts.

4.2.6 Sensitivity analysis

The *NPV* test described above tells us about the relative efficiency of a given project, given the data input to the calculations. If these data change, then clearly the results of the *NPV* test will change too. But why should data change? The main reason concerns uncertainty. In many cases where CBA is used, the analyst must make predictions concerning future physical flows (for example, traffic movements) and future relative values (for example, the price of fuel). None of these predictions can be made with perfect foresight. When environmental impacts are involved, this uncertainty may be even more widespread; for example, if a policy to reduce global greenhouse gas emissions is planned, then the impacts of this in terms of avoided damage may be subject to a wide range of predictions (Bolin, 1998). We return to this issue of environmental uncertainty below (Section 4.5).

   An essential final stage therefore of any CBA is to conduct sensitivity analysis. This means recalculating *NPV* when the values of certain key parameters are changed. These parameters will include:

   (i) the discount rate,

(ii) physical quantities and qualities of inputs,
(iii) shadow prices of these inputs,
(iv) physical quantities and qualities of outputs,
(v) shadow prices of these outputs, and
(vi) project lifespan.

One intention is to discover to which parameters the NPV outcome is most sensitive. For example, in appraising a new coalmine where the NPV has been calculated as positive, by how much in percentage terms does the world coal price have to fall before the NPV becomes negative? By how much do labour costs need to rise before NPV goes negative? By how much does our forecast of the lifetime of the pit need to fall before NPV goes negative? What is the impact of changing the discount rate? Once the most sensitive parameters have been identified, then (i) forecasting effort can be directed at these parameters to try to improve our best guess; and (ii) where possible, more effort can be made once the project is underway to manage these parameters carefully, although most will be outside the control of the decision-maker. The NPV decision will often depend crucially on the choice of discount rate: this will certainly be so for projects with long-term effects, such as woodland planting, toxic waste disposal, and research and development of alternative energy sources.

In Box 4.3, we give a worked example of a simple CBA analysis of a renewable energy investment.

4.3 Applying CBA to the Environment: What are the Problems?

THE application of CBA to environmental management is fraught with problems. Among the most serious are the following:

1. The valuation of non-market goods, such as wildlife and landscape. How should this be done, and how much reliance should society place on estimates so generated? Are we acting immorally by placing money values on such things? Chapter 3 discussed the different valuation tools available to economists, whilst we briefly outline some ethical issues in the next section.

2. Ecosystem complexity: how can society accurately predict the effects of changes in economic activity on complex ecosystems? For example, how well can we predict the effects on an aquatic ecosystem of effluent inputs? Non-linearities and surprises may be expected in many natural systems, but CBA copes with such phenomena rather badly. Ecosystem complexity can be seen as one example of uncertainty in CBA, and CBA does not cope very well with this, as we explain below.

3. Discounting and the discount rate. This raises several important questions. First,

Box 4.3 An Illustrative CBA

Consider a project to support the construction of a new renewable energy source. A plan is proposed to build a new wind farm in a scenic area. The initial construction costs are estimated to be £750,000. Following start-up, annual maintenance costs of £5,000 are expected throughout the fifteen-year lifespan of the plant. At the end of this fifteen year period, the wind farm will need to be dismantled, and the site restored, at an expected cost of £35,000. Every year after the initial construction year, the site will produce electricity with a market value of £150,000, which for now we take to be a constant flow in real terms (we will ignore the effects of inflation here). Objectors have protested about the visual impact of the windmills, and so the government has commissioned a contingent valuation study of local residents. The results suggest that the mean annual compensation demanded by locals is £25/household: there are 2,000 households thought to be affected (this mean is calculated across both those against the project and those in favour).

It is easy to set up a basic CBA of this project. The initial ('year zero') construction costs are not discounted, as they occur at the start of the project. Maintenance costs are then discounted each year using the relevant discount factor, for a discount rate of 6 per cent. Annual environmental costs of (£25 × 2,000) are also discounted over the fifteen years of the project; and are assumed to stop when the site is restored at a cost of £35,000 in year 15. This year-15 cost also needs to be discounted. Annual benefits of £150,000 get discounted each year; you can see how the present value of this fixed amount falls each year as we move forwards in time (see also Fig. 4.B3). Table 4.B3 shows all workings.

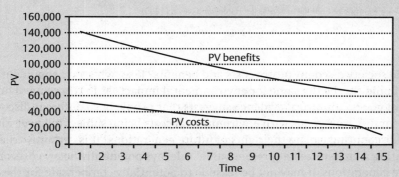

Figure 4.B3 Present values over time

As we can see, the total present value of costs is £1,275 million, whilst the total present value of benefits is £1,394 million. Thus the net present value of the project is positive at £118,351, which passes the CBA test at the 6 per cent discount rate. Notice how little the site renovation cost of £35,000 amounts to in present-value terms: less than half its future value.

Table 4.B3

Year	Discount factor at 6% discount rate $(1.06)^{-t}$	Benefits (£)	Present value of benefits (£)	Costs (£)	Present value of costs (£)
0	1		0	750,000	750,000
1	0.9433	150,000	141,495	55,000	51,881
2	0.8899	150,000	133,485	55,000	48,944
3	0.8396	150,000	125,940	55,000	46,178
4	0.7921	150,000	118,815	55,000	43,565
5	0.7472	150,000	112,080	55,000	41,096
6	0.7049	150,000	105,735	55,000	38,769
7	0.6650	150,000	99,750	55,000	36,575
8	0.6274	150,000	94,110	55,000	34,507
9	0.5918	150,000	88,770	55,000	32,549
10	0.5583	150,000	83,745	55,000	30,706
11	0.5267	150,000	79,005	55,000	28,968
12	0.4969	150,000	74,535	55,000	27,329
13	0.4688	150,000	70,320	55,000	25,784
14	0.4423	150,000	66,345	55,000	24,326
15	0.4172			35,000	14,602
Total discounted benefits/costs			1,394,130		1,275,779

For a real-life example of a similar analysis, see Hanley and Nevin (1999).

should society discount future costs and benefits? If so, what rate should be used, and should this be the same for environmental impacts as for those involving market goods? Empirical evidence suggests that people have different discount rates for different goods with environmental costs being subject to lower rates. Does discounting violate the rights of future generations? It is certainly true that operating a 'maximize net present value' rule lays potentially heavy costs on future generations. It may not be feasible to potentially compensate for these losses, due to the difficulty of signing binding intergenerational contracts, thus violating the PPI criterion.

4. Institutional capture. Is CBA a truly objective way of making decisions, or can institutions capture it for their own ends? There are many examples of agencies which are forced to undertake CBA doing so in a way which maximizes the chance of a favourable outcome to them (see Hanley and Spash, 1993). This possibility makes it desirable that CBA processes are open to external inspection, although their technical nature means it is difficult for non-experts to assess how well they have been conducted.

5. Sustainability and CBA. CBA is concerned with the efficiency of resource

allocation, whilst sustainability is an intra- and inter-generational fairness issue. This means that subjecting projects and policies to a CBA test is not a test of their sustainability. CBA explicitly allows trade-offs between natural and man-made capital (see Chapter 6), and thus can lead to violations of the so-called 'strong sustainability' criterion.[3] Some authors (e.g. Pearce, Barbier, and Markandya, 1990) have suggested imposing sustainability constraints on CBA. For example, this could include the need to undertake shadow projects to offset depletion in the natural capital stock, across some portfolio of projects/policies.

Let's illustrate these difficulties by approaching things from the other end, that is from the perspective of policy issues. First, suppose we are conducting an appraisal of a policy to introduce a tax on nitrogen fertilizers to reduce nitrate pollution in sensitive lakes and rivers. Here we must be able to predict (i) the response of farmers to the tax, (ii) where these farmers are located, and (iii) the likely consequent change in water quality. Point (ii) is important since the impact of a kilo of nitrogen fertilizer on water quality depends crucially on when and where that fertilizer is put on the land; whilst predicting (iii) will depend on a whole host of environmental factors. We must also be aware of other influences on water quality: will these change over the time-period we are considering? Once these difficulties have been resolved, we then need to be able to value the increase in water quality in money terms. This will include both market and non-market values, for example, in terms of changes in commercial fishing and changes in bird numbers and species.

Second, consider a project to flood a valley in order to generate hydroelectricity. The analyst knows that amongst the project costs will be labour and materials for construction. But wildlife will be destroyed as the valley is flooded; as we argued above, this is an economic cost which cannot be ignored. Yet some of the benefits of preserving the valley's biodiversity might be currently unknown. The dam might, for example, destroy a potential cure for cancer. Project benefits include cost-savings by generating electricity from the dam rather than by the next cheapest source. But will these cost-savings vary over the lifetime of the project? What will be the effect on the storage capacity of the dam as deforestation takes place further up the watershed? The dam will irreversibly change the valley it floods: are there special considerations in such cases? The *NPV* of the project will vary according to the discount rate, but which rate should be used?

As a last example, suppose a development authority plans to build a barrage across an estuary to increase property values and generate opportunities for marina developments. The barrage will harm waterfowl populations by flooding feeding grounds. The development authority is compelled to carry out a CBA of the project, but who will check that the benefit figures it uses are not overoptimistic, or that it has excluded important costs since they fall outside its jurisdiction? By bending the rules of the CBA procedure, the agency can maximize the likelihood that the project will go ahead. CBA can thus be used as a means for economic agents to maximize their utility (or rents): this is what was referred to above as institutional capture.

---

[3] Chapter 6 provides a detailed explanation of these concepts.

To conclude this section, we can say that there are a great many difficulties confronting the use of CBA in environmental decision-making. Some of these can be addressed by improving our skills as economists (for example, in finding more accurate ways of valuing changes in environmental quality). Some of them require action by others, for example in reducing uncertainty over global warming impacts. And some are endemic to the technique, as in its sensitivity to discount rates. However, the advantages of CBA pointed out in the previous section should be recalled: this is too powerful a technique to just throw away. Difficulties need to be addressed where this is possible and admitted where they cannot. Governments might do well to make more use of *good* CBA in environmental decision-making (see Hanley, 2000). But before seeing how CBA can be and is used, let us consider in more detail two important areas of difficulty: uncertainty, and, first, ethical worries.

4.4 Ethics and CBA

IN CBA, as in environmental valuation, the environment tends to get treated solely as a source of human satisfaction, either directly or indirectly; in this sense, the environment is treated no differently from any product or service in the economy. An important question, however, is whether the environment should always be treated as just one more consumption good, in terms of how we characterize people's value systems. Recent empirical evidence suggests that a portion of the population think of certain features of the environment in a different way (for a summary, see Hanley and Milne, 1996). The existence of such views (which are often characterized as *rights-based*) also has implications for cost–benefit analysis itself, as they challenge the PPI test on which CBA is founded.

The standard representation of how an individual values environmental quality changes rests on an assumption about the ethical beliefs of the representative agent; namely that they are utilitarian. Utilitarians place the ultimate importance on the consequences of actions; utility is the ultimate consequence, so that all such individuals are interested in is comparing alternative states in terms of the amount of utility they generate, irrespective of how this occurs (assuming they are feasible). This leads us to treat environmental benefits similarly to other benefits, by assuming that they can be traded off against other benefits (other goods).

However, some recent evidence suggests a refusal to trade off losses in environmental quality against increases in income for certain individuals (Stevens *et al.*, 1991; Spash and Hanley, 1995). Such individuals might be characterized as holding a rights-based ethic regarding environmental quality, which is at odds with the utilitarian ethic. Persons holding a rights-based ethic will refuse such a trade-off if they believe that it is our moral duty to preserve rainforests, for example. No increase in their income would compensate them (hold them on the same utility level) for a reduction in the level of rainforests, so that their minimum WTAC is infinite. Such individuals might be willing to pay some positive amount for an increase in environmental quality; it might thus be argued that WTP rather than WTAC measures should be sought, since this would minimize the extent of 'ethical protests'. However, what is easiest to measure is not the same as what should be measured, and if environmental losses are in prospect, then assuming individuals have some claim to the current level of environmental quality, WTAC is the correct measure to specify. Alternatively, people holding rights-based beliefs may be unwilling to pay for protection of the current level of environmental quality, believing that it *should* be protected (i.e. they refuse a choice over protection). However, the economist might argue that if you value something that much, you should be willing to give up something to protect it, even if you don't like the choice being placed before you.

Persons holding rights-based beliefs may do so because they believe that either all environmental resources, or some subset of these environmental resources, have values which are *intrinsic*. Intrinsic values have been defined by Callicott (1986) as values which exist independent of the utility of the object being valued to the valuer, or their use to someone other than the valuer (that is, independently of human satisfaction). Belief in such intrinsic values follows from a perspective on value that acts (such as the felling of a rainforest) are more important than the consequences of acts (utility changes following the felling of the forest), that ends do not justify means. This is the opposite viewpoint to the perspective which lies behind cost–benefit analysis. Belief in intrinsic values may, alternatively, follow from spiritual values for places and creatures.

If individuals with rights-based beliefs indeed exist, then this may invalidate PPI criteria. Recall that this states that a resource reallocation is welfare-improving if the gainers *could* compensate the losers and still be better off. But if the losers suffer environmental costs for which, due to their holding of rights-based beliefs, they would reject *any* amount of money compensation, then the possibility for compensation is violated and the principle can no longer be applied. If ethical motives dominate how we think of the environment, then in a sense in makes no sense to ask people what they are willing to pay to protect the environment; this is the wrong framing of the decision. However, three very important counter-arguments should be made. First, since resources are scarce, protecting the environment incurs costs (Chapter 1). One more rainforest protected may mean three fewer new schools being built. Clearly we need *some* way of evaluating the trade-offs here. Second, whilst the WTP 'frame' may be unhelpful for some people in some cases, this does not rule it out in many other situations. Third, 'environmental elitism', as expressed in infinite WTAC amounts, can be very undemocratic. Suppose clearing a swamp would save a whole village from malaria, yet this is opposed by one rich person who occasionally likes to visit the swamp on trips home. Should we allow his infinite WTAC to agree to the scheme overcome the benefits that all the other villagers would get in reduced disease? Most people would have a problem with that outcome.

4.5 Uncertainty

As noted above, CBA does not cope well with uncertainty. To investigate this a bit further, let us introduce some terminology by considering the example of the environmental costs of a new pollutant entering a river. Three situations regarding our knowledge of these environmental costs are possible. First, scientists may be unsure about what physical impacts the pollutant will have; this implies that not all 'states of the world', $s_1 \ldots s_n$, are known. Second, scientists may be able to identify all possible impacts $s_1 \ldots s_n$, but not be able to identify the probability distribution of these states of the world. Third, all possible states of the world and their probability distribution may be known. Most treatments of *risk* in economics are concerned with the circumstances of the third case, but not of the first two (see Chapter 5). If we know all possible states of the world and their probabilities, then expected values can be estimated. These can then form part of a CBA. However, if either not all states of the world are known, or if their probabilities are unknown, then we face a situation of true, or hard, uncertainty. In this case, which is likely to describe many environmental management situations, then CBA must fall back on sensitivity analysis, which estimates net benefits under different, known states of the world. We could then base decision-making, if desired, on tools from decision science, such as the minimax regret criterion.

As an example of CBA under uncertainty, consider the question as to what level of global response is appropriate to counter climate change.[4] Under the Kyoto agreement, signatory countries are obliged to reduce emissions of greenhouse gases by a variety of target levels (for example, by 12.5 per cent for EU countries). But is this enough or too much? One way of answering this question is by comparing the costs and benefits of reducing greenhouse gases by more or by less. Benefits include avoided damage due to climate change, plus avoided damage due to other impacts of reducing greenhouse gases. For example, in the case of CO_2, lower fossil fuel use also implies lower emissions of pollutants such as SO_2 and NO_x, with consequent savings in local air pollution problems. Costs comprise abatement costs for greenhouse gases, that is the costs associated with reducing them or with locking up more of the existing stock by creating new sinks (such as new forests). However, great uncertainty exists over the magnitude of both costs and benefits of further control. This uncertainty is greatest on the benefits (avoided damage) side. As Bolin (1998) has pointed out, there are still huge scientific uncertainties about the physical impacts of climate change, whilst there are also many uncertainties about how economies will adapt to these climatic changes (Sedjo, 1998).

Economists are divided on the best response to such uncertainty. As Tietenberg (1998) points out, we do not even know the shape of the damage curve, which may be highly non-linear. Costs of control vary according to how greenhouse gas emissions

---

[4] Chapter 12 considers these issues in more detail.

are reduced, and in terms of who undertakes the reductions (which countries, which agents). Given the huge uncertainties involved, Tietenberg argues, it is wrong to set targets for climate change policy using CBA.

Pearce (1998a), however, argues that by *not* using CBA to set targets, we risk making a very expensive mistake: the fact that uncertainty is high is a reason for doing CBA, rather than following either of two alternative decision rules: (i) act now because of the precautionary principle or (ii) do nothing now until we learn more. Pearce notes that estimates do exist of control costs and avoided damage,[5] and that the desired direction of change in emissions can be determined from an examination of these relative values. Pearce calls for a CBA which 'embodies these uncertainties'. Pearce also argues that CBA should be done because it identifies who gains and loses from climate change and by how much: for example, developed countries lose 1.3–1.6 per cent of GDP p.a., whilst developing countries lose 1.6–2.7 per cent of GDP in his analysis. This shows, according to Pearce, that developing countries should not be exempt from taking partial responsibility for reducing GHG emissions. In contrast, Tietenberg states that deciding not to reduce GHG emissions on CBA grounds would be unwise even if currently estimated marginal costs of control are less than currently estimated marginal benefits, since future damage is *potentially* enormous and also irreversible.

4.6 CBA and the Policy Process

How is CBA actually used by policy-makers? How should it be used? In what follows, we take a brief look at actual use of CBA in the OECD, before offering some suggestions on how it could be best employed.

In the UK, use of CBA was largely confined to the appraisal of certain project types, such as new roads, the infamous third London airport, and forestry schemes. In these cases, the analyses were highly partial in that environmental values were often omitted. For example, the standard CBA procedure used for new major road schemes ('COBA') included values for time saving and accident saving as benefits, but excluded landscape effects, wildlife effects, and air-pollution effects. From the early 1990s, CBAs conducted by the Forestry Commission began to include recreational and, more recently, biodiversity values for forest projects. A major impetus to the use of CBA in policy analysis came in 1991 with the publication of the *Policy Appraisal and the Environment* document by the Department of the Environment. This called for environmental effects of government policy to be included in the appraisal process in some formal way, including CBA. Such appraisals should be undertaken by all government departments whose actions had environmental impacts. Box 4.4 takes up the story of what happened next; suffice it to say here that the use of CBA within

---

[5] Pearce cites estimates of $50/t C for marginal benefits of control and $5–$20/t C for marginal costs.

Box 4.4 Assessing the Progress of Environmental CBA in The United Kingdom

A review of the effectiveness of the *Policy Appraisal and the Environment* document referred to in the main text was undertaken by consultants KPMG in 1996, five years after the document was launched. They looked at its impact on government departments. KPMG found that most consideration of environmental impacts was undertaken formally. The development of a multi-criteria analysis approach to road projects was noted. However, CBA was only found to have been used in three cases. These were the disposal of waste at sea, the design of agri-environmental policy, and the introduction of a landfill tax. In the first case, a partial analysis of the relative external costs of landfilling and dumping at sea of certain wastes was undertaken. In the second, contingent valuation studies of environmentally sensitive areas showed benefits to exceed costs : however, this had no implications for policy change. In the final case, a very detailed study of the externalities of landfill versus incineration for the disposal of municipal solid waste was undertaken. This was used to determine how large a tax to place on landfill waste. This tax was actually introduced in 1997. Recently, environmental valuation and CBA have been used by the Environment Agency to help inform decisions over abstraction licences and other actions connected with water quality; whilst valuation studies have sought to inform the introduction of a tax on quarrying (see Chapter 3). The overall impression at present is that the role of CBA in policy appraisal in the UK is small but growing.

environmental decision-making in the UK is growing, especially in the areas of the setting of environmental taxes, and in the design of agri-environmental policy. Other areas which have seen growing use of CBA include the regulation of rivers and investments in coastal defences.

In the European Union, CBA has not, until recently, been recommended as a policy appraisal tool. However, Article 13OR of the Mastricht Treaty 'requires the European Commission to carry out some (admittedly unspecified) form of benefits-cost appraisal of its Directives' (Pearce, 1998b). By contrast, CBA has been a required element of policy appraisal in the USA for some time. Presidential Order 12291 required CBA of new policy initiatives across all Federal agencies, but as Arrow *et al.* (1998) point out, some Acts specifically rule out CBA. These include the Clean Air Act and Clear Water Act. Some Acts do permit or even call for CBA—these include the Toxic Substances Control Act and the Consumer Product Safety Act. Arrow *et al.* (1998) call for much greater use of CBA to improve the efficiency of government regulation. They note that the implied cost per expected life saved varies enormously across EPA programmes by a factor of more than $10 million, from $200,000 per statistical life (see Chapter 5) under the trihalomethane drinking water standard to $6.3 trillion under the hazardous waste listing for wood-preserving chemicals, an indication that current policy is very inefficiently designed (since an efficient design would arrange things such that the value of the marginal life saved was equal across programmes). They also argue that many environmental, health, and safety regulations would fail a

Box 4.5 CBA and the 'Waste Hierarchy'

The 1992 International Earth Summit in Rio called on countries to decrease their dependence on the landfilling of waste, and employ a hierarchical approach in their waste-management practices. The waste hierarchy, as illustrated in the figure, has become the lodestar for the waste-management strategy of many national governments and international institutions, including the Netherlands, Denmark, the United Kingdom, and the European Union. The figure illustrates that source reduction is the preferred option in the hierarchy, followed by reuse, recycling, and waste-to-energy in the form of incineration. The landfilling of waste should only be considered as a last resort.

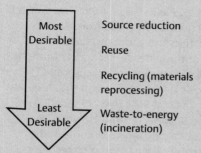

Whilst the waste hierarchy may be in accordance with green intuition, it is based on an engineering approach to the safe-rendering of hazardous waste. It has also, over the years, been adopted as the 'sustainable' way of managing non-hazardous municipal solid waste (MSW). However, this widespread adoption has taken place without any analysis of its economic efficiency.

A recent study (Brisson, 1996) used CBA to question the general applicability of the waste hierarchy in the European Union (EU). The analysis focused on recycling, composting, incineration, and landfill. The main results are summarized in Table 4.B5.

Table 4.B5 Ranking of MSW management methods based on total external and private costs

Bring systems		Co-collection at kerbside		Separate kerbside collection	
	Avg. cost ECU/tonne		Avg. cost ECU/tonne		Avg. cost ECU/tonne
1 Recycling	−170	Recycling	−131	Recycling	24
2 Landfill	92	Landfill	91	Landfill	96
3 Incineration (old coal)	115	Composting	102	Incineration (old coal)	119
4 Incineration (avg. EU fuel mix)	150	Incineration (old coal)	114	Composting	133
5 Composting	170	Incineration (avg. EU fuel mix)	148	Incineration (avg. EU fuel mix)	155

Note: negative numbers indicate net benefits

Table 4.B5 ranks the waste-management methods based on their EU-average social costs in three different scenarios. In the first scenario, it is assumed that individual householders bring both recyclable and compostable waste to central collection points.

The second scenario assumes that those categories of waste are collected at the kerbside at the same time as the remainder of the waste stream. And the third scenario assumes that they are collected at the kerbside, but in a separate collection round.

These estimates appear to confirm the position of recycling in the waste hierarchy. Indeed, the environmental benefits of recycling more than outweigh any private costs in the first two scenarios, so that considerable net social benefits are realized. However, it is noteworthy that the social benefits of recycling decrease as we move from a bring-system to co-collection at the kerbside, and in fact, turn into social costs as the recyclable (and compostable) material is collected at the kerbside, separately from the remainder of the waste. It is also worth considering that the estimated costs and benefits are based on the level of recycling that took place in 1995, when the study was carried out. Typically, at modest levels of recycling, the materials that are recycled are those relatively easy to collect and which offer good financial returns. However, as recycling efforts are stepped up, recovering the materials is likely to become more cumbersome, and the quality of the recycled materials is likely to deteriorate. Thus, we should expect the attractiveness of recycling to decline as recycling rates increase, and at some level recycling will carry greater social cost than the other options available.

The private costs of landfill, incineration, and composting appear to totally overshadow the environmental costs. This means that, although incineration under certain assumptions can lead to environmental benefits, whilst landfill carries net external costs, the fact that private landfilling costs are generally significantly lower than private incineration costs leads to landfill being ranked above incineration in all three scenarios. This contradicts the ranking in the waste hierarchy, which has landfill as the least desirable of all options. However, the data in the table are based on EU averages and thus lose the diversity between the individual countries. Indeed, in some countries, incineration, where the energy recovered displaces power that would otherwise have been generated in old coal-fired power stations, is ranked above landfill, because the environmental benefits here outweigh the private cost differential between landfill and incineration. However, when it is assumed that the power recovered through incineration displaces that which would otherwise have been generated using an average European fuel mix, incineration carries an environmental cost which adds to the private cost differential between landfill and incineration. Under this assumption, landfill is ranked above incineration in all EU countries.

Composting, which can be categorized as a form of materials reprocessing, or recycling, should according to the waste hierarchy be ranked above both landfill and incineration. However, in all three scenarios the estimated social costs are higher than those of both recycling and landfilling, and its ranking compared to incineration depends on the collection method used. This, perhaps surprisingly, low ranking of composting is to a large extent explained by the form of composting modelled. In her study, Brisson (1996) considered only municipal composting which involves a considerable degree of transportation. Indeed, the majority of both the environmental and the private costs are transport-related. If individual households were encouraged to compost at home, the social cost would be significantly reduced, and the position of composting in the ranking would improve.

The conclusion is that whilst source reduction and reuse are at the appropriate position at the top of hierarchy, the current ranking of the other waste management methods is not consistently supported by CBA. Differences in individual countries' infrastructure and cost structures affect the relative desirability of each method. Thus it is not possible to place the waste management methods in a strict hierarchy that will apply across all countries irrespective of their individual circumstances. So, rather than focusing rigidly on adhering to the waste hierarchy, authorities charged with waste management would be better advised to concentrate on devising a combination of waste-management methods that take into account local circumstances, using CBA to guide them.

CBA test. This is not necessarily bad news if regulators have no regard for efficiency. But in a world of scarce resources and unlimited wants, perhaps they should.

So how could use of CBA be improved within government? Arrow *et al.* suggest some guidelines. These are:

1. Decision-makers should not be precluded from considering the economic costs and benefits of regulation (in other words, don't outlaw CBA);
2. CBA should be an essential part of major regulatory decisions, since such decisions involve a significant opportunity cost to taxpayers;
3. Government agencies should not, however, be bound by the outcomes of these CBAs, since other criteria might be judged more important in particular instances. These other criteria might be environmental impacts, or fairness;
4. Benefits and costs should be quantified wherever possible, but uncertainties should be explicitly set out. As we have seen above, in many cases economists will only be able to produce a likely range for benefits and costs; pretending too much precision is a mistake;
5. CBAs should be subject to external review, to keep up standards of good practice and even-handedness. This is to counteract the 'institutional capture' problem mentioned in Section 4.3;
6. A 'core set' of economic assumptions should be established, which should be uniform across agencies. These include the discount rate, the economic value of a life (of avoiding a death), and the economic value of health. In this way, decisions can be made efficiently across the whole of government.
7. The CBA analysts should also present information on the distributional impacts of government regulation: whilst CBA does not employ fairness as a measure of outcomes, it can be used to show who gains and who loses.

4.7 Summary

CBA is now a well-established part of applied economics, and of policy and project analysis. CBA is useful for comparing the good and bad outcomes of policies within a consistent framework: CBA can 'set the agenda' for discussion on the merits and defects of opportunities. If a CBA approach has already been adopted, then including environmental impacts within this makes for more efficient decision-making, explicitly recognizes the impacts of the economy on the environment, and the contribution that the environment makes to the economic process. Yet including the environment within CBA is not obviously the best way of protecting the environment, since CBA explicitly permits trade-offs: the environment might thus be better served under alternative decision-rules. CBA also cannot in itself move us towards sustainable development, since that is an equity issue, whereas CBA addresses itself only to efficiency.

Most economists would still argue that CBA has a useful and important part to play in the decision-making process. As Pearce (1998b) has pointed out, ignoring costs and benefits can lead to inefficient and wasteful legislation. The CBA process itself has useful attributes, in terms of identifying costs and benefits (and who they fall on), and by structuring thinking about an issue in a way which establishes the important parameters for discussion. It is also a way of introducing public preferences into environmental policy-making, which would seem valuable in and of itself.

References

Arrow, K., Cropper, M., Eads, G., Hahn. R., Lave, L., Noll, R., Portney, P., Russell, M., Schmalensee, R., Smith, V. K., and Stavins, R. (1998). 'Is there a role for benefit-cost analysis in environmental, health and safety regulation?', *Environment and Development Economics* 2: 196–201.

Bolin, B. (1998). 'Key features of the global climate system', *Environment and Development Economics* 3(3): 348–65.

Brisson, I. E. (1996). *Externalities in Solid Waste Management: Values, Instruments and Control*, SØM publication 20 (Copenhagen: AKF Forlaget).

Callicott, J. B. (1986). 'On the Intrinsic Value of Non-Human Species', in B. G. Norton (ed.), *The Preservation of Species* (Princeton: Princeton University Press).

Department of the Environment (1991). *Policy Appraisal and the Environment*. (London: HMSO).

Hicks, J. R. (1939). 'The foundations of welfare economics', *Economic Journal* 49, 696–712.

Hanley, N. (2001). 'Cost benefit analysis and environmental policy-making', *Environment and Planning C*, forthcoming.

—— and Milne, J. (1996) 'Ethical beliefs and contingent valuation', *Journal of Environmental Planning and Management* 39(2): 255–72.

—— and Nevin, C. (1999). 'Appraising renewable energy developments in remote communities: the case of the North Assynt Estate, Scotland', *Energy Policy* 27: 527–47.

Johansson, P-O. (1991). *An Introduction to Modern Welfare Economics* (Cambridge: Cambridge University Press).

Kaldor, N. (1939). 'Welfare propositions of economics and inter-personal comparisons of utility', *Economic Journal* 49: 549–52.

Pearce, D. W. (1997). 'Benefit-cost analysis, environment and health in the developed and developing world', *Environment and Development Economics* 2(2): 210–14.

—— (1998*b*). 'Environmental appraisal and environmental policy in the European Union', *Environmental and Resource Economics* 11: 489–501.

—— (1998*a*). 'Economic development and climate change', *Environmental and Development Economics*, 3(3): 389–91.

—— Barbier, E., and Markandya, A. (1990). *Sustainable Development: Economics and Environment in the Third World*. (Cheltenham: Edward Elgar).

Sedjo, R. (1998). 'How serious are the damages associated with global warming?', *Environmental and Development Economics* 3(3): 398–401

Spash, C. L. and Hanley, N. (1995). 'Preferences, Information and Biodiversity Preservation', *Ecological Economics* 12: 191–208.

Stevens, T. H., Echeverria, J., Glass, R. J., Hager, T., and More, T. A. (1991). 'Measuring the Existence Value of Wildlife: What do CVM Estimates Really Show?' *Land Economics* 67(4): 390–400.

Sugden, R., and Williams, A. (1974), *A Practical Guide to Cost-Benefit Analysis* (Oxford: Oxford University Press).

Tietenberg, T. (1988). 'Economic analysis and climate change', *Environment and Development Economics* 3(3): 402–4.

Further Reading

■ Brent, R. J. (1990). *Project Appraisal for Developing Countries* (New York University Press).

■ Broadway, R., and Bruce, N. (1984). *Welfare Economics* (Oxford: Blackwell).

■ Hahn, R. (1998). *Risks, Costs and Lives Saved: Getting Better Results from Regulation* (Oxford: Oxford University Press).

■ Hanley, N., and Spash, C. (1993). *Cost-Benefit Analysis and the Environment* (Cheltenham: Edward Elgar).

■ Smith, V. K. (1984). *Environmental Policy Under Reagan's Executive Order: The Role of Benefit Cost Analysis* (Chapel Hill: University of North Carolina Press).

■ Krutilla, J., and Fisher, A. (1985). *The Economics of Natural Environments* (Washington DC: Johns Hopkins University Press).

Chapter 5
Environmental Risk

5.1 Introduction

A goal of environmental protection is to reduce risks to humans and the environment. By risk, we mean the combination of two elements—the *chance* that a bad event might happen, and the *consequences* that are realized if a bad event actually does occur. And although our actions to improve our lives usually are not intended to create risk to others and ourselves, we do generate pollution and accidents do happen. Cars pollute. Oil spills. Technology fails. How and when and where and by how much define the gambles that we create in a modern economy. More often than not the risks we take generate worthwhile rewards—new medicines, new transportation, new communication systems. But sometimes things go wrong—Chernobyl, Bhopal, Love Canal; or our choices are feared to have put society on the wrong path—loss of biodiversity, inhospitable climate change.

We must recognize that a zero-risk society is a noble but unattainable goal. The costs to eliminate all risk to everyone are simply too great. Even if you believe that we cannot attach a monetary value on human pain and suffering, our actions say something different. If we really were willing to pay any price to reduce risk to zero, society would for instance impose a 4-mile speed limit for all roads and highways. We would all drive slow enough that no one would ever die from an automobile accident, except perhaps from boredom. We'll never see such a rule. The costs per life saved from driving so slow are too great for most people—people are willing to trade-off more risk for quicker travel time. We make similar trade-offs all the time in our jobs, our recreation, our lifestyles. As such, understanding the nature of health, safety, and environmental risk, and looking for effective strategies that reduce risk without curtailing the rewards of our modern life is essential for better public policy.

This chapter explores the nature of environmental risk. We address how private citizens and governments confront the challenge of finding reasonable answers to three key questions:

- What environmental risks do we actually face, and how bad are they?
- How do people perceive risk, and how do they value its reduction?

- How can society manage and regulate risk?

We explore the role of economics in helping to answer these questions.

5.2 Assessing Environmental Risks

THE production of many goods we gladly consume generates waste material that can be hazardous to human and environmental health. And the more society and nature are exposed to toxic, flammable, radioactive, or corrosive substances, the greater the risk and the potential damage. For example, people often worry that hazardous material might contaminate groundwater used for drinking. Concern arises because landfill sites are the primary means of disposing millions of tonnes of hazardous industrial waste. People often believe, wrongly or rightly, that landfills have inadequate safeguards to prevent hazardous substances from seeping into water supplies. Communities are concerned that hazardous material will migrate from new or abandoned waste sites and contaminate drinking water supplies.

How should we assess this environmental risk? Recall that environmental risk can be defined by two basic elements—the likelihood an unfavourable event will occur and the severity of the event if realized. Historically, the field of economics has defined 'risk' as when a person can assign a probability to the chance that an event will occurr. In contrast, 'uncertainty' existed when a person could not or would not assign odds on any events. The economic literature currently treats risk and uncertainty as synonymous.

Risk assessment is the method used to define and estimate the likelihood of adverse consequences from exposure to an environmental hazard. Risk assessment attempts to deal with complex issues in determining whether a hazard exists and the potential adverse effects of the hazard. Although uncertainties exist due to limited data and imperfectly understood dose–response relations, risk assessment categorizes the available evidence so that regulators have better information for environmental risk management. Risk assessment provides a framework to quantify risk. With numerous levels of safety factors, quantified risk estimates generally provide policy-makers with a conservative safety level to aid decision-making. Risk assessment has four qualitative and quantitative components—hazard identification, dose–response estimate, exposure assessment, and risk characterization. Consider each in turn.

Hazard identification is a qualitative assessment that collects, organizes, and evaluates all the relevant biological and chemical information to determine whether a hazard may be a risk to public health. The goal is to determine whether a hazard warrants the attention of a full-scale quantitative assessment. If a hazard has generated evidence of cancer, genetic mutation, or development problems, quantitative risk assessment is needed.

Hazard identification is designed to present a weight-of-evidence ranking on the potential adverse health effects from exposure to a hazard. The weight-of-evidence ranking is derived from two major information sources supplemented with the evaluation of supporting information. The first major source of information is long-term animal studies. Hazards that generate evidence of positive adverse effects in long-term animal studies are generally considered high risk unless there is substantial contradictory evidence. The second major source of information is the use of human studies. Epidemiological studies are only capable of detecting comparatively large increases in relative risk. Therefore, the non-detection of adverse effects does not rule out potential health risks. To determine the effect, the human information must be examined in relation to the animal data and supporting information on the chemical-physical properties and routes and patterns of exposure. Hazard identification provides the qualitative information necessary for the risk assessor to weigh all available evidence to determine whether a quantitative assessment is warranted. By ranking the evidence in terms of uncertainties and assumptions, the decision to further assess the risk can be justified.

Dose–response estimation quantifies how health responds to various exposure levels. Dose is often considered shorthand for exposure to a hazard, and response is the percentage of the exposed population suffering death or illness. Threshold exposure levels can be determined below which only minimal health risks exist. Three primary methods exist to estimate a dose–response function: clinical human studies, inter-species comparison (toxicological method), and epidemiological studies.

Clinical human studies involve exposing human subjects to various ambient levels and determining health effects. Due to the use of human subjects, these studies are costly and controversial. Since clinical studies seldom provide sufficient information for a risk assessment, the two principal sources of toxicity data are interspecies comparison and epidemiology. Interspecies comparison and epidemiological studies both use a detailed, disaggregated research technique, but differ by animal and human data. The interspecies comparison method uses animal bioassays to determine the dose–response function. The method attempts to extrapolate the high-dose responses of animals to determine the low-dose responses of humans. The epidemiological method estimates dose–response functions by observing human health in natural surroundings.

Information on individual health is obtained through large surveys and from aggregate health statistics. Once the data are collected, epidemiological methods use multivariate econometric models to estimate the dose–response function. The dependent variable, human health, is related to the independent variables of human health determinants. Independent variables include the dose of the contaminant and lifestyle characteristics.

Exposure assessment identifies the population at risk and the likelihood of exposure to the hazard. An exposure assessment estimates the magnitude, frequency, duration, and route of exposure. Researchers begin by collecting general information about a potential hazard, including the molecular formula, chemical, and physical properties. They then examine the points where the hazard enters the environment so that they can help identify the exposure pathways and environmental fate. They also assess the potential mobility of a hazard based on the media (e.g. air, soil, water, or biological), the physical reaction to other compounds; and the temporal and spatial persistence.

Concentrations of the hazard are measured. The exposed population, both human and non-human, is identified by size, characteristics, location, and habits. Researchers then combine concentration estimates with the exposed population to determine an exposure profile—the size of the exposed population, routes of exposure, and the duration, frequency, and intensity of exposure. Finally, an exposure assessment must flag the uncertainties associated with the procedures.

Risk characterization summarizes the three-proceeding steps to generate a numerical estimate of risk. Herein researchers determine risk thresholds or 'safe' exposure levels below which further analysis is not necessary. For non-carcinogens, thresholds are bounded by two levels: the lowest exposure in which effects are seen—the lowest-observed-effect level (LOEL), and the highest exposure in which no effects are seen—the no-observed-effect level (NOEL). NOEL is generally used as threshold measure since it is a more conservative estimate.

For carcinogens and most reproductive toxins, however, regulators assume no threshold. Instead, regulators use an acceptable risk level, often selected as 10^{-6} or to 10^{-5} risk of cancer or other illness per lifetime. Safety factors are often used to compensate for scientific uncertainties and data limitations. Two safety factors are generally used for non-carcinogens: a tenfold factor to compensate for sensitive individuals (e.g. children) when extrapolating from studies of 'average, healthy' people, and a hundredfold factor when extrapolating from long-term animal experiments.

5.3 Choice under Risk

ASSESSING risks to people depends in part on how people create risk and how they react to the risks they create. This question has captivated people at least since the time humans 'discovered' that gambling was fun. And although our ancestors could buy a thrill, they had to wait until the Renaissance before witnessing the development of a systematic theory of probability. Until that time, they seemed to think that people did not create much of their own luck, and fate was the master. Their lives were linked much closer to nature, and much more exposed to its whims. Crops failed and children died without seeming reason. Most people were simply too busy trying to survive to ponder the systematic nature of risk.

As people began to grasp that they could use free trade to double or triple the value of the wealth they created, the desire to master risk began in earnest. More trade meant more wealth and more risk. Trading partners separated by unpredictable oceans had an incentive to understand how to manage and control risk. And as unruly trade routes turned into world wars and global stock and bond swaps, the gains from risk assessment and management as practical arts increased. Those who had a sophisticated appreciation of the behavioural underpinnings of risk had a better chance of winning real and metaphorical battles. This holds for environmental risk too.

To follow the intellectual history of understanding how people make choices under risk, consider three gambles:

- Gamble X is a certain payment to you of $30 — a sure bet.
- Gamble Y is a coin flip in which you win $100 with a heads, and lose $100 with a tails.
- Gamble Z is a roll of a die in which you win $2,000 if a 1 is rolled; win $1,000 with a 2; $500 with a 3; lose $0 with a 4; lose $1,000 with a 5; and lose $2,000 with a 6.

Which would you choose? Early theorists speculating on how people make choices under risk thought that many people would prefer the gamble with the highest expected value — the probability weighted average of all possible outcomes of the gamble.

Expected value = (probability of outcome 1) x ($ of outcome 1)

+ (probability of outcome 2) x ($ of outcome 2)

+ (probability of outcome n) x ($ of outcome n)

In our case,

- Gamble X: 100 per cent chance of $30 = $30 *expected value*
- Gamble Y: 50 per cent chance of $100 + 50 per cent chance of –$100 = $0 *expected value*
- Gamble Z: [1/6] chance of $2,000 + [1/6] chance of $1,000 + [1/6] chance of $500 + [1/6] chance of $0 + [1/6] chance of –$1,000 + [1/6] chance of –$2,000 = $83.33 *expected value*

Gamble Z has the highest expected value. But yet we observe that many people shy away from gamble Z and take gamble X instead. The old adage that a bird in the hand is worth two in the bush reflects the prudent strategy to go for the sure thing.

But why does the gamble with the lower expected value attract so many people? In the eighteenth century, Nicholas Bernoulli devised an ingenious example to show why. His St Petersburg paradox works as follows. Suppose you are offered the following proposition. You can buy into a gamble on a fair coin toss. If a head comes up on the first flip, you earn $2; if it takes two flips to uncover a head, you earn $4; if it takes three flips, you earn $8; four flips, $16; five, $32; six, $64; seven, $128; and so on. What is the maximum you would be willing to pay to buy into this gamble?

You probably were willing to pay an amount much lower than infinity. But infinity is the expected value of this gamble:

Expected value = [1/2] chance of $2 + [1/4] chance of $4 + [1/8] chance of $8 + . . .

= $1 + $1 +$1 + $1 + $1 + . . . = infinity.

So it seems as though you should have been willing to pay a lot more than you probably said you would. But you most likely said you would pay a few dollars. Why?

One reason is because the variance of the gamble is also infinite. Variance is often considered synonymous with risk because it reflects the potential volatility of the outcome. The variance reflects the distribution around the expected value. More variance implies more chance that bad states — low pay-off outcomes — will be realized.

Nicholas's cousin Daniel Bernoulli soon offered a reason why people will pay much less than infinity for a gamble with infinite variance: a gain of $2,000 is not necessarily worth twice as much as $1,000. That is, people seem to have diminishing marginal returns to wealth. This means that even though you prefer more money to less, the last dollar you earn gives you less satisfaction than the first dollar earned. His key insight is that a person's 'utility' [the degree of satisfaction in possessing wealth or goods] resulting from any small increase in wealth will be inversely proportionate to the quantity of the goods previously possessed.

Figure 5.1 illustrates the idea of diminishing marginal returns. Increased wealth increases total utility at a decreasing rate, which is why the utility function is curved. Therefore, gambles with high variance are less attractive — your gain from an extra dollar added to your wealth is smaller than your loss from an extra dollar taken away. One example of a useful utility function with this property is

$$u(w) = \text{square root(wealth) or } u(w) = \sqrt{w}.$$

For instance, wealth of $10,000 creates a utility level of 100, while wealth of $1,000,000 creates a utility level of 1,000. A hundredfold increase in wealth increases a person's utility by only tenfold. When a person acts this way we say he or she is *risk-averse*. A risk-averse person is more likely to take a certain pay-off over a fair bet — a

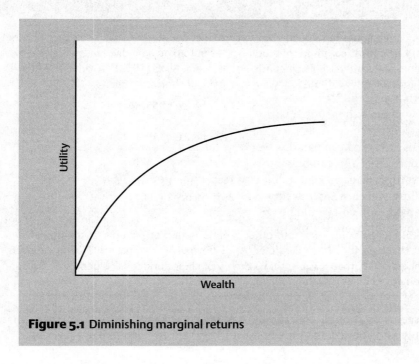

Figure 5.1 Diminishing marginal returns

gamble in which the expected value is zero, e.g. 50 : 50 odds to win or lose $1,000. Our person is *risk-loving* if he or she prefers a fair bet to a certain pay-off equalling the expected value of the gamble. He is *risk-neutral* if he is indifferent between a gamble and certain pay-off equalling the expected value of the gamble.

Bernoulli's insight was formalized into a modern analytical framework called *expected utility theory* (EU). Since its introduction in the 1940s by the mathematician John von Neumann and the economist Oscar Morgenstern, EU theory has been the most success model of how people make decisions under risk. The formal theory of expected utility reflects the idea that people who make choices about risk based their *beliefs* about the probability that good and bad events will be realized, the *consequences* of good and bad events, and the *utility* or *satisfaction* a person gets from the consequence that is realized. And despite limits to the model (see Box 5.1 on the Allais paradox), analysts continue to use the model because it is intuitive and tractable.

Consider now our three gambles from an EU perspective. Assume the person has an initial wealth of, say $2,001, and a square root-style utility function.

- Gamble X: 100 per cent chance of $\sqrt{\$2,031} = 45.1$ *expected utility*
- Gamble Y: 50 per cent chance of $\sqrt{\$2,101}$ + 50 per cent chance of $\sqrt{\$1,901} = 44.7$ *expected utility*
- Gamble Z: [1/6] chance of $\sqrt{\$4,001}$ + [1/6] chance of $\sqrt{\$3,001}$ + [1/6] chance of $\sqrt{\$2,501}$ + [1/6] chance of $\sqrt{\$2,001}$ + [1/6] chance of $\sqrt{\$1,001}$ + [1/6] chance of $\sqrt{\$1} = 40.9$ *expected utility*.

Box 5.1 The Allais Paradox

Several techniques have been used to construct counter-examples to expected utility theory. The most common method involves obtaining an individual's response to a pair of choices designed to give inconsistent answers. Allais (1953) provided the first counter-example with the following two pairs of choices:

		10% chance of $5m.
A: 100% chance of $1m.	vs.	B: 89% chance of $1m.
		1% chance of $0

and

C: 10% chance of $5m.	vs.	D: 11% chance of $1m.
90% chance of $0		89% chance of $0

If the person maximizes expected utility, he must either prefer the pair (A, D) or the pair (B, C). Allais and numerous other variations have observed that the modal, and often the majority, of people prefer (A, C), however (Machina, 1997). This suggests that expected utility theory is too thin a theory of choice under risk—people are making systematic choices that are not captured by the theory.

References: M. Allais, (1953). 'Le comportement de l'homme rationnel devant le risque: Critique des postulats et axiomes de 'ecole Americaine', *Econometrica* 21: 503–46.

From the lens of expected utility, the person clearly should prefer Gamble X to either Y or Z: 45.1 > 44.7 > 40.9. This is the key insight of expected utility theory—expected values and expected utility do not rank alternative gambles the same way.

Now consider an example of environmental risk. Travis is a carpenter who lives and works in Las Vegas, which has elevated levels of air pollution. He earns $50,000 per year. But he is uncertain as to whether he will stay healthy given his ongoing exposure to ozone and particulate matter. Suppose he believes that roughly one of two states of nature will be realized—a good and bad state. In the good state, he stays healthy and earns $50,000. In the bad state, he gets sick and earns $35,000 (= $50,000 – $15,000 in medical expenses and lost work). Let π and $(1 - \pi)$ represent his beliefs that either the good or bad state will be realized. Suppose he thinks that the odds are 70:30 that he will stay healthy, i.e. $\pi = 0.7$ and $(1 - \pi) = 0.3$.

Travis is thinking about moving to Baggs, Wyoming, which has both lower air pollution and lower wages. If he moves to Baggs, he can earn $40,000 per year in the good state, and $38,000 in the bad state. He believes his odds of staying healthy are 90:10 that he will not get sick from air pollution (i.e. π' and $(1 - \pi')$).

We can now write Travis's expected utility for both living in Las Vegas or Baggs as the probability-weighted sum of the two potential states of nature:

$$\text{EU(Las Vegas)} = \pi(w) + (1 - \pi)u(w - D)$$

$$= (0.7)u(\$50{,}000) + (0.3)u(\$35{,}000)$$

$$= 0.7\sqrt{\$50{,}000} + 0.3\sqrt{\$35{,}000}$$

$$= 213$$

$$\text{EU(Baggs)} \quad = \pi'(w) + (1 - \pi')u(w - D)$$

$$= (0.9)u(\$40{,}000) + (0.1)u(\$38{,}000)$$

$$= 0.7\sqrt{\$40{,}000} + 0.3\sqrt{\$38{,}000}$$

$$= 200$$

With these odds and earnings, Travis's expected utility is greater in Las Vegas even though the odds of getting ill are greater, 213 > 200. He is willing to trade-off the greater health risk for the higher earnings. This is common in many jobs in which workers take greater risk for more pay.

Now suppose his odds of staying healthy in Las Vegas drop to, say 50:50, holding everything else constant. Now his expected utility equals 205. But he still prefers Las Vegas to Baggs since 205 > 200. Travis would only think about leaving Las Vegas if the odds change to 30:70, in which his expected utility drops to 198. Now Baggs is the more attractive option, 200 > 198. Of course, numerous additional factors influence one's decision on where to live, such as school quality, crime, and recreation opportunities. We would have to adapt the expected utility framework to account for these other preferences. This is more complicated but doable as we saw in Chapter 3 in the hedonic pricing model.

The next step in the development of the expected utility model is to account for a person's ability to *influence* the risk they confront, either privately and collectively through market insurance, self-protection (or mitigation), and self-insurance (or adaptation). Travis is not as helpless against the risk as the model suggests. He has more options than moving to Baggs. He can purchase market insurance against illness. And he can invest in different risk-reduction strategies to change the odds of suffering from some illness due to the air pollution. He can buy an air filter for his home, or he can eat better and exercise more. His actions can reduce the likelihood that the bad state will occur or reduce the severity of the state if realized or do both. We refer to actions to reduce the likelihood of illness as *self-protection* or *mitigation*; actions to reduce the severity are *self-insurance* or *adaptation*.

Travis's economic problem now becomes a bit more complicated. Now he selects the level of self-protection and self-insurance that balances the extra gains he gets from lower odds of illness and less severity with the costs of protecting and insuring himself,

$$\text{EU(Las Vegas} \mid \text{risk reduction)} = \pi(z)u(w - z - x) + (1 - \pi(z))u(w - D(x) - z - x),$$

where $\pi(z)$ is the probability of the good state which depends on his level of self-protection, z; and $D(x)$ is the severity of illness which depends on his level of self-insurance, x. Including the private ability to reduce risk is helpful to understand choice under environmental risk because these actions link risk assessment with risk management. One must account for these actions to measure risk accurately and to manage risk effectively (Shogren and Crocker, 1999).

Although risk assessment has amassed a useful record of estimating potential threats to humans and nature, one problem permeates the risk assessment literature—the underemphasis on how people adapt to the risk they face or have created. Over the past decade scientists have increasingly acknowledged that environmental risk is endogenous. People can influence many of the risks they confront. Examples abound. People move or reduce physical activities when air pollution becomes intolerable. They buy bottled water if they fear that their drinking water is polluted, and they apply sunscreen to protect their skin from UV radiation. A person can invest in a water filter, move, buy a membership to a health club, jog, eat food low in fat and high in fibre, or apply sunscreen; each choice altering his risk to health and welfare. How a person invests resources to increase the likelihood that good things happen and bad things don't depends on both his attitudes towards risk and his ability to reduce risk.

Of course, cases do exist in which people have little time to react to protect themselves, such as Chernobyl. And some people have argued that we can redefine the problem so that risk is independent of human action. This position is ultimately self-defeating, however. Consider a situation in which bacterial groundwater contamination threatens a household's drinking water. The probability of illness among household members can be altered if they boil the water. An analyst could define the situation as independent of the household's actions by focusing solely on groundwater contamination, over which the household likely has no control. But this definition is economically irrelevant if the question is the household's response to the risks from groundwater contamination. The household is concerned about the likelihood of illness and the realized severity, and it is able to exercise some control over those events. The household's risk is endogenous because by expending its valuable resources it influences probability and severity.

People often substitute private actions for collectively supplied safety programmes. The use of stronger building materials to reduce the damage from tornadoes, storms, and earthquakes; more thorough weeding and crop storage in response to the prospect of drought; sand-bagging and evacuation in anticipation of floods; and improved nutrition and exercise regimens to cope with health threats. At the policy level, these private risk-reduction choices can affect the success of collective regulation that promote safety. Use of auto seat belts reduces both the probability and the severity of injury, but their mandatory installation cannot guarantee that passengers will choose to wear them. Highway speed limits also are effective at reducing fatalities only when drivers observe them. At work, rules promoting personal protective gear (e.g. hard hats) have the same problem: they protect only those workers who wear them. In each case, individual decisions influence both the probability and the magnitude of harm.

Endogenous risk implies that observed risks are functions of both natural science parameters and an individual's self-protection decisions. Given the relative marginal effectiveness of alternative self-protection efforts, how people make decisions about risk differs across individuals and situations, even though the natural phenomena that trigger these efforts apply equally to everyone. Therefore, assessing risk levels solely in terms of natural science can be misleading. Relative prices, incomes, and other economic and social parameters that influence any person's self-protection decisions affect risk. Just as good public policy-based economics requires an understanding of the physical and natural phenomena that underpin choices; good public policy-based natural science requires an understanding of the economic phenomena that affects risk. Accounting for private decisions to adapt can increase the precision of risk assessment. Failure to acknowledge the depths of individual choice in environmental risk will result in excessive economic expenditures at no gain in environmental quality.

5.4 Valuing Risks to Life and Limb

WE now consider how people value a reduction in risk, for both private and collective strategies. Constrained budgets and increased fiscal accountability prevent a policy-maker from reducing all risk to all individuals. Deciding which risks to reduce and by how much requires evaluation of each new or revised regulation. Comparability of value across all sectors of the economy requires that policy-makers rank regulatory alternatives in terms of a common unit. Arguably, the most common denominator is money, or monetary equivalence. Risk valuation systematically evaluates each regulation by estimating the monetary value—both benefits and costs—of a reduction in risk.

Valuing the costs and benefits of reduced risk is formidable and often controversial. While measuring the cost to control risk is more straightforward, the benefits are a challenge to quantify. Problems arise because goods associated with reduced risk—death and injury—are not directly bought and sold on the auction block. These goods often enter a private market indirectly, and remain unpriced by collective agency action.

Valuing risk reductions often requires that we place a value on death and illness. These efforts give rise to the loaded term: 'the value of life'. The idea of a monetary value of life, or more correctly the value of reduced mortality risk, raises more than a few eyebrows. Ethical and moral beliefs often force a person to balk at the idea. But our everyday choices put a value on life, whether we explicitly quantify it or not. Whenever a policy change is enacted or whenever the status quo remains, life and limb are implicitly valued. For example, a North Carolina hospital once refused to spend $150 per healthcare worker for an inoculation against hepatitis B. Given the worker's odds of catching the disease, the hospital had implicitly placed a relatively low value on life. Nothing is lost by explicitly examining the value of reduced statistical risk.

So how can we value a reduction in risk? The straightforward answer is that the value of risk reduction equals

$$\text{The value of risk reduction} = \frac{\text{Willingness to pay for risk reduction}}{\text{Change in risk}}$$

This says that a person's value for a risk reduction equals his or her maximum willingness to pay to increase the chances to stay healthy, conditional of his previous private actions to reduce risk. For example, suppose a person was willing to pay $6 to reduce the risk of death to 1 life in 1,000,000 from 4 lives in 1,000,000—a 3 in 1m. risk reduction. The value of life is then $2,000,000 (= $6 /(3/1,000,000)). If the person was willing to pay $0.60, the implied value of life would be $200,000.

This willingness to pay is called the *option price*. The option price is the maximum a person is willing to pay that keeps him indifferent between the gamble and the next-best alternative. Consider Travis again and his decision to move to Baggs. Suppose regulators are thinking about a policy that would control air pollution so as to increase the odds to 90:10 of being healthy in Las Vegas. The maximum option price, OP, that Travis would pay for this risk reduction is the amount that would make him indifferent between the *status quo* and staying and leaving Las Vegas for Baggs,

$$(0.9)u(\$50,000 - OP) + (0.1)u(\$35,000 - OP)$$

$$= (0.7)u(\$50,000) + (0.3)u(\$35,000).$$

$$0.9\sqrt{(\$50,000 - OP)} + 0.1\sqrt{(\$35,000 - OP)}$$

$$= 0.7\sqrt{\$50,000} + 0.3\sqrt{\$35,000} = 213$$

$$0.9\sqrt{(\$50,000 - \$3,000)} + 0.1\sqrt{(\$35,000 - \$3,000)}$$

$$= 213.$$

In this case, Travis would be willing to pay at most $3,000 to reduce the risk of illness in Las Vegas.

Alternatively we could ask him to reveal his minimum willingness to accept compensation, C, to forgo the potential risk reduction.

$$(0.7)u(\$50,000 + C) + (0.3)u(\$35,000 + C)$$

$$= (0.9)u(\$50,000) + (0.1)u(\$35,000) = 220.$$

$$0.7 \sqrt{(\$50,000 + C)} + 0.3 \sqrt{(\$35,000 + C)}$$

$$= 0.9 \sqrt{\$50,000} + 0.1 \sqrt{\$35,000}$$

$$0.7 \sqrt{(\$50,000 + 3,100)} + 0.3 \sqrt{(\$35,000 + 3,100)}$$

$$= 220.$$

Travis would take at a minimum $3,100 to forgo the proposed risk reduction policy.

So how do economists actually go about trying to measure the value of risk reduction? The literature on risk valuation has developed two general approaches to measuring the economic benefits of reduced risk: the human capital and willingness-to-pay approaches.

- *The human capital approach* values risk reductions by examining a person's lifetime earnings and activities. The value of a risk reduction is the gain in future earnings and consumption. The value of saving a life is often calculated as what the individual contributes to society through the net present value of future earnings and consumption. The human capital approach has an advantage in that it is actuarial, i.e. it uses full age-specific accounting to evaluate risk reductions. A major drawback of the approach is that it assigns lower values to the lives of women and minorities, and zero value to retired individuals. The approach also lacks justification based on traditional economic welfare theory. For this reason, economists have downplayed the human capital method in favour of the willingness-to-pay approach.

- *Willingness-to-pay approach.* Economists have advocated the willingness-to-pay approach since it is based on the theory of welfare economics. Welfare economics lays the foundation for estimating the value of risk reduction. People value risk reduction if it leads to a greater level of utility or welfare. The welfare change is measured by the maximum that the average person would be willing to pay to reduce risk or the minimum compensation he would be willing to accept for an increase in risk. Economists then use this willingness to pay or accept to estimate the implied value of life and limb. And although far from perfect, economists argue that the willingness-to-pay approach is preferable to the alternative—it is better to have a rough estimate of a well-grounded theory than a precise estimate of a flighty one. Four empirical approaches are commonly used to determine the willingness to pay for risk reduction: the wage-risk trade-off, stated preferences, experimental auctions, and the averting behaviour. These may be comparable with the general valuation methods described in Chapters 3 and 4.

- *Wage-risk trade-offs.* Wage-risk trade-offs are based on the theory of hedonic prices. Hedonic price theory captures the idea that a person's wage rate depends on skill, education, occupation, location, environment of work, and job safety or risk. A worker will accept a higher wage for more risk, holding all other job attributes constant. More risk, higher wages. And a worker selects his job to equate the incremental willingness-to-pay for each attribute to the incremental contribution of each attribute to the wage rate. The value of risk reduction is the incremental willingness-to-pay for the attribute 'job safety'. Workers then compare their risk-wage trade-offs to the rate that the market is willing to trade risk for wages. The market equilibrium between workers and employers then determines the risk premium—the extra compensation for risky jobs. The wage-risk trade-off is thus determined, other job attributes held constant. Wage-risk studies set the value of a statistical life between $700,000 and $16,300,000 (in 1997 dollars). But note that these values can be challenged. Critics question the presumptions that workers know all the risks in the job, and can change jobs costlessly. Also they point out the weak correlation between job safety and environmental hazards. They also stress that hedonic models only consider a segment of the population—people with a job; children and seniors are underrepresented.

- *Stated preferences.* Stated preferences methods (e.g. contingent valuation) directly ask people how much they would be willing to pay to reduce risk through a survey or interview. The approach constructs a hypothetical market, in which a person buys or sells safety. The method attempts to reveal a person's willingness to pay for a risk reduction. The challenge is to make these hypothetical markets realistic and relevant to people. The biggest complaint is that a person answers a hypothetical question that does not enforce his or her actual budget constraint. The estimated range of the value of a statistical life is $1.5–4.6 million (in 1997 dollars). The range of values is consistent with the high-range estimates of the wage-risk model, working to dampen somewhat complaints about overestimation.

- *Experimental auctions.* Experimental auction markets are a relatively recent approach to directly value reductions in risk. Experimental auctions use the laboratory to sell real goods to real people within a stylized setting. Laboratory experiments can isolate and control how different auctions and market settings affect values in a setting of replication and repetition. Experiments with repeated market experience provide a well-defined incentive structure that allows a person to learn that honest revelation of his or her true preferences is his or her best strategy. Using demand revealing auctions (e.g. the second-price, sealed-bid auction mechanism, subjects will participate in an auction market that allows for learning as participants realize the actual monetary consequences of their bidding. The non-hypothetical auctions with repeated market experience can help improve the precision of risk valuation. For example, work in experimental markets has elicited the *ex ante* willingness to pay for safer food. These experiments used real money, real food, repeated opportunities to participate in the auction market, and full information on the probability and severity of disease resulting from the food-borne pathogens. The value of statistical life implied by bidding behaviour in early

Box 5.2 Valuing Reduced Risk from Food-borne Pathogens in the Lab

What is the value of food safety? Hayes *et al*. designed a set of experimental auctions to explore this question. They constructed an experimental auction to elicit both the option price and compensation measures of value for five different food-borne pathogens. They also used additional treatments to evaluate how subjects respond to changes in the risk of illness for a given pathogen, *Salmonella*, and to explore if pathogen-specific values act as surrogate measures of general food safety preferences. All experiments used real money, real food, repeated opportunities to participate in the auction market, and full information on the probability and severity of the food-borne pathogen. The design also used a Vickrey second-price auction to provide incentive to reveal preferences for risk reduction truthfully.

Four results emerge from their experiments. First, people underestimated the objective risk of food-borne pathogens. Second, values across food-borne pathogens were not robust to changes in the relative probabilities and severity, suggesting that people place more weight on their own prior perceptions than on new information on the odds of illness. Third, marginal willingness to pay an option price decreases as risk increases, again suggesting that the people weighed their prior beliefs more than new information. Fourth, they found support that values for specific pathogens might act as surrogates for general food-safety preferences.

Overall, the results suggest that the average subject in our experimental environment was willing to pay approximately $0.70 per meal for safer food. The *Salmonella* treatments under alternative risk levels indicate that the average person would pay about $0.30 per meal to reduce risk of food-borne pathogens by a fraction of 10. If one could transfer these values to the US population, the value of food safety could be at least three times the largest previously available estimates.

Reference. D. Hayes, J. Shogren, S. Shin, and J. Kliebenstein (1995). 'Valuing Food Safety in Experimental Auction Markets' *American Journal of Agricultural Economics* 77: 40–53.

lab work often exceeds by an order of magnitude the value estimated in other valuation methods, ranging from $2 million to $70 million. (See Box 5.2 on the value of risk reduction from food-borne pathogens.)

■ *Averting behaviour*. The averting behaviour method estimates willingness to pay for risk based on what people actually pay to protect their families and themselves. People reveal their preferences for lower risk through the market for self-protection such as smoke detectors, seat belts, medicine, bottled water, and water filters. The current estimates of the value of life range from $0.72 million to $4.8 million (in 1997 dollars).

The idea that people can use private markets to reduce risk themselves raises an important issue in the value of life and limb. The value of life or limb is usually defined as the cost of an unidentified single death or injury weighted by a probability of death or injury that is uniform across people. The willingness to pay approach captures this cost by revealing the previously unobserved preferences for risk reduction. But here is the rub. These estimates actually contain more than just unobserved preferences—it captures preferences for risk reduction conditional on each person's unobserved ability to reduce risk privately.

Consider an example. Suppose people have identical preferences for risk reduction from contaminated drinking water but they differ in their ability to access private risk reduction markets. And now say each person is asked to reveal his or her value for a collective programme to reduce risk. Each person's value for this collective risk reduction is conditional on his or her private actions. Following the standard procedures to value life, one might assume that people with a low value for collective risk reduction were willing to tolerate greater risk. But in fact it just might be that they have access to effective private risk reduction and have reduced the risk themselves.

But why does this matter? This matters because the statistical value of life commonly used in benefit-cost estimates could be upwardly biased because it has not addressed these private actions. To see this, consider the value of life used by the US Environmental Protection Agency. The Agency's value of life, $5.9m. per life (in 1997 dollars), is the mid-point estimate of different valuation exercises. Implicitly, this $5.9m. value is conditional on the private ability to reduce risk in the study it was taken from. To apply this fixed value to other risk reduction policies is to implicitly assume that any other study has the identical private risk reduction opportunities. That this is always the case is not obvious. Why should the market for the private reduction of water risk be identical to the market for toxic air risk? By focusing mainly on collective risk reduction, the statistical life approach can bias the value of risk reduction, which can lead to inefficient levels of environmental degradation. Allowing a person to reveal whether he would prefer to reduce risk privately or collectively or both will elicit a more exact measure of the value of risk reduction.

The value of reduced risk depends on the willingness to pay and the change in risk. If we do not account for the fact that people start from different baselines due to their personal ability to access private markets, the value will be biased. Consider two kinsmen, Riley and Ole, who are identical in every way except for their unobserved skill or access to private risk reduction markets. Suppose they are asked to state their willingness to pay for a collective policy that will increase the odds of a gamble from 50 : 50 to a 100 per cent chance the good state of the world will be realized.

Riley says he will pay nothing for the change in risk, and Ole says he'll pay $100. The traditional estimate of the value of this risk reduction is

Value of risk reduction without private action

$$= \frac{1}{2}[\$0/0.5] + \frac{1}{2}[\$100/0.5]$$

$$= \$100.$$

But this presumes that Riley and Ole face the same baseline and the same change in risk, 50 : 50, even though their unobserved skill or market access differs. Let Riley have high skill or access, such that his real odds are 90 : 10 of a good outcome prior to the collective policy, such that he is paying for a real change in risk that equals $0.1 = 1.00 - 0.9$. Whereas Ole has low skill or access and his real odds are 10 : 90. Thus

Ole is paying $100 for a 0.9 change in risk, 1.0 −0.1. The value of risk reduction conditional on private risk reduction is then

Value of risk reduction with private action

$$= \tfrac{1}{2}[\$0/0.1] + \tfrac{1}{2}[\$100/0.9]$$

$$= \$56.$$

The value of risk reduction is lower than the traditional measure if one accounts for private actions changing the baseline risk. If the willingness to pay amounts were reversed such that Riley paid $100 and Ole paid nothing, the new value exceeds the traditional measure

Value of risk reduction with private action

$$= \tfrac{1}{2}[\$100/0.1] + \tfrac{1}{2}[\$0/0.9]$$

$$= \$500.$$

This example is less likely to be observed, however, since low skill and low risk-aversion are more likely to be correlated. Private actions affect the baseline risk, and this alters the value of risk reduction of the average person.

5.5 Risk perception

HAZARDOUS material conjures up images of either a fortified storage facility containing sanitized, air-tight receptacles, or an abandoned dump-site teeming with rusty, leaking barrels of toxic waste. The two images induce vividly different perceptions of risk to public health. Yet such a range of public risk perceptions can exist simultaneously in a community, causing considerable disagreement as to whether a risk is acceptable or not. Determining whether the risk needs to be regulated depends on how people are willing to trade-off risks for the benefits they can generate to society. Their willingness to surrender benefits for reduced risk represents the value they place on risk reduction. Estimating this value for risk reduction is a critical component of risk-benefit analysis, now commonly used in policy-making on environmental risk.

This value of reduced risk depends in part on people's *perceptions* of and *preference* for risk. People deathly afraid of the risks they see around every corner are likely to value risk reduction more than those who live to take risks. This statement seems straightforward enough, and the logic behind it guides most economists who address environmental risk. Those at most risk who are most afraid of risk and who have the most income should consistently value risk reduction the most.

Economists who work with risk most often use the expected utility framework which presumes people have well-defined preferences for risk and can logically form rational perceptions of risk. The working presumption is that people have a solid foundation that drives their choices, such that when they confront a risk, new or old, they are able to evaluate the odds and consequences in systematical and predictable way. A person's stated value for risk reduction is based on a logical foundation of choice—welfare economics, and thus economics is able to judge the overall economic efficiency of some policy decision. Without well-grounded preferences and perceptions, there is a crack in the foundation of the rational theory of choice on which the economist's risk-benefit analysis rests.

But cracks exist. Psychologists and some economists have documented numerous exceptions to the idea of a rational theory of choice. These behavioural researchers have shown how people use rules of thumb, or heuristics, to simplify their reasoning about risk. Using these rules, people often react to risk in broader patterns than predicted by expected utility theory. This suggests that the standard model used to guide risk-benefit decisions is 'too thin'—the model does not predict systematic aspects of behaviour under risk regularly observed in many situations. In fact, the evidence suggests that risk preference and perceptions seem to be systematically influenced by the context of choice.

People are complicated. People who make judgements about risk use heuristics that the popular expected utility framework fails to capture. There is a long list of behavioural anomalies and paradoxes uncovered by cognitive researchers.

One bias in judgement is when people overestimate low-probability risks and underestimate high-probability risks. Figure 5.2 illustrates the bias. The 45°-line represents the case in which the general public's subjective risk equals objective risk as defined by expert opinion. The flatter dashed line reflects the evidence from different experiments and surveys examining how people actually rank the threats posed by different risks. People seem to inflate low risks that they have little to no control over (e.g. nuclear power) and deflate high risks that they can control to some degree (e.g. driving to work). They tend to worry more about how and where a risk arises than its magnitude, e.g. synthetic versus natural carcinogens. This poor calibration between experts' objective opinions and the lay persons' perceptions can lead to rejection of potentially beneficial technologies, e.g. commercial nuclear power.

Some risks are simply more acceptable than others are. People who accept the risk of smoking or driving without seat belts may not accept the risk associated with nearby treatment, storage, and disposal of hazardous material. Voluntary risks people think they can control are more acceptable than involuntary risk they believe are outside their control. Technologies that inhibit the sense that this risk is 'voluntary' are less acceptable—e.g. nuclear power. Recent research has refined this argument with the idea that space, time, familiarity, dread, anxiety, regret, time-horizons, and perceived controllability drive the idea of voluntary risk (Viscusi, 1992).

The perception gap raises a potential dilemma for the regulation. Suppose experts argue that the risks from a certain product are unacceptable, while many people perceive the opposite. Does the policy-maker ban the product or allow people to use their own discretion? The beef-on-the-bone ban in the United Kingdom is a good example of not leaving the decision to people. The policy-maker's dilemma is to balance the trade-off between preserving individual freedom of choice and maintaining

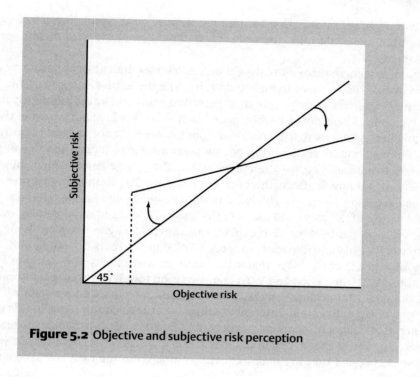

Figure 5.2 Objective and subjective risk perception

public safety. The policymaker may indeed be tempted to step in and regulate the risk in the best interest of society. Such paternalistic action, however, conflicts with many societies that are committed to consumer sovereignty—the person is best able to judge what is or is not in his or her own best self-interest.

Risk perception examines lay persons' perceptions of risky technologies, and the determinants of their relative acceptability. Using risk-benefit analysis, researchers attempt to measure the welfare benefits of risky technologies. The majority of risk acceptance research has been in the area of public perception of low-probability/high-consequence technology such as nuclear power. Lay persons often will not accept risk if the hazard is perceived as uncontrollable, regardless of expert opinion. For example, in the early 1980s, lay persons perceived nuclear power as the number-one risk to public safety, while experts ranked it twentieth—below the risk of a house-hold accident. Regardless of expert opinion, during the late 1970s and 1980s Swedish citizens perceived nuclear power risk as so unacceptable, policy-makers finally agreed to phase out the entire industry over the next quarter century.

Another risk perception effect is when people judge a risk by its familiarity with other risks they have confronted. They base their decisions on how well what they currently know represents the new event. This tendency to stick with one's preju-dices can cause people to ignore risks that have characteristics that they have not confronted before. A person might tend to underestimate the risk of radon because it is odourless and colourless, and as such, there is nothing concrete against which she can compare it. There are other occasions in which people fear the worst when given good and bad information because we seem to most readily recall bad events. People often have alarmist reactions to well-publicized risks to health or the environment.

People also seem to place more weight on small losses than huge opportunities. We tend to dislike losses more intensely than we like the equivalent gains. This 'loss-aversion' idea suggests that people treat perceived gains and losses differently in two ways. We seem to seek out risk when gambles involve only loss; but we avoid risk for the equivalent gambles that involve only gains. This evidence suggests that rather than thinking about overall wealth, people seem instead to judge the value of gains and losses from a *status quo*—a reference point. They judge risk by what they have experienced and how it affects their current standing. The context in this case is the *status quo*. A person's value for risk reduction then will depend on the reference point and the nature of the gains and losses of the lottery (Tversky and Kahneman, 1981).

Loss aversion has been used to explain the unpredicted gap between the willingness to pay (WTP) and willingness to accept (WTA) measures of economic value. The theory of rational choice says that with small income effects and many available substitutes, WTP for a good and WTA compensation to sell the same good should be about the same. But evidence suggests that a significant gap exists between WTP and WTA, maybe up to a tenfold difference. Critics of rational choice point to this gap as evidence that standard economic theory has failed, and that people instead are motivated by loss aversion, or a fundamental *endowment effect*—people are less willing to surrender a good they are endowed with compared to their eagerness to acquire the same good.

In addition, how the risk is 'framed' can affect choice in ways unpredicted by expected utility. If a person has well-formed preferences and values, a choice between two options should be independent of how they are represented or described. But again psychologists show how choice and values can be systematically influenced by different ways to frame an identical problem. A famous example illustrates the importance of framing effects with the following example. Answer the following three questions:

Q.1: Which of the following options do you prefer?
  A. A 100 per cent chance to win $30
  B. An 80 per cent chance to win $45.
Q.2: This is a two-stage game. In the first stage, there is a 75 per cent chance the game will end with no prize and a 25 per cent chance to move to the second stage. If you reach the second stage, you have a choice between:
  C. A 100 per cent chance to win $30
  D. An 80 per cent chance to win $45.

Your choice must be made before the game starts. Please indicate the option you prefer.

Q.3: Which of the following options do you prefer?
  E. A 25 per cent chance to win $30
  F. A 20 per cent chance to win $45.

Questions 2 and 3 are identical in odds and rewards, and therefore should produce identical choices from a person. But instead people treat Q.1 and Q.2 the same, not Q.2 and Q.3. People prefer option C in Q.2 and option A in Q.1, while they prefer option E in Q.3. This is the so-called 'certainty effect'—an option framed as a sure-thing appears as attractive as a genuinely certain option. All this suggests that framing matters to risk policy. Studies confirm that regulators should pay as much attention to *how* they provide the information as to *what* information they provide. People also place varying levels of trust in information on environmental risk according to the source.

People also do not deal well with ambiguity in risk. Ambiguity implies that probabilities of bad events are uncertain—the odds of a bad event might range between 1 and 10 per cent. Ambiguous risks dominate many decisions people must make, e.g. investments, health care, exercise, and food. And while the expected utility model assumes people handle ambiguous risk, consider the following example. Suppose you had the choice between choosing a ball from an urn with a known number of coloured balls and an urn with an unknown number of coloured balls in a pay-off situation. Most people prefer drawing from the urn with the known distribution, even if the expected payoff is lower. This is the Ellsberg paradox. Even in experiments using professionals who deal with risk on a daily basis, actuaries, business executives, life insurance executives, and MBA students, were averse to ambiguous risk.

Finally, people also reverse their preferences. A person is said to reverse his preferences when his ranking of two gambles differs from the selling prices he assigns to each gamble. That is, you prefer gamble A to B, but place a higher selling price on B than A. Answer the following questions:

Q.3: Which gamble do you prefer, A or B?
    Gamble A: 35/36 chances to win $4
                1/36 chance to lose $1.
    Gamble B: 11/36 chances to win $16
                25/36 chances to lose $1.50.
Q.4: Suppose you own both gambles. What is your selling price for:
    Gamble A: $_____
    Gamble B: $_____

Expected utility theory requires that you be consistent—the gamble you select should also be the gamble you value the most. So if you preferred Gamble A to B, and then assigned a higher $ value to Gamble B than A, you can add your name to the list of the surprisingly large number of people who reverse preferences.

The logical inconsistency is this: suppose you preferred A to B, and valued A at $2 and B at $8. Now if your statements are a true indication of your preferences, we can turn you into a 'money pump' in three easy steps: (1) sell you B for $8, (2) ask you to switch B for A because after all you preferred A to B, and then (3) buy A back from you for $2. Now you have neither gamble, and a $6 hole in your pocket (−$6 = $2 − $8). If you prefer more money to less, this is not a good thing. Your choices should be more consistent than that, which is what expected utility assumes. But the preference reversal phenomena has been duplicated in numerous settings including with real gamblers in Las Vegas and by sceptical economists doubtful of the earlier work by psychologists.

Efforts to eliminate preference reversals have been successful when stakes are very large and when people are clearly made aware they can be a money pump. Since these circumstances are less likely to be observed for environmental goods, preference reversals have led some researchers to conclude that standard environmental valuation exercises and surveys are unreliable and a poor guide for rational risk regulation.

In conclusion, risk perceptions matter to environmental risk policy because if people's stated values for risk reduction are inconsistent with their underlying preferences or if set preferences are a fantasy, society has less information to use to judge the relative net benefits of one environmental policy over another. If values are context-specific so that they change with the policy, then we cannot compare two policies with risk-benefit analysis because it would be like comparing apples and oranges. Economists cannot rely on standard risk-benefit analysis to guide policy if values always depend on the context. They cannot rely on the foundation of welfare economics to define a consistent ranking of environmental policy based on our statements of how much we prefer reductions in risk.

5.6 Regulating Risk

WE have thus far considered what risk is, how people make choices under environmental risk, how they value risk, and how all of this is tempered by risk perception. Managing and regulating risk in society requires regulators to integrate assessment, psychology, economics, and political factors. Risk-management policies are complicated by numerous factors: scientific complexity and uncertainty, political and economic pressure from special interest groups, financial abilities to clean up disposal sites, jurisdictional disputes, unresolved liability, and variations in local, state, and federal policy goals. Successful strategies to manage risk should address which risks we want to confront now and in the future, how we will control these risks in a cost-effective manner, and how we balance who faces what risk.

Consider several ways to select the risks we choose to face. A common first reaction is to want to set a target of *zero risk* to society. Regulation in the USA such as the Delaney Clause of the Food, Drug, and Cosmetic Act that prohibited the presence of any known carcinogen as a food additive in processed food is a zero risk regulation. As science becomes better at measuring small amounts of trace chemicals that are potential carcinogens, the zero risk approach is increasingly restrictive. If almost everything is feared to cause cancer of some form, what can we really eliminate? The costs to hit a zero risk target increase so rapidly that it often becomes prohibitive. Some actions and activities can be so risky that society should completely ban their use—zero risk because they are gone from society. But in most cases for the goods we need and want, reasonable people recognize that zero risk is a noble yet unachievable goal.

The next wave is for society to set an acceptable risk target that can be reached using current or new technology. *Technology-based standards* are a centralized process of setting permissible levels of contamination or building codes. People or firms who ignore these standards would be punished in civil or criminal court. Examples include uniform limits on total emissions per day or year, emission per tonne of input used in a production process and type of equipment used in production, such that it is the best available control technology. One argument advanced by proponents of technology standards is that only technology-based engineering decisions that construct a uniform threshold of acceptable risk have to be measured; costs and benefits are left unmeasured. But uniform standards are likely to be inefficient, as we see in Chapter 11.

A third wave is to promote cost-effective risk reduction. Dollars now enter explicitly into the picture. Costs matter. *Cost-effectiveness* allows regulators to set a target and then asks that people be allowed to find the most cost-effective path to achieve the target. The idea is to take the public's preferences and perceptions of risk into consideration. This can be accomplished through open meetings in which regulators and the public set health and safety targets. Cost-effectiveness attempts to find the least costly method to achieve the goals. One advantage of cost-effectiveness is that it does not have to measure the benefits of the target. The method maximizes lives saved given a fixed budget in which assumptions on values are built directly into the model.

If we want to consider trade-offs involved in risk management but still not explicitly measure costs or benefits, regulators can address *risk–risk trade-offs*, or *comparative risk analysis*. Risk–risk analysis compares how we trade-off one risk for another. For example, an energy policy that would switch to more nuclear power and less coal power would shift the nature of risk to radiation rather than climate change. A shift to more hydropower would shift the risk towards more endangered species protection. The framework requires estimation of the tradeoff between consumer health risks and substances that offer a direct health benefit. The health benefits of drugs, exercise, and diet, for example, fit into this framework. The benefit of the risk–risk framework is that regulators can convert health outcomes into fatality risk equivalents, which might allow more meaningful comparisons than a risk–dollar trade-off.

Finally, policy-makers can use risk-benefit or cost-benefit analyses as we saw in the previous chapter. Here we ask for dollar measures of both costs and benefits, and a direct comparison of the trade-off between risk and dollar benefits. As we discussed, economists have spent considerable effort to determine the value of reduced risk. Cost-benefit analysis can be used as a tool to measure the economic efficiency of a regulation. Cost-benefit analysis attempts to measure the costs associated with the risk regulation and the subsequent welfare benefits from a risk reduction. The costs of differing policy alternatives are then compared with their benefits to determine if and to what extent the risk will be reduced. The goal of cost-benefit is to maximize economic efficiency and make the resulting risk reductions as large as possible.

There are many controversial aspects to cost-benefit analysis. The value of risks to life must be explicitly addressed. The appropriate discount rate remains a nagging question. Exponential discount rates place less weight on the future. And we must confront equity and distributional questions—whose risk will be reduced and who will pay? Equity criterion spreads out the costs and benefits of risk based on some subjective measures to weight who gets what for which price. Risk can be evenly distributed among the population; or it can be progressively or regressively distributed based on, say wealth.

Environmental risk to children is a prime example of questions over whose risk we should be reducing. Evidence suggests that children face disproportionate health risks from environmental hazards. These unbalanced risks stem from several fundamental differences in the physiologies and activities of children and adults. As children develop, their digestive, nerve, and immune systems are more susceptible to toxic pollutants and other environmental hazards. Children eat, drink, and breathe more for their weight, and spend more time outside exposing themselves to greater amounts of contamination and pollution for their weight than adults. They also face potential exposures over their entire lifetime. They are also less able to recognize and to protect themselves. All this suggests children require special attention when dealing with environmental risk.

Based on this argument, President Clinton unveiled in April 1997 a new executive order to protect children from environmental risks. The order directs the federal government to safeguard children from environmental threats through more policy, better research coordination, and more federal regulatory analysis. All US federal agencies must now make the protection of children a high priority when implementing their statutory responsibilities and fulfilling their overall missions. Agencies promulgating major regulations that may have a disproportionate impact on children must now evaluate how regulation could affect children's risk, and then explain why the planned regulation is preferable to alternative actions that might have more cost and less risk.

This forces agencies to ratchet up their regulatory standards, with a corresponding increase in the costs and burden of regulation. The pressure to raise standards across the board may generate criticism from industry and other groups who are likely to assert that analysis of impacts on children can lead to bad decisions, i.e. costly Superfund clean-ups based on exposure of children to toxins, and analytical flaws in the public health data supporting recent Clean Air Act proposals on ozone and particulate matter. The additional burden may further delay the regulatory process, and add resource demands to agencies confronting tight budgetary constraints (see Box 5.3 on Superfund).

Regulators have many tools at their disposal to reduce risk, either to adults or children. They can impose mandates, liability rules, pollution taxes and subsidies, create new markets, and use informed consent through risk communication. We have discussed taxes and markets previously. Consider risk communication strategies.

Box 5.3 Superfund

In 1981 the US Congress passed the Comprehensive Environmental Response, Compensation, and Liability Act (CERCLA) which established Superfund. Superfund ($8.5 billion) is funded by feedstock taxes and is used to pay clean-up costs of an abandoned disposal site if it is considered dangerous to either human health or the environment. CERCLA required the EPA to select a National Priorities List of at least 400 sites, with the top priority of each state listed in the first 100 sites. As of 1988, the average clean-up costs of a Superfund site is between $21m. and $30 m.; a considerable amount more than the projected costs of $8.1m. per site.

Superfund has the right to recover costs from the owner or operator of the site, or from anyone responsible for transporting hazardous materials to the site, if identifiable. The potential responsible party is liable for clean-up costs and health damage. The government does not have to show negligence, and can request triple the costs of action. Strict liability and joint and several liability among many defendants have created a tendency to go for the firms with the deepest pockets. As such the costs of litigation have been estimated at over $8 billion, 55 per cent of the estimated direct clean-up costs of the National Priority List sites. If two-thirds to three-quarters of the Superfund litigation costs could be eliminated, then 300 to 400 additional sites could be cleaned up below the project costs of current programme.

Since the government has not been willing to settle until the identity of all major contributors and most minor contributors is well established, insurance and reinsurance markets have drastically retreated from the environment liability market. With insurers curtailing liability coverage, litigation costs will continue to increase diverting valuable resources from future clean-up operations. A goal to minimize the social costs suggests that it is still necessary to revisit the incentives behind Superfund since it is questionable that the programme has produced sufficient benefits to justify its costs.

Reference: R. Revesz and R. Stewart (eds.) (1995). *Analyzing Superfund. Economics, Science, and Law.* (Washington, DC: Resources for the Future.)

The major benefit of risk communication and informed consent is that people are allowed to make informed choices based on preferences toward risk rather than uniform government bans or regulation. The risk manager must be sure that the information consumers have will result in more accurate private decisions regarding risk. But the language of the hazard warnings often seem to maximize political interests rather than advancing the primary objective of informing consumers and enabling them to make better decisions. By ignoring fundamental economic and psychological concepts of decision-making under risk, warnings will not convey the information necessary for consumers to make sound choices regarding risks and precautions.

But regulators and the public must also be aware that risks can be regulated by simply being transformed and transferred elsewhere. Transferable risk implies that people protect themselves by transferring the risk through space to another location or through time to another generation. Most environmental programmes do not reduce environmental risks by cutting the mass of materials used or causing them to accumulate in the economy. People select a technology that transfers a risk which creates conflict and induces strategic behaviour. Some nations and states reduce their air pollution by building tall stacks such that the winds carry the emissions to those downwind. Some local governments ban toxin storage within their jurisdictions, thereby shifting the problems elsewhere. Effective risk management should address the question of transferability.

5.7 Concluding Remark

ENVIRONMENTAL risk requires we understand the nature of the risk, how people perceive and react to the risk, and how collective action can help or hinder private actions. Understanding basic economic behaviour under risk can help make our decisions to control risk more effective—reducing more risk for more people. Knowing how to assess risk accurately, whether people make risky choices with reason or at random, what people are willing to pay to reduce risk, what institutions exist to control risk can only help us make better decisions on how to save lives and reduce injuries.

Economics has a responsibility to convince the natural sciences to connect mind to matter by including economic parameters in their core frameworks that address environmental risk. We have an obligation to help define the environmental thresholds of human and ecosystem health that underpin risk reduction policies. If economics does not challenge the position that biology is independent of economics in risk assessment, we abdicate too much authority to the natural scientists to design a nation's environmental risk reduction agenda. Human actions and reactions to nature have a role in determining the risks that shape our lives, and understanding how people react to and protect themselves from risk can again result in saving more lives at less cost.

References

Allais, M. (1953). 'Le comportement de l'homme rationnel devant le risque. Critique des postulats et ascioms d'ecole Americaine', *Econometrica* 21: 503–46.

Baron, R. (1994). *Thinking and Deciding*. (Cambridge: Cambridge University Press).

Ehrlich I., and G. S. Becker (1972). 'Market insurance, self-insurance and self-protection', *Journal of Political Economy* 80: 623–48.

Hayes, D., Shogren, J., Shin, S., and Kliebenstein, J. (1995). 'Valuing food safety in experimental auction markets', *American Journal of Agricultural Economics* 77: 40–53.

Machina, M. (1987). 'Choice under uncertainty: problems solved and unsolved', *Journal of Economic Perspectives* 1: 121–54.

National Academy of Sciences (1983). *Risk Assessment in the Federal Government Managing the Process* (Washington, DC: National Academy Press).

Revesz, R., and Stewart, R. (eds.) (1995). Analyzing superfund. Economics, science, and law. (Washington, DC: Resources for the Future).

Ruckelshaus, W. (1984). 'Risk in a free society', *Risk Analysis* 4: 157–62.

Shogren, J. F., and Crocker, T. (1999). 'Risk and its consequences', *Journal of Environmental Economics and Management* 37: 44–51.

Tversky, A., and Kahneman, D. (1981). 'The framing of decisions and the psychology of choice', *Science* 211: 453–8.

Viscusi, W. K., 1992. *Fatal Trade-offs*. (Oxford: Oxford University Press).

Von Neuman, J., and Morgenstern, O. (1944). *Theory of Games and Economic Behavior* (Princeton, NJ: Princeton University Press).

Further Reading

- Crouch, E., and Wilson, R. (1982). *Risk-Benefit Analysis* (Cambridge, Mass.: Ballinger).

- Kates, R. W. (1978). *Risk Assessment of Environmental Hazard* (New York: Wiley).

- Knight, F. (1971). *Risk, Uncertainty, and Profit* (New York: Harper & Row).

- Lowrance, W. (1976). *Of Acceptable Risk* (Los Altos: Wm. Kaufman Inc).

- Savage, L. (1954). *The Foundation of Statistics* (Wiley: New York).

- Schwing, R., and Alberds, W. (eds.) (1980). *Societal Risk Assessment. How Safe is Safe Enough*? (New York: Plenum Publishers).

- Slovic, P., Fischoff, B., and Lichtenstein, S. (1982). 'Why Study Risk Perception?', *Risk Analysis* 2: 83–93.

- Starr, C. (1969). 'Social benefit vs. technological risk', *Science* 165: 1232–8.

- Sugden, R. (1991). 'Rational choice: a survey of contributions from economics and philosophy', *Economic Journal* 101: 751–85.

- Waller, R., and Covello, T. (eds.) (1984). *Low Probability/High Consequence Risk Analysis* (New York: Plenum Publishers).

Chapter 6
Economic Growth and Sustainable Development

THIS chapter discusses the general idea of economic growth and development. Section 6.1 outlines what we mean by growth, a general understanding of how economies grow, and the differences between growth and development. In Section 6.2 we review the history of the debate about the links between growth and the environment, which involves a brief survey of the origins of environmental and natural resource economics as a discipline. One controversial aspect of the debate is whether an economy can grow its way out of environmental problems, and this is covered in Section 6.3. Most debates on the links between growth and the environment are now undertaken in the context of the idea of 'sustainable development'. Section 6.4 explains how economists view this concept. The chapter closes with a review of different economic indicators of sustainability in Section 6.5.

6.1 Economic Growth and Development

GOVERNMENTS worldwide are almost always concerned with economic growth as a measure of a country's performance, both in absolute terms (how fast are we growing?) and in relative terms (are we growing faster than our neighbours?). Newspapers and TV often report actual growth figures and predictions of future growth. But growth in what? Why does it occur? Are 'growth' and 'development' the same thing? This section addresses these questions, before turning to the relationship between growth and the environment.

Economic growth is commonly understood to reflect an increase in people's living standards over time. What we want is an indicator of how well we are doing as a society. This is a hard question. Economists have answered it by defining gross national product, or GNP, a Nobel Prize-winning idea. GNP is a monetary measure of the total value of output of a country in any time-period. GNP is also a measure of national incomes to all factors of production (land, labour, and capital) and of total spending (consumption plus gross investment). GNP is often expressed in per capita terms, to allow for the effects of changes in population. If real GNP is rising, it is usual to say that a country is experiencing economic growth. We can track changes in real GNP by adjusting nominal GNP (measured in the current year's prices) according to the rate of change in absolute prices (inflation). Tables 6.1a and 6.1b show GNP per

Table 6.1(a) Real GNP per capita in selected countries

Real GNP per capita PPP$	1987	1989	1990	1991	1992	1993	1994	1995	1997
USA	17,615	20,998	21,449	22,130	23,760	24,680	26,397	26,977	29,010
UK	12,270	13,732	15,804	16,340	17,160	17,230	18,620	19,302	20,730
Spain	8,989	8,723	11,723	12,670	13,400	13,660	14,324	14,789	15,930
Poland	4,000	4,770	4,237	4,500	4,830	4,702	5,002	5,442	6,520
Thailand	2,576	3,569	3,986	5,270	5,950	6,350	7,104	7,742	6,690
Brazil	4,307	4,951	4,718	5,240	5,240	5,500	5,362	5,928	6,480
China	2,124	2,656	1,990	2,946	1,950	2,330	2,604	2,935	3,130
Kenya	794	1,023	1,058	1,350	1,400	1,400	1,404	1,438	1,190
India	1,053	910	1,072	1,150	1,230	1,240	1,348	1,422	1,670
Mozambique	500	1,060	1,072	921	380	640	986	959	740

Note: PPP means 'Purchasing power parity': this means that the GNP per capita figures have been adjusted to take into account the different prices in the countries in the table: each $ of PPP is supposed to buy the same 'basket' of goods.

Source: Human Development Reports, 1990–99.

Table 6.1(b) GNP annual percentage growth in selected countries

GNP annual % growth 1985–96	'85	'86	'87	'88	'89	'90	'91	'92	'93	'94	'95	'96	Average 1985–96	Country ranking
USA	3	3	3	4	3	1	−1	3	2	4	2	2	2	7
UK	4	4	5	5	2	0	−2	−1	2	4	2	2	2	7
Spain	3	3	6	5	5	4	2	1	−1	2	3	2	3	6
Poland	5	4	2	4	0	−11	−6	2	4	4	7	6	2	7
Thailand	5	6	10	13	12	12	8	8	8	9	9	6	9	2
Brazil	8	8	3	0	3	−5	1	−1	5	6	3	3	3	6
China	14	9	12	12	4	4	9	15	14	13	11	10	11	1
Kenya	4	7	6	6	5	4	1	−1	0	3	4	4	4	5
India	5	5	5	10	7	6	0	5	5	8	7	7	6	4
Mozambique	10	−4	20	10	7	3	7	1	22	6	−1	6	7	3

Source: World Bank, 1998.

capita and rates of GNP growth for a range of countries. GNP is a measure of living standards in the sense that it measures the size of the 'economic cake' to be divided amongst the inhabitants of a country, that is the amount of total income to be divided up. Rising GNP per capita would not necessarily mean that absolutely everyone is better off, since some could lose or stand still, whilst others gain more than average. GNP takes no account of income distribution, or equity. However, rising real GNP, that is, having allowed for the effects of inflation, might be claimed to show that, on average, people were getting better off over time.

Economic growth is important in the sense that lower growth rates have a big opportunity cost over time. By this, we mean that even low rates of GNP *growth* can imply very big increases in the absolute level of real GNP over time. The 'rule of 70' associated with compound growth tells us that an economy growing at 10 per cent could double its GNP in seven years. A country which cannot maintain growth rates falls further and further behind its competitors. However, we do need to be sure that what we are measuring (GNP) accurately presents changes in what we are interested in, which is well-being (see Box 6.1).

Many critics complain that GNP is an inadequate measure of well-being, as Box 6.1

Box 6.1 Is GNP a Good Measure of Well-being?

Since the end of World War II countries throughout the world have measured and compared their levels of well-being using gross national product (GNP), following guidelines laid out in the System of National Accounts. This seems sensible since GNP measures our income as a country, as well as the value of what we are producing. If population is changing, or we wish to compare GNP across different countries, then we can divide GNP by population to get GNP per capita, which shows how much income, on average, each person in a country has. Another measure of welfare from the System of National Accounts is net domestic product (NDP): this is defined as GNP minus depreciation (wearing out) of the stock of manufactured capital during the year.

However, GNP has been widely criticized as a measure of well-being. Some of the main criticisms are:

- The effects of the economy on the environment are not well measured by GNP. For example, if there was a major oil-spill in a country and much had to be spent cleaning it up, then GNP could rise (since the pollution clean-up industry increases its output) even if people feel worse off as a result.

- A closely related point is that changes in our natural resource stocks do not show up in NDP; for example, if farming generates high levels of soil erosion so that the productive stocks of soil in a country are significantly depleted, this does not show up in the national accounts.

- Although GNP measures the size of the economic pie, it does not tell us how fairly it is divided up. GNP per capita could be increasing but income inequalities could worsen.

- GNP does not adequately reflect changes in factors such as health and literacy which have important impacts on people's sense of well-being.

shows. However, despite these criticisms, nations still use increases in real GNP per capita to measure their economic performance over time. But how can GNP increase over time? In other words, what is the theory behind economic growth?

Economic growth over the long run is due to increases in potential output, rather than short-term fluctuations around this. If potential output rises by 2 per cent per year, then GNP will be about seven times larger within 100 years. What causes potential output to rise? Two factors are important: growth in the resources which can be devoted to production, and changes in the productivity of these resources.

Increasing resources. If a country experiences an increase in its resource base, then GNP can increase. This resource base includes capital, labour, land, energy, and material resources. Labour supplies can rise with population growth or migration, although this might not mean that GNP per capita was increasing, even though aggregate GNP was. Land resources can increase if a country exploits overseas colonies. Energy and material resources can increase through new discoveries (such as North Sea oil in Scotland in the 1970s). Technological progress can also drive down the costs of exploiting natural resources, and thus make more of the physical resource stock profitable to exploit. This increases the economic reserves of that resource.

Capital stocks can also rise. Indeed, capital accumulation is one of the earliest explanations for economic growth, put forward by the Classical economists and by Marx. Both privately and publicly owned capital accumulates over time through the process of investment. The productivity of capital means that positive net investment (that is, gross investment minus depreciation) can occur even with constant consumption. Capital productivity means that each £1 of resources invested in capital will generate more than £1 in consumption goods over time.

Productivity growth. As people learn more through education and training, the productivity of all of the resources used in economic activity increases. For example, the average productivity of miners in terms of tonnes of coal extracted per worker per annum, and the average productivity of agricultural land in terms of yields per hectare, have both risen tremendously over time. The more a country invests in its workers, through education and training, and thus in its technology, the faster we expect growth to be. Education pays by increasing the stock of human quality through increasing the skills of the workforce. Human productivity can also increase through learning-by-doing. The most famous example of this refers to steelworkers in Horndal, Sweden in the 1800s, who despite no changes in the machinery they worked with or in the size of the work force managed to increase output by 2 per cent per year, just through becoming more experienced at their jobs (Begg, Fischer, and Dornbusch, 1987).

Produced capital can also become more productive, with the embodiment of knowledge in new designs of machinery. This source of growth is endogenous in the sense that the greater are the amount of resources devoted to research and development activities, the greater will be the rate of technological innovation (other things being equal).

Not all of these sources of growth contribute equally. For example, Table 6.2 shows the varying contributions to growth in the UK economy of new resource discoveries

Table 6.2 Causes of UK growth, 1951–1985

	Growth rate of real GNP	Contributions from			
		North Sea oil	Productivity increase	Employment change	Hours worked
1951–60	2.7	—	2.3	0.7	−0.3
1960–73	3.1	—	3.8	0.3	−0.9
1973–9	1.3	0.7	1.2	0.2	−0.8
1979–85	1.2	0.3	2.8	−0.9	−1.1

Source: Begg, Fischer and Dornbusch (1987: 655).

(North Sea oil), output per employee (i.e. labour productivity), the size of the work-force, and the number of hours worked by the average worker. On the whole, labour productivity is the most important engine for growth according to these data, but it is important to note that much of this productivity increase is itself down to capital investment (e.g. better machinery, more modern factories).

Growth versus development. Growth, as measured by rising GNP per capita, is not usually assumed to be the same as 'development'. This is because development is usually interpreted much more broadly (see, for example, the *UN Human Development Report*); and because of the limitations of GNP referred to in Box 6.1. For an economy to be experiencing development, as distinct from growth, we might expect to see a whole series of indicators improving over time. These might include:

- GNP per capita; this is still important
- a reduction in income inequality
- an improvement in adult literacy rates
- a reduction in infant mortality
- reductions in morbidity (illness) and mortality (death) rates amongst adults.

These indicators are both monetary and non-monetary.

The Human Development Indicator (HDI) was introduced by the United Nations in 1990 (UNDP, 1990), and is published annually. A set of indicators was chosen to represent a set of measures of development for a nation. These include GNP. In Table 6.3 HDI rankings are compared with ranking in terms of GNP per capita. As may be seen, there is a strong correlation between the two for these countries over these years. This is because income is a very major determinant of the other measures of well-being incorporated in the HDI. However, *both* the HDI and GNP measures omit any direct account of environmental degradation. We can also see how, in terms of economic growth, countries such as Thailand and China perform best.

Table 6.3 Human development indices vs. GNP and GNP growth rates

	HDI, 1987	HDI, 1997	Average HDI 1987–97	Real GNP per capita, 1997	Average GNP growth, 1985–96	Rank on GNP growth	Rank on GNP per capita	Ranking on average HDI
USA	0.961	0.927	0.947	29,010	2	7 =	1	1
UK	0.970	0.918	0.937	20,730	2	7 =	2	2
Spain	0.965	0.894	0.924	15,930	3	6 =	3	3
Poland	0.910	0.802	0.843	6,520	2	7 =	5	4
Thailand	0.783	0.753	0.785	6,690	9	2	4	5
Brazil	0.784	0.739	0.771	6,480	3	6 =	6	6
China	0.716	0.701	0.635	3,130	11	1	7	7
Kenya	0.481	0.519	0.450	1,190	4	5	9	8
India	0.439	0.545	0.416	1,670	6	4	8	9
Mozambique	0.239	0.341	0.245	740	7	3	10	10

Source: Human Development Reports, 1990–1999, World Bank.

6.2 Predictions from the Past

ABOVE, we reviewed two main reasons why GNP per capita can grow over time, and thus why economic growth occurs. But how long can growth continue? Does continual economic growth come with a health warning? One of the biggest intellectual debates throughout the history of economics has been concerned with these questions, and a big part of this debate has been the nature of the relationship between the economic system and the environment. The earliest economists, known as the Classical School, worried about the interaction of these two systems. Adam Smith (1723–90) is generally recognized as the first economist. He was also a moral philosopher, and truly knowledgeable in many fields. Smith did not have much to say about the environment in his *Wealth of Nations* (1776), but for his followers, the impact of scarce natural resources on economic development was crucial. Thomas Malthus (1766–1834) first set out to formalize the implications of exponential population growth, coupled with linear growth in food output, for standards of living. In Mathus's world, rising living standards caused the working classes to breed more rapidly! Eventually food demand would outstrip food supply, and war, disease, or famine would occur. Population would crash, before restarting its exponential growth once food production per head recovered. It is not surprising, given this picture, that economics became known as the dismal science, since the only equilibrium situation was one of subsistence wages. Malthus's model was overly simplistic, since it ignored many of the factors we now see as important, such as technological progress. His predictions have not come true in general, but they had a great influence on later thinkers, including Darwin and Keynes. Chapter 10 makes use of Malthus's ideas in the context of rainforests.

David Ricardo's work (1772–1823) led to a similar long-run prediction as Malthus, although at a more general level. Ricardo made use of the concept of diminishing marginal returns: as wages rose above subsistence levels and population increased, the rise in food demand caused agriculture to expand onto land of lower and lower quality. Since food prices would have to rise to cover the increasing costs of producing on less and less fertile land, those farmers growing on the most fertile land would earn a profit, or rent, as the difference between price and production cost. The distributional implications were profound: as food prices rose, workers got poorer and poorer, whilst landlords earned higher and higher rents.

Summing up, Ricardo and Malthus put forward two different explanations for increasing scarcity. For Malthus, the problem was that we have a fixed amount of natural resources (land) but increasing demands on them. For Ricardo, the most important fact was that as demand for food rose, the average productivity of land fell and the cost of producing food rose. These two views, of absolute and relative scarcity, are now referred to as *Malthusian* and *Ricardian* scarcity respectively.

Ricardo's work is still very important, for example in current work on understanding the movements of cultivation frontiers in developing countries (see Chapter 10), and the costs of global warming to the farm sector (Mendelsohn, 1997). However, his gloomy predictions did not come true due to technological progress and the development of the British Empire, which effectively greatly increased the UK's productive land base as well as expanding trade opportunities. Increasing use of fossil fuels meant transportation became faster and cheaper, which also greatly expanded world trade (Common, 1988).

Two other early economists also impact on our thinking about environmental and natural resources. These are John Stuart Mill (1806–73) and W. Stanley Jevons (1835–82). Mill's *Principles of Political Economy*, published in 1857, is now viewed as the climax of Classical economics. Mill makes clear that economic growth is a race between diminishing marginal returns and technological progress: technological progress drives down production costs as increasing Ricardian scarcity drives them up. Economic growth, through capital accumulation, results in higher living standards. But Mill saw natural resources as productive (land for food, mines for coal), and as a direct source of utility in itself. He also suggested that economies would eventually evolve into a steady state, where growth ceased. This idea of a stationary long-run equilibrium was in keeping with theories of natural science at the time Mill was writing, and have become very influential in, for example, the work of ecological economists such as Daly. In the steady state, Mill saw it as important that we had not completely devastated the environment in the pursuit of growth:

Nor is there much satisfaction in contemplating the world with nothing left to the spontaneous action of nature: with every rood of land brought into cultivation and . . . every flowery waste ploughed up . . . If the earth must lose that great portion of its pleasantness . . . for the mere purpose of enabling it to support a larger population . . . then I hope (they) will content to be stationary long before necessity compels them to it.' (Mill, 1857, quoted in Common, 1988).

Jevons is usually credited as being one of the first neoclassical economists, in that he helped introduce the marginal analysis that enabled economics to become systematic and rigorous in its approach. Jevons was also concerned about the implications of limited non-renewable resource inputs for economic growth. Coal was the most important natural resource powering the British Industrial Revolution. As more and more coal was dug up, both Jevons and Mill worried that it would become more expensive to extract since mines would have to be dug deeper and deeper, increasing labour costs per ton. This is an application of the law of diminishing returns from land to resource deposits, and is an example of the concept of Ricardian scarcity. Jevons indeed viewed limited resource stocks as a great threat to UK development, as his work *The Coal Question* (1865) made clear.

With few exceptions, economists then turned their attentions away from the natural environment, and became entirely focused on building up the body of theory now known as neoclassical economics. The principal aim of this endeavour was to explain economic phenomena from a single, unified rational basis. This monistic approach was in contrast to the development of ecology, from Haekel in the 1860s. Important exceptions to the ignoring of environmental and resource issues in economics in this period include Hotelling (1931), who developed a theory of how non-renewable resource stocks should be exploited (see Chapter 14), which forms the backbone of most modern work. Hotelling's rule is that, if owners treated resource deposits as capital, the optimal extraction rate was one where the rate of return from exploiting the resource was equal to the interest rate, since this is the opportunity cost of capital. In the simplest version of the model, this implies resource rents rising over time at a rate equal to the interest rate. The other important piece of work in this period was by Pigou in his *Economics of Welfare* (1920). Pigou's work was important because it set out the problem of pollution as one of externalities (see Chapter 2), which was easily solvable by putting the right price on pollution by taxing emissions. This approach has also been hugely influential.

The upsurge in the development of environmental and natural resource economics partly began as a response to the *Limits to Growth* report, which came out in 1972. The impact of this report, produced by a systems dynamics group at MIT, is now hard to imagine. Many people then were shocked to be told that a complex computer model of the world economic system was predicting the collapse of this system in the near future. This collapse would come about through a shortage of natural resources, population growth leading to starvation, and increasing pollution resulting from initially increasing output. The feedback loops incorporated into the model meant that even if the world escaped doom through one route (say, if non-renewable resource constraints were relaxed), collapse would swiftly follow through another, say pollution). The principal implication of the Limits to Growth model was that the environment imposed very clear limits on development, and that there was a trade-off to be made between economic growth and human survival. This message found echoes in other reports published around this period, such as Goldsmith (1973) and Ehrlich and Ehrlich (1970), and earlier work such as Rachel Carson (1962). However, the Limits to Growth model was roundly criticized by economists as being 'Malthus with a computer' (Cole *et al.*, 1973). The main criticism was that the model produced obvious but very unlikely conclusions, since it incorporated an exponential growth in demand for food and consumer goods, yet had limited resource stocks to produce these with. Moreover, the absence of prices meant no rationing mechanism was present which could curtail demand or encourage new supply as scarcity increased. The model was thus bound to predict collapse.

Arguments over the Limits to Growth, rising concerns over resource scarcity generally, and increasing environmental awareness may all have contributed to the growth in environmental and natural resource economics (ENRE) as a discipline, perhaps best dated from the founding of the *Journal of Environmental Economics and Management* by Alan Kneese and Ralph d'Arge in 1974. Kneese and d'Arge had already, along with Ayres, worked on the application of the material balance principle to pollution control economics (see below). ENRE as a body of theory and methods has now greatly expanded in scope, whilst retaining its strong links with conventional economics. On the whole, the discipline is based on rational choice theory and the concept of market success and failure, linked to an understanding of how environmental systems interact with economic systems (feedback links). ENRE has followed the leads of Pigou, Hotelling, and Gordon (1954) in terms of pollution and resource issues. Another focus has been on applying cost-benefit analysis to environmental issues, which has necessitated the development of non-market valuation methods (Chapter 3). On the whole, the conclusions that emerge from this literature are that environmental issues do not change the way we do economics: environmental problems can be adequately addressed with conventional economic tools. Moreover, environmental problems can be best solved by a combination of allocating property rights, pricing, and technological progress.

A somewhat different view of how economics is best applied to the environment has emerged through the development of ecological economics. This places more emphasis on feedbacks and environmental constraints, and less emphasis on rational choice and on pricing solutions to market failure. The development of ecological economics had much in common with the development of ENRE, dating from the work of authors such Daly, Ayres, Geogescu-Roegen, and Boulding in the 1960s and 1970s. These authors emphasized the implications of physical limits and laws for analysis of the interactions between economic and environmental systems. Kneese, Ayres, and d'Arge (1970) pointed out the importance to economic systems of the first law of thermodynamics, sometimes called the *mass-balance principle*. This states that, in a closed system, matter, like energy, can neither be created nor destroyed. One important implication is that if economic growth implied rising use of inputs to production, this *inevitably* implies an increase in waste which somehow must be dealt with. Geogescu-Roegen (1971) introduced the second law of thermodynamics, sometimes known as the *entropy law*, into economics. He argued that the earth resembled a closed system, which used up its finite stocks of useful energy in an irreversible way. These stocks are contained within fossil fuel deposits. The inevitable consequence, according to Geogescu-Roegen, was that the economic system would eventually and inevitably grind to a halt, unless it transferred its energy use to renewable sources. The seriousness of these predictions has since been much debated, and it is fair to say that the implications of the second law of thermodynamics are now thought of as being much less serious for the near future of the world's economy than the first law (see, for example, Ayres, 1998).

The idea that perpetual economic growth was neither inevitable nor desirable was first introduced to economics by Mill in 1857. This idea was reinvigorated within economics in the 1970s by Mishan and Daly, particularly in the latter's book *Steady State Economics*. Daly was concerned with the implications of a finite environmental capacity, which included thermodynamic considerations, for global economic growth. His principal recommendation was that economic growth should be abandoned in favour of a steady state, but also that the scale of global economic activity should be minimized, subject to certain constraints. Scale, measured as matter-energy throughput, was seen as the main determinant of environmental pressure. This view, along with those of ecologists such as Holling, Erhlich, and Odum, was very influential in the development of ecological economics in the late 1980s and 1990s. The links between economic growth and the environment, and the concept of sustainable development, have been a crucial part of this paradigm. But before we turn to a detailed consideration of sustainable development, let us turn our attention back to the question of whether economic growth is good or bad for the environment.

6.3 Growth and the Environment: The Environmental Kuznets Curve

MANY people believe that economies can grow their way out of environmental problems. Wilfred Beckerman exemplifies this position: 'the only way to attain a decent environment in most countries is to become rich' (Beckerman, 1992).

This view is supported by international institutions such as the World Bank (World Development Report, 1992), and is often called the Environmental Kuznets Curve (EKC) theory. This was named after Simon Kuznets, who in 1955 hypothesized an inverted-U-shaped relationship between the equality of income distribution and income levels. A similar relationship is claimed to exist between income levels and environmental quality by proponents of the EKC hypothesis. This relationship was first identified empirically by Grossman and Krueger (1993).

The relationship between environmental quality and growth has been the focus of much work historically. For example, the 'limits to growth' school (Meadows *et al.*) argued strongly that this relationship is negative, in that economic growth is undoubtedly bad for the environment, as it leads to more resource use and more pollution. This is a materials balance view of the world, which allows for no negative feedback loops. The EKC hypothesis suggests otherwise. In the EKC literature, growth is usually measured as the change in income (GNP) per capita. Environmental quality is commonly measured by (i) individual pollutant emissions, (ii) by an index of pollutants, or (iii) using changes in ambient air/water quality. Most empirical EKCs are

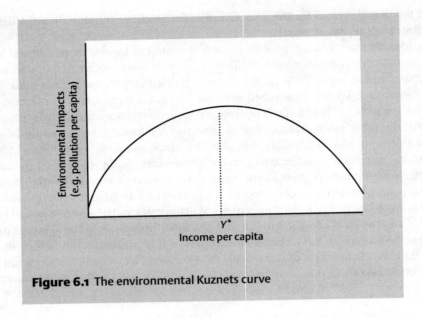

Figure 6.1 The environmental Kuznets curve

estimated for a single pollutant or ambient quality measure, with environmental impacts often being expressed as per capita amounts too.

The EKC hypothesis states that as per capita incomes grow, environmental impacts rise, hit a maximum, and then decline. This implies an 'inverted-U' shape, as shown in Figure 6.1. Two parts of the curve can be identified, before and after a turning point at Y^*. Up to Y^* emissions (say) are rising, and environmental quality is falling. Why?

- Economic growth results in an increasing use of resources and land clearance; this gives rise to an increase in waste.
- If a country starts from an early development stage as an agricultural economy, then industrialization (the Industrial Revolution) also leads to an increase in emissions, as manufacturing takes over from agriculture as the dominant economic activity.

After Y^*, though, emissions fall and environmental quality rises. Why?

- There is an increasing demand for environmental quality as incomes go up. This leads to an increase in government protection of the environment, and increasing green consumerism.
- Technological improvements over time make production per unit of output cleaner.
- Changes in the structure of the economy occur, such as moves from manufacturing to service sector or high-tech industries.
- Increasing scarcity of 'environmental quality' drives up its relative price, and this means less is 'consumed', and more is preserved.

Box 6.2 An EKC Example from the Literature

A recent paper by Cole, Rayner, and Bates looked for EKC-relationships between income and a range of environmental quality measures. Their main conclusions were that 'meaningful' EKCs only existed for local air pollutants, whereas for global pollutants either levels rise consistently with income, or turning points are extremely high or very uncertain. They also found that urban air quality responded more quickly to rising incomes than total emissions, whilst transport-generated local air pollution responded more slowly than emissions from other sources. Their results are based on data on income and environmental quality measures for up to eighty-eight countries, over varying time-periods between 1960 and 1992. The pollutants include NO_x, SO_x, PM_{10}, methane, CO, CO_2, and CFCs.

For *local* pollutants such as CO and NO_2, turning points (that is, the level of income at which emissions start to decline) were around $9,900 and $14,700 respectively in 1985 US$s. These figures can be compared with mean per capita incomes of $17,945 in the USA, $12,724 in the UK, $1,282 in India, and $408 in Chad. The implication is that we expect emissions of these pollutants to be falling in rich countries but still rising in poor ones (see Fig. 6.1). For carbon dioxide, however, the turning point was well outside the range of observed income at $62,700. For CFCs and methane, income seemed to be a rather unimportant cause of variations. Finally, three other indicators of environmental pressures were included: traffic volume, total energy use, and per capita values of municipal waste. These all rose continuously with income: in other words, no turning points could be identified.

Looked at in a dynamic perspective, the EKC thus implies a hierarchy of needs: first people want food and shelter; later on they demand amenity too. Or, to put it another way, first of all we protect ourselves from nature, and only later do we protect nature from ourselves. Figure 6.1 also shows the implications of the Limits to Growth view of development: environmental damages just keep rising with income (see Box 6.2).

6.3.1 Empirical evidence for the EKC hypothesis

What evidence exists to support the EKC theory?

Empirical evidence *for* the EKC has been found in a number of studies, mainly for local and regional pollutants. These include those looking at SO_2, urban emissions of particulates, and hazardous waste sites. The level of income per capita where the 'turning point' is reached (Y^* in Figure 6.1) varies across these studies. For example Grossman and Krueger (1995) found a turning point for SO_2 and particulates at $4,000–$6,000/year GNP/capita, when using air-quality data from around the world. In contrast, Panayotou (1995) found a turning point of $823/capita for deforestation. Others, though, find empirical evidence *against* the EKC hypothesis. This seems often to be the case for CO_2 and other global/long-term pollutants, as well as for solid waste.

For example, Cole *et al.* (1997) found no EKC for traffic, nitrates or methane, whilst Horvath (1997) discovered continually rising energy use with per capita income for 114 countries. Other researchers have found that the turning point is so high that it is irrelevant: Holtz-Eakin and Selden (1995) found a turning point for CO_2 that was $8 million/per capita!

Why are there differences in these empirical findings? These could be due to three factors. First, the nature of the pollutants studied. EKCs seem more likely to exist for local and regional pollutants (such as SO_2 and particulates) and less likely to exist for global and 'hard to spot' pollutants like CO_2. Second, other factors also drive emission levels. These factors have been found to include trade (the degree of protection); political freedom (e.g. such as measured by an index of civil liberties); and the effect of economic growth (scale of economy) independently of income per capita. Third, that for some countries and some pollutants, we are not rich enough yet to be 'over the hump'.

We might imagine a debate between a critic of the EKC hypothesis and a supporter going something like the following:

Critic: 'Although total incomes can rise with economic growth, incomes per capita might not rise if population is growing. Population changes are a very important part of environmental pressures.'

Supporter: 'Ah, but higher levels of income usually result in a slowing down of population growth rates.'

Critic: 'Not all technological change reduces environmental degradation; for example, new "exotic" pollutants may be introduced.'

Supporter: 'Quit whining! On the whole, the trends are good.'

Critic: 'The demand for increasing environmental quality argument only works for obvious, local impacts (such as smog and SO_2), but not for either (i) subtle, hard-to-notice impacts, (ii) global impacts, (iii) far-in-the-future impacts, or (iv) hard-to abate wastes.'

Supporter: 'That is a potential problem, although faster growth will give us more resources to counter these problems. We need to keep an eye on things, and intervene where necessary.'

Critic: 'At the world level, there are awkward problems over whose environmental quality and whose income we are measuring. Also at world level, the fact that the UK has got cleaner is partly because we have imported "dirty" products from elsewhere (e.g. coal-mining): but *someone* has to do it!'

Supporter: 'Yes, but trade is good,[1] so we don't want to restrict it on environmental grounds. Trade restrictions only end up hurting people more in the long run.'

Critic: 'The world has a limited carrying capacity and thresholds for total global emissions: once these thresholds/capacities are breached, environmental *impacts* must increase, and perhaps exponentially. Such dynamic "surprises" mean that the EKC is a poor policy guide.'

Supporter: 'Well, that means we should act with care and not rely on the EKC to sort all

---

[1] She has obviously read ahead to Ch. 8!

our environmental problems out. We probably need government to intervene in more difficult cases.'

Critic: 'Where environmental effects are irreversible, what if we reach the turning point after these have been triggered?'

Supporter: 'That is one of the difficult cases I referred to above.'

And so on. Concluding, the EKC hypothesis is an interesting empirical phenomenon which we can observe for some pollutants. We should probably not rely on it as a guide for how we manage the environmental impacts of growth: we would also be unwise to rely on economic growth to solve all of our environmental problems on its own, since solving them typically requires a revision of property rights or a correction of prices. In a sense, economic growth is both the cause of and cure for environmental problems: growth increases our demands on the environment, but growth also gives us the time and money to do something about its undesirable side-effects. In other words, even with economic growth, market failures still remain (see Chapters 2 and 3). Blindly promoting economic growth as the remedy for all ills is unwise: we need growth with accountability, and we need to keep our eyes open.

6.4 Broadening the Issue: The Economics of Sustainable Development

6.4.2 Definitions of sustainable development

'Sustainable development' is now a popular phrase. But what exactly does it mean? That is a difficult question to answer, since sustainable development (SD from now on) means different things to different people. People place differing emphases on different aspects of the rather vague notion which is SD. The best-known definition is that given by the Bruntland Commission in 1987: 'development that meets the needs of present generations without compromising the ability of future generations to meet their own needs.'

Another definition was offered by the Norwegian economist, Ger Asheim: 'A requirement to our generation to manage the resource base such that the average quality of life we ensure ourselves can potentially be shared by all future generations.' As may be seen, this has strong links with the material discussed earlier in the chapter, namely whether continual growth and development is both possible and desirable.

Two common features of these definitions of SD are (i) fairness across generations and (ii) fairness within generations. SD is thus principally an equity, rather than efficiency issue. However, the bigger is the economic pie (broadly defined as 'quality of life'), the more of it is there is to go around: and economic growth, as we know, can raise the average level of well-being. Economic growth can be encouraged by efficient resource allocation. There is thus a potential complementarity between promoting both efficiency and equity here. Thinking of this in another way, we can all be poor together, but would probably choose not to be.

Economists' views on what constitutes a sustainable development path for an economy over time may be divided into two broad groups. The first (the outcome approach) is concerned with how the economic process affects well-being directly. These ends-based definitions include non-declining utility per capita, and non-declining consumption per capita. Within a neoclassical model of growth it is possible to investigate whether such a sustainable time-path exists. In Figure 6.2 we show the typical result that emerges; that an economy faces a choice between an optimal rate of consumption over time, and a sustainable rate (for details, see Pezzey, 1998). As can be seen, the optimal path of consumption over time (essentially, that which maximizes the discounted value of all future consumption) starts to fall after some period t*. That is clearly not sustainable, since people living after time t* will be worse off than people living before it. This abstracts from the problem of fairness within a current time-period, though.

The second approach ('the opportunity approach') to an economic definition of SD is to consider the means which are available to society to generate well-being or consumption: its resources. 'Resources' consist of physical stocks and the technology

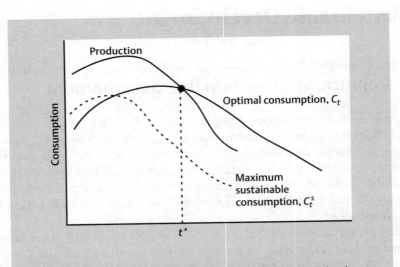

Note: In this simple economy, optimal consumption reaches a peak at t^* and then starts to fall. Production starts to fall before this. Maximum *sustainable* consumption (the highest level of consumption that can be sustained in any period) is always less than optimal consumption. Having a sustainable level of consumption therefore requires us to reduce actual consumption to below its optimal level. For detailed explanation, see Pezzey (1998).

Figure 6.2 Sustainable versus unsustainable growth

which we use to exploit them. Economists have thought about SD from this view-point in terms of capital. Three forms of capital may be distinguished:

Man-made capital, Km: this is the 'capital' that most economics students are familiar with. It is comprised of the results of past production, as the excess of output over consumption. Km includes machinery, roads, bridges, phone networks, satellites etc., and may be used up in the production of consumption goods and services. This depreciation needs to be offset with new investment or else the stock of Km will decline.

Human capital, Kh: this is labour, and includes all skills and knowledge embodied within people. The stock of Kh can also depreciate (for example, if unemployed people lose their skills), and can be added to through training and education. Julian Simon (1981) has called human capital 'the ultimate resource'.

Natural capital, Kn: natural capital comprises all gifts of nature, and so includes renewable and non-renewable energy and material resources; clean air and water; nutrient and carbon cycles; and biodiversity. Natural capital can clearly be depreciated when, for example, a non-renewable resource such as oil is used up, or when a species dies out, or when air pollution increases. Investments in Kn would include forest replanting and restocking of fisheries.

An absolutely crucial aspect of the concept of Kn is how it is aggregated. How can barrels of oil be added to hectares of forest? Or numbers of wolves to shoals of herring? Some authors have suggested an energy unit of account to permit this aggregation, but the most commonly thought of is money. If money values could be given to all elements of Kn, then we could aggregate them into a total value. Several problems exist here, however: first, although market values exist for some elements of Kn (oil, herring), these may understate true social values; second, no market values exist for a vast range of Kn, so they would have to be estimated using environmental valuation, a colossal task; and third, a money value measure conflates how much of a physical stock exists with how valuable each unit is. Thus one blue whale for which people were WTP \$10 billion has the same aggregate value as 10,000 blue whales worth £1,000 each. If Kn cannot be aggregated in this way, then it would be necessary to instead aggregate groups of elements in physical terms: for example, all woodlands in a country; all fish stocks of a certain fish; all rivers of a certain quality.

Starting from these three types of capital, two different chance-approach definitions of sustainability can be offered. The first, which has become known as 'weak sustainability', requires the total capital stock K, where $K = Kn + Kh + Km$, to be non-declining.[2] This permits natural capital to be run down (through using oil stocks, say) so long as human and man-made capital are increased sufficiently. This view clearly presumes that we can aggregate Kn, Kh, and Km in the same units; and that they are substitutes for each other. The Hartwick rule and the genuine savings measure, both discussed below, rely on this view of sustainable development. An alternative view has been to maintain that SD requires us to keep the stock of Kn as non-declining. This might be either in monetary or in physical terms. This view has been called

---

[2] See Gowdy and McDaniel (1999) for an interesting critique of the concept of weak sustainability.

'strong sustainability', and derives primarily from the view that reductions in Kn cannot be substituted for by increases in Kh or Km. A somewhat different position is taken by those who focus on 'critical' natural capital only. Critical natural capital is the subset of Kn which is either (i) essential for human survival and/or (ii) not substitutable for by increases in either other elements of Kn, or in Kh or Km. An example might be the natural climate and atmospheric composition regulation functions of the earth. Figure 6.3 illustrates these three concepts of what sustainability requires.

Sustainable development thus has two economic meanings. In the outcome approach, it means that consumption or utility do not decline over time. In the chance approach, it means we pass on to future generations at least as much capital as we have, so that they have no less a chance than us to be happy.

6.4.3 Sustainability rules?

A great myth in economics is the 'free market', since almost all markets operate under some kind of rules imposed by governments. These rules may be introduced for a wide variety of reasons, such as protecting the environment, supporting producer incomes, or keeping down prices to consumers. What kind of interventions by governments might be beneficial, though, in the cause of sustainability? We have already seen that the efficient time-path of consumption is unlikely to be sustainable,

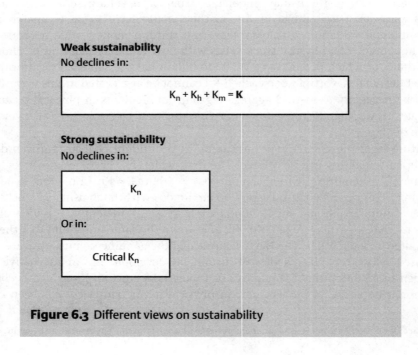

Weak sustainability
No declines in:

$$K_n + K_h + K_m = \mathbf{K}$$

Strong sustainability
No declines in:

$$K_n$$

Or in:

Critical K_n

Figure 6.3 Different views on sustainability

since consumption eventually falls.[3] This efficient path comes about through consumers maximizing the present value of future consumption. Generalizing, if the market system results in efficient outcomes through utility and profit-maximization, then it is unlikely to result in a sustainable outcome. With regard to natural capital stock-based definitions of SD, we have already shown (Chapter 2) how the market system tends to lead to the overuse of environmental resources; this will mean Kn falling over time in terms of its physical stocks, whilst the lack of a market value for many environmental resources and service flows means that this increasing scarcity is not corrected for, even at the level of efficiency, by the market. However, the market might lead to enough offsetting investment in Km and Kh even if Kn was falling over time, so that weak sustainability might be achieved even if strong sustainability was not.

But what could the government impose on markets if we want to attain a sustainable pattern of development? Four possibilities have been suggested:

1. Value all environmental goods and services at their correct prices.
2. The 'Hartwick rule'.
3. Daly's 'operational principles.'
4. Rules set in terms of natural capital itself.

Let us now consider each of these in some detail.

1. *Value all environmental goods and services at their correct prices.* As already explained, one reason why environmental resources are overused is the lack of correct prices being attached to their use. For example, a factory pays no price to use the air as a waste-disposal facility, and thus has an insufficient incentive to reduce pollution. A popular perception is that one of the main barriers to attaining SD is that too great a burden is placed on the world's ecosystems by economic activity (too much pollution, too much forest clearance). Placing the correct prices on the environment through eco-taxes, for example, might be thought to move us closer to SD, since the environment would then be less exploited. However, whilst such a move would move us in the direction of a more efficient use of the environment, and would increase the size of the economic pie (and would in all probability reduce the burdens we place on the environment), it would not necessarily address the fairness aspects of SD (Howarth and Norgaard, 1992). An economically efficient use of resources is necessarily not the same as a sustainable use of resources.

2. *The Hartwick rule.* The Hartwick rule is closely related to the idea of weak sustainability, although it precedes it historically. John Hartwick showed that an economy dependent on a non-renewable resource as one input to production could have constant consumption levels over time, provided that it followed a simple rule: reinvest all rents (the difference between price and marginal cost per unit extracted) from exploiting the resource in man-made capital. This 'zero net investment' rule can be shown to result in non-declining consumption under a range of circumstances (Hartwick, 1997). Under certain conditions, this allows the total capital stock to be held

---

[3] Although it might just be, if the rate of technological progress is fast enough, if the discount rate is low enough, and if population growth rates are low enough.

constant, and thus consumption to be sustained. The Hartwick rule is in fact the basis for the genuine savings measure of SD discussed in the next section. If we adopt a broader notion of capital, then the rents could equally well be invested in human capital. Two problems exist with the rule. First, it assumes that utility depends on consumption only, and that the environment is only important as a source of inputs to production. If the state of the environment is a direct determinant of utility, then the rule does hold *utility* constant even if consumption is not falling. Second, the rule only works if the various forms of capital are perfect substitutes for each other. We have already mentioned that this may not be true.

3. *Daly's 'operational principles'*. Herman Daly put forward a set of 'operational principles' for achieving SD. These are:

- Renewable resources: keep harvest rates less than or equal to the growth rate. This has long been a principle of fisheries economics.

- Non-renewable resources: each time-period, invest sufficient of the income from extracting the resource in renewable substitutes, and make only the residual available to fund current consumption. A sufficient level of investment here is one which, by the time when the non-renewable resource is (economically?) exhausted, a renewable substitute has been built up which has the same productive capacity as the non-renewable resource did at the time extraction started. This proposal originated with another World Bank economist, El Sarafy, but is difficult to implement in practice since this involves forecasting when the non-renewable resource will be exploited, and how quickly a renewable substitute can be developed. For some non-renewable resources it may be hard, with current technology, to imagine a renewable substitute.

- For pollutants, make sure that in any time-period emissions do not exceed the assimilative capacity of the receiving environment. Whilst this seems a sensible rule, it again has problems in that (i) for many pollutants, the assimilative capacity is effectively zero (does this mean no processes which involve the release of such pollutants should be allowed?); (ii) for many pollutants, the assimilative capacity varies both temporally and spatially, which complicates implementation of the rule; (iii) if emission rates are currently below assimilative capacity, should emissions be increased? In fact, pollution control policy is often based on the notion of assimilative capacity, for example water pollution control in the UK.

- Controls should also be placed on the scale of the world economy. Scale refers to the total matter–energy throughput of the economy, and in Daly's view increasing scale has resulted in increasing threats to human welfare. Price controls do not do so well in terms of controlling scale of activity (since it is an issue of increasing absolute rather than relative scarcity), so Daly advocates tighter quantity controls, for example on total pollution emissions, energy use, resource use, and, most controversially, population. What the welfare *losses* from such controls would be is not investigated.

Daly does not mention any rules relating to the stock of human capital, which is a clear weakness in his approach.

4. *Rules based on the natural capital stock.* The 'strong sustainability' view is that SD requires a non-declining stock of natural capital, somehow defined. It is clear that this could be a very restrictive rule for a country to impose on itself. If, for example, no trade-offs are allowed between different components of Kn (wetlands, forests, etc.), then no economic action which depleted the stock of any component could be allowed, no matter how large the economic benefits. A way around the potentially high forgone benefits this implies is the idea of *shadow projects* (Pearce, Makandya, and Barbier, 1990; Farrow, 1998). This would require any action that reduces the stock of, say, wetlands, to be offset by a physical project which generates an offsetting replacement (by creating a new wetland). Costing in such a replacement would be an essential part of cost-benefit analysis. However, considerable practical and theoretical difficulties exist here: for example, if a 500-year old oak forest is threatened with destruction by a development project, does a newly planted oak forest of equivalent size provide an acceptable offset? What if the new wood is planted on an area of heathland? Now the area of heathland has fallen, so an offset must be created for this. Finally, for many environmental effects, no physical substitute exists (for example, if a unique national park is threatened). Does this imply no development is allowed which threatens unique assets?

One answer to this question is provided by the concept of the safe minimum standard (SMS). The SMS is usually thought of as a means of assessing a proposed change which threatens wildlife or their habitats. It involves first identifying the minimum viable population or habitat size for a population, or minimum required stock of some other natural asset. Management alternatives for safeguarding this minimum are then identified, and cost estimates made of these actions. If a proposed development threatens the SMS, then decision-makers are presumed to rule against it, unless the social opportunity costs of so doing are judged to be too high. For example, Berrens *et al.* (1998) describe the means by which an SMS for endangered fish populations in the Colorado River is identified, and the costs of the management actions needed to defend these SMS values estimated. In this case, this involved costing restrictions on water abstraction and hydroelectric power station operation in order to maintain minimum in-stream flows.

The most obvious problem with the SMS principle is the difficulty of identifying how society should decide whether the cost of defending the SMS is 'too high'. This might be through a referendum or decision-maker judgement, although Berrens *et al.* (1998) suggest that if costs in terms of lost output lie within the range of historical fluctuations, then the SMS should be automatically safeguarded. A positive slant on this is to say that the SMS approach could increase democratic decision-making over the environment. Other problems with the SMS include extending the concept to elements of Kn other than wildlife populations and their habitats; and the difficulty in identifying safe minimum population/habitat sizes (which might well change over time). The approach also involves reversing the normal burden of proof in development cases, placing this on the developer rather than the conservationist (Berrens *et al.*, 1998).

6.5 Measuring 'Sustainability'

A⊤ the Earth Summit in Rio in 1992, the world's nations agreed to set about pro-ducing annual statistics on the sustainability of their economies. This has resulted in the production of a very large set of proposals for *indicators* of SD, for example by the United Nations (UN, 1995). In the UK, the government produced a discussion document in 1996 which outlined 120 different indicators to assess if Britain was on a sustainable track; this was superseded in 1998 by a revised set of thirteen indicators, the so-called 'Skylark Index', so-called because numbers of farmland birds are one indicator included. Given that SD is such a broad concept, it is unlikely that any one measure would tell us all we want to know about the sustainability of the economic-environmental system. Also, given the complexity of this system and the uncertainties that pervade its interactions, it is probably better to talk of indicators of system performance, rather than exact measures.

Indicators of sustainability have been developed from a number of different discip-linary perspectives, including economics, ecology, politics, and sociology. We now discuss two put forward by economists: green national accounts and genuine savings.

6.5.1 Green national accounts

A large literature has recently emerged on whether the System of National Accounts can be transformed to produce both a better welfare measure, and a possible indica-tor of SD (see Hanley, 2000, for a review). GNP has traditionally been thought of as a welfare measure, and as a measure of national income. By relating this to the idea of 'income' put forward by Sir John Hicks in 1930, some authors have sought to produce an indicator of SD. Hicks's view on income was that it represented that portion of the value of output which could be consumed in any year without reducing one's wealth (potential for future consumption). This clearly has resonances with some definitions of SD. In this sense, then, an adjusted national income figure would tell us the max-imum level of consumption which was sustainable in any year, in the sense that it leaves enough of a residual to be invested which preserves the national capital stock or national wealth (here, wealth is interpreted as the discounted value of future consumption). If adjusted GNP were rising, then an economy would have the poten-tial of higher sustainable consumption levels; as such, rising 'green' GNP would be an indicator of sustainability.

Why, though, is it necessary to adjust the conventional accounts? This is because, as noted in Box 6.1, these accounts omit many of the inputs which the environment provides to the economy, since they are unpriced by the market. When a country depletes its natural capital, this is typically ignored in the national accounts, even though depreciation of man-made capital is allowed for (to convert from GNP to net national product, NNP). Calculating green NNP, the value of interest, thus involves correcting for these omissions.

Two approaches have been taken to working out what corrections should be made. One, associated with Robert Repetto and the UN, involves a series of *ad hoc* deductions for depreciation in natural capital stocks, for example, to allow for deforestation, groundwater depletion, and soil erosion in Mexico. The second includes the same effects, but tries to value them in a way consistent with economic theory. This latter approach draws heavily on a paper by Martin Weitzman in 1976, and involves adjustments such as:

- For non-renewable resources, deduct from NNP an amount equal to the value of annual production (less discoveries) multiplied by the difference between price and marginal costs.

- For renewable resources, annual production is first deducted from annual growth. This amount is then valued using the same (price-marginal cost) term.

- For pollution, deduct an amount equal to the change in the stock of each pollutant multiplied by its marginal abatement cost.

This would then give us a green NNP measure equal to:

$$\text{green NNP} = \text{NNP} - (p_1 - mc_1)\Delta NR - (p_2 - mc_2)\,\Delta R - v\,(\Delta S), \tag{6.2}$$

where p_1 and mc_1 are the price and marginal cost of non-renewable resources, ΔNR is the change in the stock of non-renewables; p_2 and mc_2 are the price and marginal cost of renewables, and ΔR the change in their stock; and v is the marginal cost of abatement for pollution stock S. As you can see, the three adjustments included in equation (6.2) are identical to those described in the three bullet points above, since they adjust NNP for changes in non-renewable resources, renewable resources, and pollution stocks, in that order. In practice, one would have to aggregate over many different non-renewable and renewable resource types, and over many pollutants.

There is certainly disagreement among economists of how exactly these and similar adjustments should be made (for example, over how to treat new discoveries; and over whether an amount should be added for the value of non-market environmental services). It is also true that, for the adjustments to be correct, the price and marginal cost values used should be those which result from a competitive, dynamically optimal use of resources. Well-known problems of property rights means this is unlikely to be true, especially for fisheries. There is also dispute amongst economists about whether green NNP can be used as a sustainability indicator.

6.5.2 Genuine savings

An alternative economic indicator of SD is the genuine savings concept, put forward by Pearce and Atkinson in 1993. This statistic now forms part of the World Bank's *Annual Development Report*. Genuine savings compares reinvestment in an economy with depreciation of both natural and man-made capital. It is defined as:

Box 6.3 Sustainability Measures for Scotland

Governments are increasingly trying to set their countries on a path of sustainable development often using sustainable development indicators as a key mechanism for encouraging progress towards such development. But how can sustainable development be measured and what impact do differing attitudes and policies have? A thirteen-year study, carried out in Scotland, has critically examined various sustainability indicators, taken from different disciplines (Hanley, Moffatt, Faichney, and Wilson, 1999). Given that sustainability is such a broad concept the researchers believed it impossible for one indicator to provide sufficient data for policy-makers to act on. Seven macro-level indicators were selected: **AENP**: approximate environmentally adjusted net national product (a rough estimate of the green NNP measure discussed in the main text); **GS**: genuine savings; **EF**: ecological footprint; **NPP/C**: net primary productivity relative to consumption; **ES:** environmental space; **ISEW**: the index of sustainable economic welfare, and **GPI**: genuine progress indicator.

The two economic measures have been described in the main text. The ecological footprint (**EF**) indicator compares a measure of aggregate resource use in a country with how much land would be required if all of this resource demand was to be met by home production and through the use of renewable energy. This measure tests for whether we are exporting unsustainability to other countries. The **NPP/C** indicator is closely related to ecological footprints. It draws on the ecological notion of carrying capacity, which in turn relates energy demands to energy availability. For Scotland, it can be expressed in terms of the maximum population capable of support from net primary production, given our current consumption patterns. Environmental space (**ES**) is a measure of the fairness of resource allocation and consumption worldwide. Essentially, it will tell us whether Scotland is consuming more than its 'fair share' of global resources.

Finally, the **ISEW (**index of sustainable economic welfare) and **GPI** (genuine progress indicator) indicators are somewhat *ad hoc* socio-political measures of sustainability, which have been evaluated previously over fairly long time-periods for the USA and UK. They include allowances for fairness in the existing distribution of income, as well as measures of environmental degradation, defensive expenditure, and unpaid work.

These seven macrolevel indicators selected for the study were applied to the Scottish economy over the period 1980–93. They varied according to the extent to which they were backed up by solid theory, as well as being both empirically measurable and responsive to policy change. The summary results are shown in Table 6.B3, whilst Figure 6.B3 shows the movement over time of one indicator, namely green net national product. As may be seen, for most of the period Scotland was sustainable on this measure, and the position improves over time (as the difference between AENP and consumption increases in a positive amount). Changes in oil prices over the period turn out to be important to this pattern in AENP, since depreciation of oil and gas stocks is a major part of the 'environmental adjustment' to the conventional accounts.

Since these indicators relate to different aspects of the economic-environment system, it is not surprising that a mixed message emerges. Scotland's development is sustainable in terms of the green GNP measure for example, but not so when genuine savings or ecological footprints are used. The ISEW and GPI measures show a declining level of sustainability, due in part to increasing pollution and to increasing income inequality. These indicators also cast specific light on different policy requirements—for example, on the desirability of a switch to renewable energy sources, or for greater reinvestment in Scotland's natural and man-made capital stocks.

Table 6.B3 Summary of results

Indicator	Result
AENP	Increasingly sustainable
GS	Unsustainable, but becoming less so
NPP/C	Marginally sustainable, slight improvement
EF	Marginally unsustainable, little change
ES	Copper, lead, iron, energy: unsustainable
ISEW	Unsustainable, worsening
GPI	Unsustainable, worsening

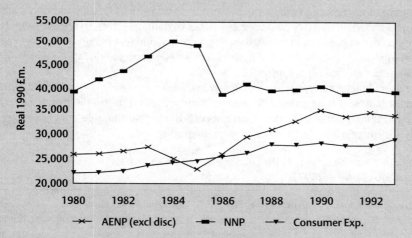

Figure 6.B3 Green net national product (AENP, excluding discoveries), net national product, and consumer expenditure for Scotland, 1980–1993

$$GS = S - \delta_m - \delta_n, \qquad (6.3)$$

where GS is genuine savings, S is total (aggregate) savings, δ_m is depreciation of man-made capital, and δ_n is depreciation of natural capital. This natural capital depreciation is typically calculated in the same manner as the environmental adjustments to NNP noted in equation (6.2), in that it includes the same components valued in the same way. To be complete, we would wish to add changes in the stock of human capital, Kh, to equation (6.3), but this would be even harder to measure. The genuine savings measure tests for weak sustainability; that is, it assumes that natural capital and man-made capital are perfect substitutes for each other. It is also an empirical test for whether a country is, on average, following the Hartwick rule. The indicator has recently been extended to allow for international trade effects (Proops *et al.*, 1999).

Genuine savings and green NNP are closely linked to each other since they are both derived from the same underlying theory. However, empirically they need not even send equal signals, as the example in Box 6.3 illustrates. In Box 6.4, we show some recent estimates of genuine savings for countries in southern Africa.

Box 6.4 Indicators of Sustainability in Africa

The World Bank now publishes annual estimates of the genuine savings (GS) measure of sustainability for a range of countries. By and large, their procedures in calculating GS follow that outlined in the main text: that is, to deduct the estimated value of depreciation in both man-made and natural capital from savings. Estimates of natural capital stock changes are, of course, highly incomplete and rather crude for the most part, tending to focus on aspects such as deforestation and soil erosion, but neglecting changes in biodiversity. As may be seen from the Table 6.B4, CO_2 damage is included, but this is based on globally averaged estimates of damage which may bear very little relation to the impact of global warming on a given country. Changes in human capital are not ignored in these calculations, as resources allocated to education (which increases human capital) are included.

The overall picture is very variable: Botswana shows a positive level of GS for 1997, whilst for Malawi it is negative. This implies that, according to this highly partial snapshot in time, Botswana's development path is more sustainable than Malawi's, which is unsustainable. All figures are given in percentages.

Table 6.B4 Genuine savings in the countries of Southern Africa (percentage of GNP in 1997)

Country	Gross domestic saving	Depreciation	Net domestic saving	Education expenditure	Resource depletion	CO_2 damage	Genuine domestic saving
Angola	27.3	6.0	21.2	2.6	20.7	0.4	2.7
Botswana	44.7	13.3	31.4	6.9	0.8	0.3	37.2
Madagascar	3.6	4.9	−1.3	2.3	0.0	0.2	0.8
Malawi	2.1	6.4	−4.3	3.2	5.4	0.2	−6.7
Mozambique	13.6	3.6	10.0	3.9	3.7	0.2	9.9
Namibia	14.2	13.8	0.4	1.7	0.6	—	1.5
South Africa	17.0	13.8	3.2	6.6	4.0	1.4	4.4
Zambia	9.8	9.9	−0.1	3.8	1.4	0.4	1.9
Zimbabwe	11.9	6.0	5.9	8.2	11.1	1.0	2.0

Source: World Bank, *World Development Indicators 1999*.

6.5.3 Other sustainability indicators

As mentioned above, indicators of sustainable development have been developed by many disciplines, including ecology. These include the net primary productivity/consumption ratio, and ecological footprints. Socio-political indicators also exist, notably the Index of Sustainable Economic Welfare. For details and examples of all of these indicators, see Moffat, Hanley, and Wilson (2000). Finally, we note that all the indicators described here are typically intended to be calculated at the national level. There is a growing literature on sustainability indicators at the regional, industry, and individual firm level, but we do not have space to discuss them.

6.6 Summary

THIS chapter has been concerned with the implications for the environment of economic growth, and the extent to which this growth causes undesirable feedbacks for people's well-being. These questions have been of interest to economists ever since Adam Smith. How to measure well-being is in itself an awkward issue: we reviewed criticisms of the 'traditional' measure of GNP, and noted some alternatives. The debate over the links between economic growth, environmental quality, and quality of life are now largely conducted under the heading of sustainable development. We reviewed how economists have interpreted this often-nebulous concept, and saw how economic indicators of sustainability can be calculated. Whilst the economic interpretation of sustainability is only one amongst many, it is at least fairly rigorous. It also recognizes that people's abilities are as important to securing sustainable development as safeguarding the environment and reinvesting in man-made capital.

References

Ayres, R. (1998). 'Ecothermodynamics: economics and the second law', *Ecological Economics* 26(2): 189–210.

Begg, D., Fischer, S., and Dorbusch, R. (1987). *Economics (2nd edn.)*. London: McGraw-Hill

Berrens, R., Brookshire, D., McKee, M., and Schmidt, C. (1998). 'Implementing the safe minimum standard', *Land Economics* 74: 147–161.

Carson, R. (1962). *Silent Spring*. London: Penguin.

Cole, H., Freeman, C., Jahoda, M. and Pavitt, K. (eds.) (1997). *Models of Doom: A Critique of the Limits to Growth*. New York: Universe Books.

Cole, M., Rayner, A., and Bates, J. (1997). 'The environmental Kuznets curve: an empirical analysis', *Environment and Development Economics* 2: 401–16.

Common, M.S. (1988). *Environmental and Resource Economics: an Introduction*. London: Longman.

Costanza, R., Cumberland, J., Daly, H., Goodland, R. and Norgaard, R. (1997). *An Introduction to Ecological Economics*. Boca Raton, Fla.: St Lucie Press.

Daly, H. (1977). *Steady State Economics*. San Francisco: W. H. Freeman.

Ehrlich, P. and Ehrlich, A. (1970). *Population, Resources and Environment*. San Francisco: W. H. Freeman.

Farrow, S. (1998). 'Environmental equity and sustainability: rejecting the Kaldor-Hicks criteria', *Ecological Economics* 27(2): 183–8.

Goldsmith, E., Allen, R., Allaby, M., Davoll, J. and Lawrence, S. (1973). *A Blueprint for Survival* (Tom Stacey Publishing).

Gordon, H.S. (1954). 'The economic theory of a common property resource: the fishery', *Journal of Political Economy* 62: 124–42.

Gowdy, J., and McDaniel, C. (1999). 'The physical destruction of Nauru: an example of weak sustainability', *Land Economics* 75(2): 333–8.

Hanley, N., Moffatt, I., Faichney, R. and Wilson, M. (1999). 'Measuring sustainability: a time series of indicators for Scotland', *Ecological Economics* 55–73.

Hartwick, J. M. (1997). 'National wealth, constant consumption and sustainable development', in H. Folmer and T. Tietenberg (eds.). *The International Yearbook of Environmental and Resource Economics*, Cheltenham: Edward Elgar.

Hotelling, H. (1931). 'The economics of exhaustible resources', *Journal of Political Economy* 39(2): 137–75.

Howarth, R., and Norgaard, R. (1992). 'Environmental valuation under sustainable development', *American Economic Review* 82 (May): 473–7.

Jevons, W. S. (1865). *The Coal Question*. Reprinted (1965) New York: A. M. Kelly.

Kneese, A, Ayres, R. and d'Arge, R. (1970). *Economics and the Environment: A Materials Balance Approach*. Baltimore: Johns Hopkins University Press.

Malthus, T. (1798). *An Essay on the Principles of Population*. Reprinted (1970). Penguin.

Meadows, D., Meadows, D., Randers, J., and Behrens, W. (1972). *The Limits to Growth*. New York: Universe Books.

Mill, J. S. (1857). *Principles of Political Economy*. London: J. W. Parker.

Moffatt, I., Hanley, N. and Wilson, M. (2000). *Measuring and Modelling Sustainable Development*. Parthenon Press.

Pearce, D., and Atkinson, G. (1993). 'Capital theory and the measurement of sustainable development: an indicator of weak sustainability' *Ecological Economics* 8(2): 103–8.

—— Makandya, A., and Barbier, E. (1990). *Sustainable Development*. Cheltenham: Edward Elgar.

Pezzey, J. (1998). 'Sustainability constraints', *Land Economics* 73(4), 448–66.

Pigou, A. C. (1920). *The Economics of Welfare* London: Macmillan.

Proops, J., Atkinson, G., Schlotheim, B., and Simone, S. (1999). 'International trade and the sustainability footprint: a practical criterion for its assessment', *Ecological Economics* 28: 75–97.

Ricardo, D. (1817). *The Principles of Political Economy*. Reprint (1926). Everyman.

Simon, J. (1981). *The Ultimate Resource*. Oxford: Martin Robertson.

United Nations (1995). *Indicators of Sustainable Development*, Commission for Sustainable Development. New York: United Nations.

UNDP (1990). *Human Development Report*, UN Development Programme. Oxford: Oxford University Press.

Further Reading

- Asheim, G.B. (1994). 'Net national product as an indicator of sustainability', *Scandinavian Journal of Economics* 96(2): 257–65.

- Beckerman, W. (1994). 'Sustainable development: is it a useful concept?', *Environmental Values* 3: 191–209.

- Cabenza-Gutes, M. (1996). 'The concept of weak sustainability', *Ecological Economics* 17: 147–56.

- Crocker, T. (1999). 'A short history of environmental and resource economics', in J van den Bergh (ed.) *Handbook of Environmental and Resource Economics*. Cheltenham: Edward Elgar.

- Hanley, N. (2000). 'Macroeconomic measures of sustainability: a survey and a synthesis' *Journal of Economic Surveys* 13: 1–30.

- MacDonald, D., Hanley, N., and Moffatt, I. (1999). 'Applying the concept of natural capital criticality to regional resource management', *Ecological Economics* 29: 73–87.

- Moffatt, I. (1996). *Sustainable Development: Principles, Analysis and Policies*. New York: Parthenon.

- Rothman, D., and de Bruyn, S. (1998). 'Probing into the environmental Kuznets curve', *Ecological Economics* 25(2): 143–6.

- Stern, D. (1998). 'Progress on the environmental Kuznets curve?', *Environment and Development Economics* 3: 173–96.

Also see the special issue of *Land Economics* on 'Defining sustainability', November 1997.

Chapter 7
Strategic Interaction

In this chapter we study strategic interactions between economic agents in conflicts over environmental resources. To this end:

- We review the origins of game theory.
- Take the prisoner's dilemma game and show how it can be applied to an open-access fishery problem and a pollution problem.
- Look at what might happen when the 'players' in a game play repeatedly through time and can form long-term agreements.
- Analyse the incentives for cooperation.
- Finally, we analyse cooperation and competition in transboundary pollution problems such as those that arise due to acid rain.

7.1 Introduction

At all levels, local, international, and global, environmental policy involves arguments and disputes between individuals and groups. Like chess-players, the 'players' in environmental conflicts develop sophisticated strategies which account for what they expect their opponents to do, what they know, and what they think their opponents know about their preferences and the issue at hand. To understand this type of conflict and how it might be resolved requires a theory of strategic interaction between *small numbers* of decision-makers. Conventional neoclassical economics predicts how markets and firms behave in the extreme cases of perfect competition, a large number of producers, and monopoly, just one producer. In 1944 a mathematician von Neumann and an economist Morgernstern (1944) introduced the theory of games to economics. Their models have revolutionized the analysis of strategic interactions between decision-makers (Dixit and Nalebuff, 1991) from both normative (that is what decision-makers *should* do) and positive (what decision makers *actually* do) perspectives.

Environmental and natural resource economists have only quite recently recognized the potential of game theory as a means of analysing and understanding a range of key environmental problems. One of the first applications to natural resources was Levhari and Mirman (1980) who model the interactions of two countries disputing the exploitation of a fishing stock, a so-called 'fish war'. The 'war' is waged through fisheries policies where a country can decide to be more or less conservationist in its setting of fishing quotas depending on how conservationist it expects other countries to be. Countries impose an externality on each other by making fish more expensive to catch. Maler (1989) considers international negotiations to reduce the level of acid rain. When countries negotiate internationally over the total levels of SO_2 emissions to be permitted, there is a strategic interaction where countries benefit from cooperation, but a mechanism has to be found to encourage those countries responsible for the externality to agree to a reduction in SO_2. A third example, Agenda 21 negotiated in Rio de Janeiro in 1992 aims to protect biodiversity (Barrett, 1994a). Biodiversity represents a global public good, but those countries who benefit most are the developed nations while the less developed countries in tropical regions are host to most of the biodiversity. The issue is how an agreement can be reached which provides an adequate incentive for these countries to reduce the rate of biodiversity loss. Finally, the 1998 Kyoto Conference on reducing carbon emissions represented a compromise agreement between countries to reduce CO_2 (Ulph and Ulph, 1994; also see Chapter 12). The problem faced by the conference was to find an agreement which satisfied the diverse interests of the countries involved. Countries formed alliances with other countries with common aims. They also used bargaining strategies which disguised what they might accept as a final solution.

In addition to *international* policy issues, game theory has been applied to analyse national environmental problems, such as the interaction between producers over a common property resource such as common land grazing (Mesterton-Gibbons, 1989) and the interaction between regulators and the regulated in pollution control (Batabayal, 1995). The key element of these problems is that the actions of one decision-maker affects the welfare of another. Problems of this general type are the subject matter of game theory.

7.2 Game theory

7.2.1 Basic concepts

The elements of game theory are that a decision-maker or player has preferences over a set of outcomes, these preferences drive the choices made, but the actual outcome depends upon what the other players in the game have chosen to do. Consider the example of two fishermen who share the fishing rights in a lake and who both want to maximize profit. The fishermen are the players and the choice they have is the level of fishing effort, but one fisherman can only catch the fish left by the other. Thus their level of profit is affected by the choice made by the other fisherman.

Game theory has developed two distinct approaches to analysing such problems. *Non-cooperative* game theory concerns how players choose strategies, whilst *cooperative* game theory concerns how players choose their allies. Non-cooperative game theory can be further classified as *static* and *dynamic* games, where static games have only one 'turn' and dynamic games have a number of stages through time. Information, or the lack of it, determines how the game is played: games of *imperfect information* are those where the players are uncertain about the outcome of a particular combination of choices. For instance in the fishing problem, uncertainty about the fish stock and harvest means that the profit is uncertain. Games of *incomplete information* are where players are uncertain about the preferences of other players. For instance a regulator may be uncertain about the cost to a firm of complying with pollution regulation, and therefore be uncertain about an appropriate level of monitoring. Modern game theory is based on some advanced mathematics and a general analysis is beyond the scope of this book. Fortunately, some simple models offer insights into a wide range of environmental problems, for example the 'prisoner's dilemma'.

7.2.2 The prisoner's dilemma

The most widely evoked game-theoretic concept in environmental economics is that of the prisoner's dilemma. The original game nicknamed a 'prisoner's dilemma' by A. W. Tucker in 1950 has the following form. Two men (Fred and George) caught with stolen goods are suspected of burglary, but there is insufficient evidence to convict them, unless one or both of them confesses. The police can convict them of the lesser offence of possessing stolen goods without any further evidence. The prisoners are not able to communicate and are kept in separate cells. The police explain the following outcomes to them: if they both confess they will both get two years in prison; if neither confesses they will both get a six-month prison sentence; if one confesses, he will go free while the other will get the maximum sentence of five years. The 'pay-offs' from this situation are represented in the *strategic form* of the game given in Table 7.1. In each of the four cells, the pay-off to George is given first and then the pay-off to Fred.

Table 7.1 The prisoner's dilemma, strategic form

Prisoner A (George):	Prisoner B (Fred):	
	confess	don't confess
confess	2-years, 2-years	free, 5-years
don't confess	5-years, free	6-months, 6-months

How might this game be played? George considers his options: if Fred does not confess then his best response is to confess, and go free, whilst if Fred confesses, then George's best response is still to confess. Therefore George concludes that his best strategy is to confess as it gives the best outcome whether Fred confesses or not. Alone in his cell, Fred follows a similar line of reasoning and comes to the same conclusion so Fred decides to confess as well. Therefore the most likely outcome of the game is that Fred and George confess and both get two years in jail. This outcome is called a *Nash equilibrium* and it represents a stable outcome for this game in the sense that there is no incentive for either player to make another choice. Figure 7.1 illustrates the game in the *extensive form*. Game theorists prefer this representation of a game as it shows the sequence of play and the information available. The circles next to players' names are called nodes—they indicate that a player has a turn. The rectangle, in Figure 7.1, around Fred's node indicates that he chooses his decision without observing George's decision.

Fred and George could have made a binding pact not to confess and to settle for six months in jail instead of two years. This represents an improvement for both players compared with the Nash equilibrium, but this kind of cooperation requires either trust or some other mechanism that enforces a cooperative outcome. This is the essence of prisoner's dilemmas that arise in environmental economics: an obvious socially optimal solution is often rejected because of distrust between the players. Examples of prisoner's dilemmas from natural resources and environmental economics include:

- countries who impose an acid rain problem on each other and would both be better off if they could agree to curtail sulphur dioxide emissions. Without agreement, it is individually rational to only account for national external costs instead of international external costs;

- urban dwellers who suffer from congested roads and air pollution would be collectively better off if they used their cars less, but with no legislative mechanism in place it may still be individually rational to use a car;

- farmers sharing common grazing land degrade the land by overstocking with sheep because they cannot agree on stocking rates;

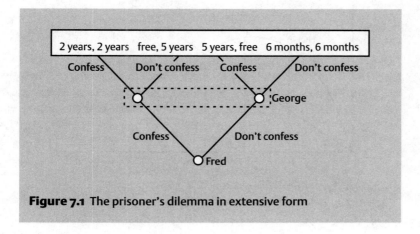

Figure 7.1 The prisoner's dilemma in extensive form

■ fishermen who share a common-property marine fishery, over-fish because they cannot devise a way of sharing the benefits of conservation.

Let us consider these problems in more detail and see how the 'dilemma' arises. In the acid rain example the lack of property rights concerns air quality: neither country has a right to control international air quality, but it may be in their interests to agree on improvement. Similarly, collective action to limit car use is often beneficial, but there is a public good (see Chapter 2) aspect to this: the benefits of improved air quality are similar to pure public goods, that is they are non-rival and non-excludable. In other words, there is little incentive for an individual to voluntarily limit their car usage unless they could be sure that everyone else would do the same. Fisheries and common land grazing are overexploited because they are either common property, (shared by a group of owners), or open access, owned by all. The problem is conventionally seen as one of an absence of, or shared rights over, a resource where each firm imposes an externality on other firms who share the resource. We now consider the last of these examples in more detail.

7.2.3 The fishermen's dilemma

Currently most of the world's marine fisheries are in a state of extreme overexploitation (see Box 7.1). In this section we offer a simple game-theoretic explanation of the problem, but before that we provide a simple model of fishing.

Fishermen share a fishery in which the stock of fish grows according to a logistic growth curve given by

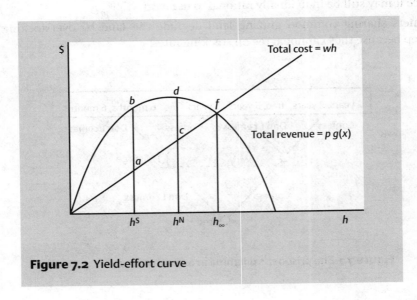

Figure 7.2 Yield-effort curve

$$g(x) = \gamma x (1 - x/K).$$

This is a standard way of representing the growth of a population. Where $g(x)$ is the growth function which gives the rate of stock growth per unit of time, x is the stock of fish, γ is a growth parameter, and K is the carrying capacity of the marine ecosystem. The total revenue in Figure 7.2 is the stock growth multiplied by the output price p. The firm's production function is given by

$$q_i = \theta\, h_i\, x, \tag{7.1}$$

that is the harvest equals a catchability constant, θ, times fishing effort, h_i, which is measured as a number of standard trawler days at sea and the fish stock, x. An important aspect of the production function is that the catch of fish for a given harvest effort depends upon the fish stock; if there are more fish they are easier to catch.

If there is just one firm then in equilibrium that firm harvests the growth in biomass so that profit

$$\pi_i = p\, q_i - w\, h_i$$

is maximized, where p is the price of fish and w is the cost of fishing effort. In a 'steady state equilibrium' where the quantity of fish caught equals the growth in population biomass, the production function becomes

$$g(x) - q_i = \gamma x (1 - x/K) - \theta\, h_i\, x = 0$$

and by solving for x and substituting into (7.1)

$$q(h_i) = \theta\, h_i\, K(1 - \theta\, h_i/\gamma).$$

This is the yield-effort curve illustrated in Figure 7.2. To maximize profit the firm equates the marginal revenue per unit of harvest with the marginal cost of harvest at h^s in Figure 7.2. This represents a social optimum where the marginal revenue from fishing equals the marginal social cost. If a regulator were to choose how to manage a fishery on the grounds of efficiency, then a total harvest effort of h^s is optimal. It is the maximum level of profit that the fishery can generate and if firms were able to

Box 7.1 The State of the World's Fisheries

Recent surveys indicate that many economically important fish stocks are in a depleted state. 'The results shown for 1994 indicate that about 35 per cent of the 200 major fishery resources are senescent (i.e. showing declining yields), about 25 per cent are mature (i.e. plateauing at a high exploitation level), 40 per cent are still "developing", and 0 per cent remain at low exploitation (undeveloped) level. This indicates that around 60 per cent of the major world fish resources are either mature or senescent and, given that few countries have established effective control of fishing capacity, these resources are in urgent need of management action to halt the increase in fishing capacity or to rehabilitate damaged resources.' (FAO, 1997).

cooperate they would choose this level of harvesting and share the profit. In an open access fishery the harvest effort increases until the profit is zero and there is no incentive for additional firms to enter the fishery. This occurs where total revenue equals total cost at h_∞ in Figure 7.2.

What happens when the resource is shared and there is no binding agreement of cooperation between the firms? Assume there are two identical firms who own the fishery, thus their production functions are identical:

$$\pi_1(q_1 \mid q_2) = p\, q_1(h_1 \mid h_2) - wh_1, \qquad \pi_2(q_2 \mid q_1) = p\, q_2(h_2 \mid h_1) - wh_2.$$

The important point to note about these equations is the profit of firm 1 is affected by the harvest of firm 2 and *vice versa*. The term $q_1(h_1 \mid h_2)$ indicates the catch of firm 1 given the fishing effort of firm 2. The prisoner's dilemma emerges when the solution is reduced down to the cooperative solution and the Nash equilibrium. If we choose some specific parameters for our simple fishery model: $K = 1$, $\gamma = 1$, $\theta = 0.8$, $w = 2$, and $p = 10$, we can produce the pay-off matrix in Table 7.2.

Comparing Table 7.2 with Figure 7.2, we see that the Nash equilibrium represents the best response to the other player's expected strategy. However, if both firms were able to agree to cooperate they would both be better off.

From Figure 7.3, the harvest rates h_1^s and h_2^s are the profit-maximizing effort that the firm would choose if they had sole ownership of the resource. Reaction curves give the Nash response of one firm to the other firm's harvest effort, that is they give the profit-maximizing harvest effort given the other firm's harvest effort. A Nash equilibrium occurs at e with effort of h_1^N and h_2^N. At this equilibrium there is no incentive for the firms to choose another strategy. The line h_1^s to h_2^s gives the Pareto optimal cooperative solutions. Along this line harvest effort is chosen so that firms maximize their joint profits. The Nash equilibrium fishing effort h_1^N and h_2^N is greater than under sole ownership but the harvest is less: this therefore represents an ineffi-cient outcome. The solution is also illustrated in Figure 7.2 where $h^N = h_1^N + h_2^N$. The fish stock is greater under the profit-maximizing harvest at h^s. A fishery regulator might prefer the profit-maximizing solution as it gives a higher level of stock.

There are two key results that emerge from this analysis. First, that if the two firms cooperate, then they stand to benefit by increasing their profit. The second point is that the problem of suboptimal exploitation becomes worse as the number of firms increases until the open-access equilibrium is reached where all firms earn zero profits. This gives a game-theoretic interpretation of Hardin's (1968) 'tragedy of the

Table 7.2 Fishery prisoner's dilemma

Firm 1:	Firm 2:	
	Nash	Cooperate
Nash	0.625, 0.625	0.791, 0.527
Cooperate	0.527, 0.791	0.703, 0.703

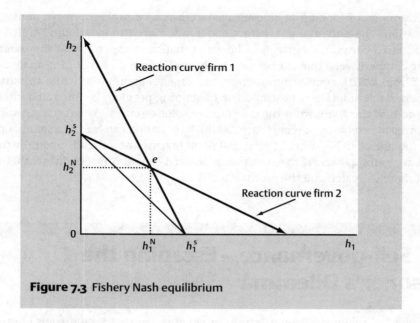

Figure 7.3 Fishery Nash equilibrium

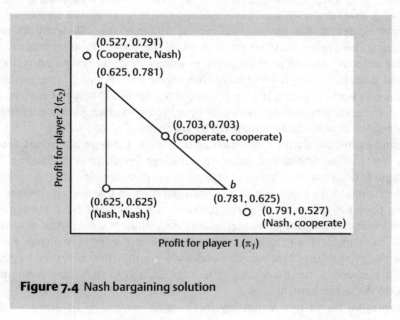

Figure 7.4 Nash bargaining solution

commons'. A prisoner's dilemma characterizes the outcome for two or more firms, but the problem only becomes severe when there are a large number of firms. Indeed with a small number of firms, a cooperative outcome may emerge as an equilibrium, especially when the game is repeated a large number of times. We discuss this further below.

Another way of looking at sharing resources is as a problem in bargaining and cooperation. The potential gains from cooperation are the maximum profit which can be shared between the players. The worst that can happen is that they continue playing competitively: that is playing a Nash equilibrium. In bargaining analysis, the pay-off from a Nash equilibrium represents a disagreement point while any share of the cooperative solution is possible. The bargaining problem is illustrated in Figure 7.4. Note that the share from the cooperative solution must exceed the pay-off that the firms can receive by playing (Nash, Nash). Negotiation can lead to a share of profit along the line *ab* in Figure 7.4. The actual point on this line depends upon the producer's bargaining power. If the bargaining power is equal for both firms, then they would share the catch and the profits equally.

7.3 Self-governance — Escaping the Prisoner's Dilemma

THE political scientist Eleanor Ostrom (1990) observes that a significant number of common property resources have avoided the tragedy of the commons by the appropriators developing institutions which increase the efficiency of resource exploitation. She argues that the predictions of the prisoner's dilemma are not an inevitable outcome for common property resources, because the potential exists for communication between players before they take their decision. Government intervention is one way of forcing producers to cooperate, but this is not necessarily the only way. Firms may be able to cooperate by agreeing to abide by the decisions of an external regulator who can be appointed by the firms.

This can be illustrated with a modified version of the fisheries dilemma game given in Table 7.2. In this new game, presented in extensive form in Figure 7.5, a Nash equilibrium is one outcome, but the players can agree to appoint an external referee, who must be paid a fee f which is shared between the two players. The referee acts by imposing penalties to ensure that the firms do not play their Nash strategies. This offers an escape route from the inefficient Nash equilibrium. Firms now have an incentive to cooperate so long as each firm's share of the fee is less than the difference between the cooperative solution and Nash equilibrium $(0.703 - 0.625) = 0.078$. The penalty agreed by the firms should be large enough so that there is no incentive to cheat on the agreement.

Ostrom (1990) found that voluntary institutions work well to manage common property ownership where a relatively small number of firms share the resource. Common property institutions tend to breakdown when the number of firms involved increases or there is a lack of family and community ties between the appropriators of the resource. Examples of where voluntary institutions have been successful include Turkish inshore fisheries (see Box 7.2), lobster fisheries in Maine, and irrigation schemes in the Mid-West of the USA (Ostrom, 1990).

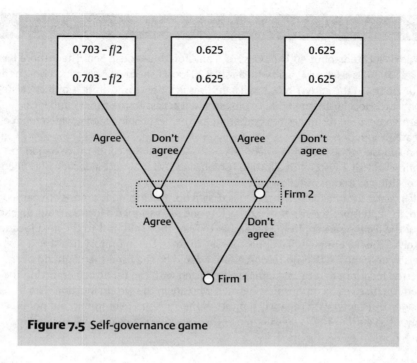

Figure 7.5 Self-governance game

7.4 Coase's Theorem and Local Environmental Problems

IN Chapter 2 pollution is seen as arising due to a market failure where property rights do not extend to the environment. Coase (1960) pointed out that if the costs of reaching an agreement (legal costs and the like) that is, *transaction costs* are zero and property rights over the environment are defined, there may be scope for the parties involved in a pollution problem to reach a negotiated settlement. Coases theorem states *that in the absence of transaction costs affected parties to an externality will agree on an allocation of resources that is both Pareto optimal and independent of any prior assignment of property rights.*

Two illustrations of Coase's theorem are offered: the first is the conventional interpretation and the second is a broader game-theoretic interpretation. Consider two firms, a farm and a fishery located on a river. The farm is upstream and the fishery is downstream. If the farm allows effluent into the river, then the fishery suffers due to increased costs of water purification. The situation is represented in Figure 7.6.

The benefit derived by the farm from pollution is given by the marginal private benefit (*MPB*) curve and the area under the curve is the total profit. If the farm has the

Box 7.2 An Example of Self-organization in a Common Property Resource

Bodrum is located about 400 km west of Alanya on the Aegean Sea. The inshore fishery (Berkes, 1986) is relatively small with about 100 local fishermen operating two- to three-person boats. In the early 1970s the fishery was in a depressed state. Conflict existed amongst the local fishermen due to unrestrained access to the fishery and local fishermen devoted resources to competing for the best fishing spots, which tended to increase production costs.

In response to this situation, members of the local fishing cooperative began to experiment with a system for allotting fishing sites. After almost a decade of refinement the resulting system is as follows.

Each year a list of eligible fishermen is drawn up. The fishing locations are named and listed. In September the fishermen draw lots and are assigned a location, but on each day of the fishing season, from September to May, they shift east to the next location. This gives the fishermen equal opportunities to catch the migratory fish stock.

This system means that no resources are wasted by the fishermen fighting over preferred locations and the system is self-policing with the fishermen enforcing the system themselves by reporting fishermen who are in the wrong location. The fishery is managed efficiently with the tacit support of the Turkish Government, but no direct policy intervention. This is an example of the self-governance game illustrated in Figure 7.5.

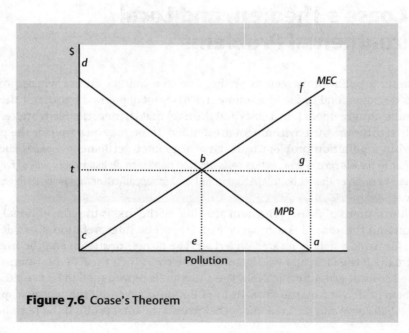

Figure 7.6 Coase's Theorem

right to pollute, then they will pollute up to *a* where *MPB* = 0 since at this point profit is maximized. The fishery suffers from the farm's pollution, this is represented by the marginal external cost (*MEC*) curve. The area under the *MEC* curve is the fishery's reduction in profit due to increased water-purification costs. If the fishery controls the quality of the river, then it would choose *c* where pollution is zero. This situation offers the potential for negotiation. If the property rights rest with the farmer, then the fishery would be willing to pay the farm up to *ebfa* for a reduction in pollution from *a* to *e*. This represents the potential for a Pareto improvement where both the farmer and the fishery owner are better off. The costs of a further abatement would not be justified, as below *e* the *MPB* is greater than *MEC*. A similar outcome can be derived for the case where the fishery holds the property rights. In this case the farmer would be willing to pay the fishery up to *cdbe* for the right to increase pollution from *c* to *e*. The importance of property rights is that they allow a legally based negotiation to take place. Zero transaction costs ensure that negotiation is viable, however, some compromise may still be reached so long as transaction costs do not exceed the potential gains.

Coase's theorem implies that there is the potential for resolving some externality problems without recourse to government intervention and the use of emission standards, taxes, and quotas. Unfortunately many real-world pollution problems involve large numbers of parties to a pollution problem and prohibitive transaction costs. As an individual citizen suffering from air pollution it is unlikely that I would be able to afford to negotiate directly with the local power station to reduce air pollution. Mueller (1989) sees this negotiation process as a role for government where the government acts as an intermediary between the parties affected by an externality as a way of focusing influence through lobbying and thereby economizing on transactions costs.

Coase's theorem can also be represented as a Nash bargaining problem; we convert the problem in Figure 7.6 to a simpler format by assuming that the optimal solution is at *b* where the *MEC* and *MPB* curves cross. The fishery pays the farm *t* per unit of pollution which gives the farm a compensation payment of *ebga* for a reduction in pollution from *a* to *e*. The pay-offs are summarized in Table 7.3. The Nash equilibrium is (negotiate, negotiate) as both the farm and the fishery are better off, and have no incentive to switch to no-negotiation. The allocation of property rights to the farm ensures that this occurs. This game is not a prisoner's dilemma as the Pareto-efficient outcome is also a Nash equilibrium.

Table 7.3 Coase's theorem: a game-theoretic interpretation

Farm:	Fishery:	
	no-negotiation	negotiate
no-negotiation	*cda*, −*cfa*	*cda*, −*cfa*
negotiate	*cda*, −*cfa*	*cdbe* + *ebga*, *bfae* − *ebga*

7.5 Repeated Games

SECTION 7.3 concludes that the mismanagement of common property resources is not an inevitable outcome. Some shared resources have been well managed without private ownership. One explanation is that the players are brought together in long-term competition rather than a single 'one-shot' game. Over time, players may develop a system of sharing the resource by agreement, but agreement would only come about because the firms expect to benefit in the long term from showing restraint. This describes a repeated game where a sequence of games is played through time. Repeated games have a much larger number of potential strategies than the one-shot game. There is the potential for observing how the other firms play, and for tacit agreements to cooperative and punitive responses. If the prisoner's dilemma is played a large number of times, then cooperation can emerge as an equilibrium. This equilibrium is reinforced by the threat that if one player stops cooperating everyone will be punished by a return to a disadvantageous non-cooperative equilibrium. This is called a 'tit-for-tat' strategy and it was found by Axelrod (1984) to be a frequently selected strategy in experiments where people play repeated prisoner's dilemma games.

In many real-life games, such as resource sharing or negotiating over fishing rights, games are repeated over and over again. It is an equilibrium to 'confess' in the one-shot prisoner's dilemma because there is no possibility of repercussions at a later stage of the game. The key result in this literature is that when a game is repeated a lot of times, cooperation may emerge as a competitive equilibrium. However, if the game is repeated just a few times, then the equilibrium is the same as for the one-shot game. If the game lasts only a few turns, then the players will reason as follows: in the last stage of the game the other player has no incentive to do anything other than not cooperate because in the last stage of the game we have a one-shot game. On this basis moving to the previous stage there is no scope for retaliation so the player chooses a Nash strategy and so on back to the start of the game. Thus in this finite game we conclude that the outcome is to play the Nash strategy in all periods. Where the game is repeated indefinitely, discounting ensures that the final period is of no importance but the prospect of retaliation is important. It turns out a policy where

Table 7.4 Fishery dilemma		
	Firm 2:	
Firm 1:	Nash	Cooperate
Nash	nn_1, nn_2	nc_1, nc_2
Cooperate	cn_1, cn_2	cc_1, cc_2

each player cooperates until the other deviates and then deviates for the remainder of the game is optimal. The reason for this is that the most the player can gain from deviating is a one-period improvement in their pay-off which is followed by a reduction in pay-offs for the remainder of the game.

Consider what happens if the fisheries game in Table 7.2 is repeated a large number of times and the player adopts a tit-for-tat strategy. The pay-offs from the fishery game are generalized in Table 7.4, where cc_1 indicates both firms cooperate and gives the pay-off to firm 1, cn_2 indicates that firm 1 cooperates while firm 2 plays a Nash strategy

---

Box 7.3 Revision on Discounting

The Basics

How do we evaluate decisions that gives rise to a flow of benefits for a number of years into the future? The problem is that $1 today is worth more than a $1 in a year's time because we can invest that $1 in the bank or in the stock market and earn interest. So when evaluating a flow of income we cannot simply sum the income in each year to obtain a total income, as this would not take account of the investment opportunities. Instead we calculate the present value of a flow of income which converts $1 in future years to its value today. For instance, if we compare $1 today with $1 in a year's time, the value of $1 in a year's time needs to be adjusted downwards to account for the fact that $1 today can be invested and earn annual interest equal to r. Let us suppose that $r = 0.1$ (10%), then after a year 1$ will equal $(1+r) \times 1 = 1.1$. The relative value of $1 after a year is therefore $(1/(1+r)) = (1/1.1) = 0.9090$. In other words the present value of $1 after a year is 91 cents. After two years of compound interest, the dollar now has grown to $(1+r)^2 \times 1 = 1.21$, the relative value of a dollar after two years is $(1/(1+r)^2) = 0.8264$. A general value for the discount factor is $\delta^t = (1/1+r)^t)$ where δ is the discount factor and t is the number of years into the future.

If a resource or an environmental asset are expected to give a constant flow of benefits for the foreseeable future, then we can actually simplify the discount formula considerably. The present value of a flow of income is given by:

$$PV_T = \delta y_1 + \delta^2 y_2 + \delta^3 y_3 + \delta^4 y_4 + \ldots + \delta^T y_T$$

If the income is constant, then the present value can be given as:

$$PV_T = \delta y + \delta^2 y + \delta^3 y + \delta^4 y + \ldots + \delta^T y$$

We can rewrite this geometric progression as

$$PV_T - \delta PV_T = \delta y - \delta^{T+1} y$$

or as

$$PV_T = y(\delta - \delta^{T+1})/(1 - \delta).$$

If we now do two things, first note that if $T = \infty$ then $\delta^{T+1} = 0$ and expand $\delta = 1/(1+r)$ to give:

$$PV_T = y/r.$$

Therefore the present value for a constant income over an infinite period is simply the income divided by the discount rate.

and gives the pay-off to firm 2. The present value of firm 1 cooperating for a long time is given by (see Box 7.3):

$$PV_{c_1} = \frac{cc_1}{r}$$

that is the sum of a discounted time-series in perpetuity, where r is the discount rate. If firm 1 deviates at $t = T_d$ and is punished by a Nash response by firm 2 for the rest of the game, then difference in the present value for deviation PV_{d_1} and for cooperation PV_{c_1} is given by:

$$PV_{d_1} - PV_{c_1} = \frac{1}{(1+r)^{Td}}\left((nc_1 - cc_1) + \frac{nn_1 - cc_1}{r}\right).$$

For the firms to gain by deviating this equation would have to be positive. The gain from deviating lasts for only one period when they receive $(nc_1 - cc_1)$, but they are then penalized for all periods after that $(nn_1 - cc_1)/r$. From this it is obvious that deviating from cooperation only pays if the benefits of deviating are very high or the discount rate is very high. The term outside the brackets on the right-hand side $1/(1+r)^{Td}$ is the discount factor for the time of deviation $t = Td$. For the example given in Table 7.2, the discount rate would have to be approximately 88 per cent for non-cooperation to be worthwhile, which implies a very low weight on future pay-offs.

7.6 Cooperative Games

COOPERATIVE games arise where players can form binding agreements in pre-play negotiations. Strictly, cooperative games are a special case of non-cooperative games, in that a non-cooperative game can be extended to include the decision to form a binding coalition. Cooperative game theory focuses on the pay-offs that different 'coalitions' can achieve rather than the details of how the game might be played. The following is a non-technical account of the basics of cooperative game theory with reference to the following example. Suppose three countries share a groundwater reservoir. They have a choice of acting individually or collaborating in various coalitions, including a grand coalition that includes all countries. Setting aside the details of how pay-offs are calculated, each country receives the pay-off indicated in Table 7.5.

Table 7.5 gives the pay-offs to different combinations of countries. Let us define a pay-off function $v(.)$ which gives the value of the game to various coalitions, for instance $v(\{A\}) = 10$ gives the value to the A from 'going it alone', $v(\{A, B\}) = 50$ gives the pay-off from a coalition between Country A and Country B, and so on. The next question is which coalitions of players are likely to form. For instance $v(\{A, B\}) = 50$ indicates that a coalition between A and B has a pay-off of 50 units, the grand coalition has a pay-off of 100, thus $v(\{A, B, C\}) = 100$. Therefore in this game the grand coalition

Table 7.5 Groundwater cooperation game	
Coalitions of countries	Value of coalitions ($ million)
A	10
B	20
C	30
A, B	50
A, C	60
C, B	70
A, B, C	100

gives a bigger pay-off than all sub-coalitions, but we have to check whether the coalition is stable. In other words do either A, B, or C have an incentive to leave the grand coalition.

Now we have set out the basic structure of cooperative games it now remains to discuss some solution concepts that determine how players divide the benefits of cooperation. The approach to this is to assume that the grand coalition forms and then assess if pay-off $\pi(S)$ (where S is a single player or a group of players) can be set which provides an incentive for the coalition to continue. The first condition is a 'budget constraint':

$$\pi(A) + \pi(B) + \pi(C) = v(\{A, B, C\}) = 100.$$

This ensures that the pay-off is shared amongst the players. Next we need to specify individual and group (or coalition) rationality. This assesses if players are able to achieve higher pay-offs outside the grand coalition either individually, or in other coalitions. Individual rationality says that $\pi(A) \geq v(\{A\})$, in other words the pay-off received by country A as part of the coalition must be no less than the amount that country A could achieve alone. This extends to group rationality as $\pi(\{S\}) \geq v(\{S\})$, thus the pay-off to the subset of players S under the grand coalition must be greater than the pay-off that could be achieved by S as a separate coalition $v(\{S\})$.

Individual and group rationality defines a set of constraints on pay-offs which would be acceptable to all players. The set of all such pay-offs which satisfy individual and group rationality are called the *core* and sets of pay-offs are called *imputations*. These concepts can be illustrated for our specific game using a diagram. Figure 7.7a illustrates the shares of the grand coalition as a triangle. In each corner, one player receives a pay-off of 100 and the others nothing. The lines across the triangle indicate individual rationality. For instance $v[\{A\}] = 10$ thus in terms of individual rationality A must receive a pay-off of at least 10 due to individual rationality, this leaves 90 units to share between C and B. The triangle *abc* is the set of pay-offs which satisfies the individual rationality constraints. Turning now to Figure 7.7b, we now introduce the group rationality constraints as well as the individual rationality constraints. This accounts for the pay-offs that the countries can obtain in sub-coalitions. The core *dfg* of the game represents a set of possible pay-offs that satisfy both the individual rationality and group rationality constraints. The actual solution would probably be determined by negotiation.

Cooperative game theory is a useful tool in environmental and natural resource economics as it helps to explain why groups with similar preferences form alliances and agree to negotiate together. For instance alliances have tended to emerge in the recent climate change negotiations in Kyoto between countries with similar interests (see Chapter 12). It also allows us to analyse how stable these alliances are which is important in predicting how successful the policy will be. These issues are picked up again in the next section on transboundary pollution.

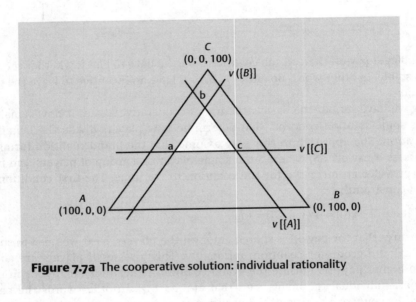

Figure 7.7a The cooperative solution: individual rationality

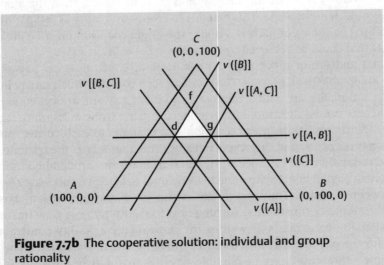

Figure 7.7b The cooperative solution: individual and group rationality

7.7 Game Theory and Transboundary Pollution Control

7.7.1 Introduction

Transboundary pollution concerns emissions that cross international boundaries. We choose to analyse this problem here because it includes elements of both cooperative and non-cooperative game theory. Non-cooperative game theory analyses the outcome in the absence of negotiation, cooperative game theory analyses how countries form coalitions and how stable these coalitions are. Transboundary pollution problems are of three broad types.

- First, there are unidirectional externalities where an 'upstream country' affects a 'downstream' country. This form of externality is characterized by water pollution where a country pollutes a river that imposes costs on the downstream country.

- Second, regional reciprocal externalities are typical of common property resources such as European air quality. The actions of a country affect not only its own costs or benefits, but the benefits of other countries as well: UK emissions of sulphur oxides acidify UK lakes and streams but also Swedish lakes and streams.

- Third, global externalities are subdivided into those which involve physical interactions between countries and those which do not. For instance chlorofluorocarbon emissions, by thinning the ozone layer, have the potential of detrimental health effects on most of the human population. Likewise greenhouse gas emissions will, through global warming, affect everyone (see Chapter 12). Non-physical effects relate to a range of goods with non-use values. These include preserving biodiversity (see Chapter 13).

All these pollution problems involve a strategic interaction between countries and can be analysed by game theory.

7.7.2 The acid rain game

This section uses a simple hypothetical two-country acid rain game to illustrate the principles of game-theoretic analysis. This problem introduces concepts from both cooperative and non-cooperative game theory. We start off by specifying the problem. There are two countries, the UK (subscript 1) and Sweden (subscript 2), which generate sulphur dioxide from coal-burning. Emissions from the UK affect Sweden and vice versa. This is a reciprocal externality. Each country has a benefit of emissions

Box 7.4 Self-Enforcing International Environmental Agreements

International environmental agreements (IEA), such as the Montreal Protocol, for ozone depleting substances and the Kyoto Protocol to limit emissions of greenhouse gases have been characterized by protracted negotiations and partial agreements. The lack of a 'higher authority' makes international environmental agreements difficult to negotiate and police. Barrett (1994b) proposes that international environmental agreements should be self-enforcing, which means that the group of countries who sign the agreement have no incentives to leave the agreement and those who are non-signatories have no incentive to join. The condition for self-enforcement for a group of N identical countries is similar to the group rationality constraint from cooperative game theory. Countries divide into signatories (s) to a IEA and non-signatories (n) to an IEA such that $N = n + s$. A coalition of signatories is stable if the following conditions are satisfied:

incentive to leave the agreement: $\pi_n(n + 1) \leq \pi_s(s)$ (1)

incentive to join the agreement: $\pi_n(n) \geq \pi_s(s + 1)$ (2)

where the pay-off to signatories is π_s, the pay-off to non-signatories is π_n. A coalition is stable if there is no incentive for a country to join the agreement and no incentive for a country to leave. Condition (1) above says that there is no incentive to leave the coalition because the pay-off to a signatory is greater than the pay-off to a non-signatory when the number of non-signatories is increased by 1. Condition (2) says there is no incentive to join as the pay-off to a non-signatory is greater than a pay-off to a signatory when the number of signatories is increased by 1.

The implications of this theoretical model are rather depressing. They imply that self-enforcing IEAs only include a large proportion of the countries when the benefits of cooperation are relatively small. Where the benefits of cooperation over non-cooperation are large, then the equilibrium tends to include only a relatively small proportion of the countries. The implication of this result is that it is going to be very difficult for countries to agree to IEAs and we may see partial agreements where one group of countries joins and another group remains outside the agreement.

function which is in terms of additional profit and an external cost function. These functions can also be given as abatement cost functions (which represents the emission benefit function) and abatement benefit function. To make this example more concrete we use the specific functional forms and parameter values in Table 7.6, but if you prefer, ignore these and look at the diagrams that come later.

The Nash equilibrium is where each country only takes account of its own external costs. The equilibrium level of abatement for a country like the UK is where:

$$MAC_1(a_1) = MBA_1(a_1 \mid a_2).$$

that is the marginal abatement cost $MAC_1(a_1)$ is equated with the marginal benefit of abatement in country 1 given the abatement in Sweden $MBA_1(a_1 \mid a_2)$. If the two countries agree to cooperate, then each country takes account of the other's benefits of abatement, thus for the UK:

Box 7.5 Montreal Protocol

Chloroflurocarbons (CFCs) have been implicated in depleting the stratospheric ozone shield since the 1970s. The depletion of the ozone layer is a truly global pollution problem in that all countries are likely to be affected, to some degree, by the health problems that the resulting elevated levels of ultraviolet light will cause. In September 1988, twenty-four countries signed the Montreal Protocol to restrict their production and consumption of CFCs to 50 per cent of 1986 levels by 30 June 1998. In London during July 1990, fifty six countries agreed to further tighten restriction on the use of these chemicals. This agreement involved the phasing out of halons and CFCs by the end of the century. An interesting aspect of this agreement is that a fund of $240 million was established to assist poorer countries to comply with this agreement. This amounts to a side payment to ensure that a negotiated settlement is achieved. The restrictions were further tightened at the fourth meeting in 1992 in Copenhagen with a ban of CFC products brought forward to 1996 from 1999 and a ban on trade in these substances.

The agreements over the reduction in substances which damage the stratospheric ozone layer represents a relatively successful international environmental policy, perhaps because the costs were potentially large and shared by all countries and the costs, due to the development of new products, were declining through time. The use of side payments also facilitated the inclusion of poorer countries in the London agreement. This outcome contrasts with the current state of disagreement over the right course of action in relation to climate change (see Chapter 14). The stability of the Montreal Protocol is strengthened by the threat of trade sanctions if countries are found to be non-compliant or refuse to sign the treaty. This has been an effective deterrent against free-riding.

Table 7.6 The acid rain game

Private costs and benefits	External costs and benefits
Private benefit of emissions:	External costs:
$B_i^e(e_i) = b_{0i}e_i - b_{1i}e_i^2$	$C_i^e(e) = c_i^e e^2$
$e_i^* = b_{0i}/2b_{1i}$	Total emissions
e_i^* is the private benefit maximizing emission	$e = e_1 + e_2$
abatement: $a_i = (e_i^* - e_i)$	$e^* = e_1^* + e_2^*$
Private abatement costs	Aggregate abatement
$C_i^a(a_i) = + (B_i^e(e_i^*) - B_i^e(e_i^* - a_i))$	$a = e^* - (e_1 + e_2)$
that is difference between maximum private benefits and	Abatement benefit function
benefits with abatement.	$B_i^a(a) = C_i^e(e^*) - C_i^e(e^* - a)$
Parameter values	$c_1^e = 0.02; c_2^e = 0.05$
$b_{0i} = 150; b_{02} = 0.15;$	
$b_{1i} = 150; b_{12} = 0.15$	

Table 7.7 Transboundary pollution—the acid rain game

	Sweden:	
UK:	Nash	Cooperate
Nash	Pay-off (£ millions) UK: 27.0 S: 6.5 UK + S: 33.5 Abatement (million tonnes SO_2): UK: 90.9 S: 227.3 UK + S: 318.2	Pay-off (£ millions) UK: 27.3 S: 6.3 UK + S: 33.7 Abatement (million tonnes SO_2): UK: 89.2 S: 241.4 UK + S: 320.6
Cooperate	Pay-off (£ millions) UK: 22.3 S: 15.9 UK + S: 38.2 Abatement (million tonnes SO_2): UK: 241.4 S: 189.7 UK + S: 431.1	Pay-off (£ millions) UK: 23.4 S: 15.4 UK + S: 38.8 Abatement (million tonnes SO_2): UK: 241.4 S: 241.4 UK + S: 482.8

$$MAC_i(a_1) = MBA_1(a_1 \mid a_2) + MBA_2(a_1 \mid a_2).$$

Using the numerical example given in Table 7.6, the results of a Nash strategy and a cooperative strategy are given in Table 7.7 and Figures 7.8.

Table 7.7 gives the pay-off and the abatement level for all the combinations of strategies. Starting with the strategy where both countries cooperate, then this gives the highest overall abatement of 482.8 and the highest aggregate welfare of 38.8. Without a binding cooperative agreement then both countries have an incentive to follow an uncooperative strategy, especially the UK which is least affected by the acid rain. For the cooperative solution to hold there would have to be a side payment from Sweden to the UK to make the agreement stable. This is a concept from cooperative game theory where it is necessary to ensure that players receive at least as much through cooperation as they do from not cooperating. In this example, then Sweden gains sufficiently from cooperation to compensate the UK and still be better off.

7.8 Summary

IN this chapter we introduce game theory as an approach to modelling the strategic interaction of a small number of economic agents. Situations where small numbers of agents or coalitions of agents interact arise in environmental economics, where

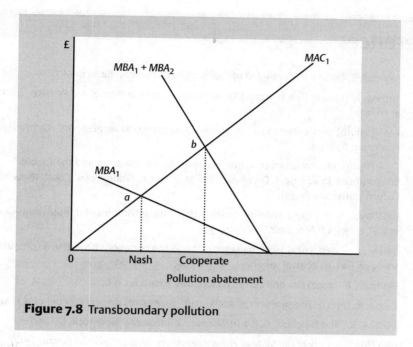

Figure 7.8 Transboundary pollution

environmental resources are shared. Environmental resources include global commons such as the atmosphere, regional air quality, and natural resources such as fisheries and grazing areas. The attributes of these problems are shared rights of ownership or poorly defined property rights where agents compete to appropriate the benefits of a resource. Game theory enables us to explore how they might interact.

The key game is the prisoner's dilemma where the 'competitive' equilibrium is one where both players are worse off than they would be if they cooperated. This is a common theme which runs through this chapter: agents are invariably better off if they can find some mechanism to cooperate. Repeated games offer a new perspective on the problem in that they imply that cooperation may actually emerge as a competitive Nash equilibrium, because through time you can punish defections by other players.

Cooperative game theory is about the formation and stability of coalitions between players. The approach can be viewed as complementary to competitive games in that it considers only the best that players can achieve in different coalitions and abstracts from the mechanics of how a solution to a game is arrived at. The importance of both non-cooperative and cooperative games is apparent in transboundary pollution and marine fishery problems where countries frequently negotiate as blocks, for example, Europe negotiates with the USA, developed countries form an alliance, and so on.

Game theory informs both how environmental conflicts and problems might be resolved, it also goes some of the way to explaining why problems have arisen in the first place when economic agents' behaviour is contrary to the common good, but is actually rational for the individual.

References

Axelrod, R. (1984). *The Evolution of Cooperation* (New York: Basic Books).

Barrett, S. (1994a) 'The biodiversity supergame', *Environmental and Resource Economics* 4: 111–22.

—— (1994b) 'Self-enforcing international environmental agreements', *Oxford Economic Papers* 46: 878–94.

—— (1999) 'Montreal versus Kyoto International Cooperation and the Global Environment' in K. Inge, I. Grunberg, and M. A. Stern, *Global Public Goods* (New York: Oxford University Press).

Batabayal, A. A. (1995) 'Leading issues in domestic environmental regulation—a review essay', *Ecological Economics*, 12(1): 23–39.

Berkes, F. (1986) 'Local-level management and the commons problem: a comparative study of Turkish coastal fisheries', *Marine Policy* 10: 215–29.

Binmore, K. (1992) *Fun and Games* (Lexington: Heath & Co.).

Coase, R. (1960) 'The problem of social cost', *Journal of Law and Economics* 3: 1–44.

Dixit, A. K., and Nalebuff, B. (1991) *Thinking Strategically* (New York: Norton).

FAO (1997) *Review of the State of Fishery Resources: Marine Fisheries* (Rome: FAO) (www.FAO.org).

Fudenberg, D., and Tirole, J. (1991), *Game Theory* (Cambridge, Mass: MIT Press).

Hanley, N., and Folmer, H. (1998) *Game Theory and the Environment* (Cheltenham: Edward Elgar).

Levhari, D., and Mirman, L. J. (1980) 'The great fish war: an example using a dynamic Cournot-Nash solution', *Bell Journal of Economics* 11: 322–44.

Maler, K-G. (1989) 'The acid rain game', in H. Folmer and E. van Ireland, E. (eds.), *Valuation Methods and Policy Making in Environmental Economics* (Amsterdam: Elsevier).

Mesterton-Gibbons, M. (1988) 'Game-theoretic resource modelling', *Natural Resource Modeling* 7: 93–147.

Mueller, D. C. (1989) *Public Choice II*. Cambridge: Cambridge University Press.

Ostrom, E. (1990) *Governing the Commons* (Cambridge: Cambridge University Press).

Von Neumann J., and Morgernstern, O. (1944) *Theory of Games and Economic Behaviour* (Princeton: Princeton University Press).

Ulph, A., and Ulph, D. (1994) 'The optimal time path of a carbon tax', *Oxford Economic Papers* (NS) 46: 857–68.

Chapter 8
Trade and the Environment

I**N** this chapter we study the interaction between international trade and the
environment. To this end we:

- Review trade theory and show why economists favour freer trade.
- Extend a simple trade analysis to include the environment.
- Briefly review the effectiveness of trade policy for achieving environmental
  objectives.
- Consider the empirical evidence on the effects of environmental policy on
  international competitiveness.

8.1 Introduction

T**RADE** economics is about how and why nations exchange goods across borders.
International trade profoundly changes what each country produces and consumes. Inevitably this change in the spatial distribution of production and consumption affects the environment nationally and globally.

Since Ricardo (1817) economists have believed that countries benefit by an increase
in welfare from freer trade and suffer a reduction in welfare when trade is restricted
through quotas and tariffs. Trade allows countries to specialize in producing goods
which have the lowest opportunity cost. This means they can achieve a level of consumption which is greater than they could achieve if they were restricted to what
they could produce from their own resources. These principles have been pursued
through the General Agreement on Tariffs and Trade (GATT) and World Trade Organization (WTO) which succeeded GATT in 1995. For the foreseeable future we can
expect to see a continued expansion in world trade that will tend to increase global
production and consumption, see Box 8.1. This growth will have an effect upon the
environment, but it is hard to say whether it will be beneficial or detrimental. On

the negative side: the first law of thermodynamics predicts that more output, by increasing the quantity of material used, will increase global pollution. The process of trade itself, which involves the physical transportation of goods to different countries, is also polluting. Environmental benefits from increased trade include: trade may lead to a reallocation of production to countries which are better able to deal with the environmental side-effects of production, whilst increased income may lead to consumers demanding higher environmental standards, this is the so-called environmental Kuznets curve effect discussed in Chapter 6.

This leads us to the question of the role, or lack of a role, for trade policy in protecting the environment. Throughout this book the message is that if you want to regulate pollution you must place taxes or quotas on emissions. Restricting production inputs or outputs is a second-best policy because these variables may not be directly related to the level of emissions. Trade policy in terms of tariffs and restrictions on the quantity and quality of goods sold in a country deals with production inputs and outputs. Therefore restricting trade in inputs and outputs is a suboptimal approach to conducting environmental policy. The fact that trade policy is often justified on the grounds of environmental protection should often be viewed with suspicion: there is often a thin line between a policy protecting the environment and protecting domestic producers from competition.

In a perfect world, a country's domestic environment should be protected by national environmental policies and the global environment protected by inter-

Box 8.1 World Trade

Table 8.B1 gives the percentage change in the volume of trade from 1990 to 1998. The average annual rate of growth of 6.5 per cent in world trade in goods, if it continues, would lead to a doubling of world trade after about eleven years.

Table 8.B1 Growth in the volume of world merchandise trade by selected region, 1990–1998 (annual percentage change)

Exports				Imports		
1990–8	1997	1998		1990–8	1997	1998
6.5	10.0	4.0	World	6.5	9.5	4.0
7.0	11.0	3.5	North America	8.0	13.0	10.5
8.5	11.0	7.0	Latin America	12.5	22.0	9.0
6.0	9.5	5.0	Western Europe	5.5	8.0	7.5
6.0	9.5	5.5	European Union (15)	5.5	7.5	7.5
5.0	9.5	7.0	C./E. Europe/Baltic States/CIS	5.0	13.5	5.0
7.5	12.0	2.0	Asia	6.5	6.0	−8.0
2.5	12.0	−1.5	Japan	4.0	1.5	−5.5
10.5	10.0	2.5	Six East Asian traders	8.0	6.5	−12.0

Source: http://www.wto.org/wto/statis/

national environmental agreements. Restrictions to trade may be warranted as the only available sanction on a country causing an international environmental problem. For instance, CITES (International Convention on Trade in Endangered Species) aims to protect species by reducing the demand for live animals and animal products. However, this Convention does not solve the source of the problem which is often the loss of habitat in the country which hosts an endangered species. Similarly the Basel Convention on the Transboundary Movements of Hazardous Waste, is an admission that some countries, unless they are protected in this way, may become a dumping ground for toxic waste. This agreement acknowledges a failure of domestic environmental policies which should price waste export and disposal at a level which did not lead to excessive dumping.

In the remainder of this chapter we analyse these issues from a number of perspectives. First, using a simple example we show why there are gains from trade. We then introduce domestic environmental policy into this model to see how the outcome might be changed. We then assess the empirical evidence on the effects of environmental regulation on competitiveness and the location of production. The next section looks at international trade policy under the GATT and WTO and how the GATT dealt with trade disputes motivated by environmental concerns. The final section considers three international environmental agreements which depend upon trade policy.

8.2 Why do Countries Gain from Trade?

ADAM Smith introduced the idea of *absolute advantage*: that is a country specializes in the good which it can produce at the lowest cost. Consider the example in Table 8.1 where two countries produce two goods, food and cloth, using a single factor of production, labour. Assume that transport costs are zero and labour can be freely allocated between the two sectors.

If each country is endowed with 120 units of labour and under autarky (no trade) both countries, on the basis of community demand preferences, allocate 60 units of labour to each sector this determines that the UK will produce 12 units of food and 30

Table 8.1 Trade and absolute advantage		
Labour per unit of output	UK	USA
Food	5 (2.5 cloth)	3 (0.5 cloth)
Cloth	2 (0.4 food)	6 (2 food)
Note: Opportunity costs are given in parentheses		

units of cloth (12, 30) and the USA (20, 10). If trade now opens up between the countries which allows the UK to specialize by allocating all labour to cloth and the USA allocating all labour to food production, this increases world production from (32, 40) to (60, 40) and as long as the exchange rate of cloth for food between the two countries is less than the domestic opportunity cost of labour there is a gain from trade. The opportunity cost is the amount of food that must be sacrificed to produce an extra unit of cloth. Thus if trade between the UK and the USA opens at an exchange rate (terms of trade) of between 0.5 units (opportunity cost of a unit of food in the USA) of cloth per unit of food and 2.5 units (opportunity cost of food in the UK) of cloth per unit of food, trade will be mutually beneficial.

In 1817 Ricardo introduced the concept of comparative advantage. This states that countries can gain from trade so long as the opportunity cost of producing goods is different, so that there does not have to be an absolute cost advantage. Consider Table 8.2. The UK has an absolute cost advantage in both sectors, however, total production can be increased if the UK transfers labour from food to cloth and the USA transfers resources from cloth to food. The outcome is illustrated in Figure 8.1.

The upper part of Figure 8.1 shows the production possibility frontiers for the UK and USA. The lower diagram shows the possible rates of exchange between the two countries and the global production possibility frontier. In the absence of trade (autarky), then the production possibility frontier also determines what a country can consume. Consider the diagram for the UK. The production possibility frontier gives the maximum combinations of cloth and food that can be produced. The slope of the production possibility frontier also tells us how much cloth the UK has to give up if it wishes to produce an extra unit of food. This is the opportunity cost of a unit of food in terms of cloth. How is this calculated? One unit of food requires 5 units of labour, cloth requires 2 units of labour per unit, therefore an extra unit of food means that the UK must forgo 2.5 (5/2) units of cloth.

The bottom diagram shows the consumption opportunities a country has with free trade. The global production possibility frontier (PPF) adds together the UK PPF and the USA PPF. Thus the maximum cloth production is 70 units which includes 60 from the UK and 10 from the USA, the maximum food is 44 which includes 24 from the UK and 20 from the USA. However, which country should specialize in food and which in cloth? It is now that we compare the opportunity costs in the two countries. The opportunity cost of food in the USA is 0.5 units of cloth while in the UK it is 2.5 units of cloth. Thus the USA specializes in food production. At point b on the global PPF the USA specializes completely in food and the UK completely in cloth.

Trade opens up between the countries and there is an exchange rate which gives the units of cloth per unit of food. A country will trade at any exchange rate which is less than the opportunity cost of production. For instance the UK will accept an exchange rate for cloth of less than 2.5 units of cloth per unit of food and the USA will accept an exchange rate of greater than 0.5 units of cloth per unit of food. These upper limits on the exchange rates are given by the lines F and C. Note that C has the same slope as the USA's PPF and F has the same slope as the UK's PPF. The actual exchange rate depends upon consumer preferences.

For instance if consumers have a preference to consume at c on the global PPF, then

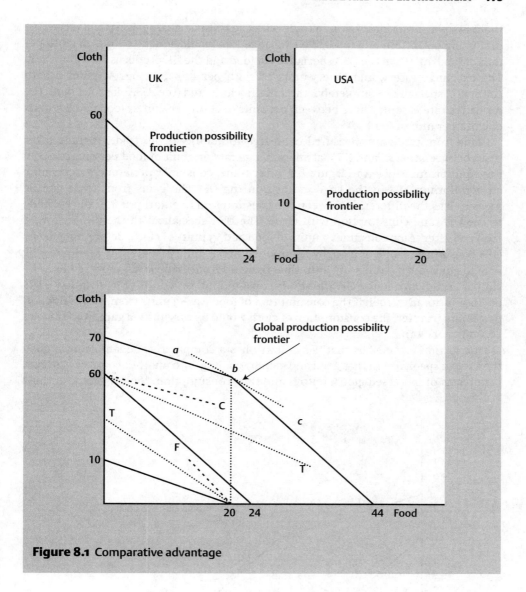

Figure 8.1 Comparative advantage

Table 8.2 Trade and comparative advantage

Labour per unit of output	UK	USA
Food	5 (5/2 cloth)	6 (6/12 cloth)
Cloth	2 (2/5 food)	12 (12/6 food)
Note: Opportunity costs are given in parentheses		

there is a partial specialization in trade with the UK specializing in cloth and the USA producing both cloth and food. The exchange rate would equal 0.5 units of cloth per unit of food. At *c* then the USA specializes in food and the UK produces food and cloth. The exchange rate would be 2.5 units of cloth per unit of food. At point *b* both countries specialize completely, the UK in cloth and the USA in food and the exchange rate is somewhere between 0.5 units of cloth per unit of food and 2.5 units of cloth per unit of food.

Gains from trade are measured compared to autarky or no trade. If trade takes place between the UK and USA, at an exchange rate of 1 unit of food per unit of cloth, the equilibrium is given in Figure 8.2. After trade, consumer preferences determine an equilibrium at *f* in the USA and at *g* in the UK. The gains from trade can be measured as the difference between the consumption in autarky at *h* in the UK and *j* in the USA and consumption with trade. The USA specializes in the production of food and after trade consumes 7 units of food and 13 units of cloth. Before trade if the USA consumed 7 units of food, by its production possibility frontier, it would only be able to consume 7.5 units of cloth, thus the gain from trade is 5.5 units of cloth. By similar arguments, in the UK after-trade consumption is 13 units of food and 47 units of cloth in autarky, then if the consumption of food was 13 units from the production possibility frontier, the consumption of cloth would be 27.5 units, a gain from trade of 19.5 units of cloth.

This section establishes that if a country has a comparative advantage in a good then it can specialize in that good and gain by trading with another country. The gain is in terms of increased global output and thus consumption. Next we consider how

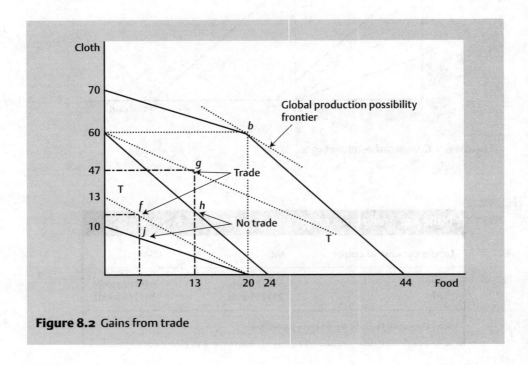

Figure 8.2 Gains from trade

this outcome changes when one or more of goods generates external costs, such as pollution, in its production process.

8.3 The Environment and Comparative Advantage

8.3.1 Extending the basic trade model to include the environment

What happens if we now introduce an environmental cost into this model? This could make the model quite complex, so let us assume that just cloth produced in the UK imposes an external cost which is confined to the UK, and that everything else is unchanged. The UK Environmental Agency has specified that 60 units of emissions from cloth production is an acceptable standard. Emissions depend upon two things: the amount of cloth produced and the labour use per unit of output. For the purpose of the example we assume that:

Emissions = 4.5 Cloth/(labour use per unit).

If the UK continues to specialize in cloth, then with a system of emission regulation through tradable permits or Pigovian taxes, the maximum amount of cloth that can be produced in the UK is reduced to 40 units and labour use is increased to 3 units per unit of cloth. These effects are given in Table 8.3 and Figure 8.3.

The impact of domestic environmental policy is to reduce the production of the polluting output. In turn, this has the impact of reducing the gains from trade. However, if the UK attempts to use trade policy in place of domestic environmental policy, then the gains from trade are reduced further. In the absence of a domestic environmental policy, the output of cloth would have to be reduced to 26.67 units as there is no means of inducing producers to use the additional labour to reduce the level of pollution, the production of food would increase to 13.3 units. Trade policy, in the form of import quotas or tariffs on food to reduce the degree of specialization in the

Table 8.3 Labour use with an environmental policy

Labour per unit of output	UK	USA
Food	5 (5/3 cloth)	6 (6/12 cloth)
Cloth	2 (3/5 food)	12 (12/6 food)

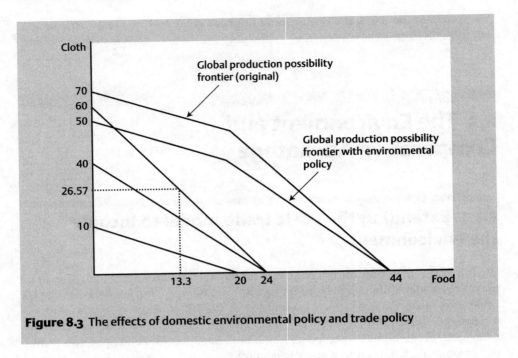

Figure 8.3 The effects of domestic environmental policy and trade policy

'dirty' good, is a 'second-best' policy as it reduces the welfare gains from specialization. In fact in this example the countries return to a pattern of output similar to that under autarky. The clear message is that trade policy is not the best way of achieving domestic environmental goals. It is more efficient to use domestic environmental policies, such as Pigovian taxes or tradable emission permits, to reduce pollution to optimal levels.

8.3.2 The interaction between trade and environmental policy

In the last section we analysed the interaction between trade and environmental policy by adapting a very simple trade model. In this section we recap on some of the main points using a more general trade model and explicitly introduce consumer preferences into the account. Instead of analysing two countries at once we just consider one country, the UK, which accounts for a small proportion of world trade (the small-country assumption). We continue to assume that cloth production is polluting and food is not, but the production possibility frontier, shown in Figure 8.4 is now concave to the origin indicating that as we devote more resources to food production the reduction in cloth output increases. This accounts for the fact that the UK economy is reallocating resources (land, labour, and capital) from food production to cloth production which are progressively less and less suitable for cloth production.

Consumer preferences are given by 'community indifference curves'. These are represented by utility contours which indicate increased levels of happiness as we move away from the origin to higher levels of consumption of both goods. Along a given curve, utility is constant. Community indifference curves, labelled U_1, U_2, etc. in Figure 8.4, represent the sum across the population of individual preferences for these goods. An economy is in equilibrium when it reaches its highest attainable level of satisfaction and this occurs where an indifference curve just touches (is tangent to) the production possibility frontier, for instance at point e. This represents an equilibrium in a state of autarky or no trade. The equilibrium is maintained by a price ratio, represented by the line dd, for cloth and food equal to the slope of the production possibility frontier and the community indifference curve at e. This implies that the rate at which it is technically feasible to trade off food against cloth is equal to the rate at which people would be prepared to trade them off against each other in terms of utility.

If the UK trades, then the comparative advantage depends upon world prices. Unlike the linear example, specialization of production is not complete. In Figure 8.5, world prices are given by the line ww. This line also represents the country's consumption possibility frontiers. The UK now specializes in cloth, but unlike the linear case, not completely. The UK produces at p, but consumes at c. This represents an increase in welfare indicated by the higher indifference curve at c rather than e. In fact, at all points along ww welfare is as least as high as it is under autarky.

If the level of production at p represents excessive pollution, then regulation can be used to adjust the production possibility frontier so that it accounts for the external

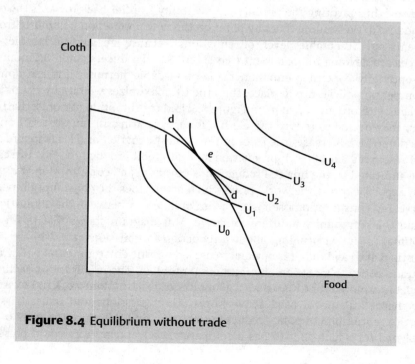

Figure 8.4 Equilibrium without trade

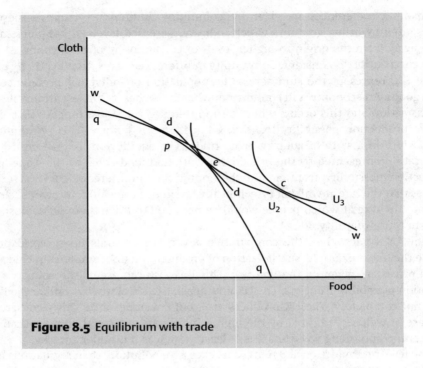

Figure 8.5 Equilibrium with trade

costs associated with cloth production. This implies resources are used for pollution abatement, thus pivoting the production possibility frontier back towards the origin from qq to q'q. We assume that any point on the new production possibility frontier represents an acceptable level of emissions because an appropriate level of resources are devoted to abatement (see Figure 8.6). Producers could be induced to abate optimally by either emission taxes or tradable permits. If these domestic environmental policies are in place, then the UK maximizes welfare by maintaining free trade, with production at p_1, in Figure 8.6, and consumption at c_1. Alternatively a country may decide to reduce the cloth output by putting an import tariff on food production which increases the price in the domestic market and leads to a reallocation of resources out of cloth production and into food production. This increase in price is indicated by the line tt. Production is now at p_2 and consumption at c_2 where the UK exports cloth at the world price which determines the consumption possibility curve, but consumption itself is at a point of tangency between the domestic price line and the community indifference curve. This diagram shows that tariffs are a suboptimal means of bringing about a reduction in emissions (the welfare at c_1 is higher than at c_2) and that it is optimal to use a domestic environmental policy rather than trade policy to tackle an environmental problem. The implications of this type of model is explored for Chile using a general equilibrium framework in Box 8.2

The theoretical model used above raises other questions and issues. First, the domestic environmental policy reduces production and therefore the level of trade in the good for which the UK has a comparative advantage. This could be seen as

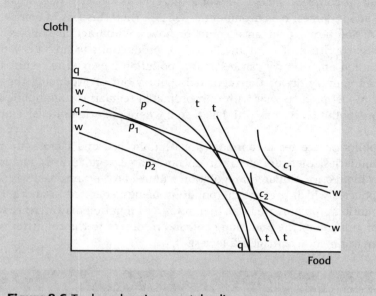

Figure 8.6 Trade and environmental policy

Box 8.2 The Effects on Chile of Trade Liberalization

Up to 1975 Chile adopted a protectionist trade policy with extensive protection for domestic industry. Following a series of reforms during the 1980s Chile has become an export-orientated economy with a high rate of export growth in natural-resource based industries such as agriculture, fisheries, forestry, and mining, all areas where Chile has a comparative advantage. These changes have led to economic growth and rising incomes. Economic growth has brought with it environmental problems (World Bank, 1994).

Using a general equilibrium model van der Mensbrugghe et al. (1998) analyse the environmental impacts of different forms of trade liberalization in Chile. They conclude that if Chile adopts 'unilateral' trade liberalization, then this would be damaging to the environment unless trade liberalization is accompanied by a more stringent environmental policy. The authors also advocate a coordinated environmental policy as they find that there is substitutability between pollutants: thus as one pollutant is targeted then producers may change production methods to generate another form of pollutant.

a reduction in competitiveness on world markets. However, if a number of other countries adopt domestic environmental policies, then this loss of competitiveness is reduced. See Box 8.3 for an account of how environmental policies may converge across countries. If we allow factors of productions to migrate between the countries, then one country can become a 'pollution haven'. The result is that the unregulated country drives the regulated country out of producing the polluting good. The model predicts that with uncoordinated regulation and mobile factors of production, 'pollution-havens' will be created where pollution-intensive production is relocated.

If the pollution creates a common global public bad and factors are immobile across boundaries, then unilateral or uncoordinated regulation is inefficient and ultimately ineffective. Unilateral regulation will need to be combined with other tax or trade policies which prevent the pollution being generated in another country. Where pollution problems are local, then resource migration may increase welfare by shifting production of the polluting good and resources to the countries where the costs of environmental damage are lowest.

Box 8.3 The California Effect

The political scientist David Vogel (1995) has coined the phrase 'The California effect' to describe the situation where environmental standards for a group of trading countries tends to converge upon those of the country with the highest standards. The 1970 US Clean Air Act Amendments allowed California to enact stricter automobile emission standards than the rest of the USA. In 1990 Congress brought national emission standards up to Californian levels and California adopted tighter standards still. American automobile manufacturers produce vehicles to the California standard to sell to that market and also in anticipation that the standards in all states will be increased to the Californian level.

The term 'California effect' is used to describe a much broader phenomenon where tighter regulatory standards are matched in competing countries. The economic explanation of this is that as one country's product standards are improved, then domestic producers have an initial competitive advantage in the market so other countries have an incentive to increase their standards so that their producers can compete.

Vogel advocates a *laissez-faire* policy to product standards where there are incentives for countries to increase their product standards to the levels required by the richer, greener nations. However, this effect is only relevant in cases where the environmental problem can be resolved by improving product standards.

8.3.3 Partial equilibrium model of trade and the environment

The last section considers the impact of trade within a simple general equilibrium model, which represents the whole economy. It is also useful to analyse the effect of trade on a single polluting product. This extends the analysis of externalities introduced in Chapter 2 to an economy which is open to trade. We use consumer and producer surplus as a measure of welfare. This analysis is based on Runge (1995).

Figure 8.7 is divided into six diagrams. The right-hand diagrams give the market equilibrium for a country which exports the commodity, the left-hand diagrams give the equilibrium for an importer. Each pair of diagrams demonstrates a particular issue: Figure 8.7(i) shows that countries gain from trade; Figure 8.7 (ii) introduces external costs by driving a wedge between the supply curve and the supply curve adjusted to account for external costs; it shows how gains from trade are less clear-cut for the exporting country; finally, Figure 8.7 (iii) shows that a tariff policy is an alternative to a domestic environmental policy, but an inferior one.

Let us now consider the details. In Figure 8.7 (i), the equilibrium under autarky is at e and the sum of consumer and producer surplus is given by the area obe. If trade opens at the fixed world price (small country assumption) p, then the countries benefit from an increase in welfare efg. In the exporting country there is an increase in producer surplus and a fall in consumer surplus and in the importing country the opposite occurs.

Figure 8.7(ii) introduces an adjusted supply curve which takes account of the marginal external cost MEC which is assumed to be proportional to output. The gains from trade for the exporting country are reduced by additional external costs equal to the ehjf. Thus whether trade brings a net increase or net decrease in welfare depends upon whether the additional producer surplus from trade efg is greater than additional environmental costs ehjf. The outcome for the importer is unambiguous. In addition to the original gains from trade efg the importing country also gains a reduction in external costs ghje. In other words by importing it has transferred some of the external costs to the exporting countries. Can the welfare gains from trade be increased? If both countries introduce domestic environmental policies, Pigovian taxes or tradable permits that force firms to account for the external costs when taking their output decisions (internalize the externality), then gains from trade can be increased in both countries. In the case of the exporting country supply is reduced from Q_s to Q'_s and welfare gains equal efg minus ehik which is clearly positive. In the importing country there is a further reduction in the supply from Q_s to Q'_s and a further reduction in external costs of mnhg which exceeds the loss of producer surplus mng.

Is a trade policy such as an export tax a viable alternative policy to a domestic environmental policy? Figure 10.7 (iii), for the exporting country, shows the case where an export tax is levied which reduces the price to producers to p". The

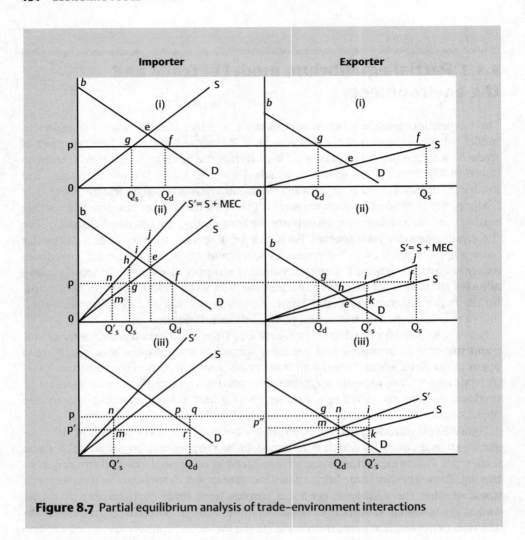

Figure 8.7 Partial equilibrium analysis of trade–environment interactions

government captures *mnik* in tax revenue, consumer surplus increases as the price to domestic consumers falls, but there is an overall welfare loss equal to *mgn*. In the importing country, the policy would involve an import subsidy, which reduced the price to p″. The component of the subsidy expenditure not captured by increased consumer surplus equals *rpq*. Therefore an export tax is inferior to optimal domestic environmental regulation as a means of protecting the environment.

8.4 Empirical Evidence on the Trade Effects of Environmental Regulation

THEORETICAL models predict the link between trade and environmental policy. First, the additional costs of environmental protection can change the pattern of comparative advantage: thus stringent environmental policies in a country can actually change the comparative advantage a country has in a product so that it no longer exports that product. Second if factors of production are mobile between countries, then this effect is reinforced and factors of production associated with a particular polluting commodity will shift to so-called pollution havens. This effect has the potential to be detrimental if the pollutant is a global bad, for instance carbon emissions, as the level of pollution remains excessive, but may be beneficial if the pollutant, for instance groundwater contamination, has only a local effect. In that the pollution has shifted to the country with lower environmental costs. The actual effects of environmental regulation on trade is an empirical issue: theoretical models are based upon restrictive assumptions which do not always hold in reality. We now review the empirical evidence.

8.4.1 The effects of environmental policy on competitiveness

In a multi-country cross-section study for 1975 Tobey (1990) uses a trade model to predict exports. He assesses the relationship between exports of a group of pollution-intensive commodities and the stringency of environmental regulation. Environmental regulation is included in the model as an index of environmental stringency for each country, as the example given in Table 8.4 shows.

The analysis is repeated for a group of five pollution-intensive industries, namely mining, paper, chemicals, steel, and non-ferrous metals. The results show that for all commodities the stringency of environmental regulation has a negligible effect on

Table 8.4 Index of environmental stringency (7 = strict, 1 = tolerant)

Developed countries		Developing countries	
Austria	4	Chile	4
UK	4	Liberia	1
Norway	6	Nigeria	2
USA	7	Israel	4

exports. Therefore this study concludes that there is little evidence that the stringency of environmental control measures caused export patterns to deviate from patterns predicted by the resource endowments of the countries. The explanation of this result, which is consistent with other studies, is that pollution abatement costs are a relatively small proportion of the total costs of production. For instance, the highest proportion of total costs accounted for by abatement costs was 2.89 per cent for inorganic chemical plants in the USA. Tobey remarks that other factor market and product market effects are likely to outweigh pollution abatement costs in the determination of competitiveness and thus export levels. See Box 8.4 for an extension of this argument.

Box 8.4 The Porter Hypothesis

In an article in *Scientific American*, Porter (1990) challenges the notion that tight environmental policies inevitably lead to increased productions costs which reduce the competitiveness of a country's industry and therefore reduce its export competitiveness. Instead, he claims that tighter environmental standards trigger innovations that may increase a firm's competitiveness and outweigh short-run costs to firms of complying with the regulation. The so-called 'Porter hypothesis' is supported by evidence from case studies which shows that some firms operating under strict environmental regulations have shown relatively high levels of performance. The empirical evidence in Tobey (1990) and Jaffe *et al.* (1995) indicates that there is very little evidence to indicate that tighter environmental regulations significantly reduce competitiveness, which may be largely explained by the small proportion of costs associated with complying with pollution standards.

The two reasons why Porter's hypothesis may be correct: first, environmental regulations make firms aware of opportunities for changing production activities in ways not previously identified; second, firms subject to stricter environmental standards than their foreign competitors may be at a competitive advantage when environmental standards are tightened in their competitors' markets.

Arguments against the Porter hypothesis include: first, why should rational firms need to be prompted by environmental regulation to find new techniques which improve their competitiveness; second, if environmental regulations are not tightened the firm operating under the lax environmental standard has a permanent competitive advantage.

At present there is no theoretical justification (Xepapadeas and de Zeeuw, 1999) for the Porter hypothesis and no firm empirical evidence. However, it received widespread attention because it provided an attractive idea to policy-makers attempting to justify tighter environmental regulations to industrialists.

8.4.2 Production location and environmental regulation

If factors of production such as labour and capital are mobile, then firms in a polluting industry will take account of the costs of complying with local pollution regulations along with factor availability and prices when deciding where to locate a plant. In a study of the decisions of firms to locate new plants in America, Levinson (1996) concludes that there is little evidence that firms choose to locate new plants in states with less stringent environmental regulations. Levinson attributes this to the small proportion of new investment allocated to pollution abatement equipment, on average 4 per cent. A further explanation is that firms operating plants in a number of states find it cost-effective to operate all plants to the same environmental standards and many firms anticipate that regulation will converge to a uniformly strict level. In common with the study by Tobey (1990) discussed in the last section there appears to be little evidence that stricter environmental regulation in a country will either reduce competitiveness or dissuade firms from locating production facilities there even in pollution-intensive industries.

The validity of arguments often pushed by some politicians and industrialists for retaining lax domestic environmental controls on the grounds of maintaining international competitiveness depends upon the costs of abatement. The empirical evidence suggests that there are often other costs which are more important in determining international competitiveness.

8.5 International Trade Agreements and the Environment

8.5.1 International trade agreements

Multilateral trade negotiations under the General Agreement on Tariffs and Trade (GATT) have their origins after the Second World War when memories of the damaging protectionism of the 1930s led the victorious countries, especially the UK and USA, to plan for more stable trade relations. The Bretton Woods Conference in 1944 proposed setting up three international organizations, the International Monetary Fund (IMF), the International Trade Organization (ITO), and the International Bank for Reconstruction and Development (IBRD). While negotiations were taking place on the form of the ITO, a group of countries recognized the need for immediate reductions in tariffs. The USA took the lead by drafting a general agreement on tariffs and trade, and later this was agreed to by twenty-three countries as the GATT. Despite subsequent negotiations, the ITO never came into existence leaving the GATT as the framework for trade relations. Currently 100 countries are signatories of the GATT accounting for 80 per cent of world trade. An additional twenty-nine countries abide by GATT rules.

In 1995 the GATT was replaced by the WTO which inherited from the GATT the following objectives. The WTO has three principle objectives. First, to provide a forum for multilateral trade negotiations. Second, to provide a framework for eliminating trade barriers. Third, to provide agreed rules to reduce unilateral trade-restricting action. These objectives are pursued by a set of thirty-eight Articles which form the basis for resolving disputes. These Articles embody three basic principles.

- Non-discrimination or the most-favoured nation (MFN) clause. This clause binds WTO signatories to treat all sources of imports for a good equally. Thus if a country reduces the tariff on timber from one country it must extend this new tariff to all countries. This principle acts as a disincentive to unilateral trade agreements.

- Reciprocity is the principle that if one country agrees to reduce tariffs, then the other country should agree to reduce tariffs to leave their bilateral balance of trade unchanged.

- Transparency, this principle in most cases, involves the elimination of quantitative trade restrictions in favour of tariffs. It is argued that a tariff is clear to exporters and domestic consumers.

When the GATT was established there was no explicit reference to environmental issues and it is only recently that the GATT has been asked to adjudicate on barriers to trade justified on environmental grounds. The GATT approach is best illustrated with some examples. Most product-related environmental policies do not conflict with GATT rules provided they apply equally to domestic and imported products. This is the principle of the most favoured nation; thus if Germany requires domestic cars to carry catalytic converters and seat belts it can impose these standards upon imports, but it cannot require imported cars to comply with more stringent standards. Countries can also adopt a range of policies to protect the domestic environment including restrictions on emissions to air and water, but they cannot extend these standards to imported products unless they physically affect the final product. An imported product should not be treated differently from an identical domestic product on the grounds that the processes employed in making it were different.

This basic principle has led countries wishing to restrict trade on the grounds of process and products to invoke Article XX which allows for exceptions to general GATT principles where 'necessary to protect human, animal or plant life or health' (Article XX(b)) and where relating to the conservation of exhaustible natural resource if such measures are made in conjunction with restrictions on domestic production or consumption (Article XX(g)). The application of this article is informative in the case of the dolphin–tuna dispute between the USA and Mexico.

In eastern tropical areas of the Pacific Ocean schools of yellowfin tuna are often found swimming beneath dolphins. When the tuna is harvested with purse seine nets some dolphins become trapped and often die unless released quickly. The US Marine Mammal Protection Act set out fishing methods that the American fishing fleet must comply with and which also extends to other countries fishing in the American zone of the Pacific Ocean. A country exporting tuna to the USA must prove that it meets the dolphin protection standards, otherwise an embargo will be placed on all fish exports from that country.

In particular, the USA banned tuna exports from Mexico and also a number of intermediary countries handling tuna from Mexico *en route* to the USA on the grounds that Mexican fishing methods were not dolphin-friendly. Mexico requested a GATT panel in February 1991 and it reported in September 1991. The panel concluded that the USA could not embargo imports of tuna products from Mexico simply because Mexican regulations on methods of tuna catching were less strict than American regulations. However, the USA could apply its regulations to the quality of the product. It also concluded that GATT rules did not permit one country to use trade policy as a means of coercing another to enforce its domestic laws in another country.

This ruling is important in that it reinforces the principle that products should be judged on their quality alone not on the process used in their production. However, the panel deemed it acceptable for the USA to allow advertising to identify brands of tuna as being 'dolphin-friendly'. Mexico's complaint was upheld by the panel, but the panel's report was not adopted and the disagreement was eventually resolved bilaterally between the USA and Mexico. Trade disputes due to domestic environmental regulation have also arisen in the European Union, see Box 8.5 for an example.

In 1995 the World Trade Organization was established as the successor to the GATT, providing the framework under which multilateral trade negotiations take place. In the preamble to the Marrakech Agreement (1994) which set up the WTO, reference is made to 'sustainable development' and environmental preservation. The WTO is set to become more involved in resolving conflicts where trade policy and environmental concerns interact. To this end WTO has established a Trade and Environment Committee to bring 'environmental and sustainable development issues into the mainstream of WTO work'(WTO, 1999, *www.wto.org/wto/environ/*). It remains to be seen if it is feasible for a trade organization to become involved in environmental policy. In another statement a more conventional approach is expressed: 'The WTO is not an environmental agency. Its members do not want it to intervene in national or international environmental policies or to set environmental standards. Other agencies that specialize in environmental issues are better qualified to undertake those tasks' (WTO, 1999, *www.wto.org/about/beyondthe*). Clearly the interactions between trade and the environment require further clarification and will be a central issue in the first round of WTO trade talks initiated in Seattle in 1999.

Box 8.5 European Environmental Regulation and Trade

Article 30 of the 1957 Treaty of Rome aimed to foster the freedom of trade between the member States of the European Community by preventing 'quantitative restrictions on trade', but Article 36 of the same treaty states that trade may be restricted on the grounds of 'public morality, public policy or public security' or for the 'protection of health and life of humans, animals or plants'. Thus it allowed countries to restrict trade so long as it was justified on one of these counts. So when is a domestic environmental policy little more than a form of disguised protectionism?

In 1981 Denmark enacted legislation requiring all beer and soft drinks to be sold in a range of reusable containers accredited by the Danish environmental protection agency. Containers used by exporters to Denmark often did not meet the strict Danish recycling requirements and their sale was prohibited. The foreign companies complained that the extra costs involved in modifying their containers and arranging collection and transporation in Denmark would reduce exports. Manufacturers took their case to the European Commission who ruled that the Danish law contravened Article 30. Not satisfied by Denmark's modification of the law in 1984, the European Commission took the case in December 1986 to the European Court of Justice. This step was taken because there was a fear that countries would justify protectionist laws on environmental grounds.

In September 1988, the Court ruled that Denmark's deposit and return system was legal under Article 36, because there was no alternative means of reducing the amount of waste. However, Denmark was required to remove the restrictions on the type of container: any container could be used so long as it was recycled.

This ruling was highly significant: for the first time the Court had sanctioned an environmental regulation which restricted trade. This led the German Government to enact very strict recycling laws which were also restrictive to trade. The implication was that, even within the Single European Market, countries could introduce legislation which restricted trade so long as it was justified on environmental grounds. See Vogel (1995: ch. 3) for a fuller account.

8.5.2 Multilateral environmental agreements and trade

The theoretical models presented in Section 2 of this chapter predict that trade restrictions offer a second-best, or suboptimal, solution to local, transboundary, and global environmental problems. The first-best or optimal solution is found by either taxing emissions or introducing a tradable permit system. Multilateral environmental agreements should ideally involve an agreement upon the required restrictions coupled with optimal national environmental policies to achieve the agreed standard for national emissions. This principle holds for both transboundary and global pollution problems.

Unfortunately there is little evidence that national economic policies even in relatively green developed countries are close to being optimal and in many developing countries environmental policies may be weak or ineffectively enforced. The first-best optimum is therefore unattainable and regulators are compelled to choose from among second-best policies an option which, at least partially, achieves environmental objectives. This argument goes some way to explain why multilateral environmental agreements include trade restrictions as the primary policy instrument. Trade flows, because they involve movement across national boundaries, provide an opportunity for monitoring and restricting the flow of materials. This may go some way to curtailing the environmental damage due to a particular product in the absence of effective national policies. We have also seen in Chapter 7 how difficult it is to set up voluntary international agreements for the control of global pollutants or the protection of global public goods, since countries have the incentive to free-ride on such agreements. Trade sanctions provide a means of encouraging participation in agreements and penalizing signatories that step out of line. The following policies provide examples.

The United Nations Convention on International Trade in Endangered Species of Wild Fauna (CITES) was ratified in 1973. It regulated trade in species which are threatened with extinction (Appendix 1 species) and those species that may become extinct unless trade is strictly regulated (Appendix 2 species). Trade is regulated by a system of export and import permits, the requirement for an import permit before an export permit is issued attempts to prevent exporters sending live animals or animal products to countries which are not party to the convention. This policy aims to reduce the incentive to exploit rare species through trade, but can be seen as a second best substitute for effective national policies which protect species and their habitats within countries.

The 1987 Montreal Protocol is an application of the 1985 Vienna Convention regarding substances that cause depletion of the ozone layer. The parties to the original protocol agreed to reduce chloroflurocarbons (CFC) by 50 per cent by 1999. Negotiations in London in 1990 agreed that production of CFCs should cease in 1996. Further meetings in Copenhagen (1992) and Montreal (1997) have increased the list of substances subject to restrictions (see www.unep.ch/ozone for details). The Copenhagen (1992) meeting agreed not to export or import restricted substances and to ban imports of products containing CFCs by 1993. This policy includes both agreements over domestic production and consumption of these products but is also backed up by trade measures which prevent countries which have not ratified the treaty becoming potential markets for these products. This is an example of where a trade policy is used as an effective complement to a multilateral environmental agreement and effective domestic policies. Trade policy is only used to prevent non-parties to the agreement eroding the effectiveness of the restrictions agreed, and signatories from defaulting on their commitments.

The Basel Convention on the Control of Transboundary Movements of Hazardous Waste and their Disposal allows restrictions to trade in hazardous waste. It forces countries to focus on national solutions to industrial waste problems and protects export countries from being used as dumping grounds. Thus the convention establishes that exports of waste should only be with the importing country's permission (as distinct from importing companies) and if an exporting country believes that waste will not be disposed of in an environmentally sound manner it should not be exported. Trade with non-signatory countries is not allowed (see *www.unep.ch/basel* for more details).

8.6 Summary

TRADE flows have a profound effect on national economies and must therefore have a significant effect on national environments. Simplistically, trade increases economic growth, production, and consumption and by the fact that more production requires more natural resources an increase in trade is likely to lead to an increase in pollution. However, increased trade also leads to a specialization of production, which may occur in countries where inputs are used more efficiently or in 'pollution havens', countries with lax environmental standards. The empirical evidence suggests that the effects of stringent environmental standards on a country's competitiveness is rather slight and that countries with lax environmental standards will not necessarily become pollution havens because firms place more importance upon factors other than environmental costs when deciding where to locate.

From the theoretical and empirical analysis there is no clear justification for restricting trade on environmental grounds. Free trade for most countries is welfare-increasing and, so long as countries have effective domestic environmental policies, there is no reason why it should be more damaging to the environment than restricted trade. Trade policies are almost always suboptimal instruments for protecting a country's environment and should be replaced by domestic environmental policies. The question arising from this is why are trade restrictions used as a major component of environmental policies? First, environmental justifications for trade restrictions are sometimes little more than covert protectionism. Second, in the case of international environmental agreements, they are a suboptimal alternative where the failure of countries' domestic environmental policies may have consequences on the global environment. Examples include, the Montreal Protocol, CITES, and the Basel Convention on Hazardous Waste. In all these cases, using trade restrictions might be the best approach that is available.

References

Andersson, T. , Folke, C., and Nystrom, S. (1995). *Trading with the Environment* (London: Earthscan).

Jaffe, A. B., Peterson, S. R., Portney, P. R., and Stavins, R. N. (1995) 'Environmetnal regulation and the competitiveness of US manufacturing: What does the evidence tell us?', *Journal of Economic Literature* 33: 132–63.

Levinson, A. (1996) 'Environmental regulations and manufacturers' location choice: evidence from the Census of Manufacturers', *Journal of Public Economy* 62: 5–29.

McGuire, M. C. (1982) 'Regulation, factor rewards and international trade', *Journal of Political Economy* 17: 335–54.

Porter, P. R. (1990) 'America's green strategy', *Scientific American* 264: 168.

Runge, C. F. (1995) 'Trade pollution and environmental protection', in D. W. Bromley (ed.), *The Handbook of Environmental Economics* (Blackwell: Oxford).

Sodersten, B., and Reed, G. (1994) *International Economics 3rd edn.* (New York: St Martin's Press).

Tobey, J. A. (1990) 'The effects of domestic environmental policies on patterns of world trade: an empirical test', *Kyklos* 43: 191–209.

Van Der Mensbrugghe, D., Roland-Holst, D., Dissus, S., and Beglin, J. (1998) 'The interface between growth, trade pollution, and natural resource use in Chile', *Agricultural Economics* 19: 87–97.

Vogel, D. (1995) *Trading Up: Consumer and Environmental Regulation in the Global Economy* (Cambridge Mass.: Harvard University Press).

Walter, L. A. (1991) *International Economics (4th edn.)* (London: HarperCollins Academic).

World Bank (1994) *Chile Managing Environmental Problems: Economic Analysis of Selected Issues*, Report 13061 (Washington, DC: World Bank).

Xepapadeas, A., and de Zeeuw, A. (1999) 'Environmental policy and competitiveness: the Porter hypothesis and the composition of capital', *Journal of Environmental Economics and Management* 37: 165–82.

Part II

Applying the Tools

Chapter 9
Transport and the Environment

IN this chapter, we review how transport affects the environment, seeing how its impact can be quantified in economic terms, and look at the use of cost-benefit analysis (CBA) to appraise investments in transport infrastructure. We will also see how economic incentives can be used to reduce the environmental costs of transport, as well as addressing other externalities associated particularly with car use, such as congestion.

9.1 The Environmental Impacts of Transport

TRANSPORT is all about getting people and goods from A to B: the transport industry 'produces' services which accomplish this purpose. Transportation services are an essential component of economic activity, and are one key to its growth. The use of transportation services continues to grow globally, as Tables 9.1 and 9.2 show.

Most people would agree that transportation is a 'good thing' which, on the whole, improves our quality of life. However, transportation has a number of environmental-side effects that people dislike. These environmental impacts arise in a number of ways:

- through the emission of pollutants by cars, lorries, buses, trains, and airplanes;
- through land-take, for example for new airports and new roads; and
- as increases in noise levels.

Economics can help us to quantify how bad these side-effects are, and can also help us design policies for reducing them. Let us first look in a little more detail at what these side-effects are.

Table 9.1 Road traffic volume in OECD countries, 1970–1992

	Passenger cars				
	Vehicle-km travelled (vkt), billions			Annual growth rates (%)	
	1970	1980	1993[a]	1970–93 vkt	Passenger cars 1970–93
USA	1,434	1,789	2,652	2.7	2.2
Japan[b]	120	241	429	6.5	6.9
France	165	245	343	3.2	3.0
West Germany	216	297	425	3.0	3.6
Italy	123	191	356	4.7	4.8
Great Britain	141	197	334	3.8	3.2
Netherlands	38	61	81	3.4	3.8
OECD	2,584	3,604	5,473	3.3	3.4

	Freight vehicles				
	Vehicle-km travelled (vkt), billions			Annual growth rates (%)	
	1970	1980	1993[a]	1970–93 vkt	Freight vehicles 1970–93
USA	346	619	1,039	4.9	4.1
Japan[b]	100	142	272	4.4	4.1
France[c]	32	49	94	4.8	3.9
West Germany	37	32	46	3.6	2.0
Italy[d]	23	33	52	3.6	4.9
Great Britain	35	41	64	2.7	2.2
Netherlands	6	8	16	4.4	3.4
OECD	656	1,086	1,807	4.5	4.1

Notes:
[a] provisional data   [b] excludes light vehicles   [c] excludes freight vehicles over 15 years old with load capacity greater than or equal to 3 metric tonnes   [d] includes three-wheel vehicles

Source: Organization for Economic Cooperation and Development, *OECD Environmental Data: Compendium 1993*, and *OECD Environmental Data: Compendium 1995* (Paris, France: 1993 and 1995). Adapted from: 'An International Comparison of Transportation and Air Pollution' (ch. 9), *Transportation Statistics Annual Report 1996*. US Dept. of Transportation.

9.1.1 Pollution emissions

Here we focus on using fossil fuels to move about, and the pollution this causes. Emissions can be categorized into three broad types according to their effects. First, local pollutants. City traffic is a significant source of pollutants such as sulphur dioxide, particulate matter, benzene, and carbon monoxide. Increases in such pollu-

Table 9.2 World motor vehicle fleet, 1970–1993

Country or region	1970: No. of vehicles (thousands)	1993: No. of vehicles (thousands)	Shares of total (%)		Annual growth rates (%) 1970–1993
			1970	1993	
OECD	211,686	469,233	86	76	3.5
USA	108,418	194,063	44	31	2.6
Other OECD	103,268	275,170	42	45	4.4
Non-OECD	34,692	147,854	14	24	6.5
Total (world)	246,378	617,087	100	100	4.1

Note: data for Mexico are included with non-OECD data

Sources: Organization for Economic Cooperation and Development, *OECD Environmental Data: Compendium 1993* (Paris, France 1993); 221; and *OECD Environmental Data: Compendium 1995* (Paris, France: 1995): 215. Adapted from: 'An International Comparison of Transportation and Air Pollution' (ch. 9), *Transportation Statistics Annual Report 1996*. US Dept. of Transportation.

tants are linked to lower local air-quality and increases in illnesses, primarily cardio-vascular and pulmonary. PM_{10}, a common measure of particulate matter (soot), has been statistically linked to increased hospital admissions for cardiovascular and pulmonary illness for older people and other vulnerable groups (such as asthmatics). A recent fourteen-year study in Edinburgh found that significant relationships existed between exposure to 'black smoke'[1] and mortality rates in the over-65 age group (Prescott *et al.*, 1998). Interactions of hydrocarbons and sunlight produce photochemical smogs, which can also be injurious to health.

The second effect is regional. Acid rain has been blamed for water pollution and fish deaths in Northern Europe and in parts of Eastern Canada and North-Eastern USA. Transport is a major source of two of the constituents of acid rain, namely sulphur dioxide and nitrous oxides. A 1989 study showed that 48 per cent of UK emissions of NO_x were from road transport, which was also the fastest-growing source of emissions.[2] Traffic can also be a significant regional source of nitrates through airborne deposition.

Finally, all fossil fuel combustion results in the emission of CO_2, and transport is a significant net contributor to emissions of greenhouse gases, especially in the West. For example, in Scotland in 1993, 32 per cent of total CO_2 emissions originated in the transport sector, with road traffic accounting for 87 per cent of this figure.[3] Airlines worldwide account for about 3 per cent of total global emissions of CO_2, a figure which is predicted to rise relatively quickly. Table 9.3 gives information on traffic's contribution to total CO_2 emissions across the globe, and how this has changed over time.

[1] Black smoke is a rather crude proxy of PM_{10} levels, and refers to the way in which measurements are taken.
[2] Royal Commission on Environmental Pollution, 1992 report.
[3] In the UK as a whole, the Kyoto baseline shows transport emitted 39 million tonnes of carbon equivalents, 38MtC of which are as CO_2. 39 MtC represents 18% of the 216 MtC total UK baseline emissions.

Table 9.3 Mobile source CO_2 emissions by region, 1971–1993 (million metric tonnes)

	1971	1980	1993	World total (%) 1971	World total (%) 1993
USA	1,079.7	1,251.4	1,489.8	39	34
Canada	88.1	129.6	129.9	3	3
OECD-Europe	575.8	611.3	873.8	21	20
Japan	150.2	160.3	244.1	5	6
Australia/New Zealand	46.2	59.0	79.1	2	2
OECD total	1940	2,211.5	2,816.7	70	65
Non-OECD Europe	79.9	86.5	68.2	3	2
Former Soviet Union	276.9	351.8	298.8	10	6
Asia	141	166.0	365.9	5	9
China	[a]	83.1	168.1	—	3
Latin America[b]	200.7	260.9	340.3	7	8
Africa	45.8	91.5	117.6	2	3
Middle East	105.3	88.8	158.4	4	4
Non-OECD total	849.6	1,128.6	1,517.3	30	35
Non-OECD without Europe and former Soviet Union	492.8	690.3	150.3	18	27
World total	2,789.6	3,340.1	4,334.0	100	100

[a] data not available for 1971
[b] data for Mexico is included in non-OECD Latin America

Source: Organization for Economic Cooperation and Development. OECD Environmental Data: Compendium 1993 and Compendium 1995. Table taken from: An International Comparison of Transportation and Air Pollution (ch. 9), in *Transportation Statistics Annual Report 1996*. US Dept. of Transport.

From a policy perspective, it is important to note that pollution from cars, lorries, airplanes, and trains share many of the characteristics of non-point source emissions (see Chapter 11). This is because there are a very large number of mobile sources each contributing a very small amount to total emissions. Policies should thus avoid being based on a need to continuously monitor emissions from individual sources, since this would be extremely costly and probably politically unfeasible too.

9.1.2 Land use

Land is a unique resource in that it is perfectly inelastic in supply; that is, it is available to society as a fixed total quantity. Adding to transport infrastructure by building new roads or new airports uses up this scarce resource, and so imposes an opportunity cost on society. This cost is made up of the value of all those services which the land could have provided had it not been allocated to this use. Building roads and airports imposes environmental costs. These include:

- reductions in landscape quality;
- loss of wildlife habitat;
- islanding effects, whereby movement corridors for wildlife are disrupted; and
- loss of cultural heritage sites, such as when new roads are built over archaeological sites.

9.1.3 Noise

Roads, airports, and railways are noisy. As traffic movements increase, so do noise levels (technological improvements notwithstanding). The disamenity effects of additional noise due to transport investments have been the focus of government compensation schemes worldwide for some time. Noise impacts from, say, an extension to an airport, are usually measured using 'A-weighted decibels', DbA, a scale which approximates the sensitivity of the human ear. Some of the earliest work on quantifying the externalities of transport was carried out for noise impacts, for example in the enquiry into the siting of a new airport for London in 1971 (Flowerdew, 1972).

9.2 Valuing the Environmental Impacts of Transport

CHAPTER 3 described several methods available to economists for estimating the monetary value of changes in environmental quality. As noted above, transport has three main types of environmental impact: on air quality, on noise levels, and as land-take. Economics can help us to quantify the welfare losses associated with these impacts, through the use of environmental valuation methods. But which valuation methods are most suitable for estimating these external costs? Table 9.4 summarizes these valuation methods.

For *local air pollution impacts*, policy-makers and researchers have focused on estimating dose–response relationships from health data. These dose–response models relate increases in local concentrations of a given pollutant to increases in both illness (often defined in terms of hospital admissions) and premature deaths. For example, for PM10, one function reported in the literature is:

$$dRHA = 0.294 * dA$$

where dRHA is the change in the number of hospital admissions per 100,000 adults, and dA is the change in ambient concentration of PM10 (Maddison, 1997). This shows that for every 1 per cent increase in pollution concentrations, we expect to see a 0.29 per cent increase in admissions. Dose–response functions have the problem that they

Table 9.4 Valuation methods and transport impacts

Environmental impact class	Specific impact	Valuation methods	Comments
Air pollution, local	TSP SO_2 NO_x	Dose–Response Dose–Response Dose–Response	Predict impacts on health (morbidity and mortality)
Air pollution, regional	SO_2 NO_x	Dose–Response, TCM, CVM	Acidification, nitrate deposition
Air pollution, global warming	CO_2	Production function, Dose–Response	Impacts on farming and forestry; health impacts
Land-take	On wildlife On landscape quality On cultural heritage	CVM CVM CVM	
Noise	Urban noise levels	HPM	Effects on house prices

Note: CVM; contingent valuation method; TCM: travel cost method; HPM: hedonic-pricing method.

often show wide variability across studies, and that many possible choices exist for the dependent variable (RHA, above). Once health impacts have been estimated, then they are given an economic value by attaching them to estimates of the monetary value of additional illness episodes (e.g. sickness days) or, controversially, a life. Chapter 5 discussed ways of estimating the value in dollars of reducing expected deaths: estimates such as these are routinely used in health economics and in transport economics to value changes in mortality and morbidity.

For *regional pollution impacts*, such as acid rain, a variety of methods could be used to estimate the costs of losses to fisheries and forests. Where market-valued crops are concerned, dose–response methods can be used which relate the dose of increased deposition/acidity to changes in crop growth; these can then be valued in money. For non-market values, such as ecosystem damage or damage to recreational fishing, methods such as contingent valuation and travel costs could be used, although it may be difficult to quantify the contribution made to regional pollution levels of a given transport sector/investment. Finally, carbon dioxide emissions from transport may be costed in terms of their *global warming potential* using standard estimates of the value of a tonne of carbon, using studies such as those described in Chapter 12.

Many transport investments involve land-take. For impacts on wildlife, cultural sites, and landscape, contingent valuation can and has been widely used as a valuation method. Box 9.1 gives one example of such an application. Respondents might typically be asked how much they were willing to pay at most to avoid damage to, for example, an archaeological site by a new road. Alternatively, they could be asked what is the least compensation they would accept to put up with this damage. Finally, for noise impact, the hedonic-pricing method can be used. This involves estimating a statistical relationship between ambient noise levels and house prices or rents. Several such studies have been undertaken worldwide, for example in Oslo, Toronto,

Brisbane, and Helsinki (Bertrand, 1997). A recent study in Neuchâtel, Switzerland found that a rise in noise levels from 45DbA to 80DbA reduced monthly rents from £243 to £176 (Soguel, 1994). Interestingly, the marginal disamenity cost of noise fell across this range: in other words, as noise levels rise, each extra increment causes less extra disamenity than at lower noise levels.

9.3 Cost-Benefit Analysis and Transport

SOME of the earliest applications of CBA have been in the transport sector. CBA is a formally required part of the procedure for licensing a new road in some countries (e.g. the UK). What will be the principal components of such an analysis, and what are the main problems in carrying it out? Table 9.5 sets out the costs and benefits of a typical road project, a by-pass around a town:

A major constituent of total benefits is often *time savings*. A bypass may reduce congestion in a town, and speed up the travel times of motorists travelling elsewhere. Time savings can be in terms of leisure time and working time. For working time, the economic value of one hour saved for any worker is roughly equal to their wage rate, since that is the value that employers place on their labour. From this we can deduce that the value of working time varies across workers. What is the monetary value of saving in leisure time? Time is scarce, thus people will value having more of it. Ideally, we would like to find out people's WTP to save one hour's leisure time. This can be done using contingent valuation-type studies, or using revealed preference data on choices made between faster, more expensive modes of travel and cheaper, slower modes. Again, this implies that the value of leisure time will vary across individuals. However, we should note that time savings may be a rather temporary effect of the new road: if traffic increases, then travelling times can increase back to or even beyond their previous duration (the so-called Downs–Thomson Paradox).

Road investments are also motivated by a desire to reduce accidents, for example by diverting through-traffic away from population centres. We have already discussed the idea of placing an economic, money value on avoided deaths and illnesses.

Table 9.5 Main costs and benefits of a new bypass

Benefits	Costs
Time savings to drivers	Land acquisition
Reductions in accidents in town	Construction costs (labour + materials)
Reduced noise in town	Annual maintenance costs
Reduced emissions in town	Environmental costs: land-take impacts
	Environmental costs: increases in emissions
	Environmental costs: noise

Box 9.1 CBA applied to New Roads: the Harrogate–Knaresborough Bypass

The earliest uses of CBA by the UK government were in the appraisal of transport projects. However, the environmental consequences of these impacts were typically omitted from the analysis. In the UK, the government developed a procedure known as COBA for assessing new road schemes. The principal benefits counted in the analysis are time savings and accident reductions; the principal costs being construction, land acquisition, and maintenance costs. Environmental costs were excluded.

One recently controversial planned road was a bypass around the town of Knaresborough in Yorkshire. The proposals were controversial because the preferred route involved bisecting an area of ancient woodland known as Birkham Wood. Birkham Wood is notably rich in species, with 140 plant species having been recorded there. There is a rare transition zone between acid soils in the southern portion of the wood, and alkaline soils in the northern part (an 'ecotone'). Thus the wood is classified as a site of special scientific Interest (SSSI). It is also relatively large as fragments of ancient woodland go, with an area of 29.5 hectares. In England and Wales, 90 per cent of ancient woodlands are less than 20ha whilst only twelve out of the 360 sites exceed Birkham in size. The wood's proximity to Knaresborough means that it also offers recreational opportunities.

The COBA analysis in fact considered four possible routes for the road, and evaluated each in terms of its net present value (NPV). This, as will be recalled from Chapter 4, is the difference between the sum of discounted benefits (here, time and accident savings) and the sum of discounted costs.

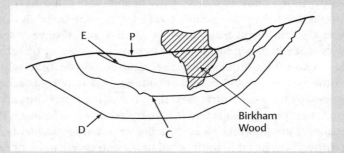

Table 9.B1 shows route P has the highest NPV and was the preferred route, even though it cuts the wood in half. The next most preferred route on NPV grounds is route E, which has an NPV which is lower than that of route P by £3.45m, even though it avoids most of the wood.

From an economics perspective, the crucial question is then whether the reduction in environmental damage associated with route E is worth more or less than the loss of net benefits in terms of the NPV difference. Hanley and Spash (1993) report the results of a contingent valuation study which tried to answer this question. They showed that if a willingness to accept a compensation measure of environmental value was used, then route E was greatly preferred to route P. This would imply that those who value the wood have the property rights, in the sense that they must be compensated for its loss. If those using the road have the rights instead, so that willingness to pay should be used, then the answer depends on the number of people who would benefit from the wood's protection. WTP was estimated to be about £19/household. Most reasonable views on the choice of the relevant population would lead one to the conclusion that the environmental benefits of avoiding damage to the wood were greater than the additional benefit in choosing route P.

Table 9.B1 Route options

	Length (km.)	Cost (£m.)	Net present value (£m.)	Woodland severance (%)
Option				
P	2.89	1.38	59.17	50
C	3.10	1.93	54.06	0
D	3.36	2.16	51.26	0
E	2.98	1.52	55.72	5

Predicted reduction in fatal and non-fatal accidents can be treated in the same way: in the UK at present, an avoided fatality is 'priced' in CBA analysis at £880,000,[4] and an avoided non-fatal but serious accident at £98,510. These figures are based partly on willingness to pay estimates for safety improvements (Jones-Lee, 1976). Estimates for the USA were noted in Chapter 5. We should note that other types of road investment, such as traffic-calming schemes, also yield benefits in the form of accident savings (see Box 9.2).

Some road schemes can reduce local environmental damage: in the case of the bypass discussed here, noise levels in town may fall as traffic is diverted to the new road, whilst emissions in town may fall too if traffic speeds up. These benefits can be counted alongside the time savings and accident reductions forecast.

On the cost side, obvious elements include the cost of acquiring land, and the predicted cost of the labour and materials used in road construction. Additional maintenance costs, net of savings in maintenance costs in the town, also count. Finally, the environmental impact discussed in the previous two sections needs to be included for a full CBA, since we assume that there is net traffic creation and that emissions and noise levels both increase overall.

Cost-benefit analysis can take into account most of the important impacts of a transport investment, and can test whether it represents an efficient use of public or private money, as Chapter 4 explained. But what are the problems here?

■ The populations of gainers and losers may be quite different, and can be difficult to identify. For example, in the case discussed in Box 9.1, gainers included motorists passing through *en route* to elsewhere, and local residents now relieved of traffic

---

[4] Although the benchmark academic estimate is currently around £2.2 million for the value of a statistical life.

Box 9.2 Road Traffic and Pedestrian Accidents: a Grim Externality

One very unfortunate externality of increasing urban traffic levels is the impact this has had on accidents involving pedestrians. A recent study by Raeside and Abdalla (reported in Hamer, 1997) has shown that for one UK city, poorer households are disproportionately affected in this way. Data on pedestrian accidents in Edinburgh was linked to home locations, and to socio-economic data on these locations. This showed that for all age groups, pedestrian casualties per 10,000 population were higher for the poorest 15 per cent of the population than for the richest 15 per cent. The gap was greatest for the 5–16 age group, with poor children in this group being eight times more likely to be injured or killed by traffic. The authors attributed this to much higher car ownership amongst richer households (so that poor children make more journeys by foot, including to and from school), and the lack of private gardens for poorer children, meaning they were more likely to be playing in the street. Overall, around 4,300 British children are seriously injured or killed by being knocked down each year. The UK child fatality rate due to such accidents is 1.3 per 100,000 children. This compares to the European average of 0.9 per 100,000, and a figure of 0.5 per 100,000 for the Netherlands.

Increases in the number of pedestrian accidents have been one factor in the large shift in the proportion of children being driven to school as opposed to walking or cycling: the proportion making their own way to school fell from 80 per cent in 1976 to 10 per cent in 1998. Partly this is a result of home relocations and schooling choices, but it is also partly a result of increased perceived risk on the part of parents. One effective way of reducing such risks is traffic-calming schemes. These slow down vehicles passing through built-up areas (the average reduction in road accidents involving children due to the installation of such schemes was recently estimated at 67 per cent). Whilst traffic-calming schemes seem expensive, they may well be economically efficient to install. A recent UK government research report suggests that a once-off investment of £2.3bn in such schemes would produce savings of £2.1bn *per annum* in health service costs (Griffiths, 1997). As we have already pointed out, the economic value of these avoided accidents would be well in excess of this, since we expect people's WTP to avoid the grief and suffering of accidents to be much greater than the value of avoided hospital spending (for evidence, see Schwab Christe and Soguel, forthcoming). Traffic-calming schemes of the type considered here seem likely, therefore, to pass the cost-benefit test.

congestion. Losers included all those who were unhappy about the landscape impacts and the destruction of an important wildlife site: but who exactly are these people?

■ Benefits gained by saving time may be temporary if building new roads encourages motorists to use the new road more. Travel times may eventually revert to or exceed their pre-project level as traffic increases, so that a short-term gain has been made, yet environmental damage may be permanent. Predicting future demand is an essential task in appraising many transport investments, but is notoriously hard to do accurately.

- Time values may in any case be used out of context. Suppose 1,000 individuals living in a city are asked their maximum WTP to save one hour's travel time to a city 300 miles away by speeding up rail links. On average, they are WTP £5 each for this saving. This value is then used to evaluate the benefits to 10,000 motorists who will save on average 5 minutes each in a journey of 2 hours, through the construction of a new road which will entail the destruction of a wetland. This is done by converting the £5/hour figure into a figure of £0.08/minute. But is this a valid benefits transfer procedure? Will people notice such a short-time saving on average? Would they be willing to accept 40p each in compensation per journey for the loss of the wetland?

9.4 Policy Options to Reduce the Externalities of Transportation

To drive our points home here, we concentrate on the car. Cars are major sources of local, regional, and global pollutants. The environmental costs associated with these emissions are externalities, since in an unregulated market car drivers pay no price to emit these pollutants. The use of cars can impose another type of externality though, congestion. As car use rises, congestion increases too (on the whole): my decision to drive to work today rather than take the train or work at home implies an increase in congestion for all drivers on my route, yet I pay only part of the cost of this increased congestion (lost time, frustration, increased pollution). Finally, car use is related to pedestrian casualties (see Box 9.2). These effects imply that in a free market, too many cars will be driven too many miles from the point of view of social optimality. The non-point characteristics of pollution from cars means it is almost impossible to choose policies which are based on the ability to continuously monitor emissions from each car, since this is impractical.

Assume that the city council wishes to cut emissions from cars in Metroville. What are the options? Policies can usefully be characterized by three possible impacts:

1. To reduce the number of cars on the road.
2. To reduce the level of emissions per kilometre driven.
3. To reduce the number of kilometres driven.

Each of these three effects would reduce pollution. Fewer cars, others things being equal, mean fewer pollution-generating units. Lower emissions per kilometre obviously reduce pollution if the rate of use of the stock of cars is constant. Finally, fewer kilometres being driven will typically mean lower emissions, since emission levels are partially a function of the amount of driving people do (they are also a function of the average speed of cars within the city). Notice that (1) and (3) also reduce congestion, but (2) does not.

Technological fixes have typified policy choice in both the USA and the EU. These include demanding that new cars be equipped with catalytic converters (which cut out most pollutants, although not CO_2), technological standards on engine perform-ance and emission levels, and technological standards on petrol/gasoline com-position. Figure 9.1 shows a possible curve relating emissions of pollutants to kilo-metres driven as E1. A technological standard might shift this downwards to E2. Such fixes may not impact on the existing car stock, but only on additions to the stock: this implies that average emissions per kilometre across the stock as a whole decline only slowly. The EU has recently negotiated a voluntary agreement with car manufactur-ers to cut average CO_2 emissions from new cars to 140 g/km by 2008 through techno-logical improvements. Technological fixes can also be inefficient if regulators insist on equal performance across all manufacturers and makes. Cathy Kling has shown that cost savings could be brought about by changing from a uniform emission stand-ard per new car sold in California to a 'fleet average' standard that allows for trade-offs across models (Kling, 1994). Alternatively, for a given total cost, such a move would allow greater reductions in emissions to be achieved.

Measures affecting the fixed costs of motoring can be effective in reducing the stock of vehicles and thus the level of emissions. Such measures include lump-sum taxes such as the Motor Vehicle Licence Duty in the UK, whereby a fixed fee of £150 a year is charged for keeping a car on public roads. Licence duties tend to have very small disincentive effects on car ownership due to their relatively low level (they are pri-marily put in place by governments to raise revenue). Fixed fees also have no impact on marginal decisions about whether to drive more or fewer miles in a year, since annual mileage is not related to the tax rate.

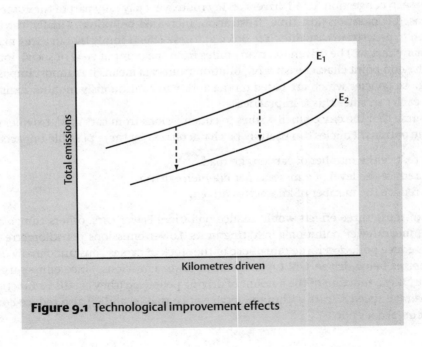

Figure 9.1 Technological improvement effects

Box 9.3 Gasoline Prices and Vehicle Use in the USA

Gasoline prices in the USA have been falling in real terms (that is, once we allow for the effects of inflation) during most of the 1980s and 1990s, and by 1997 had reached a historic all-time low at around 91 cents/gallon. This can be compared with costs of $2.29 during the Depression and $1.77 in 1948 in today's prices. As can be seen from 9.B3, falling prices have coincided with rising demand. Prices are not, of course, the only thing driving demand: rising real incomes are important too, but it is apparent that the only time when growth in demand (measured in distances driven) stuttered was during the price increases of the late 1970s. Falling gasoline prices also do little to encourage people to swap their sports utility vehicle for more fuel-efficient cars. In fact, average fuel economy of the national car fleet has improved, from 13.4 miles to the gallon in 1973 to 21.5 in 1997. This has however been outweighed by an increase in the number of cars on the road, and in an increase in how far each one is driven in a year.

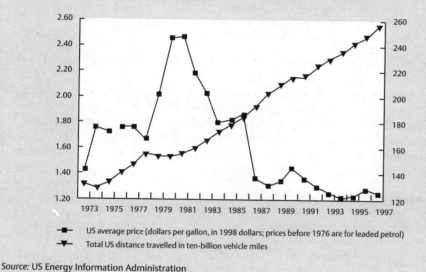

- ■ US average price (dollars per gallon, in 1998 dollars; prices before 1976 are for leaded petrol)
- ▼ Total US distance travelled in ten-billion vehicle miles

Source: US Energy Information Administration

Figure 9.B3 US Gasoline prices and vehicle miles travelled, 1973–1997

One interesting question is whether any lump-sum tax on car ownership should be differentiated according to the age or type of vehicle. Older cars tend to be more polluting than newer cars, due to both wear in the engine and advances in anti-pollution technology. Increasing the fixed cost of owning older cars might be one way of taking account of this differential impact. However, if older cars tend to be bought by poorer people, then such a move would have undesirable effects on income inequality. Engine size is another criterion for setting the car tax, since larger engines tend to be less fuel-efficient and thus emit more CO_2 than smaller engines per mile travelled. Incentives to influence the types of car (more/less polluting) that are

Box 9.4 The Impact of Increasing Air-Quality Standards on Health

As noted in the main text, the transport sector is a major source of local air pollutants such as SO_2, NO_x, and particulates. Improving air quality in a city might therefore well involve changing the way people move around. In the UK, recently announced national air quality standards for local air pollutants will require changes in transport modes. These standards are as shown in Table 9.4B.1.

Table 9.4B.1

Pollutant	Standard	Levels in Edinburgh, 1998
PM10	50g/m 24-hr mean	71 (max)
CO	10 ppm 8-hr mean	3.7 (max)
Ozone	50 ppb 8-hr mean	61 (max)
SO_2	100 ppb 15-minute mean	136 (max)
NO_2	21 ppb annual mean	25

In the city of Edinburgh, for example, meeting these targets for PM10 and NO_2 will certainly involve further restrictions on car use.

What are the expected benefits of improving air quality up to these new standards? National estimates for the UK have recently been made by AEA Technology. Predicted levels of selected pollutants were compared under business-as-usual scenarios, and compared with predicted levels under the new standards. These ambient concentrations were translated into health effects using dose–response relationships from the literature, as drawn in Table 9.4B2.

Table 9.4B.2

Pollutant	Health outcome	Dose–response coefficient
PM10	Deaths brought forward	+0.75% per $10g/m^3$
	Respiratory hospital admissions	+0.80% per $10g/m^3$
SO_2	Deaths brought forward	+0.6% per $10g/m^3$
	Respiratory hospital admissions	+0.5% per $10g/m^3$
Ozone	Deaths brought forward	+0.6% per $10g/m^3$
	Respiratory hospital admissions	+0.7% per $10g/m^3$

Using these dose–response equations, and the predicted ambient levels in 2005, gave the figures shown in Table 9.4B.3.

Clearly, these reduced deaths and reduced hospital admissions could be translated into economic values by attaching appropriate monetary values to them (see main text). In this way, the costs and benefits of the new national air-quality standards could be compared to see whether they are too strict or not strict enough, given current projections.

Table 9.4B.3

Pollutant	Reduced cumulative deaths relative to 1996 baseline by 2005	Reduced emergency respiratory hospital admissions by 2005
PM10	4,860	4,015
SO^2	9,675	6,230
Ozone	790	675

purchased can also be provided through the income tax system using differential tax allowances for workers with company cars.

Regulatory measures such as banning cars with certain number plates from entering the city on certain days of the week have also been used. Such schemes have met with rather mixed success in practice.

Measures affecting the variable cost of motoring. These variable costs include the costs of gasoline/petrol, the time cost of driving to work, and any tolls. A tax per litre of gasoline is thus an example of a measure affecting variable costs (for an empirical example, see Heringer and Shah, 1998). Petrol costs translate fairly neatly into costs per kilometre driven, for a given technology and given level of congestion. Figure 9.2 shows a demand curve D1 which gives a possible relationship between petrol prices and the number of kilometres driven. The more expensive petrol is, the less people drive their cars, and the less people own cars. Increasing the petrol price from 60p to

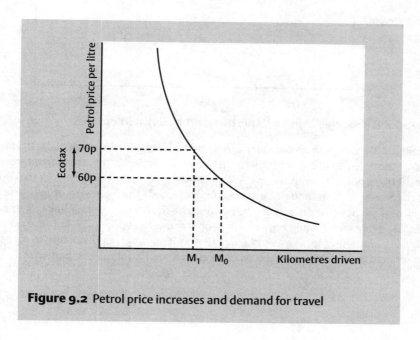

Figure 9.2 Petrol price increases and demand for travel

Box 9.5 Encouraging the Use of Public Transport: Freiburg and Zurich

Reducing congestion and improving air quality in a city may well require us to get more people to travel by public transport, and less to travel by car. But how can this switch be best encouraged? Economists Felix FitzRoy and Ian Smith have studied the apparent success stories in two European cities to find out.

In Zurich, Switzerland, car ownership is high by European standards, yet public transport use rose by 33 per cent 1985–1990 (see Fig. 9.B5). Mean trips per head by public transport are 470 per annum, compared with 290 p.a. in London and 104 p.a. in Nice. What caused this increase? First, measures were introduced to speed up journey times. These included dedicated bus and tram lanes, restrictions on parking, no-car, streets and sufficient resources to police these restrictions effectively. Automated traffic lights gave no-wait times at junctions to public transport. Second, transferable season tickets (across mode and people) were introduced. These reduced the marginal money cost of an extra journey to zero. The real price of trips fell over the time-period for all users, whilst the distance covered by the system increased. Together, these factors explain over half of the variation in demand.

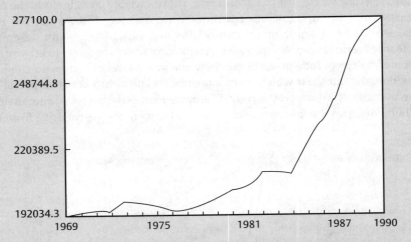

Figure 9.B5 Passenger trips by public transport in Zurich (thousands)

In Freiburg (Germany), a similar story can be told. Passenger trips on public transport in the city rose from 30 million in 1969 to over 60 million in 1993, representing an increase from 17 to 23 per cent; of total trips. In the same period, car use fell from 60 to 53 per cent of total trips, even though car ownership increased. The most important cause of this increase in public transport use turns out to be the introduction of low-cost travel cards, which are transferable across both people and service providers. Improvements in the quality of the service, as measured by the length of routes supplied, the frequency of tram services, and reduction in the real fare all had significant effects on demand.

Interestingly, public transport use was found to rise with income per head, although at a less-than-proportional rate. Other measures, such as restrictions on car speeds and car parking, and pedestrianization, are also thought to have increased demand for public transport relative to the car. Road pricing, though, was not used.

Box 9.6 Road Pricing in Singapore

The island of Singapore, with a population of 3 million people, has experienced rapid industrial growth. Singapore's road network spans 3,035 km. Its motor vehicle fleet comprises approximately 345,400 passenger cars and 141,200 commercial vehicles. To limit vehicle ownership and use, a four-pronged approach was adopted consisting of curbing car ownership, improving public transportation, improving the management of roads, and the introduction of an area licensing scheme. More specifically this includes:

(a) Very high duties on imported vehicles which comprise almost all of Singapore's cars.
(b) Vehicle registration fees are set at 195 per cent of automobile import values (Michaelis *et al*, 1995).
(c) A road tax which increases with engine size.
(d) Drivers must purchase stickers for display on windshields to access the central business district during certain hours. These can be purchased on a daily or monthly basis (Toh, 1992).
(e) In 1998 an electronic tolling system was put into place.
(f) A monthly quota system, where car ownership permits are auctioned off for thousands of dollars, was imposed in 1990 to limit the number of new vehicles.

Singapore's electronic tolling system
Cars using certain routes to enter the city centre during morning rush hour hear an electronic gadget on their dashboards beep. They then deduct the appropriate toll, adjusted depending on the time of day, from a stored-value cash card. Failure to follow this procedure leads to a fine. Evidence of violations are collected by a robotic eye spanning the highway which takes photos and also checks every car in each lane. For several months before the electronic tolling scheme became operational, motorists were given instructions for installing the devices, checking them and purchasing the appropriate value cards. The tolling system was then phased in one highway at a time to allow motorists to familiarize themselves with the system, and address any teething problems.

70p per litre through an eco-tax of 10p/litre cuts distances driven by all motorists in Metroville from m_0 to m_1. Fuel is, of course, taxed at very widely differing rates across the world. Empirical studies have found that the elasticity of demand for fuel is, on the whole, rather low (from about −0.25 to about −0.09). Demand is more elastic in the long run than the short run, since in the long run drivers can adapt by buying vehicles with more fuel-efficient engines, or relocating closer to their place of work. However, taxes on petrol may be deemed undesirable on equity grounds, since they impact disproportionately on poorer households; whilst motorists in rural areas may complain that they are being taxed for externalities (especially congestion-related) which they did not create. This is a reason for switching taxes from car ownership to car use. Box 9.3 gives information on the relationship between petrol prices in the US, and petrol consumption.

An alternative to an increase in the fuel tax is to introduce some form of road pricing. In Figure 9.3, this is represented in a similar fashion as the petrol tax if the price is set at 2p/kilometre. Here, the vertical axis measures fuel prices per km (that is, fuel prices divided by average fuel economy in litres per km). Many Western countries already use a simple form of such pricing, although tolls tend to be either restricted to a few motorways/expressways and bridges. Technological solutions are emerging which will enable more sophisticated designs of charge: for example, which enable councils to automatically monitor which cars enter into controlled zones (e.g. cross city boundaries), or which enable authorities to monitor distances driven per driver. So far, such a sophisticated use of road pricing in cities to reduce pollution and congestion problems is limited: Box 9.6 gives one example, from Singapore and Box 9.8 another from Norway. Note, though, that this is not a direct tax on emissions, but on traffic flow.

All of the options above can be made more effective if we can change the relative costs of public and private transport further by reducing the perceived cost of public transport. This might be accomplished by subsidizing fares on public transport alternatives, possibly funded from revenues raised by taxes on motoring. If part of the additional perceived cost of using public transport is the additional time a journey

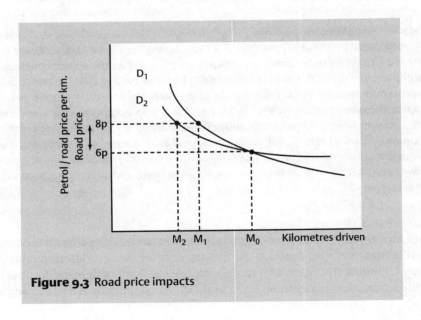

Figure 9.3 Road price impacts

Box 9.7 Environmental Taxes on the Car: the Leaded Fuel Premium

Tax differentiation between leaded and unleaded petrol has been introduced in most OECD countries where leaded petrol is still sold (it is no longer sold, for example, in Canada, Austria, and Sweden). In 1983, a report by the UK's Royal Commission on Environmental Pollution identified lead as an important risk to young children's health. In response, the UK government introduced in 1986 a tax differential, which resulted in leaded petrol costing 2.5 per cent more than unleaded, despite the fact that unleaded was (then) more expensive to produce. This differential proved to have too small an effect, especially given the cost of converting cars to run on unleaded. The differential was therefore gradually increased until it reached 9 per cent in 1994, by which time unleaded had claimed 52 per cent of the UK market. Before the tax was introduced, the government had consulted with petrochemical companies to ensure they would increase availability of unleaded fuel, at the same time as removing lower octane leaded fuels from the market. The switch in consumer behaviour and retailing practice that resulted from the tax differential helped the introduction in 1993 of an EC directive which required all new cars to be fitted with catalytic converters, since this technology requires unleaded fuel. This move increased demand for unleaded fuel still further.

Since 1993, unleaded's share of the UK market has continued to rise, whilst leaded fuel sales are being phased out in 2000. The environmental impacts of this combined effect have been large: airborne lead levels originating from transport have declined to one-third of their levels in 1984.

takes, the council could increase the number of buses, trams, and underground trains operating, or else speed them up (e.g. through the use of designated bus lanes, improvements in signalling and junction controls, or closing certain streets to cars but not to buses). Road-rationing schemes, which reallocate scarce road space from private users to public users, may be effective here. Studies have found that reducing waiting and journey times on public transport is a more effective way of encouraging switching than lowering its monetary cost (FitzRoy and Smith, 1994):[5] for example, the demand for rail travel in Europe seems to be more responsive to increases in train frequencies than reductions in ticket prices (FitzRoy and Smith, 1998). This could also reduce time spent (and thus time costs incurred) in waiting. As Box 9.5 shows, the rapid growth in public transport use in Zurich was due more to increasing the speed and quality of public transport than increasing the cost of car use. Public transport alternatives might also be seen as less desirable because they are perceived as less comfortable than cars. Again, actions could be taken to reduce these perceived costs by investing in the public transport system. Figure 9.4 sums up these alternatives as changing the balance of the relative costs of making a journey by car compared with public transport.

Taken together, measures which reduce the perceived total cost of switching to

---

[5] Technically, the cross-price elasticity of demand between public and private transport with respect to time is greater than the cross-price elasticity with respect to monetary costs.

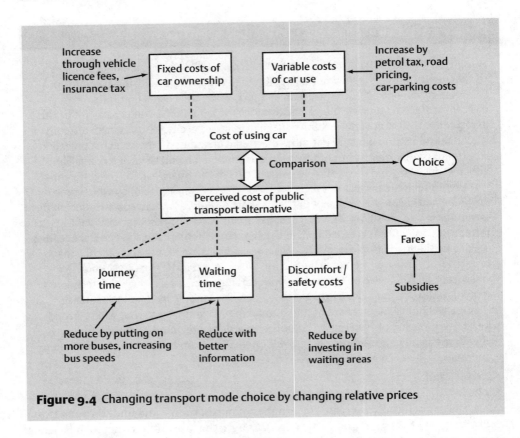

Increase through vehicle licence fees, insurance tax → Fixed costs of car ownership

Variable costs of car use ← Increase by petrol tax, road pricing, car-parking costs

Cost of using car

Comparison → Choice

Perceived cost of public transport alternative

Fares

Journey time

Waiting time

Discomfort / safety costs

Subsidies

Reduce by putting on more buses, increasing bus speeds

Reduce with better information

Reduce by investing in waiting areas

Figure 9.4 Changing transport mode choice by changing relative prices

public transport can make the demand for car journeys more elastic, so that a given increase in the price per journey (e.g. through the introduction of variable road pricing) would produce a bigger reduction in car journeys. This can be seen in Figure 9.3, where the demand curve pivots from D1 to D2, implying that introducing the road price reduces journeys by a greater amount. In practice, we would expect a package of measures to be undertaken, which both reduces demands for trips by car, but also reduces the perceived costs of alternatives. In our simple example, both of these result in lower total emissions and less congestion.

Outside the city, solutions are more difficult, since lower population densities increase the cost per passenger kilometre of public transport alternatives. This implies that the demand for car journeys is likely to be less elastic for rural dwellers than for city dwellers. This may mean facing commuters with higher drive-to-work prices than those living in the city face, for instance by imposing a differential charge on those entering the city to work each morning. Such differentials can be expected to produce changes over time in both where people choose to live and where employers choose to locate.

Box 9.8 Road Pricing in Norway

Since 1991 the city of Trondheim in Norway has imposed tolls around its central business area so that all vehicles entering the area within business hours have to pay a toll. The tolls are levied at twelve points controlling all road accesses into the central area which contains many of the main businesses, institutions, and the harbour. Approximately 40,000 people also live within this area. People who live close to the ring or whose business requires them to make frequent crossings are charged for a maximum of 75 entries per month to avoid very large toll bills. There are no tolls outside the main daily working hours or at weekends.

These tolls have resulted in a 10 per cent reduction in traffic in the central area during toll hours, an overall decrease of 4 per cent. The law under which tolls can be imposed in Norway requires that the revenues be used exclusively for transport improvements. In 1996 the tolling system in Trondheim was generating a profit of $25m., which was being used to fund new roads and the bus service.

9.5 Conclusions

In this chapter we have looked at the environmental impacts of the transport sector. These come in the form of noise, atmospheric pollution and land-take. Economic tools such as cost-benefit analysis can be used to appraise transport schemes in a way which accounts for these environmental impacts, so long as environmental valuation methods can be applied successfully. Economics thus helps us to evaluate the environmental costs of transport, and compare these with transportation benefits. Economics can also contribute to solving the environmental problems posed by transport choices, through the use of economic incentives such as road pricing to change behaviour. Road pricing could also address problems of congestion. Although full-scale road pricing has not been widely attempted, economic incentives in the form of fuel and car taxes are common. These impact on both the nature and size of the stock of cars (and other vehicles), and on decisions as to how many miles to drive. Whilst the demand for car travel is notoriously inelastic, it can be made more responsive by improving alternatives, for example by investing in public transport.

References

Bertrand, N. F. (1997). 'A meta analysis study of willingness to pay to reduce traffic noise', Unpublished M.Sc. Diss., University College London.

Department of the Environment (1994). *Making Markets Work for the Environment* (London: HMSO).

FitzRoy, F. and Smith, I. (1994). 'The demand for public transport: some estimates from Zurich', *International Journal of Transport Economics* 21(2): 197–207.

—— —— (1998). 'Passenger rail demand in 14 western European countries: a comparative time series study', *International Journal of Transport Economics* 25(3): 299–312.

Flowerdew, A. D. J. (1972). 'Choosing a site for the Third London Airport', in R. Layard (ed.), *Cost-Benefit Analysis* (London: Penguin Books).

Griffiths, J. (1997). 'Please, try to stay calm', *Financial Times*, 25 Jan. 1997.

Hamer, M. (1997). 'Mean streets', *New Scientist* (Nov.): 26.

Hanley, N., and Spash, C. (1993). *Cost-Benefit Analysis and the Environment* (Cheltenham: Edward Elgar).

Heringer, B., and Shah, F. (1998). 'Control of stationary and mobile source air pollution: reducing hydrocarbon emissions in Connecticut', *Land Economics* 74(4): 497–513.

Jones-Lee, M. (1976). *The Value of Life: An Economic Analysis* (Chicago: University of Chicago Press).

Kling, C. L. (1994). 'Environmental benefits from marketable discharge permits', *Ecological Economics* 11: 57–64.

Maddison, D. (1997). 'Valuing changes in life expectancy in England and Wales caused by ambient concentrations of particulate matter', CSERGE, UCL, London.

Michaelis, L. *et al.* (1995). 'Mitigation options in the transportation sector', in *Climate Change 1995: Impacts, Adaptation and Mitigation of Climate Change: Scientific Technical Analysis* (Cambridge: Cambridge University Press).

OECD (1997). Environmental Taxes and Green Tax Reform (Paris: OECD).

Prescott, G., Cohen, G., Elton, R., Fowkes, F., and Agius, R. (1998). 'Urban air pollution and cardiopulmonary ill-health: a 14.5-year time series study', *Occupational and Environmental Medicine* 55: 697–704.

Schwabchriste, N., and Soguel, N. (forthcoming). 'The pain of road accident victims and the bereavement of their relatives: a contingent valuation experiment', *Journal of Risk and Uncertainty*.

Soguel, N. (1994). 'Evaluation monetaire des atteinties a l'environment: une etude hedoniste et contingente sur l'impact des transports'. University of Neuchâtel.

Toh, R. (1992). 'Experimental measures to curb road congestion in Singapore: pricing and quotas', *Logistics and Transportation Review* 28(3): 289–312.

Further Reading

- Beverland, I. (1998). 'Urban air pollution and health', in J. Rose (ed.), *Environmental Toxicology: Current Developments*. Gordon & Breach: 189–209.
- Pearce, D. W. (1996). 'Economic valuation and health damage from air pollution in the developing world', *Energy Policy* 24(7): 627–30.

Chapter 10
Rainforests

IN this chapter, we analyse the economic issues which surround the loss of tropical rainforests:

- We review the costs and benefits of conserving tropical rainforest.
- Analyse why rainforest is being destroyed.
- Consider how the optimal area of rainforest might be determined.
- Finally, we discuss local and international policy responses to the problem of deforestation.

10.1 Introduction

THE destruction of large areas of tropical rainforest has become a major environmental issue. Many environmentalists believe that rainforests are being converted to other land uses too rapidly and that this process is causing profound damage to the world's environment and ecosystems.

An opposing view on deforestation is that it is a necessary and inevitable part of the development process: land under rainforest is needed for agriculture, commercial forestry, and urban growth. In fact the tropical nations are repeating a pattern of development followed in medieval times in Europe and in the more recent history of North America where forests were cleared on a massive scale for agriculture and urban development.

From an economist's viewpoint, rainforests may be excessively depleted due to a failure of market price signals to reflect the wide range of local, national, and global benefits which rainforests provide. However, the benefits of deforestation *are* expressed through timber markets and, without government intervention, rates of deforestation may continue to be above the social optimum in many countries.

Local benefits. Tropical forests are home to many millions of people including numerous indigenous groups. The forests provide a range of outputs including timber and other wood products as well as non-timber forest goods such as edible fruit, oils, latex, fibre, and medicines. Non-timber products tend to yield higher net returns per hectare than timber, and can be harvested with considerably less damage to the forest (Peters, Gentry, and Mendelsohn 1989). Local people often make their living practising shifting cultivation and collecting a wide variety of forest products to sell in the local market. The survival of poor landless farmers depends on the availability of forest resources for shifting cultivation and supplies of fuelwood.

National benefits. At a regional level, rainforests perform complex ecosystem functions including the regulation of flows of surface and groundwater, and the protection and enrichment of soils through reduced erosion and nutrient recycling. Rainforests act as a sponge, releasing water at a steady rate and evening out variable precipitation rates. Once a rainforest is cleared rainfall runs off the land more rapidly, potentially causing disastrous flooding and soil loss (for instance the disastrous floods in Venezuela in 1999 were partly attributed to deforestation). Tropical forests also maintain a balance of species by providing pest control services, and they regulate surface temperatures and local and regional climates through the process of evapotranspiration.

10.1.1 Global benefits

Greenhouse gas emissions. Atmospheric concentrations of greenhouse gases have been gradually increasing over the last century (see Chapter 12 for further details on climate change). These gases are increased by any process natural, industrial, or agricultural which leads to the net increase of greenhouse gas (CO_2, CH_4, N_2O, and CFCs) concentrations in the atmosphere. Estimates from Houghton (1993) indicate that tropical deforestation contributes 26–33 per cent of global carbon emissions through CO_2. Indirectly tropical deforestation contributes about 38–42 per cent of methane (CH_4) emissions: through forest being replaced by cattle ranching and paddy fields. Deforestation also contributes 25–30 per cent of N_2O emissions. Overall forestry made a 22–6 per cent contribution to global greenhouse gases. However, it should be noted that the impact of deforestation depends upon the fate of the carbon removed from the forest and what the land is used for. If an area is allowed to regenerate to secondary forestry, then this allows about 60 per cent of the carbon under closed rainforest to be recaptured. The conclusion from the available data is that tropical rainforests contribute both directly and indirectly to increasing greenhouse gases. Thus, through climate change, deforestation is imposing costs on all countries.

Biodiversity store. Tropical rainforests are also a rich source of biodiversity: they cover 7 per cent of the Earth's surface but contain 50 per cent of all species (Pearce and Brown, 1994). The gene base present in tropical rainforest is a commercially exploitable natural resource which contains biologically active compounds with medicinal properties (see also the biodiversity Chapter 13 on this issue).

10.2 **Rainforest Distribution and Losses**

TROPICAL forests make up just over half of the world's forest cover of about 1.8 billion ha. Rainforests are the most prevalent forest type in the tropics, covering almost 714 million ha. in 1990 (World Resources Institute 1994, 1995). Over half the world's tropical forests are located in Latin America (679 million ha., 57 per cent), primarily in the Amazon basin, with the remainder split between Africa (217 million ha.) and Asia (316 million ha.). The world lost 450 million ha. (one-fifth) of its tropical forest cover between 1960 and 1990 (FAO 1992). Asia lost almost one third of its tropical forest cover during that period, whereas Africa and Latin America each lost about 18 per cent. During the 1980s the world lost 8 per cent of its natural tropical forest cover. Regional deforestation rates were highest in Asia, where 11 per cent of this cover was lost between 1980 and 1990 (see Table 10.1).

On the basis of satellite imagery, the FAO Forest Resources Assessment Project (1990) provides an estimate of how forests in different regions are being cleared or degraded. The FAO definition of deforestation refers to the conversion of forest to other uses such as cropland and shifting cultivation. The findings of this study showed that more than 7 per cent of the 1980 forest area underwent change during the period from 1980 to 1990. Of this change less than half represented conversion to other land uses (42 per cent to agriculture and 3 per cent to plantations), while more than half represented a deterioration in forest condition.

Table 10.1 Estimates of forest cover and deforestation by geographical regions

Geographic region	Total land area (million ha.)	Forest area (million ha.)		Annual deforested area (million ha.)	Rate of change 1981–90 (per cent, p.a.)
		1980	1990		
Africa	2,236.1	568.6	527.6	4.1	−0.7
Asia	892.1	349.6	310.6	3.9	−1.1
Latin America	1,650.1	992.2	918.1	7.4	−0.7
Total	4,778.3	1,910.4	1,756.3	15.4	−0.8

Source: Singh 1993.

10.3 Why is Rainforest Lost? Economic Theories of Deforestation

In a review, Rudel and Roper (1997) assess two competing economic explanations of deforestation, the *frontier model* and *the immiserization model*. The frontier model assumes that capital investment is the main driving force for deforestation with the timber industry playing a key role. The immiserization model sees increasing population and impoverishment as the incentive to open up forest areas for agriculture. We now consider each of the models in more detail.

The frontier model. This model identifies networks of entrepreneurs, companies, and small farmers as the chief agents of deforestation. Together this group has sufficient power to raise private capital and obtain assistance from the State to open up regions for timber extraction, settlement, and deforestation. For an initial period, while roads are being established and landownership is contested, farmers have a strong incentive to clear land rapidly to state a claim or to extract resources before they are appropriated by others. This is an example of an open-access resource (see Chapter 7 for a more detailed analysis). Investment-driven deforestation will open up whole regions to settlement and agriculture; however, once this process has taken place there may be a pattern of more gradual deforestation as farmers incrementally expand their cultivated area.

The process is represented in Figure 10.1(a) where a plus sign indicates that a variable has a positive affect on deforestation. Population growth increases the size of the surplus labour force which is willing to enter remote regions and clear land. Gross national product (GNP) is a measure of the funds available to invest in large capital projects such as road-building and timber companies, and some of this capital may come from abroad. Timber companies contribute to deforestation directly by harvesting and indirectly by building roads which are then used by farmers and ranchers to gain access to remote areas.

The immiserization model. This model focuses on individual farm household decisions as the source of deforestation. In a country with low levels of GNP, foreign debts and tight fiscal policies lead to a low level of growth in non-farm employment and income. The lack of off-farm opportunities and increasing household size mean that the opportunity cost of labour is low and this provides the household with an incentive to expand the cultivated area to more marginal land areas. The immiserization model has strong Malthusian overtones (see Chapter 6), in which Malthus predicts that population growth continues until the family drives its per capita food consumption down to subsistence levels leading to a 'dismal' equilibrium where the family just meets it subsistence needs. Walker (1993) concludes that deforestation due to poverty amongst farmers tends to be more local and incremental than the frontier model in which whole regions are opened up to deforestation.

The immiserization model is represented in Figure 10.1(b). GNP (Gross National

Box 10.1 Deforestation in Rondonia: an Example of the Frontier Model

The Amazon encompasses the world's largest moist forest region, at 5.5 million sq. km. Of this roughly 3.8 million sq. km. lie within Brazil. The Brazilian forests are home to as many as one-fifth of the world's plant and animal species. Brazil has the world's largest remaining tropical forest, and by far the largest area of annual deforestation. The range of annual deforestation rates for Brazil's Amazon is between 1.7 and 8 million ha. per year. Deforestation accelerated in the early 1980s, peaked in 1987 (an estimated 9 million ha.), and declined somewhat in 1988–9 because of a combination of changes in government policies and wetter weather.

In Brazil most of the extensive deforestation of the Amazon totalling over 15 million ha. by 1987 can be traced directly to government-financed programmes and subsidies. Cattle-ranching has been the foremost cause of forest conversion, with small farmer settlements (mainly government promoted) the second largest cause of deforestation. Small farmers have accounted for about 11 per cent of the Amazon's total deforestation up to 1983. Other large projects developed partly to alleviate Brazil's foreign debt crisis have deforested more areas. These include several huge hydroelectric investments such as the Tucurui Hydroelectric Project, which cost US$4 bn, and flooded 2,160 sq. km. of forested land.

The government of Brazil has engaged in massive efforts to colonize its tropical forests with small farmers, for example along the Transamazon Highway. The Northwest Development Programme (POLONOROESTE), encompasses the entire state of Rondonia, and part of the Mato Grosso. The government undertook to demarcate plots and establish land titles, and by mid-1985 the responsible agency had awarded 30,000 titles, mostly for 100-ha. farms. Settlers only paid a nominal fee for their land (US$1) and could recover their relocation costs by selling timber. Once they had obtained title to the land they become eligible for subsidized agricultural credits. It has been estimated that subsidized settlers cleared almost 25 per cent more forests than those not benefiting from government programmes (Repetto, 1988).

Polonoroeste was intended to promote sustainable farming systems, based on tree crops, and to include environmental protection. Instead, unguided colonization took place. Settlers poured into the state of Rondonia increasing its population at an average rate of 14 per cent a year from 1980. The wave of settlers in Rondonia cleared and burnt the forest, and accelerated the rate of deforestation from an area equating to 3 per cent of Rondonia in 1980, to an area that accounting for 24 per cent by 1985 (Repetto, 1988). The deforestation was in part a direct result of existing government policies. First clearing the land was required as evidence of 'land improvement'. The settlers were then able to claim title to an amount of land in direct proportion to the area of forest cleared. Poor settlers who did not benefit from tax incentives offered at the time, gained more by clearing the land, selling it to large cattle-ranchers, and moving on, than they could from staying and farming the land.

Box 10.2 Deforestation in the Ivory Coast and the Discount Rate: an Example of Immiserization

The Ivory Coast has lost tropical rainforest at the rate of 300,000 ha. per year during the 1980s and of an original area of 16 million ha. only 3.4 million ha. remains. Deforestation is due to an increased demand for land for shifting cultivation. This demand is driven by population growth, rising poverty, and ill-defined property rights over forest land. Deforestation has led to soil erosion, a reduction in agricultural productivity, and the siltation of waterways. Attempts by government to define protected areas have been frustrated by the continued loss of forest to slash and burn agriculture.

In their paper Ehui and Hertel (1989) estimate the costs of deforestation through average agricultural yields. As deforestation proceeds average yields across cultivated land decline due to soil erosion and a reduction in soil fertility.

The socially optimal equilibrium is where both the forest area and the average agricultural yield are constant. The outcome is highly sensitive to the discount rate. For instance if the discount rate is 3 per cent ($r = 0.03$) the optimal forest area is 5.4 million ha., which implies some reforestation. If, however, the discount rate is 11 per cent ($r = 0.11$) then the optimal forest area is 2 million ha. In a country which is prone to economic instability high interest and discount rates tend to be the norm. On the basis of this analysis, without government protection the rainforest area in the Ivory Coast will continue to decline.

Product) increases will reduce the rate of deforestation in two ways: growth increases off-farm opportunities so that labour moves out of agriculture, and this reduces the incentives for deforestation. Growth may also reduce the foreign debt of a country. An increasing debt burden affects deforestation in two ways. First, the government's requirement for foreign exchange to pay debts, encourages expansion of export sectors which include cash crop production and timber. Second, the devaluation of local currency which often accompanies a debt crisis tends to increase the profits of timber companies and leads to increased investment and expansion of logging activities. Finally, rural population increase leads to the movement of agriculture to more fragile marginal land.

Testing the models. On the basis of a cross-country study, Rudel and Roper (1997) conclude that the evidence suggests that immiserization explains economic activity better than the frontier model. The main justification for this conclusion is that economic activity, as measured by the gross national product, is not found to be a significant determinant of deforestation: this counts against the frontier model as an explanation. However, the choice between the two models is not clear-cut and explanations of deforestation vary from country to country. In low-income countries with small remnant forest areas, for instance the Ivory Coast, population growth appears to increase the rate of deforestation. In countries, such as Brazil, with large blocks of forest, the frontier model is more appropriate. It is also possible to discern a progression, where initial deforestation is due to capital investment in roads which is

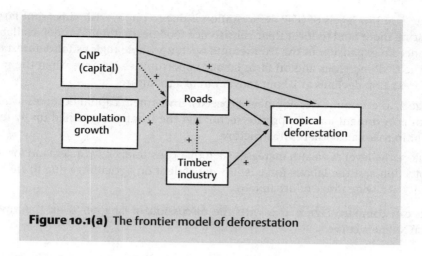

Figure 10.1(a) The frontier model of deforestation

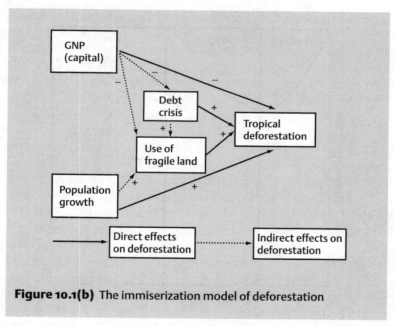

Figure 10.1(b) The immiserization model of deforestation

then followed by agricultural expansion which may be driven by population growth. Different pressures for deforestation may wax and wane depending upon cycles in a country's economy. If the economy is growing strongly, then this leads to frontier expansion and reduced dependence on subsistence agriculture. If the economy moves into recession, then frontier development declines, but deforestation for subsistence agriculture increases as a large proportion of the labour force turn to agriculture for a livelihood as the availability of urban jobs declines.

In an attempt to generalize this relationship Rudel and Roper predict the relationship, in Figure 10.3, between the proportion of the forest area logged and GNP.

- Stage 1, at low levels of GNP deforestation is due to impoverished peasant farmers clearing more land to meet their subsistence food needs. Capital is not available to finance an expansion in the frontier and open up whole regions for deforestation. As the GNP increases and off-farm labour opportunities improve, then the rate of deforestation declines as labour moves out of agriculture.

- Stage 2, as economic development proceeds, investment capital becomes available from government and the private sector and the frontier is opened up by investment in roads and other infrastructure.

- Stage 3, the level of wealth increases such that consumers have a demand for forest protection and the labour force is less dependent on agriculture due to the availability of a wide range of urban jobs.

You can compare Figure 10.2 with the discussion in Chapter 6 on the environmental Kuznets curve.

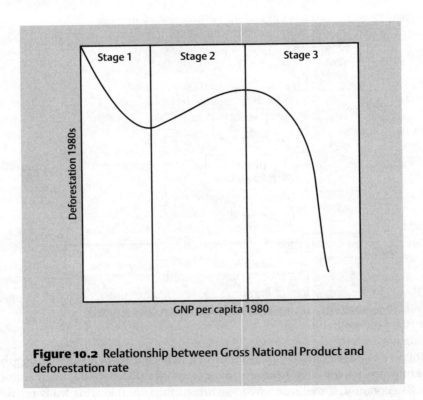

Figure 10.2 Relationship between Gross National Product and deforestation rate

10.4 Sustainable Forestry

IN the more developed countries of Europe and North America there has been a development towards making forestry harvesting sustainable. This also represents an option for tropical nations where natural forests are replaced by semi-natural or plantation forests. This section considers two questions: first, how should these forests be managed when the standing forest only has a timber value; second, how should the standing forest be managed when it has an external value (non-timber).

Forest managed for timber value. The problem of how long a forest rotation should be to maximize the present value of profits was solved in 1847 by a German forester Martin Faustmann. As a stand of single-aged trees grows through time so does their timber value $V(T)$. This is shown in the top half of Figure 10.3. The value of trees is set against their opportunity cost, that is, the return money tied up in trees could earn in an investment with a rate of return r. The bottom half of Figure 10.3 shows the rate of return on trees as the percentage growth in value. This is given as the *marginal growth in value (MVG)* divided by the value of the trees. This value is compared with r and when the two are equal, as at a in Figure 10.3, it is optimal to fell the forest. At this point the present value of the forest is maximized. Note that this is a shorter time than T_{max}, the time when $V(T)$ reaches a maximum. The original Faustmann formula includes an adjustment for the *site value*, that is, the opportunity cost of the land in terms of delaying the start of all future rotations. If the interest rate rises, then the optimal rotation length falls, for instance at r_2, the length of the rotation reduces to T_2.

Forest managed for timber and non-timber value. If the forest has a non-timber value, for instance, in terms of its recreation value or its value as a wildlife habitat, then this changes the socially optimal forest rotation. Instead of maximizing the present value of timber the forest is managed to maximize the present value of timber and non-timber values. Unlike the timber value that is only realized at the time when the forest is clear-felled, the non-timber value is given as a flow of benefits in each year. The line, $G(T)$ in the upper half of Figure 10.4 gives the non-timber benefits. Note that the non-timber benefits $G(T)$ continue to increase with the rotation length, reflecting the fact that wildlife habitat values tend to increase with the length of the rotation. This contrasts with the timber value $V(T)$ where the forest is assumed to reach an age where it starts to have a declining timber value due to tree death and senescence. The optimal rotation, where the rate of return on the total value equals the discount rate $((MVG + G)/V) = r$, at discount rate r_1 is now longer than the yield maximizing rotation T_{max} at T_3. It may be optimal, for some forests, to never harvest the timber because the non-timber benefits are so large; this is illustrated for a level of non-timber benefits G' in Figure 10.3.

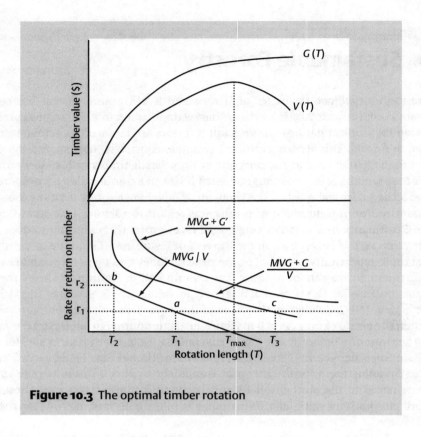

Figure 10.3 The optimal timber rotation

10.5 How Much Rainforest Should be Preserved?

10.5.1 Optimal rainforest area at the national level

In most regions the loss of tropical rainforests is either entirely or partially irreversible. Rainforests have much in common with resources like oil where extraction permanently depletes the stock. Once a tropical rainforest has been cleared and the land converted to agriculture or abandoned, soil changes and the long time-period required for the forest to return to its original state mean the rainforest is effectively lost for good. This is a simplification, since in some regions partial regeneration is possible and some of the biodiversity and ecosystem services of the original forest might be recovered in a 10 to 30-year period.

The annual benefits from a rainforest comprise three components. The aggregate market benefits (net of costs) of the annual area of rainforest felled q_t given as a function $h(q_t, x_t)$, where x_t is the remaining forest area at time t. The market net benefits derive from the net benefits of logging and increased agricultural productivity, as more land becomes available for agriculture. For any given level of deforestation the marginal benefits to the farmer of clearing decreases with the cumulative area logged. This is explained by forest clearance moving to land of progressively lower agricultural value. The benefits of preserving rainforest derive from two sources. Local benefits include the market and non-market benefits derived from forest products and flood protection $b^L(x_t)$. Global benefits include the benefits of biodiversity which include the possibility of discovering new pharmaceutical products, and the existence values to citizens of other countries derived from knowing that the rainforest is protected, this benefit is given by the function $b^G(x_t)$. Both benefit functions are an increasing function of the forest area, with a declining marginal benefit. Thus as the cumulative area cleared increases, the marginal benefit of preserving the last hectare increases. Together the net benefits of preservation are given as:

$$b(x_t) = b^L(x_t) + b^G(x_t).$$

A socially optimal forest area is one in which the marginal benefits of clearing equals the present value of the marginal benefits of preservation. The marginal benefits of clearing are of a fixed duration while the benefits of preservation are forever. Therefore the present value of preservation benefits is given by the formula $b(x_t)/r$ where r is the discount rate (see Box 7.3 about discounting). The social optimum is where the present value of the marginal benefit of harvesting, mh, equals the present value of the marginal benefits of preservation, mb:

$$mh = mb/r = (mb^L + mb^G)/r. \tag{10.1}$$

The social optimum is illustrated in Figure 10.4. The initial forest area is x_0. The optimum solution which accounts for the local and global benefits of preservation is at c with a conserved forest area of x^* where the condition in (10.1) holds. If, however, there is no mechanism to account for the global values of rainforest preservation the equilibrium is b at a lower level x^{**}. If the forest is open access and there are no effective policies for its protection, the equilibrium is driven down to x_2. Note from (10.1), the discount rate is a key parameter: if this is high, then the present value of preservation is reduced. An example of this is given in Box 10.2 for the Ivory Coast. The discount rate on which firms base their decisions will be biased upwards if there are imperfections in the capital market or the government in planning natural resource use adopts a discount rate that does not reflect people's true rate of time preference. There is no incentive for the country to account for the benefits other countries derive from the rainforest. This problem has much in common with the problems of providing public goods discussed in Chapter 2.

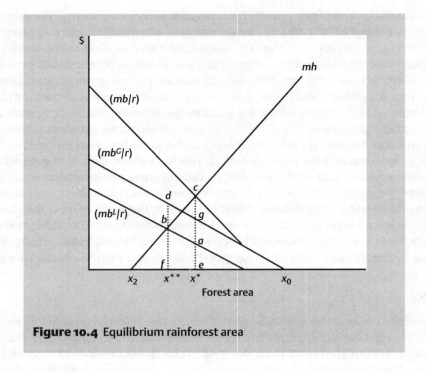

Figure 10.4 Equilibrium rainforest area

10.6 Policies for Rainforest Conservation

10.6.1 International policy

The loss of global rainforest is recognized as an international environmental problem and was a central issue at the Earth Summit in Rio in June 1992. There remains a fundamental problem that tropical rainforest is largely controlled by developing tropical nations whilst many of the benefits of preservation are global. The developed nations have the technological capacity to take advantage of gene material with commercial potential for new crops and medicines which may be discovered in preserved rainforests.

International policy to protect rainforests has a strategic dimension, as does any problem which involves the provision of a public good. There is a strong incentive for countries to benefit from reduced deforestation without paying their share of the costs. In other words there is an incentive to free-ride. Figure 10.4 illustrates a problem of strategic interaction. With no intervention from the international community then the optimum is at b since this is where only national benefits are recognized. However, this is an undesirable outcome and represents the situation if there is no agreement in negotiations to encourage tropical nations to protect more of their forest. In Chapter 7 this was introduced as a disagreement point in a Nash bargaining problem. If countries can agree to a side payment to the tropical nations, this payment must be at least the area *abc* which represents the tropical nations' net costs in terms of the reduction in the benefits of clearing. The additional benefits to the international community would be *dgef*. The tropical country may negotiate hard to make the side-payment as large a share of the additional benefits as possible. A complication in this process is that some countries may try to avoid paying their share of the side-payment in the hope that others will pay and allow them to benefit for nothing (see Sandler (1993) for a more detailed analysis of this issue).

The policy response to rainforest loss has been at the international, national, and local level. National policies are the most important as they determine the incentives that farmers and timber companies face when taking decisions to clear an area of forest. International policies have had a limited impact so far; this is largely because they express broad objectives, without the resources needed by the tropical nations to agree to reduce the rate of deforestation.

10.6.2 International agreements and policies

Since 1980 a number of international institutions have been involved in the issue of sustainable forestry including the United Nations Conference on Environment and Development (UNCED), World Commission of Forests and Sustainable Development (WCFSD), and the Intergovernmental Panel on Forests (IPF) (now the Intergovernmental Forum on Forests, IFF). The tropical timber industry has organized as the International Tropical Timber Organization (ITTO), and there are also a number of other non-government organizations including the Centre for International Forestry Research (CIFOR) and Forest Stewardship Council (FSC).

UNCED came closest to achieving a convention on forestry conservation in 1992 at the Earth Summit in Rio de Janeiro when instead a weaker Forest Principles Accord achieved consensus but not the same status as the Conventions on Biological Diversity and Climate Change. Accompanying these conventions is the Global Environmental Facility (GEF) which was established in 1991 and finances the additional cost to countries of protecting global public goods. The GEF provided $2.8bn over the period 1991–6 over half of which has been for biodiversity projects including rainforests. These sums can be thought of as a form of 'side-payment' from the developed countries to developing tropical nations. This is the only international institution that has substantial resources. Most other organizations operate by encouragement and attempting to establish standards of good forest management.

Box 10.3 The Rainforest Supply Price: Korup National Park in Cameroon

Rainforests provide significant benefits outside the country where they are located. These are in terms of biodiversity loss, carbon sequestration which reduces global warming, and their amenity value. Their importance in providing global public goods has been recognized by organizations such as the World Wildlife Fund and other development agencies that provide funds for rainforest conservation. Planners in these organizations must decide how much they are willing to pay tropical countries for rainforest conservation. Ruitenbeek (1992) analyses this issue for the Korup National Park in Cameroon.

Korup is the oldest remaining rainforest in Africa and has survived over 60 million years. It is home to over 1,000 species of plants and 1,300 animal species. Of these species sixty are unique to the forest and 170 are listed as endangered or vulnerable. The region is also the origin of one species of oil palm (*Elaeis guineensis*) and a species of insect which is important in this palm's pollination. In addition Korup helps to stabilize the water flows in the river catchment. The stability of water flow helps to maintain the Mangrove swamps 100 km. away on the Atlantic coast.

The joint scheme between the WWF and the Cameroon government involves a core rainforest area of 126,000 ha. surrounded by a 300,000 ha. buffer zone. The cost-benefit analysis for the project is given in Table 10.B3.

Table 10.B3 Korup national park cost-benefit analysis (1989 prices)

	Net present value (million CFAF Cameroonian currency)
Social costs	
Total capital costs	3,010
Total operating costs	1,465
Lost timber value	353
Lost forest use	223
Total costs (A)	5,051
Social benefits	
Sustained forest use	354
Tourism	680
Fisheries protection to Cameroon	1,770
Control of flood risk	265
Soil productivity maintenance	130
Total benefits(B)	3,199
Net benefit (B–A)	−1,852

Assumes an 8 per cent discount rate

By taking into account the local and national non-market costs and benefits, the net benefit gives the cost to Cameroon of establishing and operating a national park which will protect the rainforest. The contribution required from outside Cameroon is 1,852 million CFAF in total to preserve the rainforest indefinitely. This can be converted into an annual per hectare payment of 3,605 CFAF/ha./year; with US$1 = 283 CFAF this gives a payment of US$12.73/ha./year. This is the rainforest supply price, the price Cameroon would be willing to accept in compensation for conserving the Korup National Park. It is notable that a large proportion of the extra costs are due to park infrastructure and operation. The largest single component of benefits is due to protecting the fishery.

10.6.3 Debt-for-nature swaps

Governments and private interests exchange debt owed in return for protection of areas of rainforest. The first such exchange involved a US-based foundation swapping US$650,000 of face value of Bolivian debt for an agreement to establish and preserve 3.7 million acres of forest in Bolivia. In Madagascar an agreement was made in 1991 which involved US$120,000 of debt being acquired at a cost of US$60,000 This generated US$120,000 of conservation funds in the country. Between 1987 and 1992, seventeen countries participated in debt-for-nature swaps, and removed $100 million of face value debt at a cost of $16 million (Swanson, 1996). However to date, only small-scale debt and land areas have been involved in debt-for-nature swaps, and these agreements have not had a large direct effect on the environment or the debt burden (see Hansen (1988) for a review).

The economic justification for debt-for-nature swaps is that they represent one way of acknowledging that preserving rainforests provides a global public good. Debt-for-nature swaps should be viewed as a mechanism for contributing to the global good, in common with other development aid that includes payments for rainforest conservation.

10.6.4 National and local policies

International initiatives to conserve tropical forests depend critically upon national policies and local policies within tropical nations. The objectives of national policies should be one of reducing the adverse effects of market failure. These would include eliminating market subsidies to agricultural inputs and price support for agricultural outputs. Placing taxes on deforestation, establishing effective property rights over forest land and, where necessary, banning or regulating clearance in sensitive areas are all important initiatives.

Deforestation remains a major global environmental problem because of market distortions and market failure. Market distortions occur when governments subsidize uneconomic agricultural development, whilst market failure is where national and

Box 10.4 Madagascar: an Example of a Local Policy

Madagascar is located 400 km. from the east coast of Africa, and it is the fourth largest island in the world. It provides a unique habitat which is rich in flora and fauna. In total 5 per cent of the world's species can be found there. Three-quarters of the estimated 200,000 species of plants and animals that it provides a habitat for, are globally rare endemic species that exist nowhere else in the world. For instance, over 80 per cent of the island's 10,000 plant species are found only there. Madagascar is therefore one of the ecologically richest countries in the world, due to the high number of native plants and animals that are restricted in their distribution internationally. However, this biodiversity is under great stress as Madagascar is economically very poor, and forest clearance is occurring at an alarming rate. According to figures from the World Resources Institute (1994) the current rate of deforestation is 579 sq. mls. per year. Of the 15.3 million acres of original forest only 2.5 million acres remain.

Logging removes the damp biomass which covers the forest floor and is essential to the cycle of maintenance and regeneration of the ecosystem. Loss of cover leaves the top soil unprotected and this is prone to erosion into the sea. Madagascar has also been described as 'the red island' because the degree of deforestation is so serious that every year during the rainy season massive soil erosion in the hills shifts tonnes of red Malagasy soil into the rivers. This soil is suffocating coral reefs which provide the main breeding ground for vital inshore fisheries.

Madagascar's environmental problems are entwined with their economic problems. One of the major difficulties in Madagascar is poverty. Per-capita income is estimated at US$210 per year (WRI 1994–5). The opportunities for economic change are poor, and there are major logistical problems such as inadequate roads. The country desperately needs a solution to its terrible poverty and enormous foreign debts. Green tourism offers a promising alternative to deforestation, given the outstanding beauty of the local habitats. For instance, three hectares of rainforest preserved as a National Park in Berenty brings in more revenue than all of the surrounding 600 ha. of sisal plantation (Friends of the Earth, 1997). Furthermore ecotourism would enable the local inhabitants to have more control over any revenue generated than logging which goes directly to large landholders, sawmill companies, and governments.

To protect biodiversity in Madagascar the government is creating a system of parks and reserves, such as the Mantadia National Park. Economic estimates have been made using a combination of contingent valuation, travel cost methods, and opportunity costs to calculate some of the benefits and costs associated with the creation of such national parks (Kramer *et al.* 1993, 1994). These estimates help to put a value on the park's protection. They can measure the size of the consumer surplus enjoyed by visitors to the park, and assess the level of compensation required by local villagers in order for them to forgo access to the park.

global non-market values are not considered. There is also a third problem in that in many poor countries, government policy may be only partially implemented. International funds might be provided for rainforest conservation but, due to corruption and weak administrative arrangements may not be spent effectively.

10.6 Summary

THE international community agrees that tropical rainforests are valuable—they regulate the local environment, shelter biodiversity, and store carbon. Market failure, market distortions, missing markets, and ineffective and unstable government in many tropical countries has led to rates of deforestation that are greater than socially optimal rates of deforestation.

Those who own or who have access to the forests will cease deforestation only when it is profitable to do so (Mendelsohn, 1994). This can come about by national governments offering incentives to stop deforestation. In turn this may only happen if there are funds from the international community to account for the global public goods provided by tropical rainforests.

References

Brown, K. (1995). 'Medicinal plants, indigenous medicines and conservation of biodiversty in Ghana', in T. M. Swanson (ed.), *Intellectual Property Rights and Biodiversity Conservation* (Cambridge, Cambridge University Press): 201–13.

—— and Pearce, D. (1994). *The Causes of Tropical Deforestation* (London: UCL Press Limited).

Carson, Richard T. (1998). 'Valuation of tropical rainforests: philosophy and practical issues in the use of contingent valuation', *Ecological Economics* 24(1): 15–29.

Deacon, R. T. (1994). 'Deforestation and the rule of law in a cross-section of countries' *Land Economics* 70: 414–30.

Ehui, S. K., and Hertel, T. W. (1989). 'Deforestation and agricultural productivity in the Côte d'Ivoire', *American Journal of Agricultural Economics* 71: 703–11.

Food and Agricultural Organization (FAO) (1992). *Third Interim Report on the State of Tropical Forests*.

Forest Resources Assessment Project (1990). (Rome: Food and Agriculture Organization).

Friends of the Earth (1997). *Earth Matters* 34: 18.

Grubb, M., Koch, M., Munson, A., Sullivan, F., and Thomson, K. (1993). *The Earth Summit Agreements: A Guide and Assessment* (London: Earthscan Publications Ltd).

Hansen, S. (1988). *Debt for Nature Swaps: Overview and Discussion of Key Issues*, Environment Working Paper 1 (Washington DC: World Bank).

Hartman, R. (1976). 'The harvesting decision when a standing forest has value', *Economic Inquiry* 14: 52–8.

Houghton, R. A. (1993). 'The role of the world's forest in global warming', in K. Ramakrishna and G. M. Woodwell (eds.), *World Forests for the Future: Their Use and Conservation* (New Haven and London: Yale University Press): 21–58.

Kramer, R. A., Munasinghe, N., Sharma, N., Mercer, E., and Shyamsundar, P. (1993). 'Valuation of Biophysical Resources in Madagascar', in M. Munasinghe, *Environmental Economics and Sustainable Development*. Environment Working Paper 3. (Washington DC: World Bank).

—— Sharma, N., Shyamsundar, P., and Munsinghe, N. (1994). *Cost and Compensation Issues in Protecting Tropical Rainforests: Case Study of Madagascar*, Environment Working Paper 62 (Washington, DC: World Bank).

Mendelsohn, R. (1994). 'Property Rights and Tropical Deforestation', *Oxford Economic Papers* 46: 750–6.

Myers, N. (1989). *Deforestation rates in tropical forests and their climatic implications* (London: Friends of the Earth)

—— (1994). 'Tropical deforestation: rates and patterns', in D. Pearce and K. Brown (eds.), *The Causes of Tropical Deforestation* (London: University College Press): 27–40.

Peters, C. M., Gentry, A. H., and Mendelsohn, R. O. (1989). 'Valuation of an Amazonian rainforest', *Nature* 339: 655–6.

Repetto, Robert (1988) *The Forest for the Trees? Government Policies and the Misuse of Forest Resources* (World Resources Institute).

—— (1990). 'Deforestation in the tropics', *Scientific American* 262: 36–42.

—— and Gillis, M. (1988). *Public Policy and the Misuse of Forest Resources* (Cambridge: Cambridge University Press).

Rudel, T., and Roper, J. (1997). 'The paths to rain forest destruction: cross-national patterns of tropical deforestation', *World Development* 25: 53–65.

Ruitenbeek, H. J. (1992). 'The rainforest supply price: a tool for evaluating rainforest conservation expenditures', *Ecological Economics* 60: 57–78.

Sandler, T. (1993). 'Tropical deforestation: markets and market failures', *Land Economics*, 69(3): 225–33.

Singh, K. D. (1993). 'The 1990 tropical forest resources assessment', *Unasylva*, 44 (174): 10–19.

—— and Marzoli, A. (1995). 'Deforestation Trends in the Tropics: A Time Series Analysis'. Paper presented at the World Wildlife Fund Conference on Potential Impact of Climate Change on Tropical Forests, San Juan, Puerto Rico, April 1995: 8–9.

Swanson, T. (ed.) (1995*a*). *Intellectual Property Rights and Biodiversity Conservation: An Interdisciplinary Analysis of the Values of Medicinal Plants* (Cambridge: Cambridge University Press).

—— (ed.) (1995*b*). *The Fundamental Forces Driving Biodiversity's Decline* (Cambridge: Cambridge University Press).

—— (1996). *The Economics of Environmental Degradation: Tragedy for the Commons?* (London: Edward Elgar).

—— (1997). *Institutionalizing Biodiversity Conservation: Developing the Biodiversity Convention* (London: Earthscan).

Swanson, T. M. (1995). *The Economics and Ecology of Biodiversity Decline: The Forces Driving Global Change* (Cambridge: Cambridge University Press).

Thiele, R., and Wiebelt, M. (1993). 'National and international policies for tropical rainforest conservation—a quantitative analysis for Cameroon', *Environmental and Resource Economics* 3(6): 501–31.

Walker, R. (1983). 'Deforestation and economic development', *Canadian Journal of Regional Science* 16: 481–97.

World Resources Institute (1994). *World Resources, 1994–1995* (Oxford: Oxford University Press).

Chapter 11

Controlling Water Pollution

I**N** this chapter, we study what society should do about the problems posed by water pollution. This will entail:

- reviewing some scientific aspects of water pollution, and looking at trends in pollution over time;
- looking at what options society has to respond to this problem, and possible criteria for judging which option is best;
- looking at how governments have responded to the problem in practice; and
- seeing how they could respond better.

The chapter also introduces a useful part of the environmental economist's toolkit for looking at pollution problems in general.

11.1 Introduction

W**HAT** is 'water pollution'? For a natural scientist, water pollution is the discharge of a substance into a waterbody which results in changes in the functioning of the system. For example, the input of organic wastes to a river will speed up biological processes, and in the process use up oxygen. The input of ammonia may be directly toxic to fish. Nitrate run-off can lead to nutrient enrichment of an aquatic ecosystem, the build-up of algae, and consequent oxygen depletion.

For an economist, we require in addition that water pollution adversely affects at least one person's well-being (for instance, if people worry about sewage levels at their local beach), or that it adversely affects production, such as if a commercial fisherman suffers reduced catches as a result of a local pollution incident. This is because pollution only becomes an external cost, and thus a source of market failure, if impacts are felt by people, either directly or indirectly (see Chapter 2). Pollution is in fact the most commonly cited example of an external cost, or externality, in economics.

Water pollution problems are of two main types, each of which has rather different policy implications. These main types are:

- point-source pollution; and
- non-point, or diffuse source, pollution.

Point source pollution is defined as emissions which enter waterbodies from an easy-to-identify single source, such as a pipe from a factory or the outfall from a sewage works. In such cases, we can monitor actual emissions fairly easily. *Non-point* pollution, in contrast, enters waterbodies in a diffuse manner, such as through run-off from farmers' fields or from forests, or as pollution seeping down into groundwater aquifers. Non-point pollution emissions are very hard to measure, since they are not traceable to a single pipe or point of entry.

Water pollution may originate from many different sources, for example:

- from industry, in the form of point-source discharges of heavy metals, organic wastes and other pollutants;
- from municipal sewage treatment works or direct sewage outfalls;
- as acidic drainage waters from old mines;
- as leachate from landfill sites;
- as pathogens washing off from fields in which cattle are kept;
- as run-off of oils and solvents from city streets; and
- as run-off of fertilizers, pesticides, and soil erosion from farmland and forests.

Box 11.1 provides some example data on sources of water pollution for Scotland.

In what sense is pollution harmful? Pollutants may have their main effect on aquatic organisms by reducing the dissolved oxygen (DO) content of water. The amount of oxygen that is dissolved in water varies greatly, and the impact of pollutants on this DO can be measured either in terms of biological oxygen demand (BOD) or chemical oxygen demand (COD). Alternatively, pollutants may be directly toxic: for example, if pesticides or chlorine are spilt in a river. Pollutants can also change the acidity of a river or lake, making it impossible for certain organisms to survive. Pollution can change water temperatures, or increase bacterial levels to the detriment of human health. Finally, pollutants can change the nutrient balance of a waterbody, making it over-rich, a process known as eutrophication.

An important point to note is that the impact of emissions on water quality may be highly variable. Consider the discharge of partially treated sewage to the sea. The impact of a given quantity of discharge on water quality at local beaches as measured in bacterial counts will depend on tide movements, temperature, and sunshine, and the overall direction of water circulation. This means that a given quantity of sewage discharged at two different points on the same coastline may have quite differing effects on water quality at a local beach. Another example concerns the impact of BOD discharges on local water-quality levels (measured in DO) in an estuary. Again, the impact of one ton of BOD discharged at one point on the estuary will vary according to where we measure it (for example, upstream or downstream). It is usual to refer

Box 11.1 Sources of Pollution and Changes in River Quality over time in Scotland

Prior to 1800 and rapid urbanization, Scotland's rivers were predominantly clean and healthy. However, by 1850, rivers such as the Clyde and the Almond were rendered foul by a combination of sewage and industrial waste and this trend continued into the twentieth century. Significant efforts in restoring Scotland's rivers did not start until 1965, but, since then, progress has been considerable. The improvement has been due to a combination of causes, principally Scotland's shrinking heavy industrial base and the enforcement of new legislation.

In the Figure 11.B1.1, we show reductions in the lengths of 'downgraded' waters in the period 1985–95. This is based on the official UK classification system, where Class 1 indicates the highest quality whilst Class 4 represents gross pollution.

For the worst rivers (class 3 and 4), sources of pollution were as shown in Figure 11.B1.2.

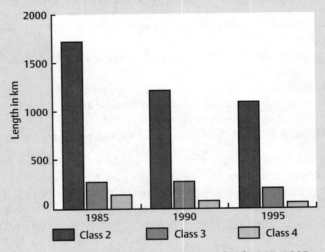

Figure 11.B1.1 Length of downgraded waters in Scotland 1985–1995

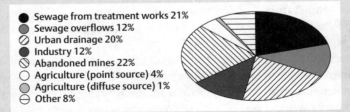

Figure 11.B1.2 Causes of low river quality: classes 3 and 4

■ Sewage remains the single most important cause of poor water quality. The impact attributable to sewage can be subdivided into two classes, that resulting from inadequate treatment at sewage works and that caused by overflows from the sewers which carry foul drainage. Poor-quality effluent from treatment works affects 21 per cent of the Class 3 and 4 river length, while combined sewer overflows impact upon a further 12 per cent.

- Urban drainage is a relatively new problem associated with the separation of surface water from foul drainage. Surface water typically suffers from contamination with metals, oil and rubber from road drainage, trade effluent from factory yards, and sewage from misconnected drains. The resultant polluting discharges contribute to the downgrading of 20 per cent of the rivers classified as Class 3 and 4.

- The impact of industry upon freshwater has been dramatically reduced over the past twenty years, although 12 per cent of the Class 3 and 4 river lengths remain affected by industrial discharges.

- Discharges from abandoned mines represent a serious threat to water quality in old coalfields. Very limited statutory control exists over this form of discharge and the problem is expected to be exacerbated in some areas as water levels in abandoned mines continue to rise. At present 22 per cent of the Class 3 and 4 rivers in Scotland are affected.

- The remaining cause of pollution, agriculture, has a limited impact upon Class 3 and 4 rivers, affecting only 5 per cent of the river length. In contrast, a separate assessment of the factors affecting Class 2 rivers suggests that agriculture is of considerable importance within this class. Point-sources were found to affect 130 km., while diffuse sources a further 150 km., 27 per cent of the Class 2 river length.

Source: Scottish Environmental Protection Agency (1996). *State of the Environment Report.*

to pollutants whose impact varies spatially as *non-uniformly mixed*. Some water pollutants do not have this property on the whole: for instance, if the concern is with nitrate levels in an estuary, it is not really important where in the catchment nitrate originates: cutting any source will have roughly the same impact on eutrophication.[1] Whether pollutants are uniformly or non-uniformly mixed is important for the design of policy.

11.1.1 Trends over time

Box 11.1 notes that water quality in Scotland worsened dramatically after the Industrial Revolution, and has only started to improve in the relatively recent past. This mirrors trends in other OECD countries. For instance, the earliest legislation passed in England (the 1876 Rivers Act) followed on from the closure of Parliament during the 'Great Stink' on the River Thames in London in 1858. Gross discharges from industrial and municipal sources (sewage works) have now largely been brought under control, as a result of legislation such as the Control of Pollution Act (1974) in the UK and the Water Quality Act (1965) in the USA. In the UK, for example,

---

[1] In fact, the way in which nitrate and phosphate pollution is treated under the North Sea Conference Agreements treats both pollutants as if they were uniformly mixed.

the length of rivers classified as 'grossly polluted' has fallen from 2,000 km. in England and Wales in 1958 to 800 km. in 1980. Since then, progress has slowed. Many localized difficulties remain, whilst diffuse-source pollution has risen in significance in both the USA and the UK. Pollution of groundwater aquifers by pesticides, nitrates, chlorinated solvents, and chlorine-rich water from old mines; and the presence of newer, exotic pollutants such as TBT (tri-butyl tin) and polychlorinated biphenyls (PCBs) raise new concerns. In many developing countries, water pollution from point sources such as industry and sewage works is still a large problem. This is also the case in Eastern Europe. Box 11.2 outlines water pollution issues in Hungary and India.

11.2 Policy Options and Criteria by which to Judge them

As Chapter 2 made clear, market failures require some kind of action to correct them. Pollution is a classic example of such a market failure: what could governments do to reduce water pollution, whether it be from point or non-point sources? Table 11.1 summarizes the policy options: regulatory options, economic incentive options, and voluntary options.

11.2.1 Regulatory options

Under regulation, the government, usually through an Environmental Protection Agency (EPA), tells firms what to do, either in terms of the technology they must use (*design standards*) or the emission standard they must achieve (*performance standards*). Design standards may be uniform across firms in a particular industrial grouping: for example, all paper mills must use a particular type of plant; or all sewage works over a particular size must use a particular design of treatment unit. Performance standards may also be uniform across firms (e.g. all firms in the estuary must cut emissions by 50 per cent) or may be varied according to the firm's location, age of plant, and previous expenditures on pollution control. Essentially, though, regulatory approaches have the characteristic that they permit firms no flexibility in how they respond. The regulator is assumed to know best.

Box 11.2 Water Quality in Hungary and India

1. Hungary

Hungary lies within the Danube basin. Three-quarters of its surface water resources are found in the channels of the Danube, Tsiza, and Drava rivers. In recent years new acts influencing environmental protection have been passed. Municipalities have been given a much larger mandate to control pollution than under the former communist system. Many community services such as water supply and municipal waste-disposal have become the sole responsibility of municipalities. However, despite the withdrawal of the State from these activities, there has been no corresponding transfer of funds to support them.

There is a large gap between the percentage of the Hungarian population with water supply and those connected to a sewage system. For example, taking the Danube watershed area of Rackeve-Soroksari alone, about three million m^3 of communal sewage is produced annually of which only about 10 per cent is treated (Csepiga, 1996). Within Budapest, only 25 per cent of sewage receives biological treatment, the remainder being merely screened for large particles before released into the river. Additional significant pollution is caused by industry. Industrial discharges from smelters, paper mills, chemical plants, and tanneries have devastated dozens of tributaries and contaminated water supplies (Tables 11.B2.1 and 11.B2.2).

In June 1994 Hungary and seven other Danubian countries with the European Union signed the Danube River protection convention, obliging members to reduce pollution and conserve water resources. In Hungary twenty-nine 'hot spots' have been identified, requiring direct investments of almost $1 bn (Woodard, 1995). Over half of this is targeted at Budapest. A large governmental programme has also been prepared which specifies that wastewater treatment should be available in all communities with more than 2000 inhabitants by the year 2010.

2. India

In India the Ganges and Brahmaputra river basins alone are home to almost 500 million people. Seasonal variation in rainfall is great, with nearly all precipitation occurring in a three-month monsoon period, and with many tributaries drying up during the winter and summer. There are over 130 large industrial units in the Indian part of the Ganges basin which account for 15–20 per cent of the river's total pollution load. Deforestation in the Himalayas leads to soil erosion, resulting in sedimentation of the river. According to a report of the Central Water Pollution Prevention and Control Board, about 0.6 million tons of chemical fertilizers and 1,300 tonnes of pesticides are being applied in the Ganges basin every year, which results in contamination of surface and groundwater by toxic substances. Table 11.B2.2 outlines industries' shares of emissions of organic water pollutants in India as a whole. The Ganges becomes most seriously overloaded in hot summer months when stream flow and turbulence are low and the effects of dilution and oxygen transfer from the air are reduced, so that the BOD of introduced wastes exceeds available oxygen (Chapman, 1995).

Industrial plants now face pressure to abate water pollution from many sources, national and local, through formal government regulation and through more informal pressure from consumer groups and concern for a firm's reputation (Pargal *et al.*, 1997).

Table 11.B2.1 Emissions of organic water pollutants in Hungary and India

	KGs per day		KGs per day per worker	
	1980	1993	1980	1993
Hungary	201,888	151,311	0.15	0.18
India	1,457,474	1,441,293	0.21	0.2

Source: World Bank (1998).

Table 11.B2.2 Industry shares of emissions of organic water pollutants in Hungary and India, 1993

	Primary metals (%)	Paper & pulp (%)	Chemicals (%)	Food & beverages (%)	Stone, ceramics, or glass (%)	Textiles (%)	Wood (%)	Other (%)
Hungary	9.9	7.6	8.1	54.9	0.2	10.8	1.8	6.8
India	15.6	8.1	7.3	50.9	0.2	12.9	0.3	4.8

Source: World Bank (1998).

Table 11.1 Water pollution control policy options

Policy option	What does the government do?
Regulatory options	
Design standards	Sets controls on how the firm produces, and on what equipment it uses for pollution control
Performance standards	Sets controls on how much pollution the firm emits, for example per 24-hour period
Economic incentive options	
Pollution taxes	Sets a tax per unit of emissions
Tradable Pollution Permits (TPPs)	Creates a market in tradable permits to pollute
Subsidies	Offers a subsidy to firms to reduce emissions
Voluntary options	
Moral suasion	Persuades the firm to reduce pollution as a 'good thing'
Voluntary sign-ups	Persuades the firm to reduce pollution in order to avoid being compelled to in the future

11.2.2 **Economic incentives**

As Chapter 2 made clear, economic agents respond to price signals. The principal idea behind economic instruments for pollution control is to change the price signals firms face, so as to give them the incentive to reduce pollution to socially desired levels. This turns out to be compatible with getting this reduction in pollution at the lowest overall cost, since economic incentives give firms flexibility in how to respond, unlike regulation. Let's look briefly at how the three types of economic instrument listed in Table 11.1 can work, although we postpone a fuller consideration of these options until Section 11.4. Pollution taxes have their effect by putting a price on each unit of emission the firm emits to the river, lake, or sea. Firms will find it desirable from a cost-efficiency point of view to cut emissions so long as this is cheaper than paying the tax. The higher the tax, the more firms cut emissions on aggregate. However, it is up to each firm to decide how much to reduce emissions, given the tax rate and its own costs of pollution control. Under tradable permits, firms are free to buy and sell the right to emit pollution, although the total amount of emissions is fixed by the EPA by fixing the total supply of pollution permits. Again, firms can decide for themselves how many permits to hold (and thus how much emission control they must undertake), taking into account the price of permits and the costs of emissions control. Finally, the EPA could offer the firms subsidies to reduce pollution. This could either be in the form of capital grants for investments in pollution treatment plants, or as per-unit emission reduction subsidies.

11.2.3 **Voluntary options**

If emission controls cost money, then firms' willingness to voluntarily undertake pollution control will be limited. Persuading them that pollution reduction is a 'good thing' may require the EPA to demonstrate that pollution control could save firms costs by making residuals handling more efficient (but if that were the case, why wouldn't firms know this already and act on it?); or persuading them that pollution control could give them an environmentally friendly image which would help their marketing. Here, consumers face problems in sorting out real from false claims ('greenwashing'). Perhaps a more effective option is to ask firms to act now to reduce water pollution voluntarily in order to escape being forced to act in the future. If firms act now, and their competitors only act later when forced to, then this *might* give firms some kind of competitive advantage. There are examples of such 'act now or be forced to later' schemes in practice, such as the US EPA's 33/50 scheme, which offers firms the opportunity to reduce pollution below their legally required level in return for less rigorous regulation in the future.

11.2.4 Non-point pollution control options

Options for the control of non-point source pollution are somewhat different, since it is hard to observe actual emissions. However, the same classification of options can be considered, namely regulatory, economic instruments and voluntary options. These can all be targetted at two possible aspects of polluters' actions:

- at their management practices, and
- at estimated emissions.

With regard to management practices, attention could be focused on the use of potentially polluting inputs, such as pesticides; on how land is managed (for example, what time of year fertilizer is applied, what kind of soil cultivation is undertaken in areas vulnerable to erosion) and on the pattern of land use itself (for example, whether forestry planting is allowed in catchments with acidity problems). Regulation could take the form of physical restrictions on input use, such as upper limits on fertilizer use, or bans on certain kinds of pesticides. However, economic incentives could also be used, for example by taxing potentially polluting inputs such as pesticides.

Controls could also be placed on emissions levels as estimated by mathematical models of pollution processes. Models exist which predict soil erosion rates under different management practices and land use; and which predict nitrate run-off to rivers and groundwater under particular management regimes. However, whilst this approach targets the actual problem (water pollution) more specifically, two problems of basing control on estimated emissions become quickly apparent: first, such schemes may be more costly and difficult to implement than controls based on management practices; and second, farmers, environmentalists, and EPA workers might all disagree on how exactly to model emissions.

But how could an EPA judge between different policy options? What criteria should be used to assess the outcomes of these options? In fact, many possible criteria exist, including:

1. Economic efficiency. This is the aspect we shall concentrate on. Economic efficiency implies that pollution control objectives should be met at the lowest possible cost to society. Costs here are defined as resource costs, that is the value of all the resources (labour, energy, equipment, raw materials, etc.) used up in pollution control, summed across all pollution sources. Put another way, we wish to buy the biggest possible reduction in water pollution for a particular level of total resource cost. Economists make most of their case for the wider use of economic incentives in pollution control on the basis of efficiency, as we shall see below.
2. Fairness: a desire to impose 'equal misery' on all polluters, or to impose equivalent emission reduction burdens on all. The impacts of a policy in terms of redistributing income between consumers, producers, and the government become important from this viewpoint.

3. Environmental performance, so that the policy option that most effectively delivers the environmental improvement is always chosen regardless of relative cost. Uncertainty over outcomes would be an undesirable characteristic of a policy option on this basis.
4. Administrative practicality, for example, in terms of actually implementing the scheme.
5. The ability to fit with existing legislation.
6. Political acceptability, which may be a combination of the preceding five criteria.

An important task of this chapter will be to show how wider use of economic incentives such as taxes and tradable permits can greatly improve the efficiency of water pollution control policy. Being good economists, we concentrate on efficiency as the main criterion by which to judge the relative merits of policy alternatives from now on. However, we will also have to take into account some of the other criteria in assessing why economic incentive policies have not been more widely used. Before accomplishing these tasks however, it will be helpful to look at how water pollution control is accomplished in practice.

11.3 Water Pollution Control Policy in Practice

CLEARLY, we cannot hope to comprehensively review actual water pollution control policy globally here, as it would take a whole book to do that. Instead, we provide two 'stylized facts' which try to sum up the current situation worldwide; and then look in some detail at actual policy in three countries, namely Germany, the UK, and the USA.

Two stylized facts about water pollution control policy:

1. Regulation, whether by performance standards or design standards, dominates. There is relatively little use of economic instruments globally.
2. However, the use of economic instruments is increasing.

11.3.1 Germany

Germany operates a system of pollution taxes, or charges, alongside a system of discharge permits which take the form of performance standards. Charges are levied on direct discharges to watercourses, including both industrial and municipal sources. The stated objectives of the charging scheme, when first introduced in 1981, were:

- to provide an economic incentive to dischargers to improve the quality of their effluents;
- to encourage older plants to upgrade their technology to the level of new plants;
- to be consistent with the polluter pays principle; and
- to recover the costs of environmental pollution control (RCEP, 1992).

The charges are calculated on a firm-specific basis, using a formula which converts different pollutants into standard pollution units. A uniform charge is levied per pollution unit, but different pollutants attract different implicit charge rates (for example, mercury is taxed 2.5 times higher than COD). Dischargers must also meet their discharge consent. To reduce their tax burden, they must seek a lower consented level of discharge: lower emissions thus translate into lower tax bills. To encourage investment, firms are offered a tax reduction three years in advance of promised capital improvements, so long as this will reduce discharges by at least 20 per cent. Tax bills are calculated using self-reported emission levels, although the regulator also performs spot-checks. To reduce political opposition, the charge has been gradually phased in. Firms can escape charges if they install technology consistent with the 'best available technology' guidelines issued by the regulator.

A report in 1990 suggested that the introduction of the charge scheme had resulted in a significant reduction in BOD, especially from municipal sewage-treatment works. However, the effects of the charge are complicated to unravel from the effects of other aspects of pollution control law. In comparison with the Dutch system of charges for water pollution, tax rates in Germany are in fact rather low (Anderson, 1999).

11.3.2 The UK

Water pollution control legislation in Britain dates back to the nineteenth century, but the most important moves came in 1951 and 1961 with the Rivers (Prevention of Pollution) Acts. These established a system of control by performance standards for all direct discharges to surface waters, known as 'consents'. Targets for water quality improvement are set locally, for example under the River Quality Objectives issued for each river in England and Wales in 1989. These translate into Environmental Quality Standards, which are usually measured in chemical terms (e.g. 7 mg/l of DO). There are also a large number of European Union directives which impact on objectives for water quality management, such as the Urban Waste Water Treatment Directive, the Nitrates Directive, and the Bathing Waters Directive. This has established a tension between the traditional UK approach of local flexibility in setting and meeting targets, and the EU approach which is dominated by uniform standards. To meet these objectives, regulation proceeds mainly through the system of consents (as noted above), although design standards are now impacting on municipal sewage works under the Urban Waste Water Treatment Directive.

Economic instruments are not really used in the UK for water pollution control.

There is cost-recovery charging for discharges to sewage works, but charges on direct emissions to watercourses are restricted to mechanisms to recover the administrative costs of issuing and monitoring consents. This is not to say that there has been no government interest in taxes or TPPs. A recent government discussion paper (DETR, 1997) laid out some of the practical issues to be addressed in bringing in economic incentives. These included the way in which taxes are calculated for point-source dischargers (the volume versus content issue), the use of product charges for non-point pollutants, and the introduction of TPP markets for BOD emissions to the River Thames and for achieving national target reductions in discharges to the sea of metals such as mercury and cadmium.

11.3.3 The USA

Water pollution legislation in the USA dates from the 1948 Water Pollution Control Act, which enabled federal loans to municipalities to invest in sewage treatment. The Water Quality Act of 1965 required states to establish ambient water quality standards, and to develop implementation plans aimed at individual sources to ensure these plans were met. These plans amounted to performance standards for direct discharges. However, dissatisfaction with the performance of this state-based system of control led to the federal government effectively taking control through the EPA under the Federal Water Pollution Control Act of 1972. State-specific ambient targets were replaced by ambitious national objectives, including the elimination of all pollutant discharges into navigable waters by 1985 (!) , and the attainment of fishable and swimable waters nationwide by 1985. The system also moved away from performance standards to design standards, with the EPA requiring firms to conform to uniform national technology standards for their type of production process. The 1977 Clean Water Act postponed some of the goals of the 1972 Act, and increased controls over so-called toxic emissions. Finally, the 1987 Clean Water Act further postponed targets set in 1972 (they were proving impossible to attain, as should not surprise us), increased federal funding of municipal sewage treatment investments, and required states to develop programmes to control non-point pollutants.

The US system of water pollution control thus gravitated in the main to a system of uniform technology-based standards aimed at meeting overly ambitious targets. Nowhere in the legislation was there a requirement to consider the relative costs and benefits of attaining these targets (although neither is there a prohibition of such a consideration). States were in fact required to develop water quality standards which would allow the national objectives, in terms of swimming and fishing, to be met. The national technology-based restrictions on firms are linked only loosely to these national objectives, since they are based on the biggest emissions reductions that can be technically achieved (tempered by some vague notion of what constituted an 'acceptable cost'), rather than the reduction required to meet a local ambient standard consistent with a specific use.

Results from this system of regulation have been mixed. There is a clear problem of

Box 11.3 TPP Applications to Non-point Pollution in the USA

One cause of eutrophication problems is excessive inputs of phosphate to a water body. Phosphate can originate from a number of sources, including farmland, urban run-off, and sewage works. If marginal abatement costs curves differ across these sources, then we would expect that an economic instrument such as Tradeable Pollution Permits (TPPs) would save costs relative to uniform performance or design standards. Indeed, in 1996 the US EPA issued guidelines to encourage the use of TPPs for improving water quality in this way. In two instances in the USA, schemes have been established to allow trading of phosphate 'allowances' between point and non-point sources.

Water quality in the Dillon Reservoir, Colorado became threatened by excessive phosphate discharges in the early 1980s. Four municiple sewage works were each allocated target reductions of around 45 per cent in phosphate inputs under the Dillon Water Quality Management Plan. However, they were also allowed to buy input reductions from non-point sources as a substitute for cutting their own emissions, provided that they have already installed best-practice technology. Emissions between non-point and point sources trade at a rate of two for one, to allow for 'greater risk' in non-point emission reductions. Only one trade has occurred so far.

The other US example concerns the Tar-Pamlico Estuary in North Carolina. Again, excessive nutrient inputs were causing water-quality problems. In this case, the main sources were sewage treatment works and run-off from farmland. In 1991, the maximum discharge from the twelve sewage works (and one firm) were capped at levels considerably below projected discharges. Nutrient credits were created which could be traded between these sources, and between these plants and farmers. This latter occurs through a payment mechanism, whereby sources can pay $29 per unit emission into a fund which then subsidizes non-point emission reduction practices. If total emissions breached the cap, then firms also pay the $29 fee per kg. in excess. The revenues from this fee are again used to subsidize emission-reducing management changes on farmland. Emission levels have fallen since the programme was introduced (by around 15 per cent for N and 30 per cent for P), although no actual trades have occurred so far between point and non-point sources. The ability to trade may become more important in the near future as emissions from point sources rise towards the cap, and as low-cost treatment options for point sources are used up. Trades between point sources are likely to have resulted in cost savings, but no published evidence exists as to how large these are.

Three lessons may be drawn from the above. First, that the volume of trading in a TPP system depends crucially on the degree to which trading is constrained by technology-based standards and mandatory performance standards at the level of each discharger. Second, that the fact that trading is low does not necessarily mean the scheme has failed, for it may have helped firms find lower-cost control mechanisms, relative to the regulatory situation. As these low-cost options are progressively used up, we might expect to see the volume of trading rise in any case. Third, both of these cases involved a relatively small number of potential traders: increasing the size of the market might well increase the scope for cost-saving trades, but market size in the water case rather depends on the physical nature of the pollution problem (e.g. in terms of the number of dischargers on a estuary).

non-compliance with discharge permits, even using self-reported data. In 1983, some 25 per cent of firms reported significant non-compliance (Freeman, 1990). In terms of water quality itself, the period 1974–81 saw an 11 per cent improvement in DO levels according to data collected by the US geological survey. Freeman reports estimates of the benefits of the 1972 Act in the order of $5 to $27bn in 1984 prices, relative to estimated costs of between $23 and $30bn. On this rough calculation, it seems the law yielded a net loss to the country.

Summing up then, we can say that in all three countries studied, regulation through design standards and performance standards dominates water pollution control policy. Most economists would argue that this system of control could be improved if more use of economic incentives were made. We now need to look in detail at the reasons behind this claim, which requires understanding exactly how such incentive schemes work, and their implications for efficiency. We also show how economics can help in setting targets for pollution control.

11.4 Improving the System: Economic Insights for Water Pollution Control

Iɴ this and the next section, two issues are examined:

1. How can economics help in deciding what policies to use to achieve pollution control objectives?
2. How can economics help in setting these objectives?

11.4.1 Deciding what policies to use

An important concept in the economics of (any kind of) pollution control is that of *abatement costs*, and the *marginal abatement cost curve*. Abatement costs are the costs of reducing emissions. Polluters can often reduce emissions by several alternative means:

■ installing 'end-of-pipe' treatment plants;
■ changing their production processes, for example by using cleaner inputs or recycling waste; and
■ reducing output.

We will assume that polluters are aware of the range of options open to them, and that they always choose the lowest-cost means. This may vary as emissions are progressively reduced. A useful way of thinking about how abatement costs vary with the level of emission reduction is shown in Figure 11.1(a). This shows a marginal

abatement curve (*MAC*) for a firm, Jones Company, for reducing emissions by installing end-of-pipe treatment. The graph is read right-to-left, since this shows falling
emissions. As can be seen, *MAC* rises as the firm progressively cuts back on its
emissions.

What does this mean? That as emissions fall, the additional cost of reducing emissions increases still further: in other words, that marginal abatement costs are rising.
This rising *MAC* curve is an almost-universal empirical finding. Marginal abatement
costs 'take-off' at a 75 per cent cut, since end-of-pipe technology cannot cut emissions
by more than this. The area under the *MAC* curve at any point gives the total abatement cost (for example, area a shows the total abatement cost of going from 100 per
cent emissions to 75 per cent emissions). Figure 11.1(b) shows the *MAC* curve for the
firm defined across all emission reduction options; this is now flatter past the 75 per
cent reduction level as the firm can choose to use other methods, such as changing its
inputs. However, the curve still takes off at very high levels of emission reduction (95
per cent), as emission reductions become extremely costly at high levels of pollutant
removal.

Another important empirical finding in the literature is that *MAC* curves can vary
enormously across firms for the same pollutant. For example, Hanley *et al.* (1998)
found that for BOD discharges into the Forth Estuary in Scotland, actual abatement
costs varied by as much as 2,500 times per kg. of BOD removed. This, in general, may
be due to firms which emit the same pollutant having very different production
processes and plant; having different levels of managerial skills; or being located in
different areas (and thus, for example, facing different transportation costs for bringing in cleaner inputs).

In Figure 11.2(a), we show the *MAC* curves for Jones PLC and another firm (Bloggs)
who both emit BOD into a river. Jones has higher abatement costs than Bloggs, since
it operates a different production process. Assume for simplicity that, in the absence
of spending any money on pollution control, both firms discharge the same level of
emissions, which we show as e^0 in the figure, equal to 10,000 tonnes/BOD week each.
The total unregulated discharge is thus 20,000 tonnes/week.[2] Figure 11.2(b) shows the
aggregate *MAC* curve, which is just the horizontal summation of the *MAC* curves of
Jones and Bloggs, referred to as MAC_I. Suppose a control authority, the Environmental Protection Agency (EPA) wants to get an overall reduction of 10,000 tonnes/
week. How could it use economic incentives to achieve this cut, and what might be
the outcomes?

Pollution taxes. In Section 11.2, the idea of a tax on emissions as a way of responding
to water pollution problems was introduced. We can now look at this in more detail.
In Figure 11.3, the *MAC* curve for Jones Company is shown again. Suppose the EPA sets
a tax of *t* on every unit of emissions from Jones. This means that if Jones emits *e'* level
of emissions, it pays (*e'* . *t*) in taxes. What should the managers of Jones do? Imagine
they are currently emitting at e^0. The best they can do is to reduce emissions to e^t,

[2] In fact, it is highly unlikely that in practice, firms would engage in *zero levels of* pollution control in the
absence of regulation, since some control might result from changes in operations motivated by cost saving,
such as recycling waste streams.

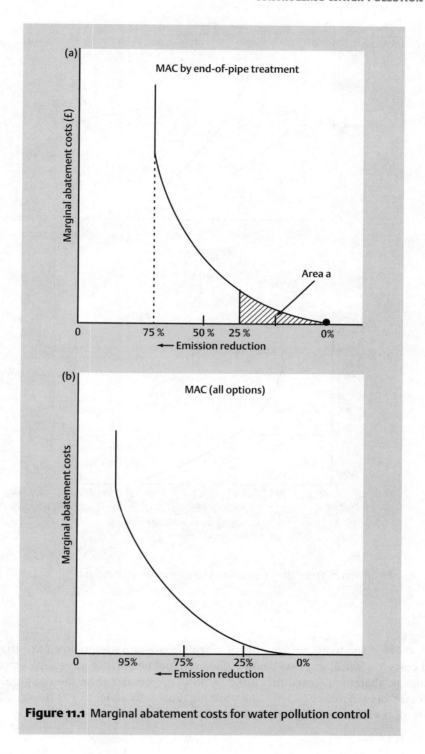

Figure 11.1 Marginal abatement costs for water pollution control

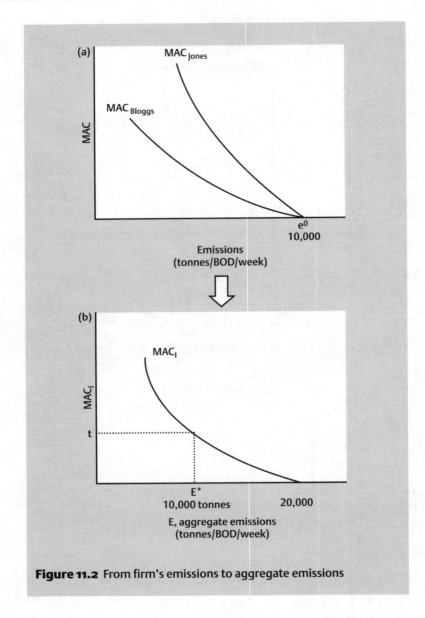

Figure 11.2 From firm's emissions to aggregate emissions

since above e^t the marginal benefits of cutting emissions are greater than the marginal costs ($t > MAC$); whereas below e^t the marginal benefits of increasing emissions (savings in abatement costs, measured by MAC) are greater than the marginal costs (increased tax payments of t per unit). Setting emissions equal to e^t is thus the firm's best response: it implies an equilibrium of:

$t = MAC.$

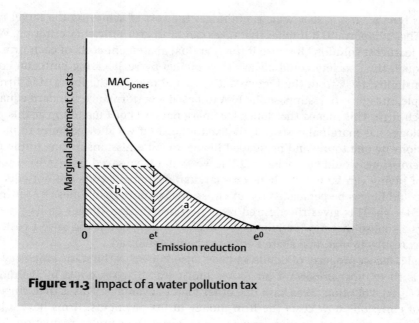

Figure 11.3 Impact of a water pollution tax

At e^t, the firm will be paying tax revenues equal to area b, and, relative to the pre-tax position, will have increased abatement spending by area a.

How does the control authority know what tax rate to set? Suppose that it knows the marginal abatement cost schedule MAC_1 from Figure 11.2. The target level of aggregate emissions is shown at E^*, equal to 10,000 tonnes of BOD. At this emission level, the aggregate MAC schedule has a value of t. This is the correct level at which to set the tax in order to achieve the target reduction. What if the EPA does not have this information? This is a rather likely scenario in practice. The EPA will now have to guess the tax rate, and observe firms' reactions. If it sets the tax rate too high, then the firms will produce too big a reduction in emissions and the target will be over-shot;[3] if the tax rate is set too low, the opposite will occur and not enough emission reduction will be undertaken. In this way the EPA can iterate onto the correct tax rate. However, firms will not favour this approach, since they will be unsure about what the future tax rate will be, which makes planning for investment more difficult.

The main attraction of taxes over regulation can now be explained. Under a tax, and as already shown, each firm's best response is to adjust its emissions so that we get:

$$t = MAC$$

for each firm. This means that for Jones and Bloggs, the tax produces the outcome:

$$t = MAC_{Jones} = MAC_{Bloggs}.$$

---

[3] It may seem odd to talk about achieving too much pollution control, but remember that each extra reduction in pollution we aim for imposes a cost on society.

This is the *least-cost solution* which minimizes the cost of achieving the target reduction. That's important: it implies that taxes can satisfy the efficiency criterion. Why is it the least-cost solution? Because if the marginal abatement costs of each firm were not equal, then society could always save money by reallocating emission control responsibility away from the higher-*MAC* firm and towards the lower *MAC* firm. For example, in Figure 11.4, suppose the EPA imposed a performance standard equal to e^* on each firm. This means that Jones has marginal costs of £100/tonne at this point, and Bloggs has marginal costs of only £50/tonne. So if we allowed Jones to increase emissions by one tonne and persuaded Bloggs to cut emissions by one tonne more, total emissions would be unchanged but we would have saved (100 − 50) = £50! This sort of saving can be made whenever marginal abatement costs are not equal. But how could Bloggs be persuaded to cut emissions by more than Jones? By setting the tax of $t = 75$. This gives the desired reduction in emissions (Jones emits 7,500 and Bloggs 2,500, so that new emissions are 10,000 tonnes), but at the lowest cost, since the tax results in marginal abatement costs being equalized.

The least-cost property of pollution taxes (also known as the static efficiency property) is their most important attribute, and it was first set down by Baumol and Oates (1971). Pollution taxes have one other major advantage. This is that, since each unit of emissions now costs the firm money in tax payments, firms have a bigger incentive to invest in cleaner, greener technology than under regulation. This is known as the 'dynamic efficiency' property of taxes, and has been argued by some to

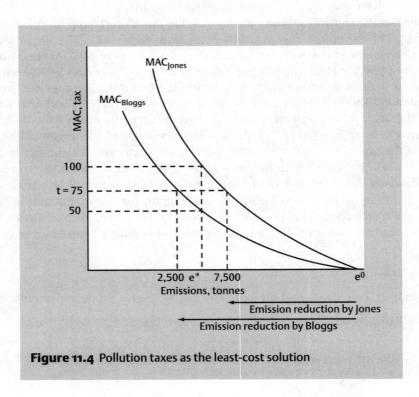

Figure 11.4 Pollution taxes as the least-cost solution

be their most important feature in the long run. Box 11.4 takes up this issue in more detail.

So what are the problems with pollution taxes as a policy solution?

- When pollutants are non-uniformly mixed, then a single tax rate is not efficient. This happens because the tax is levied on emissions rather than on their environmental impact. Firms which cause more damage per unit of emissions should be taxed at a higher rate than firms which cause lower per-unit-of-emission damage. At the limit, correcting this problem involves a unique tax rate for each firm. More pragmatically, suggestions have been made for banded tax rates to try to control for non-uniform mixing to at least some degree.

- Whilst taxes minimize the total abatement costs of hitting the target from society's point of view, they may be more expensive than regulation for firms themselves. This is because as well as paying for abatement costs, firms also have to pay the pollution tax on their remaining emissions. This tax payment may well be much greater than the abatement costs, and can result in the total financial burden of taxes (areas $a + b$ in Figure 11.3) exceeding that under regulation. This aspect of pollution taxes has, unsurprisingly, resulted in industry lobbying against their wider use.

- The EPA typically has insufficient information with which to set the tax rate correctly. We have already noted this, but we can also point here that taxes have to be frequently updated, for example as firms' abatement costs change. This makes the uncertainty problem more serious, since it means the EPA has to keep on guessing as to what the tax rate should be.

One last aspect of taxes to be mentioned is that they have the advantage of enforcing the polluter pays principle, viewed as being ethically important by some, although the polluter in fact pays twice: once in abatement costs, and then again as a tax payment on remaining units of emissions, as Figure 11.3 shows.

Tradable Pollution Permits (TPPs). The basic idea behind TPPs is to create tradable rights to pollute. Because these rights are tradable, and because cutting back on emissions is expensive, permits become valuable, and thus a price is put on the right to pollute. In the example used above, the EPA faced a situation where two firms between them emitted 20,000 tonnes of BOD per week, whereas the target level of emissions was only 10,000 tonnes. The EPA could, instead of imposing a tax, create 10,000 emission permits and then allow firms to trade them between themselves. Because it would be illegal to emit beyond one's permit holding, the target emissions reduction is reached: with only 10,000 permits available, only 10,000 tonnes of BOD can be legally discharged in total. But what advantages do TPP systems possess?

In Figure 11.5, the *MAC* curves for Jones and Bloggs are shown again. Suppose that each are given 5,000 permits. Both must cut emissions because their unregulated level is 10,000 tonnes, but by how much? Imagine that neither trades in the first instance. At an emission level of 5,000 tonnes, Jones faces marginal costs of 100, and so could save this amount if they could increase their emissions by one tonne. That would involve buying a permit from Bloggs, who would be willing to sell so long as

Box 11.4 Economic Incentives and Clean Technology

One of the most powerful arguments in favour of the greater use of economic incentives such as pollution taxes and tradable permits has been that they make the adoption of cleaner technology by firms much more likely than is the case with pure regulatory approaches. Why should economic incentives do better with regard to clean technology? The basic idea is simple. Imagine a firm that is deciding whether to invest in a cleaner technology. This will cost the firm money, but will mean that the firm can achieve pollution control more cheaply. Under a tax the firm can save both on abatement costs and tax payments, whereas under a standard it saves abatement costs only. In Figure 11.B4, the cleaner technology has a lower *MAC* schedule than the old technology. Under a regulatory standard imposed at e^*, the firm can save the area a if it invests. Under taxes levied at rate T, however, it saves the larger area $(a + b)$. What is more, emissions fall to e^{**}. Tradable permits work in a similar fashion since emission reduction frees up permits for sale.

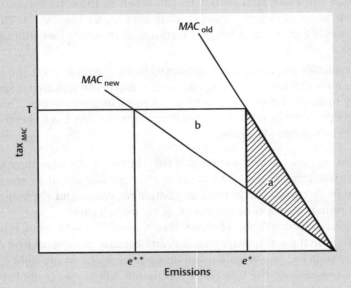

Figure 11.B4

An empirical test of the proposition that taxes encourage firms to innovate was carried out by Rene Kemp in the Netherlands. The Netherlands has a very sophisticated system of water pollution control. Control of surface water quality is the responsibility of thirty regional water quality management authorities. Each levies a tax based on the discharge of oxygen-consuming pollutants by firms to surface waters. Previous research had shown that taxes were high enough to have incentive effects on polluters (that is, made them change their behaviour). Some ninety-three firms were studied by Kemp, most of them being in the food and drinks industry. Kemp found that pollution charge levels had a significant effect on the timing of investment decisions in pollution abatement plant: as the charge level rose, so investment speeded up. However, not all of the variation in investment decisions could be explained by economic factors such as charge rates: short-term financial constraints and water-quality regulations also had an impact it seems, as did the use by firms of payback rules for deciding on potential investments.

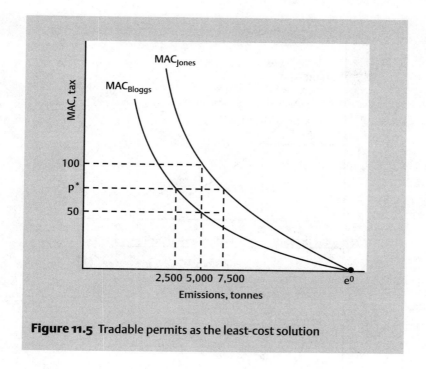

Figure 11.5 Tradable permits as the least-cost solution

the price they got was greater than the cost to them of freeing up the permit for sale by further reducing emissions. The cost to Bloggs of this sale is 50 (their marginal abatement cost at this level of emission): thus, the minimum Bloggs would take is less than the most Jones will offer, and a deal can be done. If the permit changed hands for a price of £80, then both would be better off. In fact, if all such gains from trade are exhausted, then in a competitive market for permits we expect trading to continue until *MACs* are equalized across sources. This, as has already been explained above, is a necessary condition for a cost-minimizing outcome: thus TPPs, like taxes, can offer an efficient means of controlling pollution.

Another way of looking at this is to consider how an individual firm would react if offered permits for sale at some fixed price such as p* in Figure 11.6(a). Jones would choose to buy e* permits at this price, which necessitates a cut in emissions from e^0 to e*. Why is this the case? Because if Jones bought more permits, they would find that they were spending more on permits, at the margin, than it costs them to abate. If they bought less than e*, they would find that the cost of abatement was greater than the savings in permit expenditures. Only at e* are the marginal costs and benefits of buying permits equal: e* is thus the best the firm can do. If the permit price rose, the firm would choose to buy less, and would have to spend more on emissions control (e.g. at p**). Alternatively, if the price fell, they would buy more permits and spend less on pollution control. The firm's *MAC* curve is thus its demand curve for permits.

Where does this permit price come from? One way of thinking about this is as the interaction of supply and demand in the permit market. Supply is determined by the

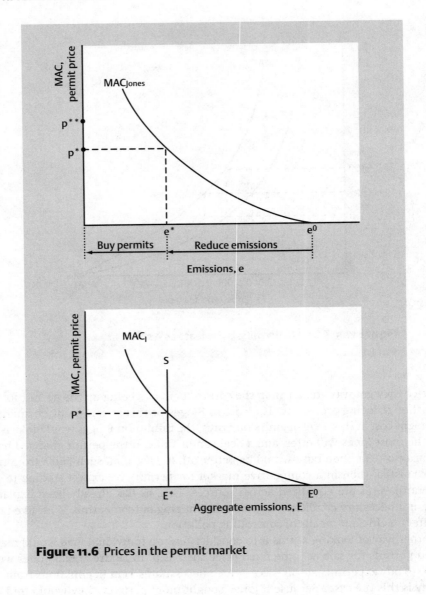

Figure 11.6 Prices in the permit market

number of permits available in total, and that is determined by the EPA when it sets the maximum desired level of emissions, E^* in Figure 11.6(b). The supply curve S is vertical at this point since no more permits are available from the EPA irrespective of the price. MAC_1 is the aggregate marginal abatement cost curve: its shows the market demand for permits. At E^*, supply and demand are equal at price p^*, and this is the market-clearing permit price. If all firms behave as Jones, then in a multi-firm market, with many dischargers (firm a, firm b, firm c, etc.), we end up with the situation that:

$$MAC(a) = MAC(b) = MAC(c) = \ldots p^*$$

which is the same efficient outcome as with a tax.

In practice, permit trading can take place in two ways. First, the EPA may decide to launch the permit market by auctioning permits. In this case, all firms need to bid for permits from a single seller. Once firms have acquired their initial holding, they can trade with each other as their circumstances change or as firms enter and leave the industry/area. In this case, the price permits trade at will depend on the bargains firms strike with each other. The EPA can also launch the scheme by simply giving permits away, a practice known as 'grandfathering'. Here, all trades will be interfirm, unless environmental groups buy up permits and withhold them (thus reducing the maximum legal level of emissions). Firms may prefer grandfathering to auctioning, since the financial burden they face will be lower on average. As with taxes, this financial burden is made up of two parts: the resource costs of pollution abatement; and payments (net of receipts) for permits.

We have seen that permits can generate a least-cost, efficient means of controlling pollution. So what's the catch?

- Transactions costs mean that fewer trades will take place than are needed to realize all potential abatement cost-savings. Transactions costs are the costs associated with finding potential buyers/sellers, and with negotiating subsequent trades. Evidence from the sulphur-trading programme in the USA suggests these can be quite a high percentage of the gains from trade.

- If there are very few firms in the permit market, then they will not behave competitively. For example, a large, powerful permit seller may withhold some permits from the market in order to keep their price high. This kind of behaviour, by both buyers and/or sellers, may result in a loss in permit market efficiency, but this depends on precise circumstances.

- Where pollutants are non-uniformly mixed, then allowing permits to trade at a one-for-one rate may result in local violations in water quality standards. Imagine that two firms are thinking of trading. In Figure 11.7, firm A is a potential buyer from firm B. However, because A is located upstream of B, each unit of emissions from A does more harm than each unit from B. If A buys 100 permits from B, then total emissions remain constant, but environmental damage rises, especially in the zone immediately downstream of A. This situation is highly likely in many cases of water pollution control, and several solutions have been proposed. One is zonal trading, which might involve banning trades between A and B, and only allowing A to trade with C. But the more trade is restricted in this way, the lower the cost-saving potential of the scheme. Another idea is to use trading rules, which would govern the rate at which A and B can trade. Suppose A's emissions are twice as harmful per unit as B's in terms of average water quality. Then an exchange rate of 0.5/1 could be imposed on trading between the two. Under this scheme, exchange rates would have to be calculated for all firms on the river, but this is possible, using water quality models. In reality, however, one of the largest actual TPP systems currently in use, sulphur trading in the USA, ignores the fact that SO_2 is a

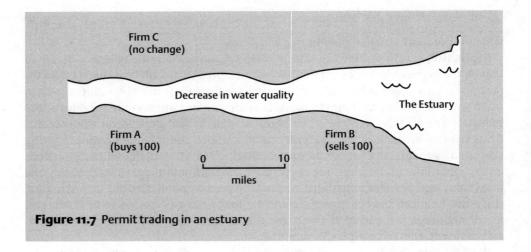

Figure 11.7 Permit trading in an estuary

non-uniformly mixed pollutant, and allows emission-based trades to go ahead at a one-for-one rate.

■ Existing firms may use permits as a barrier to entry to keep out new firms who want to set up.

However, none of these criticisms means that *all* of the cost-saving potential of TPPs is lost, so we expect some cost savings to occur if a change were made from regulation to trading. Relative to pollution taxes, TPPs possess some advantages too. Most importantly, the EPA does not need to know the firms' *MAC* curves in order to set the system up. All it does is decide how many permits to issue, what restrictions if any to place on trade, and then police the system. Firms may also prefer trading to pollution taxes especially if permits are initially allocated free of charge (grandfathered) rather than auctioned. In this case, financial burdens will be lower than with an emission tax system. TPP mechanisms also do not need updating if firms' abatement costs shift, since this merely changes the demand for permits: actual emissions cannot rise above the maximum permitted. Box 11.5 gives two empirical illustrations of potential cost-savings under TPP systems for water pollution control.

In summary, economic incentives offer the prospect of cost-savings in water pollution control, although many practical obstacles can be pointed to. This cost-saving potential can be thought of in two ways: (a) a given pollution reduction target can be achieved at a lower cost to the economy; or (b) for a given amount of resources, a greater amount of environmental improvement can be purchased.

Table 11.2 presents some evidence on the kinds of cost savings that might be expected from the wider use of economic instruments in water pollution control, based on US studies. A ratio larger than one in the third column of Table 11.2 indicates that predicted cost savings occur in switching to the economic instrument: the larger is this number, the bigger the potential savings. For instance, in the O'Neil study, the value of 3.13 suggests that the regulatory approach is more than three times more

Box 11.5 Do Tradable Permits save Money?

There is relatively little empirical evidence concerning the ability of TPP systems to deliver actual cost-savings with respect to water pollution control, since relatively little actual use has been made of them in practice. The infamous Fox River trading system was the subject of initial studies which suggested large cost-savings from permit trading (O'Neil *et al.*, 1983). However, in practice, the trading scheme was so hamstrung by regulations that only one trade ever occurred. Most 'evidence' for cost-savings from TPPs for water pollution control comes from simulation studies. In this box, we give brief details on two such studies in two European countries.

A. Scotland: the Forth Estuary

The Forth Estuary, in Central Scotland, is a tidal water body which is subject to many demands, including providing water for industrial cooling, for recreation, a habitat for birds, and a sink for waste disposal. Most waste comes from industry, notably from a large petro-chemical complex and from a yeast factory. A seasonal 'sag' in dissolved oxygen (DO) in the upper estuary due to too much pollution has been noted in many summers: this has a bad effect on salmon migrating upstream. Control is currently exercised by the Scottish Environmental Protection Agency, who use performance standards ('consents') to regulate discharges of pollution from firms and sewage works. Hanley *et al.* (1998) report results from a simulation exercise to study the potential cost-savings from introducing a TPP system to improve DO levels. They found that such a system could generate very large cost-savings over regulation, although these were reduced once uncertainty over water-quality impacts was allowed for. For example, a TPP system could achieve a 20 per cent improvement in DO in the most polluted part of the estuary at one-ninth of the cost of uniform regulation. This very large saving occurs because marginal abatement costs vary greatly over firms at the current level of control. Under uncertainty, the TPP system generates higher costs, but still achieves the target (in probabilistic terms) at a much lower cost than standards. These results were obtained by combining an economic model of polluters, based on abatement costs, with a water quality model which allows for firms located in different parts of the estuary to have different impacts on DO per unit of emission.

B. Coastal water quality in Sweden: the pulp and paper industry

Paper and pulp mills have traditionally been seen as major sources of water pollution in many countries. In Sweden, more than 50 per cent of total discharges of oxygen-depleting pollutants, and almost all discharges of chlorine-containing material come from this industry. Most plants are located on Sweden's east coast, so a lot of these discharges end up in the sea. Currently, discharges are regulated by non-tradable permits, set at the firm-specific level, as in the Scottish case above. Runar Brannlund and colleagues studied the likely impact on abatement costs of allowing firms to trade these permits. Their results are based on a study of forty-one pulp mills over the period 1986–90. They find that moving from no trading to trading increases industry-level profits by around 1.2bn SEK in 1989, a 6 per cent rise, since firms with higher abatement costs can buy permits from firms with lower abatement costs, who can profit from such sales. Some thirty-two firms become permit sellers, and eighteen firms become buyers. However, the authors note that the permit system they model could result in increased damage, since although *total* emissions are the same in the trading and no-trading cases, the impact of these emissions may vary since firms have a different environmental impact per unit of emission due to their physical locations (in other words, we are dealing with a problem of a non-uniform mixing pollutant).

Table 11.2 Simulation results for cost savings from economic instruments for water pollution control in the USA

Authors	Site of study	Ratio of regulatory cost to least-cost solution
O'Neil *et al.*	BOD in Fox River, Wisconsin	3.13 at 2 mg./l DO 1.43 at 4 mg./l DO
Eheart *et al.*	BOD in Willamette River, Oregon	4.8 at mg./l DO 1.19 at 7.5 mg./l DO
Eheart *et al.*	BOD in Delaware Estuary	3.0 at 3 mg./l DO
Opaluch and Kashmanian	Heavy metals in Rhode Island	1.8

expensive than a perfectly functioning economic instrument to achieve a target of 2 mg./l improvement in DO.[4]

11.4.2 Non-point pollution: a particular problem

We have already pointed out that non-point pollution poses special problems, but that economic instruments could nevertheless be used, based on estimated emissions or management practices. How this might work is illustrated below using the example of nitrate pollution. Too much nitrate in waterbodies can result in eutrophication, and consequent fish deaths and loss of amenity. Farming is a major source of nitrates, both in terms of artificial fertilizers and livestock waste. These are potentially polluting inputs. If some stable relationship could be found between inputs of nitrate fertilizer and nitrate levels in a polluted lake, then control could be exercised on this use of input. Essentially, this means knowing something about the 'pollution production function' (g), which relates inputs of fertilizer, N in this case, to water-quality levels, Q:

[4] These ratios are somewhat smaller than those seen for air pollutants (e.g. as quoted by Tietenberg, 1998), indicating that the relative cost-savings from introducing economic instruments seem to be higher for air pollution than for water pollution in the USA.

$Q = g (N).$

If this can be estimated, then the policy alternatives are basically the same as with point source pollutants: a tax could be placed on N, or a tradable permits system set up for purchases/applications of N. Alternatively, farmers could be regulated in terms of how much N they are allowed to apply. In Figure 11.8(a), we show the impacts of a tax on nitrate fertilizer. The initial price is P_n, at which price farmers maximize profits by applying N_1 units, since at this point the marginal cost of N (its price) is

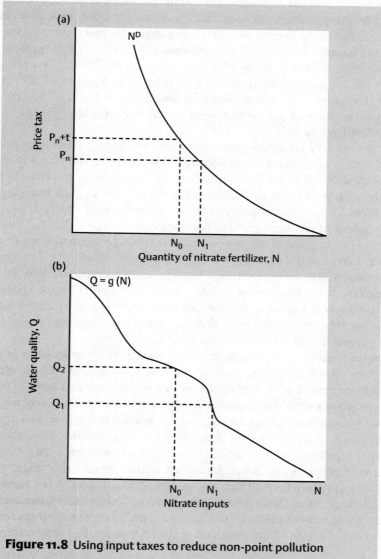

Figure 11.8 Using input taxes to reduce non-point pollution

Note: Higher levels of Q imply better water quality due to less nitrate pollution equal to its marginal benefits, measured by the demand curve N^D. Introducing a tax of t raises the price to $(P_n + t)$, and nitrate applications fall to N_o. This reduction in fertilizer use is shown in Figure 11.8(b) as resulting in a reduction in nitrate inputs to the river from N_1 to N_o, thus improving water quality from Q_1 to Q_2.

The demand curve N^D can be interpreted as the farmer's marginal abatement cost curve for nitrogen use, since each unit fewer the farmer uses costs him in terms of forgone output (as yields fall): this fall in output will vary across farms, due, for instance, to variable land productivity, varying managerial skills, and variable climate. This means that the *MAC* curve for nitrate use varies across farms, thus, just as with point-source pollution, an economic incentive approach such as a tax should give a desired reduction in emissions at a lower aggregate cost than regulation. Regulation in this instance would involve constraining all farms to apply no more than N_o nitrogen to their land. But if the N^D curve varies across farms, then this uniform regulation will be more costly (less efficient) than a tax. You should also be able to figure out that under the nitrates tax the farmer incurs a financial burden which is greater than the value of lost output since the farmer must also pay the tax on the amount of fertilizer he uses.

This all seems very straightforward, but there are huge problems in reality. The impact of each unit of nitrogen applied on nitrate levels in the lake will vary enormously, both within a given farm (according, for example, to the time of year it is applied, the crop growing in the fields, or the slope of the fields it is applied to) and across farmers. The land management regime adopted may be much more important than the amount of fertilizer applied. Technically, this means that the function $Q = g(N)$ will be very complicated. Nitrate pollution is also highly non-uniformly mixed, in that in many areas of the country there is no problem: nitrate levels in many rivers and groundwater just don't reach high enough levels to cause trouble, for a whole host of reasons. What this means is that a tax on nitrogen is far too crude a policy measure to achieve the specific, local objectives that typify many non-point pollution problems. For this reason, we need to look at other options, and see if economic incentive properties can somehow be maintained.

One option would be to provide financial incentives for management practices which reduce nitrate pollution, such as avoiding leaving land bare in winter, and avoiding nitrate applications or livestock densities which are excessive. This is in fact how the system works in the UK under the Nitrate Sensitive Areas scheme. Farmers are offered subsidies to voluntarily sign up to management practices designed to reduce pollution in highly specific areas of the country. Notice here, though, that instead of the polluter pays principle being applied we have a 'pay the polluter' principle, with property rights being assigned to the farmer.[5] This might yield cost-savings over a system where all farmers are forced to conform to the same management restrictions, since those farmers who face the lowest abatement costs are the most likely to sign under the voluntary scheme. Similar subsidy systems are used for the control of soil erosion from farmland in the USA under the Conservation Reserve

---

[5] In fact, there are very few examples of the polluter pays principle being applied to farmers: see Tobey and Smets (1996).

Programme, and a great many studies have found that such management-incentive-based approaches are more cost-effective than enforcing uniform management standards (see the suggestions for further reading). Finally, land use itself could be targetted for control, again either using economic incentives or regulation. An example of the former approach, using tradable land use permits, has been suggested by Pan and Hodge for controlling nitrate pollution (see Boxes 11.6 and 11.7).

However, one major problem that affects policies based on management practices, whether uniform-standards-based- or economic-incentive-based, is the difficulty for the government to actually monitor what farmers are doing. Consider the following. Farmers are offered a payment per hectare if they agree to a package of measures which include:

- no more than two cows per hectare;
- no fertilizer applications in excess of 110 kg./ha.;
- no fertilizer applications at all in the winter;
- no fertilizer applications within 10 metres of any river or stream.

Farmer Joe phones up to claim his payments, saying that he has carried out all the actions. But how does the agency know he is telling the truth? It could, of course, deploy a huge army of monitors to rove about the countryside checking the actions of every farmer, but this would be very costly. It would be better if incentives could be provided for honest behaviour. These can be of two types. First, the agency could sample a random, small group of farms and punish anyone who has not told the truth (e.g. with a fine). But then Joe (and his friends) can compare the benefits of cheating with the costs (equal to the expected fine times the probability of being caught), and some cheating will still occur. Or, the agency can design a payment system which is 'incentive compatible', that is, which encourages truthful behaviour. This means separating what you pay from what you say: in other words, breaking the simple link between the actions you report and the payment you receive or the tax you pay. For example, farmers could be taxed on the basis of the ambient level of water quality in their catchment, rather than on their reported contribution to this.

So: why not more use of economic incentive schemes to control water pollution? In Section 11.3, we saw that relatively little use of economic incentives to control water pollution. In Section 11.4 the potentially large cost-savings of switching to such incentive schemes were outlined. So why the big difference? Why don't policy-makers take more notice of economists' recommendations?

One possible reason is that policy-makers give a rather low weighting to the criterion of efficiency relative to the other criteria outlined in Section 11.2. For example, a tax on BOD emissions to an estuary may be efficient, but if the regulator feels its outcome is rather uncertain, or if it does not fit in well with other existing regulations, then the tax option may be rejected. Permits may be rejected because of political fears over the accusation that the government is auctioning off 'rights to pollute'. Summing up this line of argument then, we can say that few public agents are as keen on efficiency as economists (see Hahn, 2000).

Box 11.6 TPPs and Nitrate Pollution in the UK

In this section, we briefly consider the use of TPPs to control nitrate pollution. Moxey and White modelled the use of TPPs for the River Tyne catchment in Northern England. Estimates of nitrate emissions from different land types and cropping patterns were calculated using mathematical models. These were then linked into economic models of farmers in the catchment. Moxey and White then calculate the effects on farm profits of increasingly strict required reductions in ambient nitrate concentrations under two policies: a TPP market in estimated emissions, and a TPP market in nitrate inputs. Since the objective of policy is to control nitrate concentrations rather than nitrate inputs, the expectation is that the former policy will be more efficient than the latter (since there is no simple proportionality between nitrate use and nitrate concentrations due to variations in the 'transfer coefficients' which relate farm run-off to water quality). Results showed that this was so (Table 11.B6).

Table 11.B6

Abatement (%)	Profit reduction under estimated emission TPPs (%)	Profit reduction under input use TPPS (%)
10	1.34	2.74
20	6.33	9.31
30	17.75	23.55
40	38.95	46.14

It is also apparent that abatement costs rise sharply with the target reduction in ambient concentration. However, a TPP system based on estimated emissions would be much more difficult and costly to administer than a system based on input use, since for every farm estimated emissions must be predicted. A system based on input use might then be preferable, although where the degree of variation in transfer coefficients is great, a major redistribution of incomes could occur across the region. A compromise has been suggested by Pan and Hodge (1994), whereby permits would be denominated in terms of land use (e.g. growing wheat on land of a particular class). The amount of permits necessary to authorize a particular land use on a particular soil type would be calculated by the regulator on the basis of estimated emissions, but once this had been done the regulator would not need to repeat the calculation every time a trade takes place, since all that must be monitored is land use and permit holding. Pan and Hodge show that whilst such a TPP system is less efficient than an economic instrument based on estimated emissions, the cost penalty is not great, whilst the savings in transactions costs might be substantial.

Box 11.7 The Murray-Darling River Basin

Figure 11.B7

One interesting example of water quality management in Australia concerns the Murray-Darling river basin, which covers a massive 1 million sq. km. falling within the jurisdiction of four states (Queensland, New South Wales, Victoria, and South Australia). The Murray-Darling Basin Commission has been set up to coordinate the management of the area. A wide variety of demands on the water resource include industrial and municipal sewage discharges, industrial use as input waters, and irrigation for agriculture. Groundwater reserves in the area are also important. Two major environmental problems are eutrophication and increased salinity, both of which are related to the amount of water abstracted for irrigation. An innovative approach to controlling abstraction has been the establishment of the Pilot Interstate Water Trading Project. Total abstraction from the Basin is capped at 1993-4 levels; however trades are allowed within this cap. To make this possible, each of the states had to reform water entitlements, breaking the link with landownership. Trading is expected to result in water being used more productively, and is predicted to increase the value of output by around $AUS48 million annually. The scheme is currently being tested in the Mallee Region. Other feature of the scheme include:

- all trades must be approved under individual state laws for buyers and sellers;
- trades take place at exchange rates determined by the Commission; and
- in order to prevent trading from increasing salinity overall, a system of salinity credits and debits is being set up.

A second aspect concerns the political economy of regulation. Government intervention itself creates the potential for profits, thus we should not be surprised to see industry and other interest groups trying to match the manner of intervention with their own best interests. This was pointed out by Buchanan and Tullock (1975), who showed that firms could be expected to lobby in favour of regulation if their profits were higher under regulation than under a tax. In the UK, the way in which performance standards were negotiated bilaterally between firms and the regulator, and the regulator's desire to avoid court cases, combined to give firms an incentive to lobby in favour of no change in the existing system since they felt they had more room to manœuvre with regulation than with a centrally imposed tax. Firms may also see regulation as a means by which potential rivals can be stopped from entering their industry. Industry has certainly lobbied against economic instruments, as was the case with proposals for pollution taxes in the USA in the 1970s (Kelman, 1981). In Germany, there was less opposition to charges, as the government introduced them gradually over time and offered to refund revenues to industry in the form of grants for investments in abatement equipment.

How can industry affect government actions? Goodstein (1995) points to three avenues: the 'revolving door' aspect of the labour market, where EPA staff know their future lies with the companies they are supposed to regulate; through support of campaign funds for political parties and individual politicians; and through advertising campaigns. Not all industrial lobbying has been against economic incentives, though: industrial lobbies supported the introduction of permit trading into the USA in the late 1970s, and support the use of carbon credits today in the UK, since they believe it to be in their best interests to do so.

Actual economic incentive schemes can fail to realize potential cost-savings due to such schemes being overregulated. A good example is the Fox River scheme. In 1981, the state of Wisconsin introduced a tradable permit scheme for BOD discharges from point sources on the Fox River. A simulation study by O'Neil *et al.* (1985) had suggested large cost-savings if such a scheme went ahead. In practice, however, only one trade occurred, and few of the cost-savings were realized. Why did this scheme fail? Several reasons seem important. First, complex rules were imposed on trading, including a rule that trading was not allowed solely to reduce costs! Second, the dischargers affected by the scheme comprised fifteen pulp and paper plants, and six municipal sewage treatment works. The municipal sources appear to have had no difficulty in meeting their discharge targets, whilst the paper mills were in product market competition with each other. Third, permits became worthless after five years, so buying a permit would only yield a temporary property right. Fourth, sources are required to install 'best available technology' anyway, which greatly reduces the appeal of trading.

Finally, with regard to non-point pollution, the government may have to be able to prove in a court of law that there is some link between farmers' actions (both collectively and individually) and pollution levels in water if they are to be able to make economic instruments work. For example, if a lake is polluted by too much nitrogen running off surrounding land, and the government tries to introduce a TPP system to combat the problem, then farmers may be able to challenge this initiative in court if they can show that the government cannot prove where the nitrates are coming from. However, this burden of proof problem may characterize *any* move to restrict farm inputs of nitrate, not just the use of economic incentive schemes.

11.5 **Setting the Target**

M OST of the discussion so far on the contribution that economics can make to the control of water pollution has been concerned with how best to achieve a given target level of pollution control. But economics can also help in deciding what this target should be. In Figure 11.9, the aggregate marginal abatement cost for heavy metal discharges to the Great Lakes is shown. Also shown is a marginal benefits curve, MB. This shows the additional benefits of reducing pollution, which can be thought of as the monetary value of avoided damage. The function looks weird because of the very complex relationship between pollutant levels and damage. Marginal benefits are highest at high levels of emissions, and then decline, on average, as the system is cleaned up. In other words, the biggest gains in terms of avoided damage are made early on. Suppose that the Great Lakes Commission is deciding what level of pollution reduction from the no-control level of E_0 to seek. If it makes this

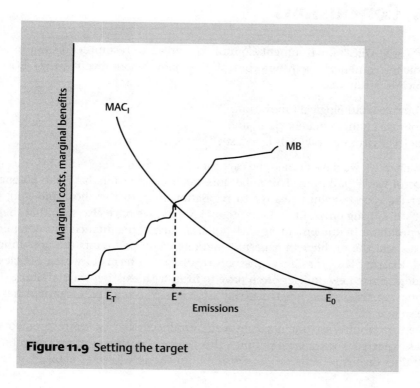

Figure 11.9 Setting the target

decision without the help of economists, it cannot take account of the balance between costs and benefits. Say it sets an aggressive target of E_T. Here, marginal benefits are less than marginal costs, and in fact the total costs of achieving this level of control exceed the total benefits. This may have been what happened under the 1972 Federal Water Pollution Control Act in the USA: see Section 11.3. From an economic viewpoint, the target is too strict. Economists, if they had the requisite information, would advise setting the target at E^*, since this is where marginal benefits equal marginal costs. This is actually the position of maximum net benefit.

In very few circumstances, however, will economists have the 'complete picture' as shown in Figure 11.9: we usually do not know enough about the value of avoided damages to compute where E^* should be. However, economists can often take a reasonable guess as to whether existing targets are set too tightly or too laxly. What is more, ignoring relative benefits and costs completely can lead to very inefficient target setting. A final point to make is that the *MAC* curve could shift according to how the pollution reduction target is achieved. Making more use of economic instruments, and thus cutting aggregate abatement costs, will increase the optimal target level of pollution control, pushing E^* to the left in Figure 11.9.

11.6 Conclusions

IN 1991, the OECD Environment Committee agreed to recommend the use of economic instruments in pollution control. The main reasons given by the OECD were that such instruments:

- encourage technological innovation,
- encourage changes in behaviour, and
- achieve environmental goals in a cost-effective manner.

In this chapter, we have argued the case for an increased use of economic incentives to control water pollution. This is because taxes and permits have the potential to deliver large cost savings relative to regulation in both the short and long term, whilst still hitting environmental targets. However, we have also seen that there are many problems in implementing such policies, such as the financial burden imposed by taxes and the problems for permit markets when pollutants are non-uniformly mixed. Existing laws may also constrain regulators in terms of which policies they can adopt, since new policies often have to fit in with existing ways of doing things. This may partly explain why relatively little use of economic incentives has been made so far.

Where economic instruments have been introduced, they have often not worked as well as expected. For tradable permits, this is often because of other environmental constraints on firms' activities, for example in the Fox River. For taxes, it is often because they are not set high enough to have incentive effects, or because they operate in tandem with regulation.

The fact that economic instruments have not been more widely used can usually be explained by criteria other than economic efficiency being judged as more important; and by the self-interests of polluters and their ability to influence regulators.

Non-point pollutants pose special difficulties. Finding cheaper ways of monitoring the performance of non-point pollution reduction schemes based on management practices is very important, and is a big issue partly due to the fact that there are likely to be a large number of relatively small firms to control, compared to the usual situation for point-source pollution where we typically have a small number of large sources. The fact that monitoring and enforcement costs are so high means regulators are often better adopting second-best, indirect policies, such as controls on land use, rather than first-best, more targetted measures such as taxing nitrate applications.

References

Baumol, W., and Oates, W. (1971). 'The use of standards and prices for the protection of the environment', *Swedish Journal of Economics* 73: 42–54.

Brannlund, R., Chung, Y., Fare, R., and Grosskopf, S. (1998), 'Emissions trading and profitability: the Swedish pulp and paper industry', *Environmental and Resource Economics* 12: 345–56.

Buchanan, J., and Tullock, J. (1975). 'Polluters' profits and political response: direct controls versus taxes', *American Economic Review* 65: 139–47.

Carling, A. (1992). *The United States Experience with Economic Incentives to Control Environmental Pollution*, Paper 230–R–92–001 (Washington, DC: Environmental Protection Agency).

Chapman, G. P. (1995). 'The Ganges and Brahmaputra basins', in G. P. Chapman and M. Thompson (eds.), *Water and the Quest for Sustainable Development in the Ganges Valley* (London: Mansell Publishing).

Csepiga, Z. (1996). 'Strategic planning in Rackeve-Soroksari (RSD) Danube-branch ecoregion', in *Developing Local and Regional Action Plans in Central and Eastern Europe: Case Studies of Bulgaria, Czech Republic, Poland, and the Slovak Republic* (Regional Environmental Centre for Central and Eastern Europe).

Freeman, A. M. (1990). 'Water pollution policy' in P. Portney (ed.) *Public Policies for Environmental Protection* (Washington, DC: Resources for the Future).

Goodstein, E. (1995). *Economics and the Environment* (Englewood Cliffs, NJ: Prentice Hall).

Hahn, R. (2000). 'The impact of economics on environmental policy', *Journal of Environmental Economics and Management* 39(3): 375–99.

Hanley, N., Faichney, R., Munro, A., and Shortle, J. (1998). 'Economic and Environmental Modelling for Pollution Control in an Estuary, '*Journal of Environmental Management* 52: 211–25.

Hanley, N., Hallett, S., and Moffatt, I. (1990). 'Why is more notice not taken of economists' prescriptions for the control of pollution?' *Environment and Planning A* 22. 1421–9.

Kelman, S. (1981). 'Economists and the environmental muddle', *Public Interest* 64: 106–23.

Kemp, R. (1998). 'The diffusion of biological waste-water treatment plants', *Environmental and Resource Economics* 12: 113–36.

Moxey, A., and White, B. (1994). 'Efficient compliance with agricultural nitrate pollution standards', *Journal of Agricultural Economics* 45(1): 27–37.

O'Neill, W., David, M., Moore, C., and Joeres, E. (1983). 'Transferable discharge permits and economic efficiency: the Fox River', *Journal of Environmental Economics and Management* 10: 346–55.

Pan, J. H., and Hoage, I. (1994). 'Land use permits as an alternative to fertilizer and teaching taxes for the control of nitrate pollution', *Journal of Agricultural Economics* 45(1): 102–12.

Pargul, S., Mani, M., and Huq, M. (1997). *Inspections and Emissions in India: Puzzling Survey Evidence about Industrial Pollution* (Washington, DC: World Bank).

Tietenberg, T. (1998). *Environmental Economics and Policy*, 2nd edn. (Reading, Mass.: Addison-Wesley).

Tobey, J., and Smets, H. (1996). 'The polluter pays principle', *World Economy* 19(1): 63–87.

Woodard, C. (1995). *Singing the Danube Blues*, (Regional Environmental Centre for Central and Eastern Europe).

World Bank (1998). *World Development Indicators*, CD-Rom (Washington, DC: World Bank).

Further Reading

■ Anderson, M. S. (1999). 'Governance by green taxes: implementing clean water policies in Europe, 1970–1990', *Environmental Economics and Policy Studies* 11: 1–25.

■ Department of the Environment, Transport and the Regions (1997). *Economic Instruments for Water Pollution* (HMSO: London).

■ Nelson, R. (1987). 'The economics profession and the making of public policy', *Journal of Economic Literature* 25: 49–87.

■ OECD (1997). *Environmental Taxes and Green Tax Reform* (Paris: OECD).

■ Royal Commission on Environmental Pollution (1992). *16th report: Freshwater Quality* (London: HMSO).

■ SEPA, (1996). *State of the Environment Report* (Stirling: Scottish Environmental Protection Agency).

- Shortle, J., and Abler, D. (1997). 'Non-point pollution', in H. Folmer and T. Tietenberg (eds.), *The International Yearbook of Environmental and Resource Economics, 1997/8* (Cheltenham: Edward Elgar).

- Svendsen, G. T. (1998). *Public Choice and Environmental Regulation* (Cheltenham: Edward Elgar).

- On the Murray-Darling Basin: *http://www.mdbc.gov.au/MDBasin/index.html*

Chapter 12
The Economics of Climate Change

12.1 Introduction

IMAGINE an invisible quilt covering the earth. Its warmth allows us to grow food, build shelters, and clothe ourselves. But a problem may exist. Mainstream scientists warn that our daily actions could influence the global climate to its detriment: developing land, raising livestock, and burning fossil fuels might be disrupting the planet's atmosphere—and the consequences could be devastating.

Their argument is based on two observed trends. First, the Earth has warmed $0.5°$ C, or $1°$ F, over the past 100 years. At the same time, atmospheric concentrations of greenhouse gases have increased by about 30 per cent over the last 200 years (see Table 12.1). A connection between these trends has been suggested, and the Intergovernmental Panel on Climate Change has in fact concluded that 'the balance of evidence suggests that there is a discernible human influence on global climate'. As a result, many scientists advocate a worldwide reduction in greenhouse gas emissions.

Such an undertaking would be enormous: possible restrictions could touch the lives of everyone on the planet. Climate change has the potential to dwarf all other environmental policy questions.

We must better understand the risks climate change presents and the choices we have to reduce them. Protecting the climate against change is a hedge against uncertainty, a kind of planet insurance, and economics offers a unique perspective to better understand such protection. This chapter examines how economics can make good climate change policy better and help prevent bad policy from getting worse.

Table 12.1 Total carbon dioxide emissions of Annexe I Parties in 1990, for the purposes of Article 25 of the Kyoto Protocol

Party	Emissions (Gg)	Percentage
Australia	288,965	2.1
Austria	59,200	0.4
Belgium	113,405	0.8
Bulgaria	82,990	0.6
Canada	457,441	3.3
Czech Republic	169,514	1.2
Denmark	52,100	0.4
Estonia	37,797	0.3
Finland	53,900	0.4
France	366,536	2.7
Germany	1,012,443	7.4
Greece	82,100	0.6
Hungary	71,673	0.5
Iceland	2,172	0.0
Ireland	30,719	0.2
Italy	428,941	3.1
Japan	1,173,360	8.5
Latvia	22,976	0.2
Liechtenstein	208	0.0
Luxembourg	11,343	0.1
Monaco	71	0.0
Netherlands	167,600	1.2
New Zealand	25,530	0.2
Norway	35,533	0.3
Poland	414,930	3.0
Portugal	42,148	0.3
Romania	171,103	1.2
Russian Federation	2,388,720	17.4
Slovakia	58,278	0.4
Spain	260,654	1.9
Sweden	61,256	0.4
Switzerland	43,600	0.3
UK	584,078	4.3
USA	4,957,022	36.1
Total	13,728,306	100.0

Note: Data based on the information from the 34 Annexe I Parties that submitted their first national communications on or before 11 Dec. 1997, as compiled by the secretariat in several documents (A/AC.237/81; FCCC/CP/1996/12/Add.2 and FCCC/SB/1997/6). Some of the communications included data on CO_2 emissions by sources and removals by sinks from land-use change and forestry, but since different ways of reporting were used these data are not included.

Source: Report of the Conference of the parties on its third session, held at Kyoto from 1 to 11 December 1997 FCCC/CP/1997/7/Add.1.

Table 12.2 Annexe B. Quantified emission limitation or reduction commitment (percentage of base year or period)

Australia	108
Austria	92
Belgium	92
Bulgaria [a]	92
Canada	94
Croatia [a]	95
Czech Republic [a]	92
Denmark	92
Estonia [a]	92
European Community	92
Finland	92
France	92
Germany	92
Greece	92
Hungary [a]	94
Iceland	110
Ireland	92
Italy	92
Japan	94
Latvia [a]	92
Liechtenstein	92
Lithuania [a]	92
Luxembourg	92
Monaco	92
Netherlands	92
New Zealand	100
Norway	101
Poland [a]	94
Portugal	92
Romania [a]	92
Russian Federation [a]	100
Slovakia [a]	92
Slovenia [a]	92
Spain	92
Sweden	92
Switzerland	92
Ukraine [a]	100
United Kingdom of Great Britain and Northern Ireland	92
United States of America	93

[a] Countries that are undergoing the process of transition to a market economy

12.2 A Global Environmental Risk

LIFE on earth is possible because certain gases trap sunlight in our atmosphere and keep us warm—like a greenhouse. Carbon dioxide (CO_2), released from burning fossil fuels, is one such greenhouse gas. But in excess, those gases may work against us, holding in too much heat, blocking outward radiation, and altering our climate.

Scientists warn that such changes could affect agricultural yields, timber harvests and water resource productivity. Results might include a rise in sea level, salt-water contamination of drinking water, and more storms and floods. Human health could be threatened by more heatwaves and spreading tropical diseases. Accurately defining the risk of such outcomes is crucial for good climate policy.

Good policy should also distinguish between stock and flow pollution. Stock pollution is concentration—the accumulated carbon in the atmosphere, like water in a bathtub. Flow pollution is emissions—the annual rate of emission, like water flowing into the tub. Because risk comes from the total stock of carbon, our focus should be on projected concentration levels. Greenhouse gases remain in the atmosphere decades before they dissipate, so different rates of emission could generate the same concentrations by a given year; policy-makers therefore have options regarding how they hit a given concentration target.

The least-cost option, as identified by economists, is a slow start with a more rapid rate of emission reductions after several decades. That would allow for a natural rate of capital depreciation and the replacement of high-carbon energy sources—like coal—for low carbon sources—like wind and solar. The 'broad, then deep' path is recommended by many researchers and policy-makers: broad participation by both

---

Box 12.1 Global Warming and Alaskan Forests

Two species of bug native to Alaska look set to cause increasing amounts of economic damage due to global warming. The western black-headed budworm *Acleris gloverana* damages spruce trees by laying its eggs in buds tied shut with silk. When the larvae hatch out, they eat the spruce needles and can kill the tree. In the last five years, 40,000 ha. of forest have been affected. The numbers of budworm seem to depend on how warm the Alaskan summer is: warmer summers mean more bugs. The last sixty years have seen an overall warming trend, whilst the IPCC has predicted warmer, drier summers in the Arctic and sub-Arctic in the future. Another native pest is the spruce bark beetle, *Dendroctonus rufipennis*, which uses chemical signals to home in on stressed or weakened trees. It then uses pheromones to attract more beetles. The beetles' life cycle has halved from two years to one recently, meaning more beetles, whilst more trees are becoming stressed due to warmer, drier summers. The combined effect of the two pests has been estimated by IPCC to mean that up to 65 per cent of the world's northern forests could be threatened due to global warming. (*New Scientist*,18.7.98).

developed and developing countries, and a gradual emission reduction path to achieve a long-term concentration target.

Good policy should also account for alternative risk-reduction strategies, such as mitigation and adaptation. Adaptation is an investment in private self-insurance to reduce the severity of realized damages. Mitigation is an investment in collective self-protection to reduce the odds that a bad state of nature is realized, and is the sum of all nations' efforts to reduce carbon emissions. Thus adaptation is mainly a private good in which the benefits of reduced severity accrue to one nation, whereas mitigation is a public risk-reduction strategy in which the benefits of reduced risk accrue to all nations.

Climate policy usually acknowledges that the climate is a global public good: everybody uses the same one. Therefore it is the sum of all the carbon emitted around the globe that matters. This is crucial because the major emitters of greenhouse gases will probably change over the next few decades. Today the industrialized world accounts for the largest portion of emissions, but soon developing countries such as China and India will be the world's largest emitters. That's why international cooperation is essential.

12.3 The International Challptice

T HE world community began responding in 1979 with the First World Climate Conference. Most recently, in 1997, in Kyoto, Japan, industrialized nations agreed to legally binding emissions reductions below 1990 levels by 2008–12. Basic provisions were made for international trading of emissions allowances and for sinks, but no agreement was reached about the responsibilities of developing countries or financial incentives to them, and no concrete measures for enforcement of the agreements were determined (see Box 12.2 on the Kyoto Protocol).

Achieving meaningful international cooperation will be an ongoing challenge. Even though nations have a common interest in climate change, many are reluctant to reduce carbon voluntarily. They realize they cannot be prevented from 'free-riding': enjoying a better climate whether they contribute to it or not. Free-riding is complicated further in developing countries where clean water and a stable food supply seem more urgent than climate change policy. The developing world also has less financial and technical capacities to act, and different perceptions about what constitutes equitable distributions of effort.

Economists and other analysts have used ideas from game theory to examine this problem and propose solutions. First, since a credible international police force does not exist to enforce an environmental agreement, such an agreement must be voluntary and self-enforcing. The problem is that the world is most likely to get a self-enforcing agreement when we really do not need it; we are likely not to get the agreement when we do need it. Consider: if the global net benefits of cooperating are

Box 12.2 The Kyoto Protocol on Climate Change

Some 150 countries met in Kyoto, Japan on December 1997 at the third Conference of the Parties (COP-3) to the United Nations Framework Convention on Climate Change (UNFCC). Their task was to create a legally binding international agreement for climate protection—the Kyoto Protocol. The Kyoto Protocol was the culmination of years of negotiations to strengthen the first international climate change treaty signed by over 160 countries at the 1992 Earth Summit in Rio de Janeiro. The original treaty, UNFCC, called on industrial nations to voluntarily reduce their greenhouse gas emissions to 1990 levels by 2000.

What does the Kyoto Protocol say?

Targets and Timetables (Article 3). The protocol set a legally binding target for thirty-nine of the world's most developed countries to reduce greenhouse gas emissions in aggregate by 5.2 per cent from a 1990 baseline for the period 2008–12. The targets are differentiated by nation, ranging from an 8 per cent reduction (the European Union) to a 10 per cent increase (Iceland) from 1990 levels. The USA agreed to a target of 7 per cent reduction; Japan a 6 per cent reduction (see Table 12. 2). Each party must show demonstrable progress towards meeting its target by 2005.

Nations can act jointly to hit their target (Article 4). The Protocol lets a group of nations form a multi-country 'bubble' in which the group has an overall target to reach. Each nation inside the bubble has its own commitment to the rest of the group. The bubble met the demand of the European Union (EU) that it should be able to comply as a group. The bubble does require the EU to adjust its commitment if its membership enlarges.

Greenhouse gases (Article 3: Annexe A). The Protocol covers six greenhouse gases, carbon dioxide, methane, nitrous oxide, hydroflurocarbons (HFCs), perflurocarbons (PFCs), and sulphur hexaflouride (SF6) as a 'basket'. The latter three use a 1995 baseline instead of 1990. The inclusion of the six gases allows for some flexibility in reaching the target. Reductions in one gas can be used to substitute for reductions in other gases.

Emission trading (Article 16). The Protocol allows for emission trading among the nations to fulfil their commitments. An emission-trading programme provides greater flexibility for a nation to achieve its target.

Joint Implementation/Clean Development Mechanism (Articles 6 and 12). Joint Implementation (JI) is when one nation gets credit for implementing a project to reduce carbon emissions in another country. A new device, the clean development mechanism (CDM), was developed for joint projects with developing nations through the payment of a special administrative fee by developed nations.

Carbon Sinks. The protocol allows for carbon sinks—land and forestry practices that remove carbon emissions from the atmosphere. Sinks could play an important role for some nations because they represent a low-cost option. Sinks are ambiguously defined in the Protocol, and will be a challenge to measure.

No harmonization of actions. The Protocol allows each nation to figure out its own best strategy to meet its commitment. Not everyone sees this as a good thing: some critics have argued that the world would have been better served by a common action rather than a common target.

What didn't the Kyoto protocol achieve?

Developing country participation. No agreement was reached in Kyoto on what commitments they should assume to reduce their greenhouse gas emissions. But it is clear to everyone that climate protection requires the participation of the developing countries because by the middle of the next century, they are predicted to generate the largest share of carbon emissions. Developing nations have no incentive to reduce their economic growth. China, for example, is the second largest emitter after the USA, but its per capita emissions are about a seventh of those in the USA. A Chinese delegate captured the sentiment underlying the opposition: "[W]hat they [developed nations] are doing is luxury emissions, what we are doing is survival emissions.' Substantial compensation might be required to induce their necessary participation.

Specifics on emission trading and the clean development mechanism. The Protocol also left the specific rules and regulations about international emissions trading to be defined at a future date.

Specifics on compliance and enforcement. The Protocol says enforcement procedures to deal with non-compliance will be established at the first meeting of the parties to the Protocol. But the details must still be fleshed out. As such, firms falling under a trading system will remain sceptical about the workability of the scheme.

large, a self-enforcing agreement cannot be maintained because there is just too much incentive to free-ride. A self-enforcing agreement can only be maintained when the global net benefits are about the same as no agreement.

If a complete agreement cannot be reached, the question becomes whether it is better to have a partial cooperation, in which some nations do a lot and others do nothing (cooperation-limited), or to have full cooperation in which all nations do a little but not the optimal amount (cooperation-lite). Which scenario leads to the most total abatement? In our example in Figure 12.1, it is cooperation-lite that has the greatest abatement, but the opposite could also hold. This issue deserves more attention.

Game theory also suggests that free-riding can be alleviated if conforming nations can retaliate against violators with trade sanctions. But the force of this deterrence is blunted in several respects. First, a nation's incentive to deviate from the agreement depends on how it views a short-term gain from cheating compared to the long-term losses from punishment. Nations that must deal today with other problems, such as clean water, might discount the threat of sanctions. Second, conforming nations must see a gain in applying punishment, otherwise their threats will not be believable. And since many forms of sanctions exist, nations would need to select a mutually agreeable approach—not a trivial negotiation. Alternatively, one could argue that the process of negotiation itself can help reinforce mutual expectations for cooperation. This perspective recognizes that unilateral confidence-building moves by some countries could inspire like-minded actions by others, and communication itself can reinforce positive expectations.

Good international climate policy should also address the implementation of cost-effective risk-reduction strategies, such as carbon taxes or carbon emission trading.

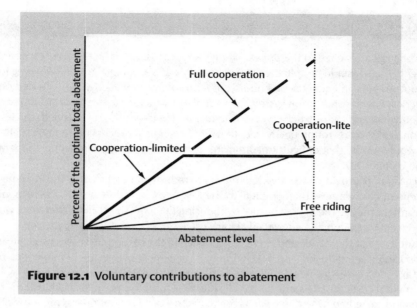

Figure 12.1 Voluntary contributions to abatement

Carbon taxes fix the cost of carbon, and allow the quantity of emissions to be determined by the private sector (see Box 12.3 on carbon taxes). Emission trading fixes the quantity of emissions and allows people to trade emission permits at a price set by the market (see Box 12.4). Such flexible mechanisms may increase the likelihood of international cooperation.

12.4 The Benefits and Costs of International Cooperation

THE conventional economics approach to assessing climate change policy is to calculate the benefits and costs of action or inaction. The potential benefits from climate protection agreements such as the Kyoto Protocol lie in what is avoided: more severe weather patterns, hobbled ecosystems, less biodiversity, less potable water, loss of coastal areas, rises in mean temperature, more infectious diseases such as malaria and cholera. Of course, climate change might actually benefit agriculture and forestry with longer growing seasons and more fertilization.

These gains (or losses) can be categorized into four broad sets of increasing difficulty to quantify: the avoided losses to market goods and services, non-market goods, ancillary effects, and catastrophes.

People usually have judged the benefits of climate protection as the incremental reduction in human and environmental risks compared to the business-as-usual

Box 12.3 Carbon Taxes

A carbon tax adds a fee to the price of fossil fuels according to their relative carbon content. The tax could be collected in various ways: as a severance tax on domestic fossil fuel output plus an equal tax on imports; as a tax on primary energy inputs levied on refineries, gas transportation systems, and coal shippers; or further downstream to homeowners and car or truck owners. The further upstream the tax is levied, the less carbon 'leaks' out through uncovered activities like oilfield processing. A fossil fuel tax also would not be that difficult to administer given the existing tax collection apparatus in the USA and EU.

A carbon tax provides incentive to emitters to reduce emissions when the incremental abatement cost was less than or equal to the tax. A tax can stimulate several responses. Firms might reduce their tax exposure by reducing CO_2 emissions. Fossil fuel users would have incentive to improve energy efficiency, use less carbon-intensive fuels, and consume less of the goods and services produced in the carbon-intensive ways. Taxes would trigger the diffusion and development of new technologies that emit less carbon. The tax is cost-effective because it sets up the institutional structure so that the incremental costs are the same across all sources—there are no gains from trade remaining to be had. One downside is that a carbon tax does not guarantee a specific emissions reduction goal.

A carbon tax could be extended to other greenhouse gases. The appropriate tax on natural gas entering the pipeline system could account for leakage, and the greater relative potency of methane. Levies also could be placed on methane releases from coal mines and landfills, and on HCFCs based on their expected venting to the atmosphere through sources like auto air-conditioners. Extending taxes to agricultural sources of methane is conceivable, but given the decentralized and difficult-to-measure nature of these sources, such an extension might be problematic in practice.

(BAU) baseline. Under BAU, modellers have estimated that carbon concentrations might be expected to double pre-industrial levels within the next half century, with mean temperatures predicted to rise by about 1° C by 2050, and 2.5° C by 2100. With Kyoto, concentrations are still likely to double, with temperatures increasing by about 0.1° C by 2050 and 0.5° C by 2100.

Researchers have estimated the impact on gross world product from climate change at around 1 or 2 per cent. The impact on gross domestic product (GDP) in the USA has been estimated to be between plus or minus 1 per cent. Most industries in the developed nations are separate from climate: less than 3 per cent of US livelihoods, for instance, are earned in agriculture and other climate-sensitive activities. And even if we include the potential non-market damage, the market and non-market benefits to the USA might be at most about 2 per cent of GDP. These impacts are not trivial, but neither are they likely to cause the next global depression. The benefits from Kyoto are most likely to accrue to the future generations in developing nations because their economies depend more on favorable climate for agriculture, forestry, and fishing. One economist has suggested that climate policy really amounts to a

Box 12.4 Tradable Carbon Markets versus Carbon Taxes

The Kyoto Protocol establishes quantitative targets for reductions in the emissions of carbon dioxide by signatory countries. Many countries, notably the USA, are supporting the use of tradable permit markets to achieve these targets. Tradable permits are attractive since they guarantee a fixed level of emission reductions, and could produce less political flak.

Some economists, however, have questioned whether this is a good idea given the great uncertainty still attached to the costs of reducing CO_2. They have promoted the use of a carbon tax. A nation sets a tax (or price) on emissions of CO_2, or on actions that produce the fossil fuels which generate the CO_2 emissions. Producers respond to the tax by seeking out the lowest means of production, internalizing the costs of CO_2 emissions.

Now if there was no uncertainty over future control costs, both tradable quantity controls and carbon taxes would produce similar outcomes. But there *is* considerable uncertainty over how big carbon control costs will be in the future, due to three factors: (i) we have little experience with such large cuts in emissions, (ii) we do not know what future technological options will be, and (iii) we do not know what the 'do nothing' level of emission will be, relative to which achievements are measured and targets set.

US economists William Pizer (1999) constructed a scenario in which there is some uncertainty over control costs, and that control costs actually turn out to be higher than thought. Under a permit system, emissions stay constant, but costs of control rise. Under a tax system, emissions are cut by less, even though the price per tonne stays constant. Permit systems thus result in more uncertainty about costs than emission reductions, whilst this situation is reversed with taxes. Under certainty, emissions by 2010 for either a $80/tonne carbon tax or a permit market with 8.5 gigatonnes or total allowances are about equal.

Pizer then subjects these alternatives to a run of 1,000 different predictions based around current IPCC calculations. He finds that emissions are below the 8.5 gigatonnes of carbon level in 75 per cent of cases with the tax, but exceed it in the remaining cases. The permit market ensures that emissions never go above 8.5 gigatonnes. However, the same simulation of possible future scenarios shows the costs of the permit scheme to be in the range of zero to 2.2 per cent of global GDP, a much larger range than that for the tax at 0.2–0.6 per cent. The variation of control costs is thus much greater under the permit system than with a tax.

Which policy option should we choose? Pizer argues that it depends on what we believe about the damage. If there is some threshhold beyond which further CO_2 emissions will impose very high (and maybe irreversible) costs, the greater certainty over emission levels that comes with permit markets is preferable. If instead, damage rises smoothly with increasing emissions, the threats are not so bad, and we prefer the greater certainty over control costs which comes from taxes. This preference for taxes over permits is re-enforced when one remembers that it is not current emissions that most worry us about climate change, but the overall stock of greenhouse gases in the atmosphere, which changes very slowly.

But carbon taxes are unpopular, and unlikely to be widely used. What to do? Pizer argues in favour of a hybrid system. In this system, the government first allocates a number of limited life permits freely, but then makes additional supplies available at a price (a 'trigger price'). This trigger price works like a tax on emissions or a safety valve, and can be gradually increased over time if we want to progressively toughen up on climate policy.

Box 12.5 Estimating the Impacts of Global Warming

Despite the considerable uncertainties surrounding climate change, policy-makers nevertheless need estimates of possible impacts to improve decision-making. These estimates are often based on complex, and often low-resolution, global circulation models which are mostly concerned with the links between stocks of greenhouse gases and climate. One particular aspect of modelling is the study of the marginal impacts of carbon emissions in terms of economic damage: this is of particular interest if we were to try and set an optimal tax on CO_2, or if we are deciding on how big a reduction in greenhouse gas emissions is warranted from an economic efficiency viewpoint. Given the uncertainties mentioned above, a large range of estimates exists for marginal damage.

PAGE (Policy Analysis for the Greenhouse Effect), developed to assist EU decision-makers in the early 1990s, is an example of a model which tries to explicitly incorporate uncertainty into its predictions (Plambeck and Hope, 1996). The model includes two types of decision variable: the level of greenhouse gas emissions over time, and the degree of adaptation to climate change. PAGE estimates climate change impacts, and the costs of achieving different adaptation/emission reduction targets.

The model is built in seven sections:

- Emissions of primary greenhouse gases
- Impact on the greenhouse effect
- Offsetting cooling from sulphate aerosols
- Regional temperature effects
- A stepped damage function, featuring a 'maximum tolerable temperature change'
- Impacts on regional GDP growth in two sectors, 'economic' and 'environmental and social'
- Adaptation investments, such as extending sea walls or investing in drought-resistant crops.

Table 12.B5 presents an example of the net present value of 'business as usual' emissions, and the effects of increasing emissions by 100 gigatonnes of carbon. The last row shows the marginal impacts. The three columns of figures show the minimum, maximum, and mean effects, which take account of the uncertainty in the model parameters. As can be seen the marginal damage ranges from $1 to $6 per tonne of carbon, with a mean of $3.

Table 12.B5

Net present value of impacts:	Minimum	Maximum	Mean
Business as usual (US$trillion)	0.8	4.6	2.2
Business as usual plus 100 gigatonnes of carbon (US$ trillion)	0.9	5.5	2.5
Marginal impacts (US$ per tonne of carbon)	1	6	3

These figures can be compared with results from an earlier version of PAGE, which left out the offsetting cooling effects referred to above: this gave comparable values of $2–7 per tonne. This makes sense, since allowing for offsetting cooling should reduce the marginal damages of carbon emissions.

wealth transfer from today's industrial nations to future generations in developing nations (see Schelling, 1997).

Two topics in non-market valuation are likely to trigger major debates: human health and ecosystem/endangered species services. Potential threats to human health include thirty diseases new to medicine, such as E. coli, hantavirus, and HIV, plus old scourges like cholera, plague, yellow and dengue fever, tuberculosis, malaria. How do we quantify such threats? Estimating the social value of ecosystem services and endangered species is another challenge. Despite the extraordinary analytical difficulties associated with measuring the social value of preserving each species, determining at least a range for these values is essential if we are to make judgements about the benefits of preservation.

One way to increase the size of the benefits of the Kyoto Protocol is to add in the potential ancillary benefits that might come from discouraging fossil fuel consumption. The Kyoto Protocol would reduce emissions of such air pollutants as carbon monoxide, sulphur and nitrogen oxides, and toxic trace pollutants in exhaust gases, thereby reducing their damage to health, visibility, materials, and crops. Studies in Europe and the USA have estimated that the non-climate benefits might be as large—or larger—than the benefits from avoiding climate change.

Finally, although modellers often presume climate change will be gradual—a slow and steady rise in temperature or precipitation—some have raised the spectre of catastrophe. They suggest there is a real risk of a sudden rupture, e.g. a structural change in ocean currents or the melting of the Western Antarctic ice sheet. The problem is that researchers do not have any reasonable estimates of the odds that these events will come to pass, but making informed policy judgements requires knowing those odds.

The costs of climate protection are unclear. Some studies suggest the USA could meet its target at negligible cost; others call Kyoto an 'economic disarmament'. A report from the White House states the costs to the USA to meet its Kyoto target are 'likely to be modest' if reductions are efficiently pursued with domestic and international emissions trading, joint implementation, and the Clean Development Mechanism (a system in which developed nations can buy the carbon reductions in developing nations). By modest, the report means an annual GDP drop of less than 0.5 per cent (roughly $10bn); no expected negative effect on the trade deficit; increased gasoline or petrol prices of about 5 cents a gallon in the USA; lower electricity rates; and no major impacts on the employment rate.

But other estimates suggest that the US GDP could take an annual hit of nearly 3 per cent, or about $250bn a year, with intranation emission trading. Plus the trade deficit would increase by billions of dollars; gasoline prices would increase by 50 cents a gallon; electricity prices would nearly double; and two million US jobs would disappear. The net global costs have been estimated at over $700bn, with the USA bearing about two-thirds of those costs.

The effects of international policy on world trade patterns are also unclear. Many leaders fear the 'pollution haven' hypothesis: domestic industry will relocate to developing countries for less stringent emissions restrictions. This seems unlikely. Except for the biggest polluting industries, the costs of complying with environmental regulations are a small fraction of total costs, and are outweighed by international differences in labour costs, capital costs, material costs, and exchange rate changes. The differences between developed nations' environmental regulations and those of most major trading partners are not that big. Besides, developed-nation firms often build state-of-the art facilities abroad regardless of the host nation's environmental regulations.

Leaders also fear carbon policy will affect the demand for domestic energy-intensive goods and cause the trade balance to deteriorate. But studies show this is not so. A related idea is the 'leakage effect'—cuts in domestic emissions could be offset by shifts in production and therefore increases in emissions abroad. On this, research has not formed firm conclusions. Studies of unilateral emissions-reduction policies in OECD countries predict leakage rates of anywhere between 3.5 and 70 per cent.

In general, cost estimates are likely to be on the low side for several reasons. Models presume the most efficient possible climate control programme, even though today only one such programme is ongoing. The models assume the control programme is announced early and maintained indefinitely, even though governments will be hard pressed to maintain consistent control over the decades. Many models focus on long-term equilibrium and do not address the short-run adjustments, such as the oil shocks of the 1970s, which could raise cost estimates by a factor of one to four. This factor would cause Kyoto to reduce GDP by 1–10 per cent from baseline. Compare that to the 2 per cent of GDP the USA now spends on all environmental programmes combined.

12.5 Economic Issues Underlying Benefit and Cost Estimates

How one sees the benefits and costs of international cooperation depends on what one believes about the nature of three elements that underlie climate protection: the cusp of a catastrophe, the degree of flexibility, and the origins of technological advance. We now take a brief look at each of these issues.

If you believe catastrophe is imminent, emission reductions cannot come soon enough. If you don't, it is hard to justify the likely costs of the Kyoto Protocol without global trading. Reliable information is needed to help people understand the nature of climate change. Right now we do not know which regions will get warmer or cooler; which will get wetter or drier; which will get stormier or calmer. Climate policy debates eventually reach the point in which the modeller is asked whether he or she has accounted for the likelihood that a change in the ecosystem will be discontinuous—in other words, a catastrophe. Most modellers acknowledge their models do not address the potential for discontinuous shocks, like a sudden shift in the Gulf Stream or an unravelling of the web of life due to the loss of some keystone species.

Experience tells people little about low-probability risks like climate change. They must rely on outside sources of information to help them make judgements about the likelihood that a bad event will actually come to pass. If that information stresses severity without giving some notion of the odds, people systematically bias their risk perceptions upward. Numerous studies have revealed that people commonly over-estimate the chance that they will suffer from a low probability/high severity event, e.g. a nuclear power accident.

Second, the costs to meet a policy depend on how quickly society wants to change its energy systems and capital structure. A stringent, inflexible carbon policy will induce greater economic burden than a loose, flexible policy, since more flexibility allows firms greater agility to search out the lowest-cost alternatives. Estimates suggest that any agreement without the flexibility provided by trading will at least double the costs.

Flexibility here means the ability to reduce carbon at the lowest cost, and three issues are relevant. We first need to work through how the trading system would be designed before alternative policies can be usefully evaluated. The Kyoto Protocol does not have a set position as to what either a domestic or international trading system would look like. Defining the rules for flexibility incentive systems is wide open, and experimental economists could play an important role in reducing the uncertainty. This holds for joint implementation and the clean development mechanism as well.

We then need to address the role of 'carbon sinks', which remain the wild card in the search for flexible, low-cost solutions. A sink is a process that destroys or absorbs greenhouse gases, such as the absorption of atmospheric carbon dioxide by trees, soils, and other types of vegetation. In the USA, forests are an important terrestrial sink since they cover about 750 million acres. A few studies have found that carbon sequestration through sinks could cost as little as $25/tonne in the USA. But serious uncertainties remain about how to measure and account for estimates of net carbon.

We also need to address the idea that the costs of climate protection might be amplified by the existing tax system. Labour and capital taxes distort behaviour because they reduce employment and investment levels below what they would have been otherwise. If we add on a carbon tax that discourages consumption and production, we further reduce employment and investment, which then exacerbates the labour and capital tax distortions, maybe by as much as 400 per cent. One could reduce these extra costs by channelling the revenue from the carbon tax, if any existed, to reduce the labour and capital taxes.

Box 12.6 The UK Climate Change Levy

The UK climate change levy will apply to energy used in industry, commerce, and the public sector. Following the recommendations in Lord Marshall's report on Economic Instruments and the Business Use of Energy, in 1999 the government announced the introduction of the climate change levy that will come into effect in April 2001. The government subsequently announced a package of modifications to the design of the levy that will improve its environmental effectiveness and protect competitiveness. As a result, electricity generated from new forms of renewable energy, like solar and wind power, and good quality CHP plants will be exempt from the levy. The structure of the levy will continue to be kept under review in the light of developments as the UK moves towards the Kyoto commitment period.

Revenue from the levy will be recycled to business via a 0.3 percentage point cut in the main rate of National Insurance Contributions and additional support for energy-efficiency measures. The cut in National Insurance Contributions will lower the cost to firms of hiring workers and will help promote employment opportunities. The levy is intended to be 'revenue-neutral'.

Finally, the costs of climate protection depend on what one chooses to believe about the origins of technological advance. Some people argue that those origins are firmly rooted in non-price responses: people do the right thing for the right reason. Most economists disagree. They see the origins of advance as driven by changes in relative prices. Even if new technologies are available, people do not switch unless prices induce them to switch. People behave as if their time-horizons were short, perhaps reflecting their uncertainty about future energy prices and the reliability of the technology. The high initial investment costs also slow down adoption of new technologies, e.g. replacing all lights at once.

If people did switch to new technologies—such as compact fluorescent light bulbs, improved thermal insulation, heating and cooling systems, and energy-efficient appliances—studies suggest 20–25 per cent of existing carbon emissions could be eliminated at low costs. Another study has shown that if historical rates of cost reduction in the production of solar energy are maintained (30–50 per cent per decade), more than 90 per cent of the world's coal will never be used. The world will make the transition to solar from coal and oil even without a carbon tax. Global temperatures will increase by 1.5–2°C by around 2050, and will then decline to pre-industrial levels.

12.6 The Flexibility-Stringency Trade-off

THE climate change debate often focuses on the trade-off between the stringency of a nation's emissions reduction path, and how much flexibility a nation has to reach its target. A stringent, inflexible carbon policy creates a greater economic burden than a loose, flexible policy. If the goal is to keep costs down to some politically acceptable level, the push for a more stringent target requires more flexibility in how a nation can achieve the target. If market or institutional imperfections restrict flexibility, policy-makers can loosen the stringency of the target to keep the costs down. Figure 12.2 illustrates this stringency–flexibility tradeoff; the iso-cost curves represent different combinations of flexibility and stringency that generate the same given cost to the economy.

Now consider the policy options from Kyoto, using points A and B in the figure. Both points are on an iso-cost curve representing a relatively low cost to the economy. Point A could represent the US position going into the Kyoto negotiations: stabilize US emissions at 1990 levels (a reduction of over 30 per cent from business as usual), with the highly flexible policy of international emissions trading. Point B represents the same total cost to the economy except that now emissions trading is prohibited. This point is consistent with the negative reaction of many developed and developing

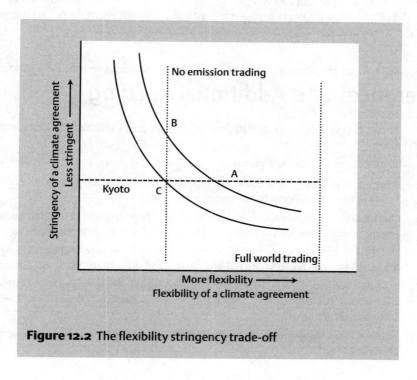

Figure 12.2 The flexibility stringency trade-off

countries towards emissions trading. To maintain the same cost as at point A, point B must necessarily involve a weaker target. If you lose flexibility, you have to give up some stringency to keep costs fixed. What emerged instead from Kyoto was something like point C, with both a less policy flexibility than some nations initially sought and a somewhat more ambitious emissions control target. Point C is on an iso-cost curve with higher cost to the economy than points A and B.

12.7 Concluding Comments

CLIMATE change is a historical fact, but its connection to human actions is not perfectly understood. Questions about whether humans really emit too many greenhouse gases, or what will happen to the global climate, or how changes will affect humans and the environment, remain unanswered.

Some useful points that emerge from the economic perspective might help create a more effective climate change policy. Carbon concentrations are what matter—and a cost-effective emissions path. Nations have an incentive to free-ride on the actions of others. People can adapt and that will change the effectiveness of international mitigation efforts. The costs and benefits depend on whether you believe we are on the cusp of a catastrophe, what level of flexibility is available to people and society, and how responsive people are to changes in the relative price of high- and low-carbon energy. Finally, policy-makers confront a political trade-off between the stringency of a climate target and the flexibility allowed in reaching it.

References and Additional Reading

Barron, E. (1995). 'Climate models: how reliable are their predictions', *Consequences* 1: 16–27.

Blinder, A. (1997). 'Needed: planet insurance', *New York Times*, 22 Oct.

Brown, S. *et al.* (1997). 'The economic impact of international climate change policy', Australian Bureau of Agricultural Resource Economics.

Chakravorty, U., Roumasset, J., and Tse, K. (1997). 'Endogenous substitution among energy resources and global warming', *Journal of Political Economy* 105: 1201–34.

IPCC (1996). *Climate Change 1995: Economic and Social Dimensions of Climate Change*, (J. P. Bruce, H. Lee, and E. Haites (eds.)) (Cambridge: Cambridge University Press, Cambridge).

Jaffe, A., Peterson, S., Portney, P., and R. Stavins (1994). 'Environmental regulation and international competitiveness: what does the evidence tell us?', *Resources for the Future*, Discussion Paper 94–08.

Jepma, C., and Munasinghe, M. (1998). *Climate Change Policy* (Cambridge: Cambridge University Press).

Manne, A., and Richels, R. (1997). 'On stabilizing CO_2 concentrations—cost-effective emission reduction strategies', *Energy Modeling Forum* 14.

Parry, I. W. H. (1997). 'Reducing carbon emissions: interactions with the tax system raise costs', *Resources* 128. 9–12.

Pizer, W. (1999). *Choosing Price or Quantity Controls for Greenhouse Gases*, Climate Issues Brief 17 (Washington, DC: *Resources for the Future*).

Plambeck, E., and Hope, C. (1996). 'An updated valuation of the impacts of global warming', *Energy Policy* 24: 783–93.

Repetto, R., and Austin, D. (1997). *The Costs of Climate Protection: A Guide for the Perplexed*, World Resources Institute, Report: 31.

Schelling, T. (1997). 'The costs of combating global warming', *Foreign Affairs*, Nov./Dec.: 8–14.

Shogren, J., and Toman, M. (2000). 'Climate change policy', in P. Portney and R. Stavins (eds.), *Public Policies for Environmental Protection*, 2nd edn. (Washington, DC: Resources for the Future): 125–68.

Weyant, J., and Hill, J. (1999). 'Introduction and overview. Special issue on the costs of the Kyoto Protocol: a multi-model evaluation' *Energy Policy* pp. vii–xlix.

Wigley, T., Richels, T., and Edmonds, J. (1996). 'Economic and environmental choices in the stabilization of atmospheric CO_2 concentrations', *Nature*, 379: 240–3.

Chapter 13
Biodiversity

IN this chapter we explore the economics of biodiversity conservation.

- The starting point is some fundamental biological principles such as species and diversity.
- Next we consider which species should be protected.
- We then consider how species and ecosystems are valued.
- Finally, we review the policy response of national governments and international institutions to preserve biodiversity.

13.1 Introduction

THROUGH the ages the processes of evolution have driven innumerable species to extinction and, by spontaneous mutations, created new species which are better suited to the evolving environment. This process, for most species, has proceeded gradually. Evidence from fossil records suggests that millions of years may separate one distinct species from another and new species are often only slightly genetically different from their predecessors. Periodically, about once every 26 million years, there have been mass extinctions (Raup, 1988) when a large number of species disappear. In the past these were due, it is thought, to meteorite strikes which briefly plunged the whole earth into winter. This theory has been put forward to explain the rapid extinction of the dinosaurs. Many biologists (May *et al.*, 1995) believe that we are currently witnessing a wave of mass extinction but this time the sudden loss of biological diversity (biodiversity) is due to human actions.

The exact rate of extinction is difficult to assess because we do not know how many species there are, see (Box 13.2). Estimates range from 3 to 25 per cent of species loss between the mid-1980s and 2015. The key determinant of the rate of species loss is the destruction of rainforest habitat, as rainforests have such high levels of biodiversity, see Barbier *et al.* (1994) for a review.

Biodiversity can be defined as:

the variability among living organisms from all sources, including *inter alia*, terrestrial, marine, and other aquatic ecosytems, and the ecological complexes of which these are a part: this includes diversity within species, between species and of ecosystems. (UNEP, 1993)

Biodiversity loss involves more than the loss of a few high-profile species such as elephants and rhinos, it concerns any regional loss of species or any reduction in the geographical range of species which reduces their genetic diversity.

Why is accelerated biodiversity loss a cause for concern? The loss of a species is a cost to society for three reasons. First, the species lost may have a direct value in terms of, for instance, genetic material for food crops, or as a source of medicines. Second, a species may play a critical role in maintaining an ecosystem and providing humanity with a range of ecosystem services such as nutrient cycling, and water catchment regulation. Finally, a species may have aesthetic and non-use benefits, for instance people like to see 'charismatic' species such as birds and butterflies in the wild.

Why are species lost? By taking land for agriculture and other uses mankind is gradually using up the habitats which support biodiveristy. Particularly at threat are rainforests, old-growth temperate forests, rangelands, and coral reefs, which together provide habitats for over 50 per cent of known species. By deciding to protect some habitats and depleting others man decides which species become extinct and which survive. Collectively society acts in the role of Noah deciding which species should be allowed on the Ark and which should be allowed to perish in the rising flood waters (see Box 13.1).

Human actions have increased the rate of extinction, therefore economics should be involved in finding solutions. Shogren *et al.* (1999) highlight the importance of economics to decisions that society makes concerning biodiversty:

- economic activity determines the risk a species faces of extinction;
- protecting a species has an opportunity cost in terms of reduced resources for other valued public goods such as hospitals and education and private goods such as food production. Unlike Noah we do not have the resources to fit all the species on the Ark;

Box 13.1 Noah's Library

Metrick and Weitzman (1998) employ the following metaphor to explain the problem of choosing which species to preserve. Consider a species as if it were a library full of books. Each book is a gene. Common books (genes) are housed in many libraries (species) others in only one. Resources can be used to protect libraries and reduce the probability of destruction by fire, but at a cost. The problem then is how should the fire-fighting resources be distributed amongst the different libraries.

A library has two attributes, the building (the phenotype of the species) and the information contained within it (the genes). We value the species for its aesthetic appeal or its use value. We may value the books (genes) for the diversity they bring to species in terms of colour and form, or we may place a utilitarian value upon them for the ideas they may contain for future medicines and food crops.

■ incentives matter, and economics tells us how people may respond to policies designed to protect biodiversity.

Some of these points appear obvious but they need to be emphasized because, thus far, the debate surrounding biodiversity has been dominated by scientific and not economic priorities. However, given that biodiversity loss is due to commercial activities, that protecting species is expensive and that conservation policies have been prone to failure due to a failure to understand incentives, it is perhaps time that economists took a more active role in finding the solution to this key environmental problem. This chapter gives an economist's perspective on this problem.

13.2 Which Species to Preserve?

THE issue of which species to preserve might, in economic terms, be judged on the basis of whether the benefits of preservation exceed the costs. This calculation is complex because both benefits and costs are difficult to estimate. Weitzmann (1992) developed a theory of which species should be preserved, based on a measure of distinctiveness; see also Metrick and Weitzman (1998). Distinctiveness can be interpreted as the 'genetic' difference between a species and its closest relative. However, distinctiveness says nothing about how much people actually like a species or how effective a species is in providing ecosystem services; it may say something, in the case of higher plants, about its potential medicinal value or about its importance in filling a particular niche within an ecosystem.

Policy-makers often have to make choices between species or ecological communities when allocating conservation funds. In an ideal world they might be able to use the following formula:

$$w(a, d) = p(a)(v_d(a, d) + v_e(a, d) + u(a, d)) - cd(a),$$

where $w(a, d)$ is the expected net benefit of conserving a species. We do not include discounting explicitly to keep the formula simple, but it should be calculated as a net present-value over a very long time-period, to account for the fact that once a species is lost it is lost for good.

Natural species populations are highly variable and it is impossible to ensure that a species will survive. The term $p(a)$ gives the probability of a species surviving. The probability of survival depends upon the decisions of landowners and policy-makers to conserve the habitat. In this simple model it is a function of the remaining area of habitat a.

The value of conserving a species or an ecological community has three components. The direct value of distinctiveness $v_d(a, d)$ is due to the expectation that a species will provide chemicals with medicinal properties or genetic material with commercial value. This is an expected value because we cannot be certain that a

Box 13.2 How Many Species?

A species is a population or series of populations within which there is free gene flow
(by reproduction). Species breed with each other but not with other species. Typically
new species emerge when a population becomes isolated due to some natural barrier
such as a mountain range or river. Due to this separation and differences in the
environment experienced by the species the two separated populations evolve separately
and eventually form two distinct separate species which are incapable of inter-breeding.

So far, 1.7 million species have been described (Stork, 1996). These include about
250,000 plants, 44,000 vertebrates, and 751,000 insects. We know with some
confidence that the 4,000 mammals described are an accurate estimate of the total,
but the numbers of described insects, fungi, and other primitive species are a gross
underestimate of the total number of species. Other groups such as viruses, bacteria,
and algae have been relatively unexplored (Colwell, 1996) and their species number
probably exceeds that of all other species combined. Some recent work on the insect
group in the Amazon by Erwin (1983) illustrate the problem. An estimated 41,389
new species of arthropod were discovered per ha. of tropical rainforest and, by an
extrapolation based on the rate of discovery, the total number of arthropod species
is predicted to be around 30 million. Choices are being made which extinguish large
numbers of species some of which have not been identified, other known species may
be identified, but very little is known about their genetic make-up or behaviour. As
biodiversity-rich habitats are converted to other land uses we might lose an unknown
number of species of unknown importance to mankind.

species or a group of species will provide commercially valuable material. We consider the nature of this component of value later in this chapter. Species distinctiveness d is important in determining this value as distinctiveness measures how close a
species is to related species which may have similar properties. If two species have
very similar genotypes, then they may be close substitutes in terms of their chemical
constituents.

The other component of value, the ecosystem service value $v_e(a, d)$, gives the contribution of the species to ecosystem services by increasing ecosytem resilience. As we
discuss later, this value depends upon how many substitute species there are within
an ecosystem which are capable of taking over the niche occupied by the species.

Finally, the aesthetic and non-use value $u(a, d)$ depends upon people's preferences
for a species or an ecological community. The species contributes to the aesthetic
value of the conserved area.

Costs $cd(a)$ are in terms of forgone development opportunities as a function of the
area of habitat preserved. This reflects the fact that as the area of habitat increases
then this increases the opportunity cost of lost development opportunities. Figure
13.1 shows the trade-off between costs and the probability of survival. We can also
think of the probability of survival representing the area of land devoted to a species
or an ecosystem. The status quo is the remaining area of habitat. If the habitat is
unprotected, then, over time, development will destroy the habitat. The cost at the

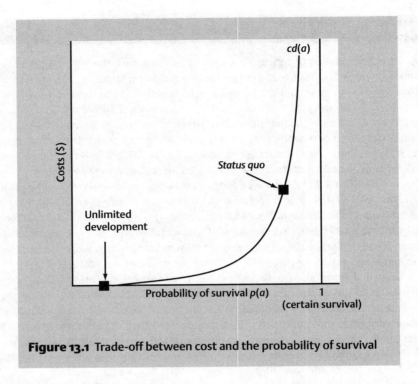

Figure 13.1 Trade-off between cost and the probability of survival

status quo represents the opportunity cost of habitat in terms of its development potential. As more habitat is preserved, or even recreated, then the probability of survival approaches one, but never reaches one because there is always some possibility that a species will become extinct. To the right of the status quo the cost curve becomes steeper as society transfers progressively more valuable land, for agriculture, forestry, or development, to restore the habitat. In fact, due to the irreversibility of destruction for many habitats, it may be impossible to restore some of the original habitat at any cost.

One approach to protecting biodiversity is to set a *safe minimum standard* which gives an acceptable probability that a species will survive (see Chapter 5). Consider the following example. Agricultural production in a region depends upon the forest area which remains in the region to moderate the hydrological cycle and reduce the intensity of flood events which in turn reduces agricultural output. The costs of conserving forest is the opportunity cost of development $cd(a)$ forgone by farmers which we draw as a quadratic shape. This is illustrated in Figure 13.2.

Farmers would choose to produce at a_p^*, since this maximizes profits. However, increasing agricultural production causes an external cost which has a threshold at a_s^{sms} where the external cost switches to a much higher level which exceeds the maximum profit. Society aims to maintain agricultural land use below this critical level. If society is uncertain about a 'safe' agricultural area, then the policy may be set at a safe minimum standard level of area at a_s^{sms}. This standard may reflect society's aversion towards the risks of an ecosystem 'collapse' and the uncertainty over how

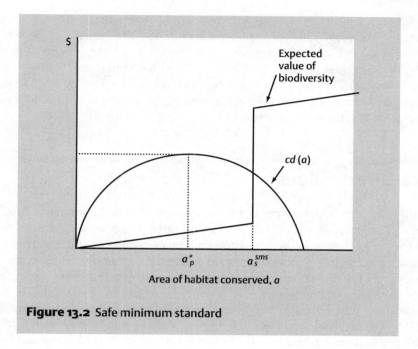

Figure 13.2 Safe minimum standard

much habitat can be destroyed before there is a catastrophic breakdown of the ecosystem. The safe minimum standard can be interpreted as an area of preserved habitat which ensures a reasonable probability of external costs staying below an acceptable level.

13.3 The Value of Biodiversity

13.3.1 Different sources of value

The total value of all biodiversity is the sum of all human welfare for current and all future generations. Without any biodiversity, then humanity would probably cease to exist. However, this self-evident truth does not help us with more relevant questions about the value of marginal changes in biodiversity, which species should be protected and which neglected. Commercial activities which may push species to extinction such as agricultural expansion and intensification, deforestation and urbanization have costs and benefits which, at least in part, are measured by market prices. Valuing a loss of biodiversity is more difficult because markets for its preservation are either missing or incomplete. The interesting economic questions concern the marginal value of biodiversity itself and the benefits of preserving a particular marginal species or community. As noted earlier, the benefits of preservation derive from three sources: first, direct values due to medicine and agriculture; second, ecosystem services such as recycling nitrogen, filtering sediment, and decomposing waste, and third, aesthetic use and non-use values. We consider each of these sources of value in more detail.

13.3.2 Direct values

Currently we use approximately 40,000 species of plants, animals, fungi and microbes (Elridge, 1998). Organisms have a vast range of uses some of which are often taken for granted. For instance the bacteria *actinobacteria* is used to produce a common form of antibiotics. From the fungi we obtain the common mushroom and *Genea hispidula* provides the structure in legumes for nitrogen fixation. Useful insects include silkworms and ladybirds that predate upon aphids. Useful animals include sheep for food and fibre and buffalo who provide meat, milk, draft power, transportation, leather, and fertilizer. The higher plants provide crop plants, timber, insecticides, and fodder, and are also an important source of traditional and modern medicines. In this century these compounds have provided the basis of many common drugs including aspirin which comes from willow bark, and taxol, an ovarian cancer treatment, derived from the pacific yew.

Over time we have become adept at finding and developing species which are useful to us, and this continues as we search for new crops, and new genetic material for existing crops and new medicines. Biotechnology has made it possible to take traits such as disease resistance from close relatives to crop plants, and incorporate these traits into commercial varieties. For these genes to be discovered they must already exist in wild or cultivated species. By destroying a habitat we may inadvertently destroy a close relative to a crop species which contains valuable genetic material. An example is *Zea diploperennis*, a rare relative of commercial maize (*Zea mays*) which was unknown and on the verge of extinction in its last remaining habitat in the Sierra de Monantlán in Mexico. This plant shows resistance to many of the diseases which afflict the commercial crop, and therefore may provide genetic material for new maize varieties in the future.

As diversity amongst wild relatives of crop plants is lost we are in danger of depending upon an increasingly small number of supercrops. But in the future these crops are at risk from disease and pest species which can evolve resistance to pesticides. Without genetic diversity from older crop varieties and wild relatives the plant breeder is restricted to the gene pool available in known varieties.

13.3.3 Bio-prospecting for drugs

The genetic codes of organisms contain the instructions to synthesize biologically active chemicals. Some of these chemicals can be exploited as the blueprint for drugs that are then produced synthetically. Often the naturally occurring substance gives the medicinal chemist a 'lead' to the likely form of promising molecules, but these need to be modified before they can be used as medicines. Preserving biodiversity maintains the number of species available to use in this way. See Box 13.3 for an example where biodiversity is exploited commercially. However, there is also substitutability between organisms in an ecosystem. First, organisms may occur across a wide ecological range. Second, different plants may produce chemicals that have similar medicinal properties.

The value of a new drug is measured by its contribution to improving the treatment of disease. For instance a new cancer drug may increase remission rates, reduce the costs of treatment, and improve our quality of life. Its value is measured by how much better the new drug is than its closest substitute in the treatment of a particular disease.

Consider the following simple analysis of the value of species (Simpson *et al.*, 1996). The value of a new product is given by the return R from the new drug and the costs of analysing a specimen c. The probability of finding a new drug is given by p. Therefore the expected value of analysing a single plant specimen, $v(1)$, is the expected revenue less the costs, that is:

$$v(1) = pR - c.$$

For instance if R = $10 million, c = $0.5 million, and p = 0.1, so that is a 10 per cent chance of finding a substance which will form the basis of a new drug, the expected value of the specimen is $(0.1)10-0.5$ = $0.5 million If there is more than one candidate

Box 13.3 INBio: Bioprospecting in Costa Rica

The Instiuto Nacional de Biodiversidad (INBio) in Costa Rica (Aylward *et al.*, 1993), by collecting and cataloguing the endemic plant species of Costa Rica's rainforests, hopes to be able to market genetic information as a means of financing conservation. In addition to government support, INBio has commercial contracts with Merck & Co. and the British Technology Group for the exclusive rights over tested samples.

This type of contract is unlikely to provide significant funds for conservation until the host countries derive more benefits from the discovery of such material Swanson (1994). Despite its financial backing and worldwide publicity since 1991 INBio has generated a surplus of US$2.5 million from bioprospecting. This does not suggest that the total value of the institute's work in helping conserve the biodiversity of Costa Rica is equal to this amount. However, it does show some of the difficulties of converting unique genetic material into substantial profits through commercial contracts.

organism to produce a similar drug, then we identify a search procedure in which searching stops when a discovery is made. Therefore with two organisms the expected value is given by

$$v(2) = pR - c + (1-p)(pR - c),$$

where the second term gives the expected value of the second organism and the term $(1 - p)$ is the probability of no compound being found in the first organism. For instance, if $p = 0.1$, then the probability of the second organism needing to be analysed is 0.9 or 90 per cent. The value of having this extra species to analyse is simply the expected value of the second species $(1 - p)(pR - c)$.

The formula can be generalized to give the expected value of any number (n) of species as:

$$v(n) = pR - c + (1 - p)(pR - c) + (1 - p)^2 (pR - c) + \ldots + (1 - p)^{n-1} (pR - c).$$

The value of the 'marginal' species is

$$(1 - p)^n (pR - c),$$

that is the expected value of having one more species to test for the medicinal product. The expected value of the marginal species is inversely related to the probability of success and the number of species. For instance, if there are 1,000 species and a 10 per cent ($p = 0.1$) success rate, $(1 - p)^n = 1.747 \times 10^{-46}$ (a very small number). If the success rate is only one-tenth of 1 per cent ($p = 0.001$), then $(1 - p)^n = 0.3677$, at the same time the $(pR - c)$ term declines, but not as quickly as $(1 - p)^n$ increases. If the number of species is reduced from 1,000 to 100 and assuming a one-tenth of 1 per cent success rate, then $(1 - p)^n = 0.904$. In ecosystems there are often large numbers of species, and as the number of candidate species increases, then the value of the marginal species falls close to zero. This implies that the 'bioprospecting' values for the marginal species in a rainforest, say, may be quite low (see Box 13.4 for an example).

13.3.4 Ecosystem service values

Ecosystems provide us with numerous direct and indirect services, including waste assimilation, water purification, and nutrient cycling. Complex ecosystems provide these services but we are often unable to assess the value of a particular species within an ecosystem. It is helpful to think of organisms being divided into different roles within the ecosystem. These include primary producers (higher plants), primary consumers (herbivores), secondary consumers (predators), and tertiary consumers (scavengers). Completing the cycle are the decomposers that feed on dead and decaying material. These groups transfer material, energy, and nutrients through the ecosystem. The ecosystem can be seen as an energy cycle that assimilates solar energy through photosynthesis. Energy then passes inefficiently to successive levels of consumers, first the plant eaters, then different levels of predators. In turn the plants and the consumers provide food for the decomposers who are able to reduce organic

Box 13.4 Biological Prospecting—an Example

The higher plants have, historically, produced the largest number of new drugs. So how do we value one plant species in terms of its potential medicinal value. Simpson *et al.* (1996) suggest the following approach and parameters.

There are 250,000 (n) species of plants known to science (Wilson, 1992). On average between 1981 and 1993, 23.8 new drugs per annum were approved by the US Food and Drug Administration. This is an approximate measure of world discovery rates as drugs first sold in other countries need to gain approval before being sold in the USA. Of these new drugs approximately one-third are derived from higher plants (Chichilnisky, 1993), thus about eight new drugs (λ) are discovered from higher plants each year. The cost of discovering a new product is around $300 million. The expected revenue (R) is $450 million, which assumes that the drug companies make a 50 per cent return on research costs. The cost of evaluating a single sample (c) is $3,600. Using the formula for the value, v, of an individual species

$$v = \frac{\lambda}{r}(pR - c)(1-p)^n,$$

where r is the discount rate which is set at 10% (0.1). This gives an estimate of preserving an individual plant species on the basis of its medicinal value of $7,109.

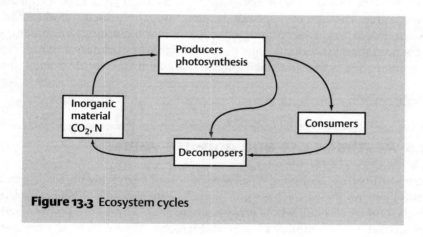

Figure 13.3 Ecosystem cycles

matter to simpler inorganic components (see Putman and Wratten (1984) or any standard ecological textbook for a more detailed account).

The number of species in an ecosystem occupying these roles varies. Diverse ecosystems may have a large number of species in a particular role and may be able to lose a number of species and still function. Damage to one part of the ecosystem may be compensated for by adjustment in another part. One way of thinking about an ecosystem is as flows of energy through a web of interacting species. If one of these energy pathways in the web becomes blocked, for instance by a species becoming extinct, then it may not affect the whole system so long as other pathways remain open. Hopkin (quoted in Putman and Ruttan, 1984: 350) uses the analogy of the blood circulation system. If a capillary is blocked or damaged, the body adapts by developing more capillaries or using existing capillaries. If main veins or arteries become blocked, then the body is damaged and finds it impossible to adapt. Thus diversity leads to resilience and resilience is important if the system is to continue functioning when subjected to a shock such as loss of land to agriculture or an extreme climatic event. In contrast, impoverished ecosystems tend to be more fragile and less resilient to the loss of key species.

Consider some examples of ecosystem services and how they might be affected by species loss. Trees in a rainforest act like a sponge and moderate the local water cycle by retaining water in the soil and transpiring (evaporating) rainfall. In this way they reduce the frequency and intensity of floods. The loss of forest tree species would significantly reduce this ecosystem service, whereas the local loss of a species of monkey would not directly affect this service. Coral reefs provide protection to coastal areas and protect delicate coastal wetlands and mangrove swamps from storms. The loss of a significant part of the coral reef by pollution, sedimentation, or a sea-level rise would result in a significant loss of ecosystem services, whereas the local loss of a species of shellfish would not directly.

The general point here is that the fewer close substitutes a species has in terms of its ecosystem functions, the more damaging is its loss. For instance, mangrove trees are critical to the functioning of mangrove swamps as they stabilize sediments and filter the water. The loss of a species of mangrove, the primary producer in that ecosystem, would have a devastating effect on the local marine environment, since there are no close substitutes for this species in its role as a primary producer capable of surviving in salt water and stabilizing the sediment in coastal swamps (see Box 13.5).

13.3.5 Aesthetic use and non-use values

We derive utility from observing species in the wild or even knowing that a particular species is being protected. People value individual species such as bald eagles, tigers, elephants, and whales and whole ecosystems such as rainforests, prairies, and heather moorland. For a summary of values which have been estimated for individual species, see Bulte and van Kooten (1999). These values tend to favour the more 'charismatic' species and ecosystems. Thus large mammals, birds, and brightly coloured flowering plants, tend to be valued more highly than species of fungi, amphibians, and grass species even though these species may be essential to the functioning of an ecosystem.

What is likely is that we obtain estimates of the amenity value of individual species and/or individual habitats, rather than of biodiversity itself (Hanley, Spash, and Walker, 1995). These values may be either use or non-use values (see Chapter 3). However, given the usual approaches taken to estimating these values including

Box 13.5 Mangrove Fisheries Linkages in the Campeche of Mexico

The high productivity of the Gulf of Mexico fishery is partially attributed to the extensive areas of coastal lagoons and estuaries which are dominated by the mangroves. Mangroves provide ideal breeding grounds for commercially exploited shrimps and finfish. Mangrove in this region of Mexico is under threat from mariculture and urban encroachment. In their study of the Campeche fishery Barbier and Strand (1998) estimate that the Campeche fishery loses, on average 0.19 per cent of its annual revenue for each km². of mangrove deforestation. This estimate is based upon a simulation model which assumes that the loss of mangrove swamp reduces the carrying capacity of the shrimp fishery and that the fishery is open access.

   An interesting conclusion of their study is that the cost of mangrove deforestation and indeed the fishery as a whole would be greatly increased if the fishery was converted from open access to a regulated fishery. The problem is an example of two missing markets: there is no market for the ecosystem services provided by mangrove forests and no market for the shrimp stocks. The lack of a market for shrimp stocks, due to open access, leads to a reduced value of the mangrove swamp.

travel costs and contingent valuation, it is highly unlikely that values will account for the complex web of interdependencies between species since these are too complex for most people to appreciate during the course of a brief contingent valuation interview (Spash and Hanley, 1995).

13.4 The Policy Response

DECLINING levels of biodiversity has led to policy responses at three levels, international, national, and local. International agreements on biodiversity often provide a guiding framework for national and local policies. In the future international policies may become more important in providing funds for conservation in developing countries where biodiversity is concentrated. We now consider different types of policies in turn.

13.4.1 International policy

Convention on biological development. In Rio de Janeiro on 5 June 1992 the Convention on Biological Diversity (CBD) came into being at the United Nations Conference on Environment and Development (UNCED). The convention was signed by 154 countries and recognizes the need to preserve biodiversity not only in terms of reducing the rate of species extinction, but also in terms of preserving ecosystems and genetic variability. The broad objectives of the convention are the conservation of biological diversity, the sustainable use of its components, and the fair and equitable sharing of benefits from the use of genetic resources.

The objectives of the convention are far-reaching, but what tangible benefits have there been? There is a danger that a convention with such sweeping objectives, backed up by limited funding will be ineffective. There is a need to translate international policy into national and local policies which provide additional biodiversity protection.

The CBD includes the General Environmental Facility which provides funding from developed countries for projects in developing countries which protect biodiversity. The economic rationale for transferring funds to developing countries to preserve biodiversity is that biodiversity is a global public good and should be paid for by all countries not only those countries which 'host' the biodiversity. The principle behind this fund is that it pays for the incremental costs of projects which provide additional global benefits. Between June 1992 and November 1998 the GEF has provided a total of US$1.74bn for biodiversity projects (COP4 Report). The replenishment of the fund was expected to be in the region of US$2.75bn. However, this sum is small relative to the size of the problem and the potential value of biodiversity. In a recent paper Costanza *et al.* (1998) put the global annual value of ecosystem services at US$33 trillion (1994 prices) and an annual global GNP of US$18 trillion. Even given that these figures are highly inaccurate the funds available relative to the scale of the problem and the value of global biodiversity are small and will not be sufficient to compensate the developing countries for the likely costs they face in conserving biodiversity. Box 13.7 gives an example of how this funding has been used in Pakistan.

International Convention on Trade in Endangered Species (CITES). The International Convention on Trade in Endangered Species (CITES) is the most important international agreement relating to the protection of biodiversity. The convention was signed in March 1972 and came into force three years later. It aims to protect endangered species by restricting trade in those species, effectively reducing or withdrawing demand for a species through trade. The mechanism is that endangered species are listed in Appendix I and potentially threatened species are listed in Appendix II. These lists are revised at biennial meetings. An Appendix I species

Box 13.6 Valuing Biodiversity

McFadden (1994) in his study of the Selway Bitterroot wilderness area in Idaho gives respondents the choice to pay for the preservation of the wilderness area from timber harvesting. No information is given as to the ecological impacts of timber harvesting, thus the respondents value the good on the basis of their own familiarity with the region, occasional use value, and limited information on the impacts that timer removal would have on the long-term resilience of the ecosystem. In this case most respondents would base their valuation on their own partial understanding of the probable damage to the ecosystem.

Box 13.7 Community Development in Pakistan

The project described for Pakistan is an example of how the GEF funds under Convention for Biological Diversity have been employed. It also illustrates how global, national, and local policies interact to determine the success or otherwise of conservation projects. Economic incentives at the local level are critical (UNEP, 1998).

Pakistan is biologically diverse. The country hosts 5,700 species of plants, of which 372 are endemic, and 188 species of mammals representing ten orders, against a global total of 4,100 species and eighteen orders. The total number of bird species in the world is 8,600 and 666 of these are found in Pakistan. The number of reptiles, mostly snakes and lizards, is 176, against a total of 6,500 for the world. A total of 525 species of amphibians and fish found in rivers, lakes, and sea are indigenous to Pakistan (400 marine and 125 freshwater), while the number of insect and invertebrate species is about 20,000.

Seventy-two per cent of Pakistan's population live in rural areas, and increasing population and rural poverty have placed great pressure upon forest and land resources. In recognition of these problems and in line with Pakistan's commitment to Convention on Biological Diversity, especially Article 8 (*in situ* conservation) the Pakistan government initiated in 1995 a wide-ranging conservation project which was partially administered by the IUCN (International Union for the Conservation of Nature and Natural Resources) in Pakistan. The project was partially funded by GEF, but also received co-funding from the Pakistan government.

The project aimed to provide incentives for the protection and sustainable use of biological resources by the rural communities themselves. One example of an incentive scheme is trophy hunting. A quota of five ibex trophies was set for the areas where biological diversity conservation initiatives have been taken by the community. A fee of US$3,000 for foreigners and PRs. 20,000 for Pakistani hunters has been fixed, from which 75 per cent will go to the communities and 25 per cent to the government. Further a quota of six markhor trophies has also been approved by CITES for Pakistan.

In addition, plant species traditionally used as medicines will be screened to assess if they have international economic value. Rights to use those resources are retained in Pakistan.

The provision of technical assistance to the local communities to enhance their income from their own resources helps to secure their cooperation in conservation. It is recognized that different incentive measures designed for the communities living in and around biological resources areas should be specific to the cultural and socio-economic conditions of Pakistan.

It is not appropriate to impose a total ban on trophy hunting or the trapping of wildlife for sport and trade. A healthy population of wildlife produces a harvestable surplus. Furthermore, the number of animals taken legally are a small fraction of those taken illegally and the presence of legal hunting can deter illegal hunting. Accordingly, the sustainable utilization of wildlife may be allowed by regularizing trophy hunting. In this way, considerable funds can be generated.

requires a permit from the exporting country to ensure that trade will not be detrimental to the species survival and a permit from the importing country to guarantee that the species will not be used for commercial purposes. This is effectively a ban on commercial trade. An Appendix II listing is less restrictive: it only requires a permit from the exporting country. The CITES Secretariat is also an important source of information on the state of endangered species as it receives annual reports from member States on the level of trade in listed species. The listing is an official declaration that a species is endangered and this may be beneficial in reducing demand or, in the case of an Appendix II listing, may actually increase speculative demand.

Restrictions on trade provide, at best, a suboptimal approach to wildlife conservation. By reducing demand, they provide no incentive for landowners or governments to devote resources to protecting habitats for the species. For instance, banning trade in ivory gives no incentive to rural populations to protect elephant habitat. However, in some instances an Appendix II listing may be more effective in terms of conservation than an Appendix I listing, as there is some incentive in regulated trade to actually protect the habitat (Bulte and van Kooten, 1999).

Some of these unanticipated perverse incentive effects have started to be addressed by delegates from developing countries. The 1981 New Delhi meeting 'downlisted' some species from Appendix I to Appendix II for the purposes of managed exploitation. For instance the Zimbabwean population of Nile crocodile was downlisted so that its commercial utilization could be expanded to provide funds for habitat protection. In 1983 this approach was extended to include trade quotas, for instance, the African leopard was allocated a quota. This approach was further extended in 1985 when downlisting was allowed on a range of species so long as a quota on trade was accepted. See Box 13.8, for a discussion of the effectiveness of the ban on ivory trade.

Swanson (1994) assesses what form CITES should take to represent a 'constructive wildlife control mechanism'. He identifies two key attributes: demand-side policies, which work to increase the individual value of species; and supply-side policies to ensure that the species traded are taken as part of a sustainable management plan. These two policy approaches would provide the incentives through trade for long-term habitat management for endangered species. The current policy fails on both demand- and supply-side counts as it provides little incentive for constructive management.

13.4.2 National policies

US Endangered Species Act. In 1973 the Endangered Species Act acknowledged that the 'ecological, educational, historical, recreational and scientific value' of species diversity was inadequately accounted for in the process of 'economic growth and development'. The stated purpose of the Endangered Species Act is 'to provide a means whereby the ecosystems upon which endangered and threatened species depend may be conserved'. The Act is administered by the Fish and Wildlife Service and the National Marine Fisheries Service. Administration involves: first, listing a species as

Box 13.8 Saving Elephants

In December 1989 CITES placed the African elephant on the Appendix I list of endangered species. This decision made trade in ivory with the main consuming nations, USA, Japan, and the EU illegal. This decision was prompted by a 50 per cent decline in the elephant population between 1979 and 1989 down to 609,000. The decline was due to illegal hunting for ivory and a loss of elephant habitat to agriculture.

Has the ban succeeded in increasing the probability of long-term elephant survivial? The population estimates give a mixed picture. The Zimbabwe population has increased and this led in 1997 to a downlisting by the parties of CITES to Appendix II. This allows trade with Japan subject to quotas. The situation in the other countries apart from Kenya is one of further population decline.

How can this be the case when the trade in ivory is banned? The answer is that as with any criminal activity, the level of poaching effort depends upon the potential cost and benefits. So long as an illegal world market remains in ivory and some countries are relatively lax in enforcing anti-smuggling and anti-poaching legislation, then an incentive will remain for elephant hunting.

Consider the following simple model. The profit from poaching is given by:

$$\pi = p\,q - costs - prob \times fine,$$

that is the profit from a poaching trip is equal to the revenue from ivory sales where p is the price of ivory and q is the quantity of ivory. The costs are the costs of labour and transport on a poaching trip, $prob$ is the probability of getting caught and $fine$ is the fine charged for poaching when the poachers are caught (Burton, 1999).

To reduce the incentive for poaching to zero then the profit must be zero. How can this be achieved? First, by reducing the effective ivory price by making smuggling more expensive, second, by increasing the resources devoted to catching poachers which increases the probabiliy of being caught $prob$. Finally, increasing the size of the fines charged when a poacher is caught.

If a country is not committed to either catching poachers or imposing large fines or custodial sentences upon them when caught, then it is likely that poaching will remain profitable. One role of international agencies might be to provide resources to catch poachers. However, a more constructive approach is to provide local people with benefits for protecting elephants and elephant habitats. If this system works, then perhaps local people will sort out the poachers themselves!

endangered or threatened—endangered being at greatest risk; second, designating habitats critical to a species' survival; third, banning activities which threaten the species; fourth, developing and implementing a recovery plan, and fifth, removing a species from the list when its population has recovered sufficiently for it not to be in danger of extinction.

The stated intention of the Act is to save *all* species. Nothing in the original wording of the statute requires that benefits or costs of species extinction should be taken into account. Although the Act treats all species as equal, budgetary restrictions force the regulatory authorities to identify priorities and thereby run the risk of some species becoming extinct. Of the 1,104 species in the USA listed as threatened and endangered by July 1997 just over 40 per cent have approved recovery plans. The existence of a recovery plans does not guarantee that funds will be available to implement its recommendations. Evidence from Carroll *et al.* (1996) and Tear *et al.* (1993) suggests that survival prospects for just less that 60 per cent of listed species are actually deteriorating. Further, some approved recovery plans entail significant risks of extinction.

The status of US wildlife is further complicated by a lack of information on a list of 3,600 'indefinite' species that may be threatened or endangered. The listing process itself is partly the product of the preferences of the specialists in the Office of Endangered Species, and this may account for the high proportion of mammals, birds, and flowering plants listed and a low proportion of spiders and amphibians. This situation was partially rectified by the 1982 Congress amendment which required scientific 'objectivity'. This led to the development of an 18-point scale which included measures of the 'degree of threat', 'recovery potential', 'taxonomy', and 'conflict with development'. Recovery expenditure (Metrick and Weitzman, 1996) is correlated with the level of conflict between a habitat and development and whether or not the species is megafauna, such as bears, wolves, and eagles.

Economic considerations are accounted for implicitly in species listing, since the role for economics only emerges at the stage when a critical habitat is designated. Under a 1978 amendment the Secretary of the Interior may exclude a critical habitat on cost-benefit grounds so long as that exclusion does not lead to extinction.

The power of the Act rests with its powers to restrict the activities of private parties and public agencies. Private parties cannot harass, harm, or wound a listed species, where 'harm' includes damaging the ecosystem. It is backed by fines between $1,000 to $50,000 and jail sentences of between 10 to 1,170 days (GAO, 1995). See Brown and Shogren (1998) for a fuller account of the US Endangered Species Act and its performance.

UK biodiversity policies. The two mainstays of UK biodiversity policy are Sites of Special Scientific Interest which originated with the 1949 National Parks and Access to the Countryside Act and Environmentally Sensitive Areas which were initiated under EU regulation 2078/92. Both these policies contrast markedly with the US Endangered Species act. SSSI, following the amendments introduced by the 1981 Wildlife and Countryside Act, allowed for compensation to be paid to producers in return for forgoing potentially damaging actions. Inevitably this gives producers an incentive to seek plausible damaging actions in order to gain compensation (Spash and Simpson, 1994). Although restrictions are placed on landowners to prevent damage there is a right to negotiated compensation. This differs with the US Endangered Species Act where costs are borne by landowners who have an incentive to destroy a habitat before it becomes listed as critical to a species' survival.

The Environmentally Sensitive Areas scheme introduced in 1987 aims to provide broader habitat protection within designated areas. The scheme is voluntary and farmers can often choose the severity of restrictions they accept. This differs from US Endangered Species Act in two ways: first, it is voluntary, and second, farmers are compensated for forgone profits. The weakness of this policy is that the farmers who are attracted to the scheme tend to be those who can enter at the least cost in terms of profit reduction. Thus the scheme often generates little extra in terms of biodiversity relative to the status quo. However, there is some evidence that the environmental benefits of ESAs are considerably in excess of their costs (Hanley, Whitby, and Simpson, 1999).

Local policies. International and national conservation policies can be well intentioned, but if they have little support from local communities they are unlikely to be effective. This is critical for the success of conservation schemes as the burden of the costs tends to fall upon the rural populations who previously benefited by exploiting the protected resources. In Africa and other developing countries these are often amongst the poorest people. By establishing conservation areas through national parks and the like we are excluding people from the resources which had previously sustained them by providing food or income. There is thus a strong incentive for these people to turn to poaching or to allow their cattle to encroach on protected areas.

Is this outcome inevitable? Drawing on examples from Africa, McNeely (1993) proposes that the solution to the problem of providing biodiversity is to design conservation schemes which:

- provide incentives for local communities to protect resources;
- avoid perverse incentives which actually encourage people to exploit the resources more than they would otherwise;
- and establish disincentives which penalize damaging actions.

Let us consider some examples for conservation schemes in Africa.

Kansunga National Park in Malawi provides an example of positive incentives for conservation, where local people have been given the right to collect tree caterpillars and establish beehives in return for curbing damaging actions. The income from these activities, US$198 per ha. for tree caterpillars and US$230 per ha. for beekeeping, provides cash for agricultural inputs which allowed some farmers to produce more cash crops (Mkanda, 1992). In Zimbabwe, to encourage wildlife conservation on communal lands, private game reserves have been established and hunting revenues paid to the local community. Over a seven-year period this scheme paid out a total of US$4.5m. (Child, 1988). Tourism can also provide a strong incentive for conservation. Kenya's economy earns US$250 million from tourism and the Kenyan Wildlife Service earns US$18 million directly. Some initiatives involve transferring resources from harmful activities into tourism. For instance, fishermen were damaging coral reefs in the Kenyan Marine park. The government advised them to convert fishing boats into glass-bottomed tourist boats. This gave the fishermen an alternative income and an incentive to protect the coral reef (Asava, 1992).

Unfortunately, examples of *perverse incentives* are also common. Often these represent government failure where natural resource or agricultural policies give an incentive to degrade the environment. For instance, in Botswana, prices for export beef supported by the EU combined with subsidized inputs including fencing, veterinary services, and, borehole development have led to widescale overgrazing which benefits a small number of ranchers (Perrings *et al.*, 1988).

Incentives need to be reinforced by *disincentives* that discourage damaging actions. However sympathetic a conservation scheme is to the economic well-being of the local community, there is almost always an incentive for people to misappropriate open-access or common property resources, to catch more fish than is their right, to poach, or allow their cattle to overgraze. Hannah (1992) found that the stronger were the enforcement procedures in place, then the more effective were conservation projects in relation to their objectives. Enforcement may be in terms of conventional monitoring backed up by legal action. Misappropriation of resources may also be reduced by community opprobrium. If a community has a sense of shared ownership over a resource, then they are more likely to protect it themselves.

13.4 Summary

THE earth is currently undergoing a phase of mass species extinction. Unlike previous mass extinctions this current episode is due to the disruptive activities of just one species, man. Mankind, by appropriating rich and diverse habitats for agricultural production and other disruptive forms of land use, influences which species survive, which thrive, and which are extinguished. In taking these decisions we are determining which species survive to provide future generations with new drugs, crops, genetic material, aesthetic values, and ecosystem services. These decisions are often taken without any sense of their gravity; instead mankind often blunders on in profound ignorance of what species are being destroyed in terms of their genetic make-up, their form, their behaviour, and their role in the ecosystem in which they are embedded.

The economics of biodiversity should attempt to value biodiversity in all its complexity including the possibility that a species contains information that is irreversibly lost by extinction. Unfortunately, we are a long way from being able to do this. We can roughly assess the value of biodiversity in terms of its potential medicinal value. We can value some ecosystem services especially where those are associated with market values. However, we have a problem in valuing a species or a group of species in terms of their role within a complex ecosystem. Ecologists acknowledge that they have an imperfect understanding of all but the simplest experimental ecosystems, therefore valuations should account for this uncertainty and complexity. This presents one of the greatest challenges to non-market valuation methods. The other challenge for economists is to design policies which present landowners and land users with an incentive to protect valued species and habitats in an efficient and effective manner.

References

Asara, W. W. (1992). 'Locaur fishing communities and marine national parks and protected areas', Paper presented at IV World Congress on National Parks and Protected Areas, Caracas, Venezuela.

Aylward, B. A., Echeverría, J., Fendt, L., and Barbier, E. B. (1993). *The Economic Value of Species Information and its Role in Biodiversity Conservation: Case Studies of Costa Rica's National Biodiversity Institute of Pharmaceutical Prospecting.* Report to the Swedish International Development Authority (London: Environmental Economics Centre).

Barbier, E. B., Burgess, J. C., and Folke, C. (1994). 'Paradise Lost?', *The Ecological Economics of Biodiversity* (London: Earthscan).

—— and Strand, I. (1998). 'Valuing mangrove-fishery linkages—a case study of Campeche, Mexico', *Environmental and Resource Economics* 12(2): 151–66.

Bromley, D. W. (1995). 'Choice without prices without apologies', in D. W. Bromley (ed.) *The Handbook of Environmental Economics* (London: Blackwell).

Brown, G. M., and Shogren, J. F. (1998). 'Economics of the Endangered Species Act', *Journal of Economic Perspectives* 12: 3–20.

Burton, M. (1999). 'An assessment of alternative methods of estimating the effect of the ivory trade ban on poaching effort', *Ecological Economics* 30: 93–106.

Butte, E., and van Kooten, C. (1999). 'Marginal valuation of charismatic species', *Environmental and Resource Economics* 14: 119–130.

Carroll, R., Augspurger, C., Dobson, A., Franklin, J., Orians, G., Reid, W., Tracy, R., Willcove, D., and Wilson, J. (1996). 'Strengthening the use of science in achieving the goals of the Endangered Species Act: an assessment by the Ecological Society of America', *Ecological Applications* 6: 1–11.

Chichilnisky, G. (1993). 'Property rights and biodiversity and the pharmuceutical industry', Working Paper (New York: Columbia University Graduate Business School).

Colwell, R. R. (1996). 'Microbial biodiversity and biotechnology', in M. J. Readka-Kudla *et al.* (eds.) *Biodiversity II* (Washington: James Henry Press).

Costanza, R. *et al.* (1997). The value of the world's ecosystem services and natural capital, *Ecological Economics* 25:(1): 3–15. (Reprinted from *Nature*, 387: 253).

Elridge, N. (1998). *Life in the Balance: Humanity and the Biodiversity Crisis* (Princeton: Princeton University Press).

Erwin, T. L. (1983). 'Tropical forest canopies, the last biotic frontier', *Bulletin of the Entomological Society of America* 29: 14–19.

Farmer, M. C., and Randall, A. (1998). 'The rationality of a safe minimum standard', *Land Economics* 74: 287–302.

GAO (1995). *Endangered Species Act: Information on Species Protection on Non-federal Lands RCED 95–16* (Washington, DC: US General Accounting Office).

Garrod, G. D., and Willis, K. G. (1997). 'The non-use benefits of enhancing forest biodiversity: a contingent ranking study', *Ecological Economics* 21: 45–61.

Hanley, N., Spash, C., and Walker, L. (1995). 'Problems in valuing the benefits of biodiversity protection', *Environmental and Natural Resource Economics* 5:(3): 249–72.

——— Whitby, M., and Simpson, I. (1999). 'Assessing the success of agri-environmental policy in the UK', *Land Use Policy*, 16(2). 67–80.

Hannah, L. (1992). *African People, African Parks* (Washington, DC: Conservation International).

Kahneman, D., and Knetsch, J. L. (1992). 'Valuing public goods: the purchase of moral satisfaction', *Journal of Environmental Economics and Management* 22: 57–70.

McFadden, D. (1994). 'Contingent valuation and social choice', *American Journal of Agricultural Economics* 76: 689–708.

Mcneely, J. A. (1993). 'Economic incentives for conserving biodiversity—lessons for Africa', AMBIO 22 (2–3): 144–150.

May, R. M. (1972). 'Will a large complex system be stable', *Nature* 238: 413–14.

——— Lawton, J. H., and Stork, N. E. (1995). 'Assessing extinction rates', in J. H. Lawton and R. M. May (eds.) *Extinction Rates* (Oxford: Oxford University Press).

Metrick, A., and Weitzman, M. L. (1998). 'Conflicts and choices in biodiversity preservation', *Journal of Economic Perspectives* 12: 21–34.

Mkanda, C. X. (1992). 'The potential of Kasanga National Park in Malawi to increase income and food security in neighbouring communities', Paper presented at IV World Congress on National Parks and Protected Areas, Caracas, Venezuela.

Perrings, C., and Pearce, D. (1994). 'Threshold effects and incentives for the conservation of biodiversity', *Environmental and Resource Economics* 4: 13–28.

Putman, R. J., and Wratten. S. D. (1984). *Principles of Ecology* (London: Croom Helm).

Raup, D. (1988). 'Diversity crises in the geological past', in E. O. Wilson (ed.), *Biodiversity* (Washington, DC: National Academy Press).

Shogren, J. F. *et al.* (1999). 'Why economics matters for endangered species protection', *Conservation Biology*, 13(6): 1257–61.

Simpson, R. D., Sedjo, R. A., and Reid, J. W. (1996). 'Valuing biodiversity for use in pharmaceutical research', *Journal of Political Economy*, 104: 163–85.

Spash, C., and Hanley, N. (1995). 'Preferences, information and biodiversity preservation', *Ecological Economics* 12(3): 91–208.

——— and Simpson, I. (1994). 'Utilitarian and rights-based alternatives for protecting sites of special scientific interest', *Journal of Agricultural Economics*, 45(1): 15–26

Stork, N. E. (1996). 'Measuring global biodiversity and its decline' in M. J. Readka-Kudla *et al.* (eds.), *Biodiversity II* (Washington: James Henry Press).

Swanson, T. M. (1994). *The International Regulation of Extinction* (Macmillan: Basingstoke).

Tear, T., Scott, J., Hayward, P., and Griffith, B. (1993). 'Status and prospects for success of the Endangered Species Act: a look at recovery plans', *Science*, 262: 976–7.

United Nation Environment Programme (UNEP) (1993). *Guidelines for Country Studies on Biological Diversity* (Nairobi: UNEP).

—— (1998). Conference of the Parties to the Convention on Biological Diversity, Fourth Meeting, Bratislava.

US General Accounting Office (GAO) (1995). *Endangered Species Act: Information on Species Protection on Nonfederal Lands* (Washington, DC: GAO/RCED-95016).

Weitzman, M. L. (1992). 'On diversity', *Quarterly Journal of Economics* 108: 157–83.

Wilson, E. D. (1988). 'The current state of biological diversity', in E. O. Wilson and F. M. Peter (eds.), *Biodiversity* (Washington, DC: National Academy Press).

Chapter 14
Resources and Energy

ARE we running out of resources? Do oil deposits get depleted too fast as oil countries try to maximize their oil earnings? What will happen to future world energy demand and supply? In this chapter we:

- Discuss what is meant by 'resources'.
- Explain a simple economic model of how resource extraction should be managed.
- Critically appraise different measures of resource scarcity.
- Analyse the special role of energy in the economy.
- Discuss what a nation's energy policy might want to address.

14.1 Natural resource types

WHAT do we mean by 'natural resources'? A distinction is often made between 'material' and 'energy' resources. This distinction relates to the conventional end-uses of these resources, in that material (or mineral)[1] resources are used as part of the physical constituency of commodities (iron ore, converted into steel, in car bodies, or copper in pipes); whilst energy resources are converted into heat and other forms of energy. Thus the chemical energy in natural gas is converted into heat energy when gas is burnt in domestic central-heating boilers. Clearly, some resources are used both as materials and as energy sources; oil is the prime example here, being used for propulsion in internal combustion engines, and to make plastics. Conversion of material resources into usable forms also requires inputs of energy resources (for smelting and mining). There are some eighty-eight minerals occurring on earth. Of these, only twelve make up 99 per cent of the earth's crust: the most common of these are silicon (27 per cent), aluminium (8 per cent), and iron (6 per cent).

One obvious distinction between resource types is in terms of their potential for natural growth. A fishery is different from a deposit of iron ore, in that the former

---

[1] A mineral is defined as a solid crystalline chemical element or compound in fixed composition. Rocks are aggregates of one or more minerals. A mineral deposit is an accumulation of a specific mineral.

exhibits a natural rate of growth, whilst the latter does not. It is thus usual to distinguish between 'renewable' and 'non-renewable' resources, with the former classification reserved for those resources exhibiting a positive natural rate of growth. This is a clearer distinction than the classification into 'exhaustible' and 'non-exhaustible' resources, since even a renewable resource can be exhausted (by continuing to harvest in excess of the natural rate of growth, for example), and a non-renewable resource may not be exhausted if it becomes uneconomic to extract.

14.2 What Determines the Rate of Resource Extraction?

14.2.1 The simple case

Consider now the most important economic model which addresses the question of what determines the rate of resource extraction: the Hotelling model. Imagine an oil market made up of a large number of firms, each owning their own oil wells. All firms want to minimize the *present value* of their profits, where profit is the price of oil times the quantity extracted (remember from Chapter 4 that the present value is the discounted sum of all future values). We assume, for the time being, that oil can be produced at zero cost. The problem the firms face is how much oil to supply in each time-period. The use of a present value of profit implies that delaying oil extraction has an opportunity cost in terms of the return (r) that money tied up in oil reserves could earn from alternative investments (such as money in the bank). So why do these firms not empty their oil wells in the first year and live off their investments?

A similar question led Hotelling (1931) to develop a model of how non-renewable natural resources are extracted through time. The key result is now known as *Hotelling's rule*. The general version of the rule is complex (see Hanley *et al.* (1997: chs. 7 and 9) for a fuller account), but the basic idea can be explained in a simple two-period example. What we seek to define is an equilibrium where the producer is indifferent between selling the last unit of oil in the current period or in the next period. For this to be the case the present value of a barrel of oil would have to be the same in both periods. If the price in period 1 is give as p_1 and the price in period 2 is given by p_2 then this condition is given by:

$$p_1 = p_2/(1 + r) \tag{14.1}$$

where $1/(1+r)$ is the discount factor. What does this condition imply? Suppose the discount rate is 10 per cent ($r = 0.1$), this implies (by rearranging this formula) that:

$$(1 + r)p_1 = p_2$$

the price in period 2 must be 10 per cent greater than the price in period 1. Another way of representing this formula is as

$$\frac{p_2 - p_1}{p_1} = r, \tag{14.2}$$

that is, the proportional price rise for oil equals the discount rate. Hotelling's rule therefore predicts that the oil price will rise through time. The next question is what actually drives the price increase? The answer is market demand combined with all firms reducing their output through time. Collectively firms continue extracting in each period until they expect the above condition (equation 14.2) to be met.

We now have a basic condition to determine the price and the quantity of oil pumped in each period. However, this is not enough to determine the life-cycle of oil reserves since we also need to know the initial stock of oil and the price at which demand falls to zero. The price at which demand falls to zero is known as the 'back-stop price' and it can be interpreted as the price of a substitute for the non-renewable resource. For instance in the case of oil it might be the price at which demand switches to a renewable alternative such as petrol made from alcohol.

Once we know the backstop price and the initial stock, on the basis of Hotelling's rule, we can calculate the price and quantity through time. This can be represented in a four-quadrant diagram (Figure 14.1). The north-west quadrant of Figure 14.1 gives the demand curve, and the north-east quadrant the extraction path. Note that through

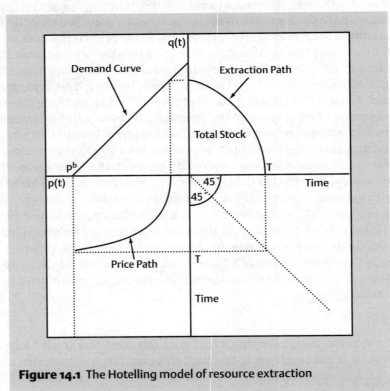

Figure 14.1 The Hotelling model of resource extraction

time the quantity extracted falls and reaches zero at the end time T when the resource is exhausted. The area under the extraction curve is the total initial stock which is the sum of all extraction through time. As the rate of extraction falls then the price, in the south-west quadrant, rises at a rate which satisfies Hotelling's rule until at time T it reaches the backstop price p^b when demand falls to zero. The south-east quadrant contains a 45-degree line which simply transfers time from one axis to the other.

Is this resource extraction plan socially optimal? The discount rate reflects the current generation's preferences for resource use through time. If this is accepted, then so long as the discount rate is the social time preference rate then the resource extraction path is at least efficient. However, if firms face imperfect capital markets and interest rates or returns on other assets are distorted, this may lead firms to extract the non-renewable resource either too rapidly or too slowly. In many countries the interest rate tends to be higher than the social discount rate due to the inclusion of a premium to cover risk. Therefore this implies that firms may be inclined to extract a non-renewable resource too rapidly. This is predicted by Hotelling's rule: high discount rates lead to more rapid equilibrium rises in the price and thus a more rapid decline in the rate of extraction and more rapid exhaustion.

14.2.2 Resource extraction and the monopolist

In contrast to the example in the previous section, the structure of many real-life non-renewable resource industries is typically highly concentrated. For instance, OPEC represents a significant proportion of world oil production, whilst South Africa has a high proportion of the world's gold and diamonds. An interesting question is how a monopoly would decide to extract a non-renewable resource. The answer is that the profit-maximizing zero cost monopoly follows a slightly different version of Hotelling's rule. Instead of equating the present value of price through time, it equates the present value of the marginal revenue,[2] thus:

$$\frac{MR_2 - MR_1}{MR_1} = r. \qquad 14.3$$

In practice the monopoly acts as a price discriminator where the market is separated through time. The implication of this rule is that a monopoly extracts relatively slowly compared with firms in greater competition with each other. In fact we may view the activities of members of OPEC as being 'conservationist' in the sense that by acting as a cartel they reduce the supply of oil and thus extend the life of the resource.

[2] Remember that marginal revenue is the change in total revenue when we increase output by one unit.

Box 14.1 Testing Hotelling's Rule

Hotelling's rule is remarkable as an example of a dynamic model which is able to trace out the life cycle of a non-renewable resource industry from the current time to the time when the last drop of oil that is worth extracting is extracted. As a model it has two possible applications. It can be used *prescriptively* to inform non-renewable firms how they should schedule resource extraction through time or it can be used to predict how firms *actually* behave. In the first of these roles, the model might clearly be useful as a guide to extraction rates so long as the firm is able to predict how the oil price changes through time. However, even a monopoly firm faces a demand curve which changes through time due to changing tastes, technology, and general economic conditions. A number of authors have tested how good Hotelling's rule is at predicting the behaviour of firms (see Hanley *et al.* 1997: ch. 9 for a review), and the overall conclusion is that the standard form of Hotelling's is not very good at explaining how firms actually behave. Why should this be?

Pesaran (1990) outlines what a model of non-renewable resource extraction should take into account. First, the model should represent the fact that the firm aims to maximize profit through time. Decisions include extraction, exploration, and development. Hotelling's rule only accounts for extraction. Second, attention must be given to how firms form price expectations (that is, guesses about future prices). Hotelling's rule says nothing about how firms form price expectations. Third, the model should account for the geology of the non-renewable resource. Geological characteristics determine the form of the cost function, and this may mean costs are a rising function of the remaining reserves and that adjusting production exactly to price expectations may not be possible. The fact that many of these attributes of real resource problems are difficult to measure using existing data explains why the relatively simple versions of Hotelling's rule that have been tested perform badly as predictive models.

14.2.3 Including extraction costs

Hotelling's rule has so far been described for a zero-cost firm, which is clearly unrealistic. The model can be easily modified to include costs. Note that in the zero-cost case, the price can be interpreted as the marginal profit, that is the addition to profits for each extra unit extracted. If we introduce costs, then the marginal profit becomes the price minus the marginal cost, given as $M\pi = p - MC$. Hotelling's rule with costs is then given as:

$$\frac{M\pi_2 - M\pi_1}{M\pi_1} = r,$$ 14.4

that is, instead of the price increasing by the discount rate, the marginal profit must increase by the discount rate. This means that the rate of increase in prices now depends partly on how costs change over time. Costs for non-renewable resource firms are typically given as an increasing function of the rate of extraction (q) and a declining function of the remaining reserves (x) that is, $c = c(x, q)$. This form of cost function explains the geological reality that extraction tends to move to progressively more costly deposits as reserves are depleted: mines move further underground, oil extraction moves to remoter fields in Alaska and the North Atlantic (see Box 14.2). The marginal profit ($M\pi = p - MC$) also gives a measure of resource scarcity, in that it is the value of the marginal unit of the resource stock. We can see that scarcity increases as the price increases, but falls as the marginal cost increases. Measures of scarcity are discussed in the next section.

14.3 Measuring resource scarcity

ONE of the most common questions in debates over the use of natural resources is 'are we running out?' For any non-renewable resource, a positive rate of extraction means that the physical stock of the resource is reduced in size. But (i) there are major problems in defining what this physical stock should represent; (ii) the economic measure of the size of the reserves of this material is not the same as the physical size of the reserves; (iii) the value of the economic reserve will change over

---

Box 14.2 Why is Resource Scarcity so Difficult to Measure?

The value of a unit of resource stock in the ground is the marginal profit that it earns:

$$M\pi = p - MC,$$

thus we can approximately measure resource scarcity by either costs or prices, but neither is ideal, as the discussion in Section 14.3 suggests. Empirical studies tend to arrive at conflicting conclusions: why might this be?

Farzin (1992) explores the impact that new technology has on costs. The cost curve for a renewable resource firm depends on the rate of extraction, q, the remaining reserves x, and the state of cost-reducing technology z. Thus the cost function is $c(q, x, z)$, where costs are increasing in q, decreasing with the size of the stock, and decreasing in z. The reason costs are decreasing with the size of the stock is that as extraction proceeds, the firm shifts to reserves which are more costly to exploit. What happens to costs through time? New technology reduces costs, and thus increases the value of the resource stock. This might be characterized as a 'race' between depletion and technological change to keep costs down.

What is the evidence? Lasserre and Ouellette (1991) show that, even with technical change, the decline in the grade of asbestos ore extracted still increased marginal costs.

time; and (iv) there are alternative measures for the *scarcity* of this economic reserve, which may well give different answers to the above question.

Consider Figure 14.2. The two axes show the influence of physical and economic parameters. As the ratio of the price of the resource to its marginal extraction cost falls, then clearly extracting the resource today becomes less attractive. The term 'economic reserves' is often used to describe that portion of a deposit (or collection of deposits) which it is profitable to extract, given current prices and costs. Costs depend partly on the state of technology, and on cumulative extraction: clearly these costs will be changing over time. Prices will also change, in response to the decisions of extractors over extraction rates (which might depend, for example, on the agreement reached by a cartel of producers, such as OPEC), demand for the material, and government intervention on prices.

Thus the dashed horizontal line in Figure 14.2 will move up and down over time, changing the measured level of 'economic reserves' as it does so. For example, the minimum concentration of copper in a copper deposit required for profitable extraction fell from 3 per cent in the 1800s to 0.5 per cent in the mid-1960s with technological progress, which at constant real prices would result in the size of the economic reserve increasing over time.

There is also uncertainty over the actual amount of a resource in a given geographic area. For example, it is not known with certainty how much oil lies under the North Sea. Some oil deposits have been found and are in production, others have been found and are not in production. Other deposits are thought to exist given the nature of the surrounding geology. But the total size of deposits may be greater than this. However, even with respect to defining the physical size of a deposit, or of all deposits for a particular material, difficulties arise. For example, should all amounts of copper be counted, irrespective of their concentration, or of the form in which they are present?

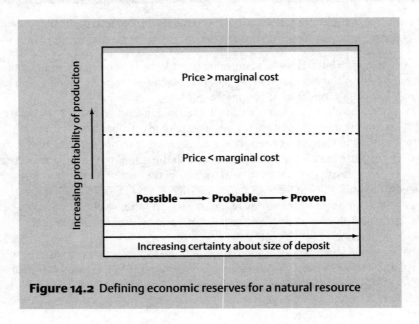

Figure 14.2 Defining economic reserves for a natural resource

Several writers have argued that a crucial concept here is that of the 'mineralogical threshold' (e.g. Harris and Skinner, 1982). Below this threshold, minerals occur as silicates, in that they are chemically bonded to silica. The total amount of a mineral which exists on earth is known as its 'crustal abundance', also referred to as the resource base. However, only a small fraction (roughly 3 per cent on average) of the crustal abundance of most minerals exists in non-silicate form, as oxides, sulphides, or carbonates. For some minerals, very few deposits exist which are in non-silicate form. Skinner (1976) calls these minerals 'geochemically scarce'.

To take the example of lead, its average concentration in the earth's crust is 0.001 per cent, but extraction currently takes place in ore deposits where lead is found in concentrations of between 2 and 20 per cent. Once these ore deposits have been worked out, then vastly more energy would be required to extract lead from its silicate form, where it is trapped by atomic substitution. Their extraction would also produce large quantities of geochemically abundant minerals as a by-product. Geochemically scarce minerals include copper, lead, mercury, and gold (Anderson, 1985). For geochemically abundant minerals, such as iron, the energy required to extract the mineral increases smoothly as the purity of the ore declines, as Figure 14.3 shows; for geologically scarce minerals, energy use jumps at the mineralogical threshold. A prediction from the mineralogical threshold model is that geochemically-abundant minerals will be substituted for geochemically-scarce minerals as the threshold is

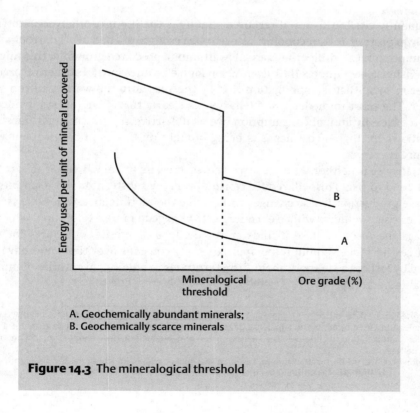

A. Geochemically abundant minerals;
B. Geochemically scarce minerals

Figure 14.3 The mineralogical threshold

Table 14.1 World reserves, reserve bases, and crustal abundances of selected materials

Material	Economic reserves (000 metric tonnes)	Reserve base (000 metric tonnes)	Crustal abundance (million tonnes)
Aluminium	21,800,000	24,500,000	$1,990,000 \times 10^6$
Iron	151,000,000	229,000,000	$1,392,000 \times 10^6$
Coppper	321,000	549,000	$1,510 \times 10^6$
Lead	70,000	120,000	290×10^6
Mercury	130	240	2.1×10^6
Zinc	144,000	295,000	$2,250 \times 10^6$

Source: World Resources Institute (WRI) 1992.

approached. Table 14.1 gives recent estimates of world economic reserves,[3] the reserve base[4] and crustal abundance, for a range of materials. We now review four alternative measures of resource scarcity.

14.3.1 Resource lifetime

A frequently cited measure of resource scarcity is the lifetime of a resource. This is usually expressed as the economic reserve of a resource divided by its current annual consumption rate, with perhaps an allowance for a predicted growth in this rate over time. Fisher (1981) quotes (but does not endorse!) a measure of forty-five years for copper in 1974: that is, a prediction that by the year 2019 the world will run out of copper. The most immediate problem here is clearly that if we instead divided the resource base by annual consumption, we would arrive at a much larger figure, one that allows for higher-cost deposits being brought on line as prices rise; but which measure is correct?

The answer is neither. As a resource gets scarcer, its price will, other things being equal, tend to rise. This will reduce consumption (by substitution, for example), and increase production. These changes will change the lifetime measure. What is more, as prices rise producers will be encouraged to engage in more exploration, which will increase the resource base if finds are made. In fact, lifetime measures for many resources have been found to be approximately constant over time, and have been argued by Fisher to say more about firms' attitudes to holding inventories of minerals than about scarcity.

---

[3] Defined in the data source (WRI, 1992) as 'those deposits whose quantity and grade have been determined by samples and measurements and which can be profitably recovered at the time of the assessment. Changes in geologic information, technology, costs of extraction and production, and prices of mined product can affect the reserve.'

[4] Defined as 'the portion of the mineral resource that meets grade, thickness, quality and depth criteria defined by current mining and production processes. ' It includes measured and indicated reserves, and does not take account of profitability of extraction (WRI, 1992).

14.3.2 Unit cost measures

Some of the earliest arguments in natural resources economics about scarcity centred around the costs of extraction. As a mine is depleted, miners have to travel further and further underground to recover coal, causing labour costs per unit of output to rise. As a country mines its copper, it has to move onto less and less pure grades of ore. Cumulative production thus increases average costs, which are therefore an indicator of scarcity.

In the 1960s, Barnett and Morse (1963) studied trends in average costs over the time-period 1870–1957 for a variety of primary products. With one exception (forestry), they found that an index of real unit (capital plus labour) costs had declined over the period, indicating decreasing scarcity: real capital-plus-labour inputs declined by 78 per cent for the minerals sector and 55 per cent for the total extractive sector. Barnett and Morse's work was repeated by Johnson, Bell, and Bennett (1980), who found that if anything the rate of decline in unit costs had increased over the period 1958–70.

Are these results proof that these materials were becoming less scarce over this time-period? Unfortunately, this unit cost measure has problems. First, technological progress has undoubtedly reduced unit costs over this time period (see Norgaard, 1975 for empirical evidence from the oil sector). This will also have the effect of increasing the size of economic reserves. Second, the unit cost hypothesis relies on the assumption that firms will always deplete the lowest-cost deposit first; yet to know which deposit is the lowest cost implies a perfect knowledge of the characteristics of all deposits, some of which are yet to be discovered! Norgaard (1990) has termed this the 'Mayflower problem':

[I]f the pilgrims knew where the best places for an agricultural colony were, they would not have gone to Plymouth Rock . . . Many generations passed before American agriculture shifted from the relatively poor soils of the east coast to the more productive mid-west.

Third, while unit capital and labour costs may have been falling, this might be due to substitution of some other input for capital and labour. The obvious missing input here is energy. Hall *et al.* (1986) recomputed Barnett and Morse's figures for the coal and petroleum sectors, including energy use with capital and labour use: they found that whilst the Barnett and Morse data showed a 35 per cent decline in unit costs for the petroleum sector, including energy use changed this to a 10 per cent *increase*. Fourth, unit costs are a poor predictor of future scarcity, since they are based entirely on past experience, and are not 'forward-looking': technological advances could increase future economic reserves even if, historically, unit costs have risen.

14.3.3 Real prices

Prices are well established in conventional microeconomics as indicators of scarcity. For natural resources, a rising real price has been argued by many to be a potentially good measure of increasing scarcity (e.g. Fisher, 1980). This will be so when prices signal all future and current opportunity costs of using up a unit of a non-renewable resource today. In simple versions of the Hotelling model the price of a resource rises at the rate of interest along an optimal depletion time path, until it is equal to the price of the 'backstop resource': its closest substitute.

Several empirical studies have looked at real price data. The earliest comprehensive study was by Barnett and Morse (1963), who found that for most primary products, real prices had remained approximately constant from 1870 to 1957. Slade (1982) suggested that the time path of prices might follow a u-shape, as an initial decline in prices due to technological progress was eventually overcome by the tendency for increasing cumulative production to increase costs, and by the desire of resource extractors to see rents rising at the real rate of interest. Slade found that a u-shape fitted the price series of twelve materials better than a linear form, indicating that for aluminium, for example, real prices started to rise in the 1960s. Finally, Anderson and Moazzami (1989) repeated Slade's analysis, using a somewhat different statistical technique. They found strong evidence of increasing scarcity for some materials (such as coal and copper), but only weak evidence of increasing scarcity for others (such as aluminium and iron).

But many criticisms can be levelled at the use of real prices as scarcity measures. First, the influence of producer cartels on prices of primary products can be great, and yet not reflect scarcity changes. For example, the large oil price increases produced by OPEC in 1974 and 1979 were more to do with a voluntary reduction in supply to increase oil revenues than an increase in scarcity. Other commodities (such as tin) have been similarly affected. Second, governments intervene in resource markets, imposing price controls which distort price signals. An example here is actions by the UK government in the 1970s and 1980s to keep gas prices high in order to reduce a loss in sales by the nationalized electricity companies (gas is a substitute for electricity in domestic heating and cooking). Tietenberg (1992) documents distortions caused by the imposition of maximum prices (price ceilings) by the US government for natural gas.

Third, natural resource prices do not measure social opportunity costs, partly because producers are not forced to pay for the environmental damage caused by the extraction and processing of these resources. For example, oil prices could be argued to be too low since not all of the external costs associated with oil-drilling and refining are imposed on producers; whilst a similar statement could be made for aluminium extraction (via bauxite-mining) and processing. Natural resource prices therefore do not measure one element of social opportunity costs, namely the environmental benefits forgone in their production.

14.3.4 Economic rent

Economic rent is defined as the difference between price and marginal cost. One result from the Hotelling model described above is that an efficient depletion path involves resource rents rising at the rate of interest. The intuition behind this is clear: if resource rents represent the rate of return on 'holding' a non-renewable resource deposit, then this should be equal at the margin to the return on holding any other kind of asset, such as a savings bond. Rising rents are thus an indicator of scarcity.

But several problems exist with this measure. First, empirical data are scarce. Economic rents are the difference between price and marginal extraction costs, but are not the same as accounting profits. Neither firms nor governments are in the habit of recording these data. Empirical economists have thus often relied on proxy measures, such as exploration costs. The argument here is that rational firms will spend no more on exploration than the expected net benefits (i.e. the expected future rents) to be thus gained. Devarjan and Fisher (1980) measured average exploration costs for oil in the USA over the period 1946–1971, and found them to be rising, an indicator of increasing scarcity despite the fact that no such trend exists in oil prices over that period. Yet as expected prices are a component of expected rents, the criticisms of the real price measure given in the previous section also apply to the rent measure.

Second, the use of rent as a scarcity measure assumes that firms are following optimal depletion plans (Faber and Proops, 1993). Yet there is very little evidence that this is so in reality (see Box 14.1). What is more, to be able to follow the optimal depletion plan, firms need to be fully informed about future prices and extraction costs: a rather more extreme version of the Mayflower problem (although it is certainly possible to define a best-depletion programme under conditions of uncertainty). Interest rate movements will also affect optimal depletion programmes, such that changes in rent will pick up these macroeconomic effects too.

Rent is perhaps the best scarcity indicator from a theory point of view. After all, it shows that gap between what society is willing to pay for one more unit of the resource and the cost of extracting that unit. But it suffers from empirical drawbacks. It is possible for the rent on a resource to *decrease* even though its physical abundance is falling.

14.4 Global Energy Demand and Supply

W^E care about scarcity and using our natural resources efficiently because they provide the energy that drives our modern economy. Energy plays many roles in our lives.

- *Energy is a consumer good.* The energy derived from renewable and non-renewable resources like petroleum, natural gas, coal, hydro, nuclear, biomass, geothermal, solar, and wind helps grow and cook our food, warm and light our homes, and power our cars.
- *Energy is a factor of production.* Energy, combined with capital, labour, and land, is an essential input in the production of nearly all goods and services around the globe.
- *Energy is a strategic resource.* Energy also has enormous strategic value for a nation, and the threat of its loss has led to war. People and governments follow energy prices with intense interest because it is so vital to our daily lives.

Today the world produces and consumes nearly 400 quadrillion British thermal units (Btu) of power. As a comparative benchmark, energy use in 1970 was about 200 quadrillion Btu. China, Russia, and the USA are the biggest producers and consumers of world energy. Together these three countries account for about 40 per cent of the world's total supply and demand for energy. Five nations currently produce about half of the world's energy— Canada, China, Russia, Saudi Arabia, and the USA. The USA alone produced over 70 quadrillion Btu of energy; Russia and China produced over 40 and 33 quadrillion Btu. And five nations consume nearly half of the world's energy—China, Japan, Germany, Russia, and the USA. The USA consumes nearly 95 quadrillion Btu, three and four times that demanded by China and Russia at 34 and 26 quadrillion Btu. The next big consumers are Brazil, Canada, France, India, and the UK.

As the world economy continues to grow so does the demand and supply of energy. Expanding economies demand more energy. Consider now how energy supply and demand has changed by region over the last two decades, 1980 to 1998. The largest regional increase in energy production occurred in the Far East and Oceania region— production increased by nearly 40 quadrillion Btu, over a 100 per cent increase in two decades (Table 14.2). Their energy consumption also doubled with an increase of 50 quadrillion Btu, again the largest change during this period (Table 14.3). This increase in energy use matches the rapid increase in this region's economies over the last two decades.

In North America, overall energy production and consumption did not grow as fast as in Asia, but it still increased by about 16 and 22 quadrillion Btu. The Middle East increased its production and consumption by 13 and 10 quadrillion Btu. Africa increased production and consumption by 9 and 5 quadrillion Btu. In Central and South America, production and consumption increased by 13 and 8 quadrillion Btu. Western Europe increased supply and demand by about 13 and 11 quadrillion Btu. In

Table 14.2 World primary energy production (quadrillion Btu)

Region	1980	1990	1998
North America	83.25	91.8	99.28
Central and South America	12.09	16.7	24.86
Western Europe	30.65	38.4	43.55
Eastern Europe and former USSR	67.79	81.9	58.32
Middle East	42.26	41.0	54.54
Africa	17.40	21.6	26.24
Far East and Oceania	36.04	59.6	75.41
World total	289.49	351.3	382.18

Source: US Energy Information Agency

Table 14.3 World primary energy consumption (quadrillion Btu)

Region	1980	1990	1998
North America	91.70	100.02	112.57
Central and South America	11.47	14.16	19.73
Western Europe	58.74	63.99	69.52
Eastern Europe and former USSR	61.38	74.11	48.96
Middle East	5.88	11.13	15.90
Africa	6.80	9.34	11.77
Far East and Oceania	49.18	74.09	99.27
World total	285.16	346.83	377.72

Source: US Energy Information Agency

Eastern Europe and the former USSR, both energy production and energy consumption declined by about 12 quadrillion Btu, the only region to witness a decline in energy demand.

Energy is not a homogeneous input. Different primary energy sources will be used based on the relative energy prices. Cheaper energy sources will dominate the mix, and continue to do so until there is a change in relative prices—either through increased scarcity or a change in technology. People made changes in their energy mix and use when the Organization of Petroleum Exporting Countries (OPEC) restricted energy supply causing oil prices to spike in the 1970s. Technological progress and innovation also induce people to switch towards less expensive energy sources over time as old capital is retired and new technologies prove themselves to be effective and reliable.

What is the current mix of primary energy supply around the world? Table 14.4 shows that the non-renewable resources of petroleum, coal, and natural gas are the big three energy sources today. Petroleum remains the most important source, producing nearly 40 per cent (152 quadrillion Btu) of energy today. Saudi Arabia, the USA,

Table 14.4 World production of primary energy (quadrillion Btu), 1990 and 1998

Primary energy	1990	1998
Petroleum	136.35	151.96
Natural gas	75.91	85.49
Coal	92.28	88.61
Hydroelectric power	22.56	26.63
Nuclear electric power	20.37	24.48
Biomass, geothermal, solar, and wind electric power	1.70	2.47
Total energy	351.39	382.18

Source: US Energy Information Administration (EIA)

Table 14.5 World production of primary energy (quadrillion Btu), 1990 and 1998

Primary energy	1990	1998
Petroleum	134.87	149.73
Natural gas	74.78	84.40
Coal	90.41	87.53
Hydroelectric power	22.65	26.84
Nuclear electric power	20.37	24.48
Biomass, geothermal, solar, and wind electric power	1.70	2.47
Total energy	346.83	377.72

Source: US Energy Information Administration (EIA)

and Russia are the three largest suppliers. Coal is second, capturing 23 per cent (89 quadrillion) of production, although it did decline by about 5 per cent from 1990 levels. China and the USA are the leading producers. Natural gas ranks third, supplying about 22 per cent (85 quadrillion Btu), and has increased its share over the last decade. Russia is the leading producer. The remaining energy sources, hydro, nuclear, biomass, geothermal, solar, and wind make up the balance. Together they accounted for a combined total of 54 quadrillion Btu. While currently a small share, these other sources of energy have increased significantly over the last decade.

Understanding how prices drive the mix of energy has implications for the future of global energy use (see Table 14.5). As we showed earlier in the chapter, the most relevant economic model is Hotelling's rule for pricing non-renewable energy resources. So how well has Hotelling's rule explained price movements? Economists have had mixed success in empirically validating the rule. The needed data are difficult to come by, and have forced most studies to use proxies for user rents and expectations of future interest rates. Since user rents are usually confidential and we do not observe expectations in practice, whether the Hotelling rule is a reasonable guide for the future remains an open question.

What does the future of energy demand look like? The US Energy Information Agency's *International Energy Outlook 2000* (IEO2000) predicts that world energy demand will increase by about 60 per cent over the next two decades. The outlook forecasts that worldwide energy use could increase to over 600 quadrillion Btu in 2020 from 380 quadrillion Btu in 1997. While developed nations have long been the dominant users of energy, developing nations are predicted to drive much of the future growth in demand. Energy use in Asia and Central and South America is projected to more than double.

What does the mix of energy sources look like into the future? Oil currently supplies the largest share of world energy consumption, about 70 million barrels per day. The IEO2000 predicts that worldwide oil demand will hit about 110 million barrels per day by 2020, about 38 per cent of total energy consumption. Growth in oil use in the developed nations should come from the transportation sector, since the few alternative sources are expensive. Oil demand in developing countries could come from both transportation and heating demand (see Table 14.6).

Natural gas will remain the fastest-growing component of world energy demand. Gas use is projected to more than double by 2020. The IEO2000 predicts, for instance, that natural gas use in China could grow at a rate of over 11.2 per cent per year. *Coal* will continue at its historical share, about 22 to 24 per cent of energy demand. The main reason why coal will continue to meet the exploding energy demand is that the developing Asian nations like China and India are predicted to account for 97 per cent of the increased world demand for coal. The future of *nuclear power* is less clear. The IEO2000 shows an increase in nuclear power with the expansion of use in developing Asian nations, and then a decline as plants are retired in many developed nations like the USA. *Renewable resource* development will be slow if the expected price of fossil fuels remains relatively low in the near future. Renewables cannot compete with low fossil fuels prices. The IEO2000 projects modest growth in renewable energy,

Table 14.6 Energy consumption (quadrillion Btu) by region, 1990–2020

Region	1990	1997	2010	2020
Developed	183	204	239	260
East Europe/Former USSR	76	53	63	76
Developing				
Asia	51	75	126	173
Middle East	13	18	26	34
Africa	9	11	16	21
Central & South America	14	18	30	45
Total	87	122	198	273
Total world	346	379	500	609

Sources: History (1990, 1997): Energy Information Administration (EIA), International Energy Annual 1997, DOE/EIA-0219(97) (Washington, DC, April 1999). Projections 2010, 2020: EIA, World Energy Projection System (2000).

covering about 8-per cent of total energy demand. Large-scale hydroelectric projects in developing nations are likely to drive any significant world growth in renewables.

14.5 Global Issues in Energy Policy

WE care about the future trends of energy because it plays such a crucial role in the modern world. As such, governments have always been tempted to intervene in energy markets. Policy-makers have long wanted to control energy for national security reasons. Many reasonable arguments exist to justify government intervention on national security grounds, i.e. to reduce the odds of another 'energy crisis', to promote the public good of research and development into new technologies. Now policy-makers have added environmental concerns as a justification to intervene in energy markets. As we have seen throughout this book, private markets often fail to provide the socially desired level of a good or service, and energy markets are no exception.

Global climate change, regional acid rain, and local air pollution problems are all linked to fossil fuel use. Petroleum and coal, no matter how efficiently burned, all produce the carbon dioxide feared to be warming the planet to unacceptable levels;

Box 14.3 Energy Facts

- Global petroleum production increased by nearly 9 million barrels per day over the last decade. The USA consumed about 19 million barrels per day of petroleum—about 26 per cent of world consumption. Japan was second in consumption, with 5.5 million barrels per day.

- The USA was the leading consumer of natural gas, and Russia followed, and together they accounted for 43 per cent of world demand.

- China was also the largest consumer of coal in 1998, using 1.31 billion short tons, followed by the USA, which consumed 1.04 billion short tons, India, Russia, and Germany. These five countries together accounted for 65 per cent of world coal consumption.

- Canada, the USA, Brazil, China, and Russia, were the five largest producers of hydroelectric power. Their combined hydroelectric power generation accounted for 51 per cent of the world total.

- The USA led the world in nuclear electric power generation, France was second, and Japan ranked third.

- The USA led the world in biomass, geothermal, solar, and wind electric-power generation. Japan was second, then Germany, Brazil, and Finland. These five countries accounted for 65 per cent of the world's biomass, geothermal, solar, and wind electric-power generation.

they also produce the sulphur oxides and nitrogen oxides that lead to the acidification of soils and surface water; they also produce smog and particulate matter that affect human health. People have also worried about the health and safety issues from the actual mining of energy sources, e.g. black lung disease, and impacts of strip mining.

The question is should governments intervene in energy markets for environmental protection, and if so, how? Justifiable intervention for environmental protection depends on whether one can reasonably argue that the gains of new rules and regulations outweigh the risks of slowing down the productivity that drives the development of an economy. If the gains dominate the costs, the government has three general ways to intervene in energy markets: change economic incentives by taxing fossil fuels and subsidizing renewable fuels, expand technological options by promoting and subsidizing R&D, and provide information about options that promote energy efficiency.

Changing economic incentives. Relative prices drive the mix of energy demand. Energy prices encourage people to make the least costly adjustments based on their own personal information. Governments that wish to alter this mix can change the relative prices through economic incentives like taxes and subsidies. Energy policy could provide economic incentives in a variety of ways. A typical economic incentive policy is to increase the private cost of fossil fuels, forcing users to address the social costs of emissions. This policy raises the price of emissions, by either taxing emissions based on their potential to cause environmental harm, removing existing subsidies that increase fossil fuel use (e.g. parking subsidies), or by adding new subsidies that promote renewable fuels and lower-emissions fuels or technologies (see Box 14.6). Another policy to change relative prices is to limit emissions or energy use, and let people trade permits to pollute.

Box 14.4 World Estimated Recoverable Coal (million short tons)

Table 14.B4

Region/Country	Recoverable anthracite and bituminous	Recoverable lignite and subbituminous	Total recoverable coal
North America	131,807	153,390	285,197
Central and South America	8,641	15,140	23,781
Western Europe	29,022	70,636	99,658
Eastern Europe and former USSR	124,354	164,032	288,386
Middle East	213	0	213
Africa	67,420	276	67,695
Far East and Oceania	203,321	118,934	322,255
World total	564,777	522,408	1,087,185

Source: US Energy Information Agency

Box 14.5 World Crude Oil and Natural Gas Reserves (January 1999)

Table 14.B5

Region/Country	Crude oil (billion barrels)[a]	Crude oil (billion barrels)[b]	Natural gas (trillion cubic ft.)[a]	Natural gas (trillion cubic ft.)[b]
North America	73.8	55.0	291.4	257.9
Central and South America	89.5	63.4	219.1	226.1
Western Europe	18.9	19.8	161.5	159.8
Eastern Europe and former USSR	58.9	67.9	1,999.4	1,916.2
Middle East	673.6	627.1	1,749.5	1,853.2
Africa	75.4	77.2	361.1	377.9
Far East and Oceania	43.0	57.1	359.6	354.0
World total	1,033.2	967.5	5,141.6	5,145.2

[a] *Oil and Gas Journal*
[b] *World Oil*
Source: US Energy Information Agency

Changing the relative price of fossil fuels would give people an incentive to reduce their energy consumption—they drive less, they turn down the thermostat. People would also have incentives to buy more efficient energy equipment, e.g. more insulation, a car with better gas mileage. Sellers would also adjust if the demand for energy-inefficient goods declined. Everyone now has incentives to develop more energy-efficient technologies, and find low-emission energy sources.

Expanding technological options. Governments can intervene in the energy market by promoting the research and development of new technologies that address the environmental problems associated with fossil fuel use. The private sector generally underinvests in this type of R&D because it cannot capture all the benefits. These public programmes include government-funded programmes and subsidies for private R&D. Options include R&D into fossil fuel technologies with greater conversion efficiencies and non-fossil fuels such as biomass, wind, solar, geothermal, and nuclear energy.

Information programmes. Governments can also try to alter the energy market by providing information to people about different energy-efficient options. Policies that promote the market penetration of new technologies include information and outreach programmes, green programmes (for example, offering electricity supplies from renewable sources at higher tariffs), market identification, and targeting. Governments can form partnerships with industry and others to promote less environmentally damaging fuels. For example, governments can try to overcome the information problems associated with landowners and renters. Both have no incentive to invest in energy efficiency because the landowner does not pay the utility bill, while the renter might not get reimbursed for investments in energy efficiency.

However, as we discussed in Chapter 12, the ability to cause much change through

Box 14.6 Renewable Energy in the UK: Promotion and Impacts

The UK Renewable Energy Advisory Group have defined renewable energy as 'those energy flows that occur naturally and repeatedly in the environment and can be harnessed for human benefit' (REAG, 1992). Europe has a great and largely untapped potential for the generation of power and heat from renewable sources of energy. Renewables currently supply 5.3 per cent of the EC's energy consumption, but only 1 per cent in the UK. In a 1996 green paper the EC suggested a target to increase renewables' share of gross energy consumption to 12 per cent by 2010 (ENDS, 1996). Achievement of this target would reduce the EU's annual carbon dioxide emissions by around 250 million tonnes (ENDS, 1997). Although renewable energy technologies are being continually developed, many are still significantly underutilized due to financial, technical, environmental, and social factors.

Private sector development of renewable energy is promoted in the UK by guaranteeing a certain portion of electricity demand from electricity supply companies for renewable sources, and offering a higher payment to renewable operators per kilowatt supplied, compared to the price of fossil fuel electricity. This difference is funded by a fossil fuel levy on consumer's electricity bills. The two schemes which implement this policy (in England and Wales, the Non-Fossil Fuel Obligation, and in Scotland the Scottish Renewables Orders) have been successful in increasing private sector investment in renewables. In Scotland, this has mainly taken the form of windfarms, biogas plants, and small-scale hydro schemes.

However, whilst the environmental benefits of renewable energy are well known (mainly avoided emissions from fossil fuel power stations), the environmental costs of renewables receive less attention (European Commisson, 1995). In Scotland, these include landscape impacts from windfarms, local disamenities from waste-to-power schemes, and ecosystem impacts from hydro plants. Hanley and Nevin (1999) report some results from a study of these environmental costs for a range of alternative renewable energy investments in the crofting community of Assynt, in the North-West Highlands. This is an interesting case, since the investments would be made on behalf of the local community. However, there is a concern that tourists could be put off by such changes. An energy audit and environmental impact analysis were carried out, which resulted in three main viable options being identified: a small windfarm, a small-head hydro, and a biomass planting scheme. Contingent valuation was used to study impacts on local residents: this revealed community views which differed across the three options. A tourist survey was also undertaken to estimate the differing impacts on tourist spending of each option. Results were then presented as a ranking of options:

Table 14.B6.1 Energy options and potential tourism effects

Renewable energy option	Possible effect on total season's income from tourism if trips were shortened by 1 day	Possible effect on total season's income from tourism if trips were shortened by ½ day	Implied ranking
Wind farm at Raffin	−£2,590	−£1,295	1
Small scale hydro on Loch Poll	−£17,208	−£8,604	2
Biomass development at Culkein/Stoer	−£26,829	−£13,415	3

Table 14.B6.2 Energy options and WTP of residents

Renewable energy option	Percentage in favour of scheme	Proportion of those opposed would accept compensation[a]	Implied community willingness to pay (per annum)[b]	Implied ranking
Wind farm at Raffin	78	3/10	£13,585	2
Biomass schemes at Culkein/Stoer	42	7/26	£6,642	3
Small-scale hydro on Loch Poll	87	0/6	£14,282	1

Notes: [a] sum of those willing to accept personal income compensation and local jobs compensation
[b] based on population of 260 adults living on the Estate.

The relationship between support for renewable energy options and number of years in residence on the Estate was interesting. With respect to both the wind and hydro option there was less support amongst those who had lived on the Estate for ten years or less. In contrast, a low level of support for biomass development was evident among residents who had lived in the area for many years. The taking of land from traditional crofting areas which this option would require may have been a factor in this result.

information is an open question. Optimists stress examples of unexploited opportunities to use cost-reducing technologies and apparent market failures that impede the realization of these opportunities. Others note that more people will respond to changes in energy prices and clearer information on the potential to remove the hidden costs of technology switching not addressed in engineering cost estimates. Economists counter that the choice of energy technology offers no free lunch. Even if new technologies are available, many people are unwilling to experiment with new devices at current prices. Factors other than energy efficiency also matter to consumers, such as quality, and the time and effort required to learn about a new technology and how it works. People behave as if their time horizons are short, perhaps reflecting their uncertainty about future energy prices and the reliability of the technology. Some people will move to less fossil fuel use just because it is, in their opinion, the right thing to do; others will need more convincing or a change in prices.

14.6 Concluding Remarks

Resources and energy drive our economy. In this chapter, we have looked briefly at the main economic model which shows how resource extractors *should* manage their resource deposits, although as Box 14.1 explains, it is almost certainly too simplistic as a view of what drives extraction. We also reviewed different measures of resource scarcity, and saw the problem in using resource lifetimes as a measure of scarcity. We examined the role of energy in the world economy, and likely changes in global supply and demand. Finally, we looked at alternative tools with which governments can implement an energy policy, which tries to reduce the environmental costs of energy use. Economics turns out to be very useful in developing an understanding of the factors which both limit and promote a move to a more environmentally friendly energy future.

References

Anderson, F. (1985). *Natural Resources in Canada* (Toronto: Methuen).

—— and Moazzami, B. (1989). 'Resource scarcity re-examined', Discussion Paper 11–89, Lakehead University, Ontario, Canada.

Barnett, H. J., and Morse, C. (1963). *Scarcity and Growth: The Economics of Natural Resource Scarcity* (Baltimore: Johns Hopkins University Press).

Devarjan, S., and Fisher, A. (1980). 'Exploration and scarcity', Working Papers in Economic Theory IP-290, University of California, Berkeley and Los Angeles.

ENDS (1996). *The Ends Report* 263: 17–18 (Environmental Data Services Ltd).

—— (1997). *The Ends Report* 275: 43–4 (Environmental Data Services Ltd).

European Commission (EC) (1995). *Eastern Externalities of Energy*, vi: *Wind and Hydro*, Report 16525 (Brussels: EC)

Faber, M., and Proops, J. (1993). 'Natural resource rents, economic dynamics and structural change', *Ecological Economics* 8(1): 17–44.

Farzin, Y. H. (1992). 'The time path of scarcity rent is the theory of exhaustible resources', *Economic Journal* 102: 813–31.

Fisher, A.C. (1980). *Resource and Environmental Economics* (Cambridge: Cambridge University Press).

Hall, D., Cleveland, C., and Kaufman, R. (1986). *Energy and Resource Quality: the Ecology of the Economic Process* (New York: John Wiley).

Hanley, N., and Nevin, C. (1999). 'Appraising renewable energy developments in remote communities: the case of the North Assynt Estate, Scotland', *Energy Policy* 27: 527–47.

—— Shogren, J. F., and White, B. (1997). *Environmental Economics: in Theory and Practice* (Basingstoke: Macmillan).

Harris, D., and Skinner, B. (1982). 'The assessment of long-term supplies of minerals', in V. K. Smith and J. Krutilla (eds.), *Explorations in Natural Resource Economics* (Baltimore: Johns Hopkins University Press).

Hotelling, H. (1931). 'The economics of exhaustible resources', *Journal of Political Economy* 39: 137–75.

Johnson, M., Bell, F., and Bennett, J. (1980). 'Natural resource scarcity: empirical evidence and public policy', *Journal of Environmental Economics and Management* 7: 256–71.

Lasserre, P., and Ouelette, P. (1991). 'The measurement of productivity and scarcity rents: the case of asbestos in Canada', *Journal of Econometrics* 48: 287–312.

Norgaard, R. (1975). 'Resource scarcity and new technology in US petroleum development', *Natural Resources Journal* 15: 265–282.

—— (1990). 'Economic indicators of resource scarcity: a critical essay', *Journal of Environmental Economics and Management* 19: 19–25.

Pesaran, M. H. (1990). 'An econometric analysis of the exploration and extraction of oil in the U.K. Continental Shelf', *Economic Journal* 100: 367–90.

Renewable Energy Group (REAG) (1992). *Energy Paper 60* (London: HMSO).

Slade, M. (1982). 'Trends in natural resource commodity prices: an analysis of the time domain', *Journal of Environmental Economics and Management* 9: 122–37.

Skinner, B. (1976). 'A Second Iron Age?' *American Scientist* 64: 258–69.

Tietenberg, T. (1992). *Environmental and Natural Resource Economics* (London: HarperCollins).

United States Energy Information Agency (2000). *International Energy Outlook 2000.* (Washington, DC: US Department of Energy).

World Resources Institute (1992). *World Resources* (Oxford: Oxford University Press).

Zwartendyk, J. (1973). 'Mineral wealth: how should it be expressed?', *Canadian Mining Journal* (April): 44–52.

Additional Reading

■ Dasgupta, P., and Heal, G. (1979). *Economic Theory and Exhaustible Resources* (Cambridge: Cambridge University Press).

■ Hartwick, J. (1990). 'Intergenerational equity and the investing of rents form exhaustible resources', *American Economic Review* 57: 972–4.

■ Kolstad, C. (1994). 'Hotelling rents in Hotelling space: product differentiation in exhaustible resource markets', *Journal of Environmental Economics and Management*, 26: 163–80.

■ Kolstad, C. (2000). 'Energy and Depletable Resources: Economics and Policy, 1973–98, *Journal of Environmental Economics and Management* 39(3): 282–305.

■ Krautkraemer, J. (1998). 'Nonrenewable resource scarcity', *Journal of Economic Literature* 36: 2065–107.

■ Solow, R. (1974). 'Economics of resources or resources of economics', *American Economic Review* 64: 1–14.

■ Velthuijsen, J. W., and Worrell, E. (1999). 'The economics of energy', in *Handbook of Environmental and Resource Economics* (J. van den Bergh, ed.) (Cheltenham: Edgar Elgar): 177–94.

■ Withagen, C. (1999). 'Optimal extraction of non-renewable resources', *Handbook of Environmental and Resource Economics* (J. van den Bergh, ed.). (Cheltenham: Edgar Elgar): 49–57.

Chapter 15
Epilogue

Economics is a discipline of limits. Economics works for the environment by explicitly addressing how people define, confront, and overcome the limits they face now and in the future. And while for simplicity's sake it is more convenient to keep the study of these economic and environmental limits separate, this disconnection is ultimately self-defeating. To see this, we conclude by asking two basic questions.

What happens when the environment gets left out of economics? People know and yet still often take for granted in the modern world that the economy operates within the environment (Chapter 1). The environment provides humanity with a wide range of valued goods and services a large number of which are left unaccounted for through the market system either because of missing markets or because they are public goods (Chapter 2). If these goods and services are not accounted for, then economic analyses that underpin public policies can make society worse off. The likelihood of bad choices increases the more we promote policies that try to increase the value of market goods by reducing the value of environmental goods.

The importance of accounting for the environment goes beyond the problem of environmental valuation (Chapter 3). Some environmental goods and services are so all embracing and complex (for instance, climate regulation, biodiversity, and nutrient cycling) that they are incompatible with sensible monetary valuation since they form our life-support system. The economist then must define the limits under which economic activity should operate. Recognition that environmental limits are critical has led to calls for sustainable development and safe minimum standards for environmental protection (Chapter 6).

Economic analysis should thus account for the environment through valuation or an appreciation of what natural scientists say about the limits of the environment. Those who account for only market-valued goods in cost-benefit analysis and who do not address the environment, are likely to recommend more rainforests be felled for timber and agriculture than might be socially desirable, especially if the actions drive a large number of species with no obvious economic value to extinction. Accounting for the environment in economic analysis involves a blend of valuation, defining our limits, and explaining the uncertainties which surround our understanding of the biosphere.

Second, what happens when economics gets left out of the environment? Omitting economic behaviour from decision-making over how we manage environmental resources, and how we achieve environmental objectives, makes it very likely that society will use its scarce resources inefficiently—expending extra costs at no gain in environmental protection. This ultimately translates in people being less well-off than they could otherwise be. In Chapter 11, we discussed how using economic instruments such as tradable permits and emission taxes allow pollution reduction targets to be achieved at a lower cost than under more usual regulatory approaches. In many cases, these cost savings are substantial, for instance as has been experienced in the US sulphur trading programme for cutting emissions that lead to acid rain. Economically efficient policies make buying environmental protection a better deal, and reduce all-too-familiar conflicts between protecting environmental quality and promoting economic growth.

Economics can also strengthen the case for conservation. Chapter 3 showed how environmental values, even when ignored in the market-place, are real economic values. Estimating how big these benefits can be makes an economic case for conservation as a welfare improvement for society. Cost-benefit analysis of projects and policies with significant environmental impacts that incorporates the monetary value of these impacts improves decision-making by showing how conservation can generate positive benefits for society.

Economics also helps us to understand the trade-offs and opportunity costs which characterize *all* problems of environmental protection. Aside from helping us understand *why* environmental problems occur, economic concepts also help in designing effective policy. For instance, recognizing that elephant conservation imposes costs on local people due to forgone farming output helps in designing more effective elephant conservation policy which compensates local people for these costs and gives them positive incentives to safeguard elephants and their habitats (Chapter 13).

In addition, economics puts meat on the bones of sustainable development—the new buzz-phrase of many government departments, international agencies, and the environmental movement. Whilst many disciplines have contributed to understanding what this means, how we measure it, and how we achieve it, economics enables us to formally characterize a set of minimum requirements for long-term sustainability (Chapter 6). Economics also helps to explain why a country's environmental impacts change over time as economies grow and develop, which helps us better understand and predict future trends.

Sustainability stresses the links between the local and the global. Some of the most serious environmental problems now facing us—climate change, biodiversity loss, ocean fisheries declines—require global actions to counter them effectively. Through the study of strategic behaviour and human interaction, the economic theory of games helps to illustrate why international agreements on these issues are so challenging to construct, and what can be done to maximize the chances of success (Chapter 7).

Economics thus provides a useful set of concepts and tools that can improve how society protects its environment. And environmental and resource economics has made significant progress in a relatively short period of time. The main achievements include:

- Developing sophisticated methods to value environmental protection; methods capable of producing numbers useful to cost-benefit analyses for a wide range of issues.

- Proposing to use the market to achieve environmental objectives at lower cost than traditional command and control policies.

- Defining the economic basis of sustainable development, including guidelines and indicators based on a solid theory of economic welfare.

- Understanding people's behaviour in the face of environmental regulation and environmental risks.

- Explaining how game theory can help us to understand strategic behaviour in a wide range of contexts, notably in global environmental agreements.

But of course much work remains. Economists still would benefit from:

- Improving how we value ecosystem services and resilience.

- Increasing our understanding of the problems of non-point pollution control.

- Expanding our understanding of the role of transactions costs and how to cope with imperfect information.

- Understanding the political economy of regulators.

- Moving away from a concentration on weak sustainability, and finding better ways of measuring changes in the natural capital stock.

- Expanding our understanding on how to deal with true environmental uncertainty or ignorance in which the odds of catastrophe cannot be defined with any reasonable degree of accuracy.

The obvious limits to the rational choice theory that underlies neoclassical environmental economics have opened the door for numerous frustrated critics. Some have put forward a paradigm of *ecological economics* as an alternative way to handle these deficiencies (see, for example, Faber, Manstetten, and Proops, 1996). But we view the distinction between environmental and ecological economics as artificial and unhelpful, since we are all after the same thing—better choices made on a more solid framework with more useful information. Both economics essentially cover the same problem areas and the same techniques. The main difference is of emphasis, with ecological economists emphasizing environmental limits more than human adaptation and response. And while ecological economics claims interdisciplinarity as a distinguishing feature, it will be apparent from this book that environmental economists *cannot* carry out much of their work without inputs from a wide range of other disciplines, including ecology, market research, hydrology, and atmospheric science. All good economics for the environment is interdisciplinary.

It is also important to state that economics does not try to provide all the answers to environmental problems. It cannot: many types of problem are way outside of its purview, such as those that require social decisions of morality, or require specific biological or genetic dose–response estimation. What happens to asthma if particulate matter in the air increases? How does the pollutant tri-butyl tin affect shellfish?

Even in terms of human interaction with the environment, other world views exist with conflicting ethical beliefs. No policy-maker believes that economic efficiency is the sole or most important criterion on which to compare policy options, preferring other criteria such as fairness or political acceptability. Ethical systems which prioritize rights over outcomes also sit uneasily with economics, as was pointed out in Chapter 4. Yet in a world of scarce resources, choices must be made, and choices involve trade-offs. We need some way to frame and evaluate these choices. Economics is one such way.

The best way to think about environmental economics is probably as a useful set of tools to address important and necessary questions of limits—both human and natural. Economics does not provide all the answers. But economics can provide insight to improve both human and environmental well-being by showing how we can achieve more environmental protection at less cost, thereby freeing up resources to take on all our other challenges in modern society.

Reference

Faber, M., Manstten, R., and Proops, J. (1996). *Ecological Economics: Concepts and Methods* (Cheltenham: Edward Elgar).

Index

An understanding of economics is vital to any understanding of why environmental problems occur and what best to do about them. This book provides an introduction to the subject of environmental economics which does not assume any in-depth prior knowledge of economics. Part one explains the fundamental economic concepts, using environmental examples, including markets, environmental evaluation, risk, and trade. Part two then sets these concepts to work in understanding and developing policy responses to some of the major environmental issues of our time. Examples are drawn from all over the world and include such vital global issues as climate change, water pollution, and the loss of biodiversity.

Clearly written, global in approach, and theoretically broad-minded, this new text is an ideal introduction both to the study of environmental economics and to the question of how economics can provide tools for improving our global environment.

- Coverage of problems such as climate change, water pollution, and loss of biodiversity provides an invaluable global overview of the most pressing environmental issues of our time

- Assessment of different theoretical approaches to environmental economics provides a key to understanding the various possible policy responses to major environmental issues

- Case studies of environmental problems from across the world combine a global picture with in-depth descriptions of specific concrete examples

Nick Hanley is Professor of Environmental Economics at the University of Glasgow.

Jason F. Shogren is Stroock Distinguished Professor of Natural Resource Conservation and Management and Professor of Economics at the University of Wyoming.

Ben White is Senior Lecturer in Agricultural Economics at the University of Newcastle and Adjunct Senior Lecturer in Agricultural Economics at the University of Western Australia.

Cover photographs © PhotoDisc, Inc.

OXFORD
UNIVERSITY PRESS

www.oup.com

ISBN 0-19-877595-4

9 780198 775959